Hippies, Indians, and the Fight for Red Power

SHERRY L. SMITH

UNIVERSITY PRESS

Oxford University Press, Inc., publishes works that further
Oxford University's objective of excellence
in research, scholarship, and education.

Oxford   New York
Auckland   Cape Town   Dar es Salaam   Hong Kong   Karachi
Kuala Lumpur   Madrid   Melbourne   Mexico City   Nairobi
New Delhi   Shanghai   Taipei   Toronto

With offices in
Argentina   Austria   Brazil   Chile   Czech Republic   France   Greece
Guatemala   Hungary   Italy   Japan   Poland   Portugal   Singapore
South Korea   Switzerland   Thailand   Turkey   Ukraine   Vietnam

Copyright © 2012 by Oxford University Press, Inc.

Published by Oxford University Press, Inc.
198 Madison Avenue, New York, NY 10016

www.oup.com

Oxford is a registered trademark of Oxford University Press

All rights reserved. No part of this publication may be reproduced,
stored in a retrieval system, or transmitted, in any form or by any means,
electronic, mechanical, photocopying, recording, or otherwise,
without the prior permission of Oxford University Press.

Library of Congress Cataloging-in-Publication Data
Smith, Sherry L. (Sherry Lynn), 1951–
Hippies, Indians, and the fight for red power / Sherry L. Smith.
p. cm.
Includes bibliographical references and index.
ISBN 978-0-19-985559-9 (hardcover : alk. paper)
1. Indians of North America—Politics and government.
2. Indians of North America—Government relations—1934–
3. Indian activists—United States—History—20th century.
4. Church work with Indians—United States—History—20th century.
5. Counterculture—United States—History—20th century.
6. Social movements—United States—History—20th century.
7. Protest movements—United States—History—20th century.
8. Alcatraz Island (Calif.)—History—Indian occupation, 1969–1971.
9. Wounded Knee (S.D.)—History—Indian occupation, 1973. I. Title.
E98.T77S57   2012
323.1197—dc23   2011038767

1 3 5 7 9 8 6 4 2

Printed in the United States of America
on acid-free paper

*For
my sister, Reverend Barbara Arlite SilverSmith
and
my brother, Brian Atwood Smith*

CONTENTS

Acknowledgments ix

Introduction 3

1. The Salmon Wars of the Pacific Northwest 18

2. The California Scene 43

3. Politics, Parks, and Alcatraz 78

4. Back to the Land 113

5. From Coast to Coast 145

6. On to Wounded Knee 183

Epilogue 213

Notes 221
Index 259

ACKNOWLEDGMENTS

To the historian, writing about the recent past poses particular challenges. Not the least of them is the fact that much of the documentation, which will eventually end up in historical archives, currently remains in private hands. Many of the people who figure in this book's story, and are part of that generation whose name baby boomers evokes perpetual childhood, are only beginning to realize they have become "historic." They have yet to collect, organize, and donate their papers to libraries. But studying them has its advantages. Many remain alive, engaged in the issues, and willing to talk. I am forever indebted to those who welcomed me to their homes or offices, answered my e-mails, or talked with me on the phone including Stewart Brand, Barbara Brenner, Marilyn Clement, Peter Coyote, Bill Davis, Candra Day, Alyce and Larry Frank, Craig Glassner, Wavy Gravy (Hugh Romney), Stuart Hardy, Eric Lambert, Lisa Law, Jack Loeffler, Peter Mackaness, Joseph Quinones, Diane Reyna, Sylvia Rodriguez, Joe Sando, Robby Stern, Dolores Martinez Romero Struck, Timothy Troy, and Richard White. I am particularly appreciative of Richard White's generosity in sharing his unpublished memoir of his Frank's Landing experiences and in bringing to our conversation the remarkable ability to separate the insights he offered as a "primary source" from the thoughtful analysis he provided as a fellow historian.

Of course archives and libraries proved essential to this project as well. Teresa Salazar and Walter Brim provided enormous help during an extended visit to the Bancroft Library at the University of California, Berkeley. Others who went beyond the call of duty to find sources include Debbie Miller, Minnesota Historical Society; Nurah-Rosalie Jeter, New York Public Library's Schomberg Center for Research in Black Culture; Donald Davis, American Friends Service Committee Archives in Philadelphia; Brian Deshazor and Phil Robison at the Pacifica Radio Archives in Los Angeles; Ann Massman, University of New Mexico's Center for Southwest Research; Sandra Kroupa, University of Washington Special

Collections; Louise Richards, University of Washington Fisheries and Oceanography Library; Daryl Morrison, Special Collections, University of California, Davis; Linda Long, University of Oregon Special Collections; Nita Murphy, Southwest Research Center of Northern New Mexico; and the staffs at the Seattle Municipal Archives, San Francisco Public Library, Taos Public Library, Santa Fe Public Library, Southern Methodist University's Fondren and DeGolyer Libraries, Stanford University Special Collections, and the National Archives in College Park, Maryland (where the Nixon Presidential Papers were housed during my research for this book). The librarians at the Teton County Library, Jackson, Wyoming, Inter-Library loan service efficiently handled my many requests during summer sojourns in Jackson Hole.

Several fellow historians and scholars in other disciplines led me to some wonderful sources I would have missed without their help. Fred Turner, Stanford University Communications Department, helped me negotiate the Stewart Brand Papers at Stanford. SMU Anthropology Professor Ben Wallace allowed me to read his unpublished manuscript interviews with Taos, New Mexico, commune dwellers, gathered in the early 1970s by Wallace and his research assistants. Historian Thomas Sugrue encouraged me to use the American Friends Service Committee archives in Philadelphia (a fabulous resource) and Western historian Leah Glaser shared some Hopi articles on hippies, from her own research in Arizona. Historian John Findlay suggested some Pacific Northwest sources I had missed. I am also grateful to Jeff Schulze, SMU Ph.D. and lecturer at University of Texas, Dallas, for providing me with a CD of Neil Young songs with Indian-related themes. Collecting photographs and images for this book has left me indebted to Stewart Brand, Lisa Law, Debbie Miller, Dean Rader, Ann Massman, Bree Stein, Claire-Lisa Benaud, Carolyn Marr, Christina Moretta, Mary Ann Kramer, David Kessler, Owen Luck, and Amanda Williford.

The research took me from coast to coast. Friends and family who generously shared their homes during some of my trips include Reverend Barbara Silver-Smith in Annapolis, Maryland; Drs. Brooke and Ed Love in Seattle, Washington; Dr. Ron and Bonnie Sanders in Palo Alto, and Guy and Gigi Anthony in Hillsborough, California. I first began this project at the University of Texas, El Paso, where a Dean's Faculty Development grant funded my initial foray into New Mexico's counterculture past. Among my UTEP colleagues who encouraged this topic from the start were Cheryl Martin, Charles Martin, Sandy McGee-Deutsch, Carl Jackson, Kenton Clymer, Chuck Ambler, Ernie Chavez, and Nicole Etcheson. Although I left UTEP one dozen years ago, I still miss my UTEP friends and our Friday afternoon "seminars." Most of the work on this book, however, took place after I moved to Southern Methodist University, a generous benefactor. Funds from the William P. Clements Department of History, the University Research Council, and a Gerald J. Ford Research Fellowship

Acknowledgments

allowed research excursions as did the support I continue to receive as a University Distinguished Professor and the 2011 Dedman Family Distinguished Professor. Two Dean's Special Research Leaves provided the essential time away from teaching and administrative duties to conduct research and write chapters. Thank you to History Department Chairs Jim Hopkins and Kathleen Wellman for supporting my leave requests and to Dedman College Deans Jasper Neel and Cordelia Candelaria and Provosts Ross Murfin and Paul Ludden for granting them. Mildred Pinkston, Administrative Assistant to the Chair in SMU's History Department, has helped me negotiate the administrative and bureaucratic processes at SMU with grace, wisdom, and skill. SMU History Department Administrative Assistant to the Faculty Sharron Pierson helped pull the manuscript and ancillary elements together for final production.

Although I was a bit reluctant to move east of the 100th meridian—with its absence of mountains and more humid climate—when I first migrated from UTEP and El Paso to SMU and Dallas, I have greatly appreciated the intellectual climate of my new academic home. David J. Weber encouraged me to join him at the Clements Center for Southwest Studies and his presence alone made that an incredibly attractive choice. That each year we would be joined by a dynamic, fresh batch of scholars working on their own projects, yet sharing our collective purpose of investigating the American West and Southwest, made it irresistible. I will be forever grateful for David's invitation and his deep, sustaining support and friendship once I arrived. His death in August 2010 left me bereft for the loss of a valued colleague and collaborator. Ben Johnson joined our faculty and the Center in 2002 and immediately displayed a lively presence, keen intellect, and became a valued friend. I appreciated his interest in my research and thoughtful suggestions of ways to conceptualize it and sources to consult. Andrea Boardman and Ruth Ann Elmore, Clements Center Executive Director and Assistant to the Director respectively, not only run the center with professionalism and efficiency, they create a working environment of scholarly support, genuine friendship, laughter, and fun. I appreciate all they do for the Center, SMU, and me on a daily basis. Ruth Ann's expertise with digital images was a huge help at the end stage of this project.

The outstanding group of scholars that have been in residence at the Clements Center since my arrival in 1999 have greatly enriched the intellectual life at SMU. It has been my great fortune to read Fellows' manuscripts and participate in their workshops, at least when I'm "in residence" myself. I have learned much from every one of them. Those whose research interests are closest to mine (the Indian historians and New Mexican historians, for instance) have proven especially helpful over the last decade as I have wrestled with "hippies and Indians." Conversations with Bill DeBuys, Julianna Barr, Colleen O'Neill, Tisa Wenger, Flannery Burke, David Wallace Adams, Brian Frehner, Andy Graybill, Brian

Delay, Deborah Kang, Marsha Weisiger, Martin Padget, Joaquim Rivaya-Martinez, Andrew Needham, Sylvia Rodriguez, Cynthia Radding, and Julia Maria Schiavone-Camacho have been especially helpful. I also appreciate the comments the Dallas Area Social History (DASH) group provided when I presented my research to them, as well as those History Department faculty offered at a seminar on my topic, particularly my fellow Americanists Ed Countryman, John Chávez, Crista Deluzio, Tom Knock, and Alexis McCrossen. But colleagues who cover other parts of the world have been generous in their interest as well. I particularly thank John Mears, Jim Hopkins, Kathleen Wellman, and Dennis Cordell. In Jackson Hole, I have cherished conversations with fellow historians and good friends Mike Cassity, Marly Merrill, and philosopher Dan Merrill about this project—and theirs.

My arrival at SMU coincided with the creation of a new Ph.D. program emphasizing the American Southwest and Borderlands. The intellectual excitement and enthusiasm the SMU graduate students bring to my classes in Western and Native American history is infectious and remind me what a great job I have. Not the least of its pleasures is shepherding new scholars into the profession and learning from them. I am particularly appreciative of the opportunity to have directed (or worked closely on) dissertations with Kerry Oman, Clive Seigle, Jimmy Bryan, Jim Dudlo, Jeff Schulze, Helen McClure, Alicia Dewey, Paul Nelson, John Gram, Anna Banheygi, Jenna Valadez, Anne Albright, and Derek Kutzer.

Reading and critiquing Clements Center Fellows' and graduate students' manuscripts is an outstanding way to sharpen one's own thinking...and writing. It can also prove to be a major impediment to finding the time to complete one's own projects. Huntington Library Director of Research Roy Ritchie came to the rescue with a wonderful gift: the *Los Angeles Times* Distinguished Fellowship at the Huntington Library for 2009–10. I used my time there to complete a draft of this book and to begin research on another. My fellow Fellows, a coterie of fabulous scholars, provided ongoing, stimulating conversations in the wonderful Huntington rose garden lunch spot (and elsewhere). I will forever be grateful for the companionship of that year's Huntington group: Elliott West, Kevin Leonard, Carl and Jane Smith, Kathy Olesko, Nick Rogers, David Igler, and Susan Gilman. The Huntington's Roy Ritchie, Susie Krasnoo, and Caroline Powell provided everything I needed to have a delightful and productive Huntington stay, ranging from an office with a window to a wonderful New Year's Eve dinner. H. Russell Smith Foundation Curator of Western Historical Manuscripts Peter Blodgett is a splendid colleague and friend. Peter and Sue Hodgkins, Huntington Literary Manuscripts curator, not only directed me and my husband, Bob Righter, to the library's rich resources, they also introduced us to some of the finer Pasadena area eateries.

During the course of this project, invitations to speak about it have been very useful as I tried out my ideas on audiences. Dan Cobb and Loretta Fowler organized a wonderful seminar at Miami of Ohio University and published the group's papers in an excellent volume, *Beyond Red Power*. I particularly appreciated the suggestions for improvement that Dan, Loretta, and participant Don Fixico provided. SMU professors John Ubelaker and Mike Adler invited me to present a lecture on the New Mexico aspect of this story at SMU-in-Taos' Fort Burgwin campus as part of their annual summer lecture series and Virginia Scharff hosted me for the Calvin Horn lecture sponsored by The Center for Southwest at the University of New Mexico. More recently, Jay Gitlin, John Mack Faragher, and George Miles invited me to talk about Indians and the counterculture for the Betts Lecture at Yale University. I was inspired and energized by all my hosts' interest and audience members' questions. Amy Scott, Andy Kirk, and I pulled together a session for an Organization of American Historians' conference on various aspects of the counterculture. I learned a great deal from Amy and Andy as well as from the insightful commentary provided by Michael Doyle. Mary Murphy and Laurie Mercier's suggestions in the context of a Western History Association conference session were also most welcome. Providing commentary on papers written by Dan Cobb and Paul Rosier at an American Historical Association conference gave me the opportunity to get to know better these two outstanding scholars of post–World War II Indian history and benefit from the insights of their work.

Through the long gestation period of this book, Oxford University Press Executive Editor Susan Ferber consistently expressed interest in the project and patiently waited for its completion. Her impeccable editing skills and speedy responses to my queries made the publication process go smoothly. She is the best. Oxford's anonymous readers made helpful suggestions about substance and style.

On a more personal level, I am grateful for the interest and support my "Righter" relatives have shown my work. Bonnie, Ron, Zachary, and Sarah Sanders along with Trisha, Loy, Benjamin, and Dylan Lack have heard me talk about hippies and Indians during our annual Righter Rendezvous in Jackson Hole. They also provided a wonderful excuse to put work aside and play for a while during their visits. The Dayton Righters—Dick, Willie, Lisa and Karen—have dedicated their lives to social justice. While I chose to study and write about a chapter in that larger story, they have chosen to act. I appreciate their respect and interest in my work; I deeply respect and remain always interested in theirs.

The Smiths currently span four generations. My father, Atwood Smith, continues to teach me how to live through his personal example as he closes in on age one hundred: with quiet humility, kindness, and humor. He remains the pinochle champion of the family and urges me and Bob to keep working, keep writing. My nieces and nephew, Brant Silvers, Brooke Silvers Love, Sara Smith Serafinski, and Amanda Smith Jackson, have enriched our family circle through marriages to Gaylea, Ed, Jason, and Tommy. They have also added a new generation: Abraham, Madeleine, and Jasper who may someday read this book, too.

It was my great good fortune to grow up as the youngest child in a family of interesting, smart siblings. My sister, Reverend Barbara SilverSmith, and my brother, Brian Smith, experienced the 1960s in different ways, places, and angles of vision than me. We now live scattered across the continent. But we get together regularly, forever linked by the bonds of family love, shared memories, and the Indiana Dunes where that fourth generation is now experiencing the joy of "sand in their shoes," to quote family friend Maida Dudley. I am grateful for all Barbara and Brian have given me over our lifetimes and so have dedicated this book to them: our generation of Smiths.

Finally, my husband, Bob Righter, remains my best friend, closest advisor, and partner in life and love. He helped me with research from Harlem to Seattle, encouraged me when my own commitment occasionally flagged, read the entire manuscript, and promised me this was going to be a "best seller." While his powers of prediction may be faulty, I do not doubt his commitment to me, my professional achievements, and our wonderful life together. I hope I have returned, at least in some measure, all the gifts he has given me.

Hippies, Indians, and the Fight for Red Power

Introduction

In January 1966 Stewart Brand found himself in the perfect place for a young man bent on pushing boundaries. San Francisco was a mecca for youthful rebels, and Brand, who would become well known as the creator of the 1970s best-selling *Whole Earth Catalog*, was in the thick of it. Brand was riding the countercultural wave that was about to crest in that city's Haight-Ashbury neighborhood in the 1967 Summer of Love. He joined the loosely knit group called the Merry Pranksters with its dazzling cast of characters including writer Ken Kesey. The Pranksters aimed to shed their parents' supposedly repressive and conformist ways through experimentation with psychedelic drugs, sexual freedom, and music. They lived in the present moment, hoping to break with the past. Brand embraced all this with one noteworthy exception: he appreciated history, at least that aspect linked to Native America.

A son of the Midwest and of privilege, Stewart Brand might have seemed, at first glance, an unlikely recruit to hippiedom. Looking like a cross between a blond California surfer and a long, lanky, youthful Abraham Lincoln, he first graduated from Phillips Exeter prep school and then from Stanford University. A two-year stint in the early 1960s with the U.S. Army followed. The military uniform neither defined nor confined him, however. While stationed in New York, Brand linked up with a community of artists who stressed connections to the natural world and its systems; an approach that resonated with the former biology major. They also expanded the definition of art, creating events or "happenings" that broke down the barriers between artist and audience through electronic light shows, psychedelic drugs, and communal togetherness. Brand's contribution to this "artistic tribe" was through photography.[1]

It was the camera that brought him to Indian tribes, as well. After the army, Brand returned to the Bay Area where he studied photography at San Francisco State University, participated in a legal LSD study at Menlo Park's International Foundation for Legal Study, experimented with peyote, and launched his personal odyssey with Indians and the counterculture. When Brand landed a photography job on Oregon's Warm Springs Reservation (home to Warm Springs, Wasco, and Paiute tribes), he came face-to-face, for the first time, with Indian people and discovered "a different America." He found their ideas about land and nature especially inspiring and quickly concluded "America needs Indians." Native Americans were the ones to teach America how to listen to the "voice of the Continent" and learn its laws of harmony. Moreover, they had rich cultures and deserved to live on their own terms and for their own purposes. With those concepts as his inspiration and motivation, he began a multiyear project visiting Indian reservations, photographing native people, and creating a multimedia show about them. In fact, on the first night of the famous 1966 San Francisco Trips Festival, designed to replicate an LSD trip without the LSD, Brand presented his show, which he titled "America Needs Indians," to the audience.[2]

In the years to follow, Brand's interests evolved in other directions, most notably toward environmental concerns and the publication of his *Whole Earth Catalog*, which offered tools for communards and others interested in a more environmentally sustainable life. Yet, as it turned out, many other West Coast counterculturists shared Brand's attraction to Indians. Although Brand decided Indian politics was not an arena he cared to enter, other hippies felt differently. In fact, the rise of Red Power, a pan-Indian movement that demanded recognition of treaty rights, tribal sovereignty, and self-determination for native people, found counterculture types among its earliest allies. From the early 1960s fish-ins of Washington state through the American Indian Movement (AIM) occupation of Wounded Knee, South Dakota, in 1973, counterculture and other non-Indians enthusiastically applauded and actively supported Indian demands for radical change regarding their place and power in America.

It is noteworthy that in the aftermath of the Wounded Knee occupation, a Federal Bureau of Investigation photographer systematically documented the buildings which had sheltered the protestors. Those images depicted the chaos and violence that characterized the tension-filled weeks when AIM and its allies faced off against the Pine Ridge Ogalala Sioux tribal and federal governments. Among the objects the government photographer found inside the compound was a pennant with a simple declarative statement: "America Needs Indians" (see figure 0.1). The flag, which harkened back to the theme of Stewart Brand's multimedia show, did more than remind its viewers that the United States *had* Indian people. It declared the country needed to keep them. Between 1963, when Brand began his photography project, and 1973, when the Wounded Knee occupation ended with a photograph of a pennant proclaiming that resonant statement, many people in the country finally seemed convinced that not only did America need Indians, but also that it should back that rhetoric with action. It was a transformational moment in American history. This book investigates that transformation.

Figure 0.1 A photographer discovered this banner in the Wounded Knee compound after the occupiers evacuated. From Stewart Brand's early 1960s multimedia show and celebration of Indians to the siege at Wounded Knee, the phrase "America Needs Indians" resonated with many. Credit: United Press International, photo held by Minnesota Historical Society Library's Wounded Knee Legal Defense/Offense Collection.

For centuries, most Americans and their government believed Indians were an obstacle to national progress or, by the mid-twentieth century, anachronisms which had no place in the modern world. Extinguishing all remnants of native life characterized federal policy by the 1950s. Of course, Native Americans did not agree and fought for survival. By the 1960s, they found support outside their communities. Who were these new allies who not only thought about and expressed interest in Indians, but also sought them out and then assisted them when they asked for help? How, why, and where did Indians and non-Indians come together, join forces, and create change? It started in peoples' hearts and minds; and as attitudes changed, so too did action. As more and more people accepted Brand's premise, political support for policy transformation followed. Behind the statement "America Needs Indians" loomed the unspoken assumption: America's Indians were endangered, could disappear, and non-Indians could and should do something to assure their survival. A first step was fighting the post–World War II termination policy: its long-term goals included eliminating tribal governments, liquidating reservations, ending treaty rights forever, and destroying native cultures. The next step was championing Indian self-determination, sovereignty, treaty rights, and cultural revitalization. By the early 1970s, that is exactly what happened.

The turbulent period of reform encapsulated in the "sixties," then, is central to understanding this remarkable, even revolutionary, shift in attitude, practice, and policy. Yet, historians of sixties social movements have slighted Native American activism. And students of Native American history have not paid sufficient attention to the crucial interplay between Indians, on the one hand, and Anglo-dominated counterculture types, left-leaning political organizations, progressive religious groups including the Society of Friends, or Quakers, other liberal denominations, civil rights advocates, Mexican American activists, and black nationalists, on the other.[3] Out of this period of intense turmoil, experimentation, and barrier-shattering change came the cross-fertilization of ideas, techniques, and partnerships. At a time when Americans were coming to terms with the shortcomings of their political and social system, Indian challenges to conformity and demands for economic and political justice resonated and found supporters. So too did acknowledgement of greater cultural diversity. At a time when the world witnessed global decolonization movements and the United States' involvement in the Vietnam War elicited foreign and domestic condemnation of American imperialism abroad, Indians were a reminder of imperialism at home and an opportunity to redress those wrongs. The parallel development of anti–Vietnam War and pro–Native American rights sentiment was no coincidence. The movements were simultaneous and often quite consciously related. The particular confluence of contemporary issues made Indians especially interesting, appealing, and relevant to the nation's restless, reform-oriented, discontented, outraged, and alienated souls. Native Americans—or perhaps more accurately peoples' rather fuzzy "understandings" of Native Americanness—suddenly had particular panache. By acknowledging non-Indians' role in this story, my intention is not to diminish the achievements of Native Americans but rather to add an additional cast of characters to our understanding of this remarkable chapter in Native American and United States history.

This argument might surprise those who see the non-Indian sympathizers featured in this book, particularly those from the New Left and counterculture, as doing more harm than good in Indian communities. Many consider these non-Indians' interests as superficial, ephemeral, and myopic at best; exploitive, self-serving, and damaging to Native Americans at worst. This now-familiar critique of the counterculture focuses on their ignorance, naiveté, and even their own brand of cultural imperialism. Undoubtedly such criticism has validity. It was there from the start. In 1967 Buffy Sainte-Marie, a Cree folksinger, noted in an interview during San Francisco's Summer of Love that the hippie interest in emulating and identifying with Indians and their customs "doesn't make any sense to me. The white people never seem to realize that they cannot suck the soul out of a race. The ones with the sweetest intentions are the worst soul suckers. It's the weirdest vampire idea." The critique only grew from there. Others denounced poetry written by non-Indians with Native American themes and the proliferation of faux Indian healers or white shamans who claimed to be authorities of Native American religion but were, in fact, fakes.[4]

Despite their obvious shortcomings and limitations, though, people identified as counterculturists or hippies, as they came to be known in the sixties, were among the first non-Indians of the postwar generation to seek out contact with Native Americans, learn about their grievances, and join their call for reform. They did so in large and significant numbers, which, in turn, caught the attention of the rest of the nation. Far from being merely superficial and marginal, such attention turned out to be of great importance to the broader cultural and political shifts relevant to Indian issues. Hippies "discovered" Indians and found them attractive *because* they presumably offered an actual, living base for an alternative American identity. Challenging bourgeois culture's values and beliefs in progress, order, achievement, and established authority, the youthful counterculture advocated freedom from discipline and convention.[5] Many looked to Indians as symbols of, and even models for, alternative ways of life. Native Americans seemed like perfect foils, in fact, to all that these predominantly Anglo Americans disdained about their own culture. Indians, supposedly, were not only spiritual and ecological but also tribal and communal. Further, they were genuine holdouts against American conformity; the original American "long hairs." Counterculture iconography, consequently, became drenched in images of Indianness, reflecting, of course, a superficial perspective on Indian peoples' lives and contemporary problems; and yet one that carried cultural and political potency.

Something of the same phenomenon operated among white middle-class New Leftists who may, or may not, have also defined themselves as counterculture. Feelings of alienation fueled the 1960s version of the American Left, as well. Part of it was alienation from the political system but part was alienation from their culture and selves. They had experienced a loss of inner wholeness and authenticity—a yearning that stretched back across the history of American industrialization. However, what had been a preoccupation among the Anglo upper class earlier in the century had, by the 1960s, sifted down to the middle class and involved many more people. Alienation and authenticity served as the two poles between which this generation spun. One outcome, early in the decade, was a student Christian movement that sought a therapeutic quest for authenticity through political action, especially in the African American civil rights movement. That, in turn, led to an extraordinary amount of interaction between blacks and whites and then, as the 1960s moved along, between Indians and non-Indians.[6]

As New Leftists sought community or solidarity with others, African Americans pulled away, moved toward being "authentically black," and urged white allies to address the racism within their own community. Some black activists even insisted on separation of races, pushing whites out of black organizations. At that point, at least some Anglos who remained committed to racial justice in America turned to Indian issues. Anglo New Leftists, meanwhile, edged toward a greater critique of capitalism and a more secular orientation. Yet, the search for authenticity through exploration of non-Western spiritual traditions continued. This impulse, joined with a belief that marginal groups seemed more culturally authentic, led some to seek out Native Americans, updating the old leftist tradition that assigned people of color sought-after authenticity. Defining African Americans or Indians as more culturally authentic, of course, carried its own form of racism and colonialism. To trap Native Americans in conceptions shaped by non-Indian assumptions about them ('spiritual," "traditional," "precapitalist," for example) was exceedingly limiting, even dehumanizing, particularly at a moment when many Indian people were generating new ways of living in a changing world. To establish a litmus test of cultural purity, based on deeply flawed notions of native histories and cultures, was absurd. Yet, sometimes Indians played along and even exploited non-Indians' definitions of authenticity for their own purposes. Often the concepts created division, dissension, and damage within native communities or individual Indian's psyches. At the time, however, most leftists did not understand their adulation and reverence carried this darker undercurrent.[7]

Moreover, if the impulse to seek authenticity among people of color was not particularly new, the number of people who embraced it was and the political consequences, thus, more far-reaching. If not all New Leftists turned to Indians, those who did—particularly in California and the far west—helped reshape national sentiments about race and justice in Native America. Based on romantic yearnings for authenticity, Anglo counterculture and New Leftists began drifting to Native American Church ceremonies and eventually to reservations. Many Indians did not welcome these newcomers. But that did not stop the migration. Further, other tribal members proved more willing to interact and eventually enlist some of these youthful seekers in efforts to promote their own political goals, including treaty rights, cultural revivals, and tribal sovereignty. These more politically oriented hippies and elements of the New Left eventually came to a more sophisticated understanding of the issues at stake for Native Americans. They formed the most vibrant and visible alliances with activists, including some reservation-based leaders, though more often with urban Indian communities and organizations. Underground newspapers provided one means by which these various groups and movements learned about one another and spread the word to national and even international audiences. The opportunities to engage with one another in cities such as San Francisco, Seattle, Denver, and Minneapolis and on university and college campuses all across the country reinforced the inclination to share "the struggle" against oppression with Native Americans.

Equally responsive to activist Indians, but more practically and immediately useful than the counterculture and leftists, were church-based organizations that backed Native American reform. They brought to their relationships with Indians greater financial and political power, experience with funding organizations and legislative procedures, maturity, and stability. Still, the connection did not seem a natural one. What could be more counterintuitive than mainstream churches, which had sent missionaries into Indian communities for centuries to stamp out native religions, appearing to reverse course and working to support and sustain these same cultures? Vine Deloria Jr. one of the most influential Native American intellectuals of the late twentieth century, made churches and missionaries a particular target in his widely read 1969 book *Custer Died For Your Sins*. "It has been said of missionaries," he wrote, "that when they arrived they had only the Bible and we had the land; now we have the Book and they have the land. An old Indian once told me that when the missionaries arrived they fell on their knees and prayed. Then they got up, fed on the Indians, and preyed." The son of an Episcopal minister and grandson of a Sioux Episcopal missionary, Deloria concluded that Christianity was "a sham" to hide the white man's shortcomings and true motives.[8] So, what possible common ground could be found between, say, the American Indian Movement and Quakers, Baptists, Methodists, or Presbyterians? Yet, common ground they found.

The turn among progressive churches to the more radical elements in the Native American rights movement came, for most denominations, near the end of the 1960s. By this time, liberal churches had much experience in the African American civil rights movement. Moving into Indian affairs seemed a natural extension and offered one more meeting ground where Anglos, Indians, and African Americans came together. Further, the churches' long-standing presence on reservations and relationships with Indians in urban communities provided other points of contact and opportunities to grasp the nature of political change these communities were experiencing. On the churches' part, what altered was not their interest in Indian peoples' well-being, but their fundamental understanding of what constituted that well-being. Challenged to listen, rather than speak, liberal-leaning denominations came to understand their role differently. Rather than focus on conversion, they shifted their efforts to justice. Moreover, they were coming to recognize (along with other non-Indians) that they were not the central figures in this drama nor did they have the clearest vision of what needed to be done. They would, in fact, follow not lead. Native Americans would provide the leadership. As John P. Adams, a United Methodist Church minister put it, "the aggrieved speak for themselves when they have the opportunity." The churches' proper role was to provide a podium where those who suffered injustice could speak and a place where congregations could hear them. Adams believed many people were more willing to listen in forums provided by churches.[9]

Finally, African Americans and Mexican Americans, engaged in their own movements for civil rights, assisted Native American activists as well. Anglos had long feared the potential for cross-racial and ethnic groups to put aside differences and join forces. Historically, it rarely happened. But starting in the 1930s—at least in parts of California—African, Mexican, Japanese, Jewish, and white Americans collaborated and cooperated to achieve shared civil rights goals. They achieved some victories, particularly in the realms of electoral politics, police brutality, school desegregation, fair employment practices, and fair housing. But cross-racial and ethnic tensions never disappeared, and the communities often divided over how to prioritize specific antidiscrimination measures. The multiplicity of races in places such as Texas and California and the push for racial liberalism, defined as both nondiscrimination and equal opportunity, led to contentious conflicts among them. Rather than blending into one river of reform, each group represented a separate stream in the civil rights struggles.[10]

Notably, none of the recent studies that track the story of civil rights era interracial cooperation and conflict incorporates Indians. This would not surprise Vine Deloria Jr. who, at the time, criticized those who expected racial coalitions and who saw civil rights as an issue they could all back. Their mistake, he explained, was assuming Indians, blacks, and Mexican Americans shared the same problems. They did not. The conflation of civil rights and race was deeply flawed because it obscured the real issues and meant solutions always had a "black orientation." Churches and the government defined the problem as race, saw race as black, and consequently excluded Indians from consideration. But the bigger problem was this overlooked the critical importance of difference. Indians had land bases or homelands, treaties, and cultural independence. Blacks did not. "Historically each group has its own road to travel. All roads lead to personal and group affirmation. But the obstacles faced by each group are different," Deloria explained, "and call for different solutions and techniques." Although he did not argue Indians, blacks, and Mexicans had nothing in common, Deloria believed their differences more important. People "fool themselves when they visualize a great coalition of minority groups" coming together. Indians, in particular, would never work with others on an "ideological basis foreign to them."[11]

And yet, despite all the reasons why they should not have done so, African Americans and Mexican Americans periodically joined forces with Indians. Even the more radical among them stepped up. By the late 1960s, as long-simmering tensions among races flared up and ethnic communities sharpened the division lines between their respective identities and distinctive strategies for reform, if not revolution, representatives from these groups all supported Indian reform. Black Panthers and Dick Gregory appeared at fish-ins in the Pacific Northwest. African American communist Angela Davis and the Southern Christian Leadership Conference's reverend Ralph Abernathy made appearances at Wounded Knee, in solidarity with AIM. Corky Gonzales's Mexican American

Crusade for Justice provided supplies and support for the Wounded Knee occupation, as well. In fact people from all these quarters, races, and ethnicities supported the Indian rights movement with their money, pens, talents, skills (especially the lawyers among them), and bodies in demonstrations. It was as if they all agreed on, at least, this: Indians were among the most aggrieved Americans and their claims to justice indisputable. Moreover, Indians' demands for treaty rights and sovereignty would be realized in mostly rural reservation areas, far away from the urban centers where other "minorities" sometimes found themselves in contention with one another over political power, access to resources, and conflicting goals. Finally, they did so as part of a larger effort in post–World War II America to confront the nation's failure to ensure the rights (in their various manifestations) of all its citizens, to challenge American imperialism at home and abroad, and to push beyond cultural pressures to conform to one way of life and one set of values.

Meanwhile, inspired in part by the rise of black nationalism, Chicano-Chicana, student, and anti–Vietnam War movements, some (particularly young, student, and urban-based) Indians consciously and purposefully sought out partnerships with these activists. They intended to strengthen their own power through loose coalitions with them. To ignore these initiatives is to miss an important element of Indian activists' strategy . . . and agency. They patterned tactics and rhetoric on models from these other social justice movements, although for distinctively Indian goals.[12] Beyond the youth rebellion, they found a powerful contemporary model to follow in forging partnerships in the civil rights movement. At least since the 1930s, churchgoers, lawyers, socialists, communists, and some Democrats and Republicans formed a national, united front pushing for racial, political, and economic equality. A shared vision of a just society motivated them, and the African American civil rights movement provided the fulcrum for their efforts.[13] Native American activists observed this and worked to create similar coalitions. As Deloria predicted, cooperation would prove short-lived and episodic. The shared experience of oppression and racism went only so far. Distinctive historical experiences, interests, and goals worked against consistent or permanent alliances. Racial or ethnic nationalism encouraged separation over integration. And individuals in these groups carried their own reservations and even racist disinclinations about engaging with one another. Still, those moments of solidarity were significant.

Of course, the strategy of creating alliances with non-Indians was not a new idea. A handful of primarily Anglo American organizations designed to support Indian political reform had existed since the nineteenth century and survived into the twentieth. As recently as the 1950s, the Association on American Indian Affairs (AAIA), a New York-based group of primarily academic scholars and former government bureaucrats, worked with the National Congress of

American Indians (NCAI) and local Indian communities to fight the termination policy and promote sovereignty and economic self-sufficiency in tribal communities. The partnership, however, attracted little attention or support.[14] A decade or so later, the number of organizations seeking to cooperate with, or respond to initiatives from, Native Americans had grown. What was new? They were no longer solely Anglo American, and they were willing to engage in more confrontational politics. Organizations cropped up, particularly from the Left, to meet new legal challenges; for example, defending individuals prosecuted by the federal government for their actions at Wounded Knee and supporting litigation related to treaty rights. Nor did the AAIA disappear. It proved to be quite important, in fact, in helping Taos Pueblo regain control of Blue Lake in 1970.

Just as with the African American civil rights movement, misunderstanding and miscommunication plagued efforts to join forces with Native Americans. Not the least of the problems, historically, had been control of reform goals, messages, and rhetoric. As in missionary circles, Anglo American political reformers had always assumed leadership roles in Indian issues. Believing they knew best what Native Americans needed, and ultimately holding the reins of power, the arrogance and condescension of such friends could be as destructive as that of enemies. By the late 1960s, however, that too changed. Native Americans now insisted on control, on leading and speaking for themselves, and on articulating the goals and purposes of actions. This time, non-Indian reformers willingly took positions behind the scenes. Despite its weaknesses and problems, in the end, the effort to reach out to non-Indian allies brought successes.

Finally, Indians realized they could not achieve their goals, including observance of treaty rights, outside the U.S. political and legal structures that gave those claims their meaning and legitimacy. If Indian sovereignty was inherent and pre- or extra-constitutional, its explicit recognition in the commerce clause of the United States Constitution and ratification in treaties, agreements, federal legislation, and case law thereafter solidified its validity. Its authority came from the established political system, not from outside of it. Reform, radical as it might appear, required realization of the political processes' past promises, not rejection of the system itself. Further, more than three hundred federally recognized reservations, originally created by the federal government to serve as "laboratories" for forced acculturation, had become the geographical sites for cultural survival. They were the places where meaningful political power was exercised and tribal economic development occurred. Reservations had been transformed into important homelands whose boundaries, resources, and jurisdictions needed protection from individuals and interests who wanted to destroy them. Native Americans had, in other words, learned to *use* the political system, laws, and bureaucracies for their own purposes. Ironically, they found themselves relying on non-Indian bureaucratic institutions and legal concepts to assert difference and separation, but they had few options.

By the late 1960s, then, opportunities for cooperation among groups and interests pushing for change in Indian country exploded, and the boundaries among them proved porous. Influences moved in all directions. What activists of all kinds, colors, and inclinations shared was a deep discontent with conventional values, viewpoints, and politics. The tendency of historians and others, in retrospect, to separate them from one another, however, does a disservice to the tenuous and temporary but powerful intersections which took place. It ignores the collaborations that occurred in a constellation of overlapping interests and issues. In short, the political and social movements of the 1960s and 1970s were very much intercultural and interracial—an insight the more recent trend toward identity politics has obscured. None of this is meant to suggest the moments of convergence among these unlikely coalitions were peaceful and harmonious. Tensions frequently characterized the interactions. Opportunities for misunderstanding abounded. Moments of cooperation came and then vanished. Connections often proved ephemeral. Some historians will emphasize the limitations of these coalitions. I prefer to emphasize the remarkable fact of their existence at all.

And, of course, Native Americans themselves were not in agreement. The same fissures dividing the rest of America in this period—generational tensions, racial misunderstandings, class divisions, and gender conflicts—cropped up among Indian people too. None were immune from the confounding troubles and turbulence of changing times. Perhaps the most volatile division within Native American communities concerned the proper tactics to pursue in the course of fighting for legal, political, and cultural rights. If they agreed on the goals, they divided on the means or methods of achieving them. Some adhered to more conventional approaches, relying upon tribal governments, the Bureau of Indian Affairs (BIA), Congress, and the U.S. justice system to create change. Others, frequently the younger men and women, preferred more direct and confrontational action—whether challenging state fishing laws that violated treaty rights along the rivers and streams of the Pacific Northwest or taking over the BIA Building in Washington, D.C. The more confrontational or militant actions garnered more publicity and sometimes sparked violent reactions, particularly from law enforcement officers. That, in turn, often attracted more media interest and sympathy from the public than did the less dramatic, but ultimately more substantive, legal and legislative approaches. Such actions played an enormously important role in capturing non-Indians' attention and support, and provide the backbone, or structure, of this book.

Yet, in the end, claims to sovereignty and treaty rights could only be realized at the tribal level. Youthful, urban Indians might attract the necessary attention, but they could not exercise legitimate political power rooted in tribal and treaty systems. Although it may not have seemed so at the time, the relationship between the "militant" elements of the Red Power movement and the reservation-based activists turned out to be symbiotic. The former's actions awakened people to Native American issues, claims, and concerns. They helped revive terms such as "treaty rights" and "tribal sovereignty" and make them part of the American lexicon once again. They also made the tribal governments and groups such as the NCAI appear moderate and relatively easy to work with. Meanwhile, it was the tribes, and their tribally based coalitions, who worked the mainstream political channels, consistently and patiently pressing for legislative reform, and pursuing judicial decisions favorable to Indian rights. In the end, it was the tribes—as it had to be—who reaped the benefits of heightened awareness and ultimately significant policy changes.

To be sure, Native Americans' demands for self-determination, observance of treaty rights, and tribal sovereignty have a long, long history. For centuries, the United States and its citizens ignored them. In the 1970s, though, these demands turned into the keystone of federal-Indian relations.[15] Its core is the idea that each tribal nation has an inherent right as a sovereign entity to exercise political and economic power. Each is entitled to practice its own cultural and spiritual values without government interference. Treaties are constitutionally acknowledged federal pledges, the supreme law of the land, and remain legally binding. All of this means a commitment to Native Americans' continued existence, as *they* define it. It also means Indians are not simply another "minority" but rather, through their tribes and their history, maintain unique government-to-government relationships with federal, state, and local governments.

Of course, since the 1970s implementation of this new approach, the policy has been challenged. Branches of the federal government have disagreed with one another about how to interpret it, and courts have not always sustained its principles. State and local governments and special interests have defied tribes over issues of political jurisdiction and economic power. Tribes have had to compromise in the course of defending their sovereignty. For example, the increased transfer of federal power to the states, particularly during the 1980s, has led some to emphasize the devolving federal arrangement. The 1988 Indian Gaming and Regulatory Act, for instance, forces tribes to negotiate compacts with states on issues regarding governance, taxation, and economic development on reservations. Critics see this "forced federalism" as a serious challenge to indigenous nationhood.[16] But, so far, the basic policy remains in place. Indian tribes, treaties, reservations and cultures are here to stay.[17]

Without doubt, this fundamental and dramatic shift in national policy and sentiment emerged because of Indians' initiatives, political skills, and indefatigable determination. Native Americans deserve the credit for this important development and many have recounted the dramatic episodes, Indian groups, and individuals linked to the headline-grabbing Red Power movement. More recently, the quieter but more sustained political activism of tribal councils and organizations such as the National Congress of American Indians, the National Indian Youth Council, and the National Tribal Chairman's Association have received attention, as well.[18] These groups eschewed the drama of direct actions and media-attracting occupations in favor of steady judicial and legislative actions, applying quiet but constant pressure for change. They pursued their ends in courtrooms and Congress rather than in streets or along streamsides. These tactics went largely unnoticed by the public but led to practical, solid results.

But whatever the strategies and tactics, given Native Americans' relative demographic insignificance, they all realized they could not do it alone. Non-Indians had to be reckoned with, educated, and enlisted. In short, the support and even active participation of sympathetic non-Indian people proved essential to any possible reform. The latter's willingness to listen and respond positively to Native American demands for justice was a necessary, even crucial, step toward the restoration of Indian power in this country. Such a cultural and political development among non-Indians is especially noteworthy precisely because acknowledgement of Native American rights represented a fundamental and dramatic reversal of centuries-long efforts (with the brief exception of the 1930s Indian New Deal years which attempted to shore up tribes, reservation land bases, and societies) to extinguish Indian people, cultures, and tribal governments. Further, it required acknowledgement of a distinctive *kind* of rights. By the post–World War II era most Americans understood "rights" as the rights of citizenship—voting, serving on a jury, and so on. A second broad conception of rights, President Franklin D. Roosevelt's second Bill of Rights, included entitlements to decent housing, recreation, work, and freedom from fear of old age and poor health, provided by government. These were rights to equality and security.[19]

The issues raised by Indian activists, however, were not about voting rights (although, admittedly, some fought for the franchise in some corners of the country) nor did they seek integration.[20] Instead, they demanded acknowledgement of cultural and social difference and realization of past promises that codified a unique status for tribal people. Indeed, Native American treaty rights were "special," pertaining only to members of particular tribes. Rather than seeking a rightful place within the mainstream, many Indians demanded their right place outside of it. It took, then, concerted effort to educate the public about history and about concepts such as treaty rights and sovereignty. To acknowledge and reinvigorate the legitimacy of treaties required non-Indians to think even more expansively about "rights." And they did.

But first, Indian activists had to capture other Americans' attention. In the sixties, at the beginning of this story, the points of contact between Indians and most non-Indian sympathizers came most prominently at places of public protest. Such events represented an increasingly common way for the dissatisfied to register their complaints and gain an audience to hear them. Starting with civil rights marches in the South and on Washington, D.C., the protest at the Pentagon in 1967, and moving on to the bloody protests and counterprotests during the 1968 Democratic National Convention, America had become "a society of the spectacle."[21] Indian activists followed that pattern. Their protests, their flash points, existed precisely to garner attention and, hopefully, national sympathy. This book, then, uses as its organizational framework a series of such spectacles, at sites such as Frank's Landing on the Nisqually River, Alcatraz Island in San Francisco Bay, the commune country of northern New Mexico, the BIA Building in Washington, D.C., and Wounded Knee village on the Pine Ridge Reservation. These places are both actual and representative landscapes of interaction. They are the geographic and symbolic points of connection. They signify the temporal framework of the story, as well, beginning with some of the earliest demonstrations and ending with one of the most famous and, as it turns out, one of the last.

The chapters often begin with cultural developments and flow into the more political activities that followed. These categories, of course, are not truly separate. To think anew about Indians was in itself a political act. But to encourage significant change on the ground required behavior more generally understood as political: staging a demonstration, providing financial support, writing a letter to a senator or the president, or serving as counsel for a tribe in a treaty rights case. The episodes chronicled here, then, investigate such activities. The story begins in the West and then goes national and even global. The fish-ins took place in the far northwest corner of the country, but the movement for treaty rights and other forms of political and cultural power caught on and wound down the coast into California, across the Southwest, out to the nation's capitol, and back to the Northern Plains—all the while gathering growing national and international audiences, sympathy, and support for Indian causes. No single event changed things. No one action moved the nation. It was, rather, the cumulative effect of Native American articulation of needs and demands over the decades matched with non-Indians' realization of their legitimacy during the 1960s and 1970s that finally led to substantive, meaningful reform in Indian affairs. While these reforms failed to solve all of Native America's problems, they set tribes on a firmer foundation than they had had since conquest and positioned them to build upon that foundation in the twenty-first century.

This process was far from tightly organized or managed. Instead it was haphazard, episodic, often spontaneous and chaotic. No single group orchestrated the protests, spoke for all Native Americans, gathered allies, or maintained cohesion. Rather, things heated up in one location, sparked attention, and eventually cooled down. Action and interest then moved elsewhere. Tracking the non-Indian response is, consequently, a challenge. It too was haphazard, episodic, and spontaneous. But evidence that non-Indians sympathized and supported Indian demands for change can be found in a variety of places. Underground and mainstream newspapers covered the issues, informing their readers of Indian demands and printing editorials as well as readers' letters of support. Dee Brown's *Bury My Heart at Wounded Knee*, intended as a Western history from the Indians' points of view, and Vine Deloria's political manifesto, *Custer Died For Your Sins* became national sensations, while periodicals ranging from *Playboy* to Stewart Brand's *The Whole Earth Catalog* covered Indians too. The memoirs of movie stars and celebrities such as Marlon Brando and black comedian Dick Gregory; commune dwellers such as Peter Coyote and Wavy Gravy; and government officials such as Richard Nixon, White House staffers Bradley Patterson and Leonard Garment provide insight into the temper and turmoil of the times. Personal papers of counterculture types and the Nixon Presidential Papers as well as documents from disparate organizations, ranging from the American Friends Service Committee to the Interreligious Foundation for Community Organization and the Wounded Knee Legal Defense/Offense Committee, offer much evidence of interest and political commitment. Interviews with a wide cast of characters who not only lived "the sixties," but also *do* remember it, does the same. Yet, while the research is wide-ranging and thorough, more remains to be done. This study does not, for instance, investigate the critically important actions of lawyers, legislators, and judges who worked diligently to realize demands for change in trials, legislation, and judicial decisions. Instead it emphasizes the front wave of interest and support, the early episodes of activity and action. But much followed that was substantive, critical, and long lasting. It remains for others to dig into the lawyers' briefs, court cases, and legislative hearings to carry on the tale.

In the end, this book is meant to be part of an ongoing conversation about partnerships in social and political change. Problems are shared and solutions require cooperation, a willingness to engage with those who are different, to breach the boundaries that keep people apart, and to collectively push the nation toward final realization of its promises. It happened before, and it can happen again.

1

The Salmon Wars of the Pacific Northwest

No one was paying much attention to the Pacific Northwest, let alone to the Native Americans of Washington state, in the early 1960s. In fact, the nation's back figuratively turned on that region while Americans watched people challenge southern forms of racial hatred in a struggle conceptualized as white against black. Indians remained well below the radar screen of national consciousness during what were, in fact, the twilight years of federal termination policies designed to end tribes as legal, cultural, or political entities. The hope and expectation was that Indians would disappear from the landscape as reservations evaporated and their inhabitants, at government expense, moved to cities where they would become Americans shorn of distinctive Indian identity.

Meanwhile a non-Indian writer from Oregon and Native American activists in Washington state engaged in a radical rethinking of the cultural meaning and political place of Indians in contemporary America. The writer, Ken Kesey, articulated an Anglo American's sense of Indians' significance, particularly for the emerging youth culture that eventually spawned San Francisco's Haight-Ashbury hippies, Berkeley's New Leftists, and New Mexico's communitarians. The Indians, whether Nisqually or Lummi, Puyallup or Makah, focused on their economic and political tribal interests as they articulated a renewed and pathbreaking insistence that treaties mattered, enduring arrests and challenging state laws that ignored them.[1]

Among the first non-Indians to signal an interest in Pacific Northwest Indians were counterculture types. And among the first to define that difficult-to-define cultural movement and link it to Indians was Ken Kesey. By making an Indian the narrator and centerpiece of his first novel, *One Flew Over the Cuckoo's Nest*, he placed his readers on the periphery of American society. As counterculture people careened across the landscape looking for alternatives to their parents' lives, Kesey's Chief Broom, a half-blood member of a fictional and defunct Columbia River tribe, may have been their first engagement with a contemporary Indian figure and with contemporary Indian political issues. The hero of *Cuckoo's Nest* is Randall

McMurphy, who challenges the brutalizing power of authority in the form of Big Nurse and consequently serves as inspiration to the other inmates of the mental hospital where he has been incarcerated. He is lobotomized and ultimately dies.

The observer, interpreter, narrator and ultimate survivor of the novel, however, is the supposedly silent and schizophrenic "Chief Broom" Bromden, the book's most fully developed character and the only one with a history.[2] He is also the one who observes, interprets, understands, evolves, and ultimately takes positive action. Under intense government pressure, Bromden's tribe has disintegrated; their village inundated by a federally financed Columbia River dam. For years, his father, a full-blood named Tee Ah Millatoona fought the hydroelectric project with its attendant pressures to give up ancestral fishing rights and retreat to government housing. Government agents beat Bromden's father and cut his hair. Still, Tee Ah Millatoona resisted until other members of the tribe sold out; some of them going to work on the dam construction with their "faces hypnotized by routine." Moreover, his own wife, a white woman, pressured him to submit, making him "too little to fight any more." Only then did he give up, turn to alcohol, and die.[3]

What remains, however, are the son and his memories. The rebellious McMurphy not only helps Bromden revive his history but also regain his voice: "I still hear the sound of the falls on the Columbia, always will . . . hear the slap of the fish in the water, laughing naked kids on the bank, the women at the racks." He begins to speak, telling McMurphy his family history, as both explanation and cautionary tale about the risks of fighting a dominating power. The "Combine" beat his father, he warns. "It'll beat you too." This proved prophetic for the red-haired Irishman, but after joining McMurphy's fistfight with the hospital attendants, standing up for the patients' dignity, and being subjected to one last shock treatment, Bromden concludes he will never again be lost in a fog. This time he will beat *them*. Using the powers McMurphy helped him understand he still had, Bromden lifts the heavy control panel from the ward's tub room, heaves it through the window, and realizes his escape. His destination? Canada eventually. But first he will go to the Dalles, seeking his Indian friends. "I'd like to see what they've been doing since the government tried to buy their right to be Indians. I've even heard that some of the tribe took to building their old ramshackle wood scaffolding all over that big million-dollar hydroelectric dam, and are spearing salmon in the spillway. I'd give something to see that."[4] And so the story ends. The hope for the future rests with an Indian as he strides through the moonlit night . . . flying, free.

It might seem surprising that Kesey chose a Native American narrator for his 1962 novel. Why use an Indian perspective—and a fishing tribe, to boot, complete with current political issues—to frame a novel populated otherwise by Anglo and African Americans? Was Kesey aware of the cluster of termination policies bent on eliminating Indians? Did he know about the Army Corps of Engineers' Dalles Dam, built on the Columbia River after World War II to provide electricity for the growing Northwest, which had flooded Celilo Falls destroying a prime fishing place used by Umatilla and Warm Springs tribes of Oregon, the Yakima of Washington, and the Nez Perce of Idaho? The tribes fought the dam but failed to alter the government's course.[5] If so, he did not say. Rather, Kesey's explanation came in a light-hearted, playful way: peyote inspired Broom.[6] An alternative explanation for the inspiration and centrality of Chief Broom rests on two things: Kesey's western background and experience, and a long-standing literary tradition. Born in Colorado but raised in Oregon, Kesey certainly knew Indians still existed, and he apparently had some familiarity with ongoing conflicts between Indians and the government regarding fishing rights in the wake of hydroelectric dam construction.[7] The details of Bromden's tribal life revealed, in fact, a remarkable awareness of and sensitivity to native politics in the twentieth century.

More than that, who is a more appropriate representative of the outsider, historically resisting the omnipotence of expanding national power, than the Native American? What greater hope for this country than that supposedly offered by indigenous people? Kesey, and many others before him, associated Native Americans with the beauties of the natural world, genuine freedom, life apart from the machine, and an organic community free of industrialization's alienation. Despite his countercultural inclinations, Kesey, in choosing an Indian narrator, was connecting with a time-honored tradition of associating Native Americans with resistance to modernity.[8] Yet, in linking up, perhaps unconsciously, with this literary convention, Kesey provided his readers with a symbol that served the purposes of a new generation. "Indianness" proved to be a powerful concept that inspired the emerging counterculture from that point forward. Moreover, it was a story with political implications. The novel's end promised Indian resistance, renewal, and renaissance in the erection of ramshackle wood scaffolding over the modern hydroelectric dam. If powerless Indians could fight the "Combine," surely others could too.

It would be difficult to overstate Kesey's contribution to the counterculture. He served as a bridge between the Beats and the hippies of Haight-Ashbury. He was the "Pied Piper of psychedelia" who with the Merry Pranksters "brewed the cultural mix that fermented everything from psychedelic art to acid-rock groups [and] in the process of his pilgrimage blew an entire generation's mind."[9] He was also, through this widely read novel, among the first of his generation to turn to Indianness as inspiration for social criticism, political action, and cultural release.

The month President John F. Kennedy died in Dallas was the month Hank Adams dropped out of the University of Washington. A Sioux-Assiniboine who grew up on Washington's Quinault Reservation (his mother married a member of that tribe), Adams decided to ditch college and instead engage in direct action and organize protests. He found the most pressing issue at hand was treaty-assigned fishing rights. Over a century had passed since Territorial Governor Isaac Ingalls Stevens signed federal treaties with Northwest tribes in the 1850s, promising them, as they ceded huge swaths of property, the right to continue fishing in their "usual and accustomed places." But over time, Washington and Oregon ignored those rights; attempted to expand their jurisdiction over tribal members; and eroded sovereignty by harassing, and sometimes arresting, Nisquallys, Puyallups, Muckleshoots, and others as they dropped nets on rivers, at times outside reservation boundaries and beyond state-determined seasons. Indians maintained that the nineteenth-century treaties provided immunity from state rules and regulations; they continued to fish these spots wherever and whenever they wanted. Sports and commercial fishermen supported Washington State's efforts to prosecute, claiming Indian fishing threatened the fisheries for everyone. By the early 1960s, with the lines now firmly drawn, some Indians continued to challenge Washington State's interference with their treaty-guaranteed rights.[10]

In 1963 Hank Adams attended his first National Indian Youth Council (NIYC) meeting, where he came into the orbit of Clyde Warrior, a Ponca from Oklahoma, who helped found the group in 1961. The National Congress of American Indians (NCAI), had been established in 1944 by tribal leaders and former employees of the Bureau of Indian Affairs (BIA), and the World War II generation dominated the group. Younger Indians, inspired by the same impulse that prompted other members of their generation to create new organizations with more activist agendas, began to press for more assertive and aggressive strategies. When NIYC met on the Ute Reservation at Fort Duchesne, Utah, during the summer of 1963, Warrior invited actor Marlon Brando to join them. Brando had recently participated in the March on Washington and urged NIYC's leaders to participate in civil rights protests. Not all were interested, but Hank Adams and Bruce Wilkie, a NIYC founder, argued that black activists' methods, if not their goals, could be applied to Northwest Indian problems. By the following March, Adams and other Youth Council members convinced Brando to participate in what the media would call a "fish-in." For several decades, Indians such as Billy Frank (Nisqually), Bob Satiacum (Puyallup), and others had fished and experienced arrest, assault, and imprisonment—accompanied by little media attention and resulting in no change in state policy. Adams wanted to ratchet up the pressure. Not all local Indians welcomed NIYC's involvement, viewing its members as "college kids with sports jackets who showed up merely to make themselves look good."[11] Not all advocated direct action, preferring to resolve differences in courts of law.

Meanwhile, Brando, although not a counterculture figure, embraced the persona of a rebel *with* a cause. He supported Israel, and African American civil rights, and then moved on to Indian affairs after reading books by former Commissioner of Indian Affairs John Collier, and D'Arcy McNickle, a Flathead tribal member who worked for Collier. Brando sought out McNickle who encouraged him to contact the National Indian Youth Council. That, in turn, led to Adams's invitation to join the fish-ins. Brando consequently spent several days in Washington, in early March 1964, and stayed consistently "on message" regarding the legitimacy of treaty rights. He understood what was at stake and the fish-ins marked the beginning of Brando's life-long commitment to Indian issues. Joining him on the Puyallup River were Bob Satiacum and Episcopal priest John Yaryan of San Francisco's Grace Cathedral (see figure 1.1). Yaryan had formerly served at a church in Auburn, Washington, working among the Muckleshoot Tribe and learning about treaty rights. He returned to Puget Sound to participate in this action. "Once you get into this whole problem," Yaryan told a reporter, "you realize that the Indians' treaty has suffered complete abrogation." The decision to enlist Brando proved to be gold. The nation noticed.[12] And the lessons were clear: to get widespread *white* attention, get white participation; to get widespread *media* attention, get celebrity participation.[13]

Figure 1.1 Actor Marlon Brando joined Robert Satiacum (Puyallup) on the Puyallup River in 1964. Brando's presence brought media attention to the Northwest Indian tribes' demand for recognition of their long-overlooked treaty rights to fish in their "usual and accustomed places" and without interference from the State of Washington. Credit: Museum of History & Industry, Seattle, Washington.

After Brando left, Pacific Northwest Indian activists continued their fish-ins and added marches and demonstrations to their repertoire of techniques. In May 1966 about fifty people participated in a "Treaty Trek" designed to bring attention to Muckleshoot fishing rights. About one-half of the marchers were University of Washington students who described themselves as "human rights advocates." Other protestors gathered on the capitol building steps in Olympia with signs reading "Ho Chi Minh: Beware of U.S. Treaties" and "Custer Died For Your Sins" (several years before Vine Deloria Jr.'s book of that title). Still others established encampments on the capitol grounds and the Thurston County Courthouse grounds complete with tipis—fast becoming the universal symbol of Indianness, despite not being used by Northwest Indian people.[14] Non-Indian celebrities, however, garnered the most media attention. In February 1966 Dick Gregory, a thirty-three-year-old black comedian and candidate for mayor of Chicago, arrived in Washington to fish the Nisqually River. He came at the invitation of Adams and the Survival of American Indians Association (SAIA), a group dedicated to the Indian fishing rights battle. SAIA used direct action and civil disobedience to capture public attention and embraced the image of "militant." The organization sought partners from the local civil rights movement, enlisting African American Jack Tanner, attorney and regional director of the National Association for the Advancement of Colored People (NAACP), in their cause. Around the same time the American Civil Liberties Union (ACLU) joined in, providing legal services to those arrested in fish-in protests.[15]

Meanwhile, for the next two years Dick Gregory's activities dominated the news coverage of the fishing rights controversy. That Gregory was neither an Indian nor a fisherman did not escape local law enforcement. For several days they ignored him even though news photographers showed up to snap pictures of him holding dead fish. His motive, Gregory explained, was to see the federal government live up to its treaties. But in a statement which, although well-meaning, suggested a limited understanding of the distinction between treaty rights and civil rights, Gregory indicated he preferred to see them receive full constitutional rights. Until then, their treaty rights should be honored. Drawing a parallel between freedom rides and sit-ins of the civil rights protestors to the fish-ins, Gregory thought the Indians' "plight" had many of the trademarks of southern blacks' position of earlier years. He also predicted college kids and easterners would join the cause. "It's about time the civil rights front shifted to this part of the country," he told reporters. After several days, state game officials finally arrested Gregory and his wife, Lillian, for setting illegal gill nets. Although the New York Times failed to cover Marlon Brando's support of the fish-in protestors, the paper did run a small story on Gregory's arrest and faithfully covered the ensuing saga over the next two years. Initially eschewing bail, Gregory began a publicity campaign from prison, eliciting supportive telegrams from British philosopher Bertrand Russell, Dr. Martin Luther King Jr., and James Farmer, executive director of the Congress of Racial Equality. The Nisqually Tribal Council, meanwhile, disclaimed any connection between them and Gregory or the "renegade" Indians who participated in the fish-ins. Tribal Chairman Elmer Kalama told reporters the controversy should be settled in the courts, without any help from Gregory. "He is trying to turn this into a civil rights issue," Kalama said. "We are fighting for our fishing rights, and he is hurting our cause."[16]

By the fall of 1966 even his Indian allies became critical of Gregory, expressing disappointment in his actions and rhetoric. According to Janet McCloud (Tulalip), a co-founder and the first director of SAIA, his activities received publicity primarily in black magazines, which advanced his career but not their cause. Although she believed "the American Negro's revolution has necessitated a change in the white man's mental picture of the colored people of the world," the treaty rights issue was now getting lost in the mix. Furthermore, the publicity discouraged small, local donations.[17] In an attempt to undo some of this damage, SAIA invited Jay Silverheels, who played Tonto on the television show *The Lone Ranger*, to attend an Indian unity meeting. A Mohawk from Ontario, Canada, Silverheels arrived and posed for a photograph with Native American proponents and opponents of the fish-ins.[18]

When Gregory returned to Tacoma for sentencing, the judge slammed him with a six-month jail term, suspending half of it. June 7, 1968, he began serving time in the Thurston County jail. Gregory's attorney, Jack Tanner, warned that black power advocates H. Rap Brown and Stokely Carmichael, as well as the Reverend Ralph Abernathy, would show up to protest the sentence. He predicted the Peace and Freedom Movement would demonstrate on behalf of Gregory, their candidate for president, and would boycott Washington state products such as apples as well as Rainier and Olympia Beer. A group of Quakers paraded around the courthouse with "Set Dick Gregory Free" signs, having spent the preceding week discussing the Vietnam War and minorities' problems. Some sported Eugene McCarthy for president buttons and sang "We Shall Overcome."[19]

Increasingly, as McCloud noted, the press coverage turned away from Indian fishing rights and toward Gregory and African American issues. Gregory sent telegrams to President Lyndon Johnson, Secretary of State Dean Rusk, North Vietnam's Ho Chi Minh, China's Mao Zedong, and twenty-four other heads of state in order "to tell the Indians' and *his story* [my emphasis] to the world literally." According to one account, Gregory was particularly miffed that Johnson and Rusk had not included him in a meeting with six other presidential candidates, a slight he characterized as "a racial insult." Further, Gregory decided to consume only distilled water and bread during his incarceration, describing his hunger strike as a protest against the denial of fishing rights, the war in Vietnam, and other issues. Newspapers regularly reported on his weight loss and one journalist even mused on the political costs to Republican Governor Dan Evans should the activist die in custody. In the meantime, during a news conference that Lillian Gregory and Jack Tanner called, Janet McCloud tried to return the focus to the Indians' issues, reminding the state that she, as one reporter put it, "hasn't buried the hatchet." Nonetheless the story's headline announced "Gregory Tells World He's Alive, Hungry."[20]

On July 17, 1968, Judge Hewitt Henry released Gregory from prison. About twenty pounds lighter than when he entered jail six weeks earlier, Gregory left the courthouse in the company of Anglo television star Robert Culp and his actress-wife France Nuyen. (Bill Cosby, Culp's African American co-star in the television series *I Spy* had been unable to make the trip to Washington). Insisting that his purpose all along remained publicizing "the plight of the Indians," Gregory told reporters that he hoped Indians would not have to become "as militant and violent as black people are for America to wake up" and that Washington state would solve its black problems and become a model for the rest of the nation. For now, he intended to turn his attention to a "world fact-finding tour" that would take him to North Vietnam, China, and North Korea, where he hoped to talk with crew members from the recently captured U.S. Navy vessel, *The Pueblo*. With that, Gregory left the Northwest.[21] Without doubt, Gregory's sympathies for Indian fishing rights were sincere. Still, this particular cross-racial partnership had proven problematic and possibly counterproductive, diverting attention from treaty rights and diffusing it into a kaleidoscope of other issues.

About the time Dick Gregory left the Pacific Northwest, a University of California, Santa Cruz, undergraduate named Richard White migrated to the region. White, who would eventually become an eminent historian of Native American and Western history, quit his summer job on Independence Day, 1968, and agreed to join a friend, Joseph Quinones—a Yaqui from California—on a road trip to the Democratic National Convention meeting in Chicago that summer. They never made it. The young men instead found their way up to the Sky River Rock Festival in Washington state where Rolling Thunder, a Cherokee medicine man who lived on the Shoshone Reservation in Nevada and had been appearing at counterculture events since the 1967 San Francisco Be-In, said to Quinones upon learning he was Yaqui: "You have to go Frank's Landing. Your people need you." The next day White and Quinones drove to Frank's Landing, a center of fish-in activity and an Indian settlement downriver from the Nisqually Reservation and outside Olympia. They ended up staying into the winter.[22]

What they found when they first arrived were members of the Billy Frank and Al Bridges families and their Indian supporters. They also found non-Indian communists, Black Panthers, Students for a Democratic Society and Peace and Freedom Party members, unaffiliated radicals from the University of Washington and Portland's Reed College, alienated Indian and non-Indian Vietnam War veterans, Quakers from Seattle, counterculture types passing through from all over the country—in short, "whoever they [the Nisqually activists] could get." Sometimes several hundred non-Indians would camp there, other times, only a core group of thirty or forty. Joseph Quinones, as a Native American, sat in on strategy sessions with the Bridges, Franks, and Hank Adams. They put him to work recruiting supporters among area high school and college students. He visited campuses and talked about treaty rights and fish-ins, collecting names and phone numbers of people who would mobilize for demonstrations. They called these groups Indian Rights Committees. Quinones found allies everywhere and invited the students among them to stay at Frank's Landing. Those who did found their job was to "give bulk" to the Indians' demonstrations, help keep the cause in the public eye, and potentially reduce violence against Indian demonstrators because law enforcement officials would presumably show more restraint with non-Indians. "We might be hippies and we might be worthless," as White put it, "but we still had the privilege of our whiteness and parents who might cause trouble [if we were beaten]."[23]

The camp dwellers also guarded the fishing nets (although they often proved hapless in protecting them from confiscation), drove members of the Bridges and Frank families to town and to meetings with other allies in their "hippie" vans and cars, collected firewood, fed people, took drugs, experienced several raids on the Landing by state and county law enforcement officers, and sometimes carried arms themselves (see figure 1.2). The newcomers to the Frank's Landing encampment lived like "they imagined Indian people lived," sleeping in tents, occasionally eating venison ("salmon was far too valuable to eat"), and waiting for the next demonstration. Of course not all counterculture visitors joined the political fight. For some, Frank's Landing was just another place on the road—a temporary haven to use drugs (despite the Frank and Bridges families' best efforts to keep drugs out) and live beyond the boundaries of conventional life. Such passers-through were not committed to Indian treaty rights and just got in the way.[24]

Up to that point, White, who traveled in both counterculture and radical circles yet retained a distance from both, had thought little about Indians or their politics. His presence at Frank's Landing was completely accidental. But once there he became drawn in by "the most interesting people [he] had ever met." Expecting to find "spear-wielding Indians, leaping deftly from rock to rock, thrusting quickly to impale giant salmon who churned in the river's foam," he found instead men who fished with nets, drank beer, and risked police harassment, beatings, and imprisonment. Al Bridges, however, "looked like the Indian

Figure 1.2 A fish-in on the Nisqually River. Washington State officials arrested and prosecuted fish-in participants until the federal court case *U.S. v. Washington* ruled in favor of treaty rights and ended the protests. Credit: Museum of History & Industry, Seattle, Washington.

every young radical automatically retrieved from his childhood. Whole psychic histories came down on his shoulders." White saw Bridges and the others as "incredibly rooted" to their place, understood they had been fighting for something for a century, and noted that they "didn't become distracted by the [counterculture] circus around them."[25] White was not privy to the strategy meetings or part of the inner circle. Nor did he expect to be. In fact, sometimes he felt like a parasite "living off the faith of the Indians. Fighting because they had something worth fighting for." Yet he also knew he could leave anytime, whereas they lacked options. The fundamental justice of their cause, however, and his personal commitment to the Bridges family, in particular, kept him there.[26]

While the Nisqually and Puyallup men, and a few women, fished, endured harassment, and arrests, the women's responsibilities included keeping the camp and political activities going by raising bail, contacting sympathetic people to contribute food and supplies, selling salmon caught to willing buyers, and occasionally setting nets and then enduring beatings and jail. Maiselle Bridges, Billy Frank's sister and Al Bridges' wife (Al was Nisqually-Puyallup-Duwamish), "was the one you saw best and remembered," according to White. "She had calmness and a dignity that had seen outrages and survived intact." Maiselle and others like her kept the Indian nations alive in the midst of what seemed to be minor arrests in insignificant towns. But she understood there was a part of the land that whites could never possess.[27] Her daughters, Valerie, Suzette, and Alison, participated in all aspects of the camp's political activities, while Hank Adams spent much of his time typing at the Bridges' kitchen table, strategizing, and negotiating complicated arrangements that often fell apart. White found him quiet and determined but not charismatic. "He inspired respect, but not adoration." Among Adams's strategies: escalating the conflict by bringing in non-Indians for large protest demonstrations as a way to make it more costly to the state. Adams himself was not a "radical," but he used radicals to buy time, get concessions, and garner publicity.[28]

In early September 1968, Students for a Democratic Society (SDS), Peace and Freedom Party, and other leftist organizations announced an alliance with the "renegade" Nisqually fishermen. As Robby Stern, prominent member of the University of Washington SDS, saw it at the time, the state and federal governments had been systematically extinguishing Indians' cultures for years and the "Red people are clearly among the most oppressed people in this society. They represent another important group that will join with other oppressed people of the society to destroy their oppressors." He also acknowledged the significant backdrop to all politics by the fall of 1968: the Vietnam War, noting that it was twice as deadly to be an Indian in America in 1965–1966 as a soldier in Vietnam. Others too, noted parallels between Indian issues and those of the war in Vietnam. To Richard White, Frank's Landing represented "the backwater of Vietnam"; another place where things had gone terribly wrong and the nation committed grave injustices. Inclinations to join the issues found reinforcement from bitter Vietnam veterans in the camp and from Hank Adams who identified a "commonality of historic and collective experience [which] established an affinity" between Indians and Vietnamese.[29]

Stern who, like White, understood the fight was the Nisqually's, still believed non-Indians could be of help. His own trajectory of activism began at Syracuse University where he became involved in civil rights and anti–Vietnam War activities. Not long after moving to Seattle to begin law school, he mobilized an effort to protect counterculture people from police harassment in the University District and somehow eventually found himself at Frank's Landing. Stern did not remember, later, how it was he came to visit the site but once there, he found himself moved by the effort and concluded that a contingent from the University of Washington's SDS needed to help out. When Stern made the offer, the Nisqually at Frank's Landing accepted.[30] His job, beyond guarding nets and helping garner publicity, was to attempt to impose order on the assorted types gathered there by creating committees for each fishing site and a master committee to coordinate them all. The internal committees, however, quickly fell apart. Meanwhile the Indian Rights Committees outside the camp raised money to replace confiscated fishing equipment and provide legal defense and bail. The Seattle-based underground newspaper, the *Helix*, sympathetically covered the fishing rights story and provided information on how non-Indians could provide support by coming to demonstrations on the rivers or at the state capitol. Its articles invited readers to bring tents, sleeping bags, and food to share communally and included maps on how to find Frank's Landing. Beside publicizing the "actions," one September 1968 story promised the fish-in on the Nisqually would feature workshops on fishing rights, Indian history, dance, and "basketweaving." It also hinted that folksingers Pete Seeger and Buffy Sainte-Marie might appear.[31]

Fish-in organizers, encouraged by local support, hoped to recruit people from all over the country to come to Frank's Landing. Suzette Bridges traveled to Denver to meet with Chicano activist Corky Gonzales, "the Guevara of the Rockies," who promised a busload of demonstrators for a mid-October demonstration.[32] Gonzales's Denver-based Crusade for Justice movement and Native American activists had first joined forces in 1968 at the Southern Christian Leadership Conference's Poor People's Campaign, a major national event designed to demand the federal government address the needs of the nation's poor and to demonstrate racial and class solidarity for nonviolent solutions to the problems of human rights. It consisted of a march on Washington, D.C., followed by creation of Resurrection City, a multiracial, rather ramshackle, encampment quickly constructed on fifteen acres of West Potomac Park, stretching from the Washington Monument to the Lincoln Memorial.[33]

Hank Adams, Al Bridges, and a group of Indian activists from the Pacific Northwest joined the campaign, linking up with other native caravans that funneled into Washington, D.C., from points west. More than two hundred Native Americans participated from all over the country: Mandans and Hidatsas, Cherokees and Poncas, Pomas and Pimas, Senecas and Tuscaroras (see figure 1.3). The southwest contingent of the Poor People's Campaign included Native Americans from Colorado, New Mexico, Arizona, Nevada and Oklahoma; California-based Diné or Navajos and Brown Berets; New Mexico land-grant heirs; Anglo hippies and radicals; and Gonzales's Crusade for Justice. The loose coalition quickly dispersed, however, once they reached Washington. The Chicano and Indian participants refused to move to Resurrection City, which was a muddy mess. Most of the Native Americans found housing at the St. Augustine's Episcopal Church, which offered dry beds, bathrooms, and a kitchen to prepare food. But they did not forsake the campaign itself. Some erected tipis at Resurrection City as a symbol of Indian presence and support, participated in planning meetings, and marched or demonstrated in all the events. Moreover, the Chicanos and African Americans reciprocated, lending their bodies and voices to an Indian march. Corky Gonzales, New Mexico-based activist Reies Tijerina, and the Southern Christian Leadership Conference's Reverend Ralph Abernathy joined Hank Adams, Al Bridges, and about three hundred people in a protest at the Supreme Court Building on May 28, 1968, that focused on fishing rights.[34]

With his arms around Abernathy and Tijerina and a cigarette dangling from his left hand, Adams stood before the cameras and objected to a Supreme Court ruling of just the day before, the *Puyallup* decision, which upheld Washington State's right to specify when and where Indians could fish. This was a critical blow to the fishing rights movement. Adams contended that treaties from the 1850s took precedence over state laws and that the federal government did not grant fishing rights. Rather, the treaties acknowledged tribes already possessed

Figure 1.3 The 1968 Poor People's Campaign brought thousands of people to Washington, D.C., including some Native Americans. This event encouraged cross-racial communication and cooperation about both shared and distinctive issues. Credit: Center for Southwest Research, University Libraries, University of New Mexico.

them and the government simply, but solemnly, promised to protect them. He demanded that he and the entire Indian delegation be allowed inside to present their petition to the Supreme Court. While officials denied that demand, he and twenty-one members of the group eventually gained admittance to the building and presented the petition to clerk of the Court. Meanwhile, in keeping with the multiracial nature of the demonstration, the protestors engaged in "long Indian chants, a few freedom songs, and shouts in Spanish," as they occupied the building's steps. Abernathy made clear the primary purpose of the event was to publicize an Indian issue and he was there to support, not lead. It was a memorable moment of interracial cooperation with a focus on treaty rights. It would not be the last. Abernathy, for one, would reappear at Wounded Knee five years later (see figures 1.4 and 1.5).[35]

Vine Deloria Jr. later claimed that most Indians were "extremely suspicious" of the Poor People's Campaign because it lumped people together indiscriminately on the basis of economic status when the most important issue for Indians, "tribal existence within the homeland reservation," was ignored. Only a few

Figure 1.4 During the 1968 Poor People's Campaign, Chicano activist Reies Tijerina (*right*) and civil rights leader Ralph Abernathy (*left*) joined Hank Adams (*with cigarette*) in a march on the Supreme Court Building to protest violation of treaty rights.
Credit: Center for Southwest Research, University Libraries, University of New Mexico.

Indians attended, Deloria claimed, funded by churches who wanted to get Indians involved in the Campaign. As for those who demonstrated for fishing rights while in Washington, Deloria believed they betrayed the proper ends with inappropriate means. Participation in any way seemed to be "a surrender to white society because the basic thrust of the campaign was to endorse middle class values through pointing out their absence in the life of the poor." At the time, Hank Adams admitted the Indians who participated in the Poor People's Campaign did not achieve their immediate goals. But he did not consider it a total loss either, claiming that it had sparked a "responsible revolution" in tribes and created a "committee of 10,000" that would pressure Congress for policy reform and the overhaul of the Bureau of Indian Affairs.[36]

Back on the banks of the Nisqually River, having tasted this moment of interracial cooperation and national attention, Adams and others continued to seek support, wherever they could find it and deployed what materialized. During the autumn of 1968, once Indian leaders decided on a demonstration date and site, SDS leader Robby Stern called a meeting of non-Indians to decide if any would be arrested (although, as it turned out, police ultimately arrested whoever they chose). The attempted orchestration was far from smooth. Even an approving underground-newspaper reporter admitted the "monumental lack of organization" when 250 Indians and non-Indians gathered at Frank's Landing in

Figure 1.5 Symbolizing cross-racial solidarity, Hank Adams (*far left*) and Ralph Abernathy (*right*) flank Reies Tijerina (*center*) at a Poor People's Campaign press conference in Washington, D.C., in 1968. Credit: Center for Southwest Research, University Libraries, University of New Mexico.

October 1968. An organizer from the Southern Christian Leadership Conference was on hand to lead the group in some riverside singing as a steady drizzle fell. The demonstrators debated whether to turn the "sit-in into a resistance situation" or pursue the nonviolent route preached by the SCLC organizer. Finally, they all adjourned to the grounds of the capitol building in Olympia where the Native American leadership reasserted control; auctioned off an illegally caught salmon; and gave speeches noting, among other things, that this demonstration signaled a "new period of protest" because so many non-Indians had joined them. In the end, White concluded, the non-Indian camp was "ineffective, disorganized and tumultuous, but its weakness became its strength." Law enforcement officers and locals in Olympia were fearful of what might happen at the Landing. Assuming they were dealing with "unpredictable, drug-crazed maniacs, they gave the camp more power than it ever had in reality . . . They feared hundreds of freaks and radicals in Olympia. This was Hank's success. It was one of the few things he had to bargain with."[37]

Most people had no idea what was actually happening at Frank's Landing and took their information from newspaper accounts of the demonstrations. Just as Marlon Brando's and Dick Gregory's participation assured front-page coverage, the hundreds of people who supported Billy Frank and other fishermen as they strung their nets at the spillway from the Deschutes River and Capitol Lake, September 8, 1968, found their photo on the *Daily Olympian*'s front page the following day. The accompanying article claimed that the Indian fishermen's supporters were "goateed, long-haired, barefoot and bare-chested hippies from as far away as Los Angeles and Alabama, singing, swinging, and carrying signs protesting restrictions of civil rights and Indian rights." Police arrested only six people, including Joseph Quinones who, upon being booked on the fifth floor of the county courthouse, opened up a window, flung his hat into the crowd below, and shouted, "Freedom now!" Robby Stern was also arrested that day.[38]

One month later, state and county officers seized a net at Frank's Landing and subsequently confronted about thirty people camped there, "mostly non-Indians, long-haired, bearded youths and their girls." Officers arrested fisherman George Meskuotis, but the featured photo in the Olympia paper depicted non-Indian men and women "lecturing" Bruce Gruett, assistant chief of the Fisheries Patrol. The story focused on the "hippies'" verbal abuse of the lawmen. The same day, the *Seattle Post-Intelligencer* printed a photo of Quinones and Stern delivering a dead salmon to the Governor's Mansion and another of two hundred young people, mostly non-Indian, sitting in on the state's Temple of Justice in support of fishing rights.[39] Most news accounts, in fact, led with sentences noting the presence of Black Panthers, Socialist Worker Party members, and SDSers, as a way to underscore the radicals' presence and, perhaps, discredit the Indians' position.

Such alliances most assuredly carried costs. No doubt many readers, including Native Americans, found the hippies and political radicals quite distasteful. Yet when the Seattle Liberation Front joined the Puyallups at their encampment, Bob Satiacum answered a reporter's query about how he liked such volunteers with the pointed comment, "Well, you don't see any of the good church people down here helping us, do you?"[40] Quite simply, supporters from most any political stripe and race were welcome. Plus, the presence of middle-class Anglo "kids" catapulted these events into peoples' consciousness. Observers might not particularly like them, but the protestors must have seemed familiar—like their own children or their neighbors'. As Joseph Quinones put it, "it pulled us out of isolation," helped get the word out about treaties and the living conditions of many Northwest Indians, and "lifted the morale" of the activists.[41] It brought home to people in the Northwest that challenges to the status quo regarding race relations and Indian politics were real, immediate, and gaining strength. The story was no longer about a handful of so-called renegade Indians demanding treaty rights. Non-Indians from across racial, ethnic, religious, geographic, and generational lines were joining them. Something significant was happening here and the word reached well beyond the Northwest.[42]

Simultaneously, other non-Indians including "some good church people" supported the fish-ins in less public ways. Adams, Janet McCloud, Ramona Bennett (Puyallup), Guy McMinds (Quinault), and others had for years been establishing relationships with church groups and gathering their support. Episcopal Canon Yaryan's participation in the 1964 fish-in signaled an early response. The following year the Episcopal bishop of the Diocese of Olympia made a one thousand dollar donation to SAIA. By 1968, at the invitation of Olympia's Episcopal bishop, Adams and Bennett were meeting with various Protestant leaders seeking continuous, not just crisis, involvement. Bishop Ivol Curtis acknowledged his denomination operated a church on Puyallup land and thought it could become a political sanctuary for Indian fishermen, much as other Episcopal churches had been used by conscientious objectors to the Vietnam War. At the end of this particular meeting, the Indians had a check for five hundred dollars from an anonymous donor and a promise of five thousand dollars more.[43]

More impressive and more sustained was Quaker support, particularly through its American Friends Service Committee (AFSC). Quakers pushed more aggressively for racial equality than any other religious group in the country. The combination of their ubiquity and zeal made them the most visible, white-dominated group in the civil rights movement. And their interests extended to Native Americans' rights.[44] The AFSC originated in 1917 when Quaker groups wanted to promote nonviolent solutions to human problems, in general, and provide alternative service for World War I conscientious objectors, in particular. Not until thirty years later, however, did AFSC enter the Indian affairs arena at the request of its own Pacific Southwest Regional Office. Alarmed at the destitution on the Navajo and Hopi reservations, brought to national attention by a 1947 devastating winter storm, the western Quakers mobilized. They established an Indian Program office in Pasadena and later moved it to Flagstaff; donated clothing, medicine, and food to these two reservations; established sewing rooms for Navajo women to repair the clothing donations that had come in; and organized summer visits for children to non-Indian families. They also issued a press release stating it was imperative Congress appropriate sufficient funds "to keep our treaty pledges with the Navaho [sic] Indians." From these rather inauspicious beginnings, the AFSC gradually established projects on other reservations and supported or created several urban centers for Native Americans, including the Intertribal Friendship House in Oakland, which opened in 1955. That same year the organization created a national desk for Indian projects. Although the organization maintained an interest in national affairs and the federal decision-making process, it viewed its primary role as encouraging education and community development on reservations and established a presence only where invited. AFSC's work in Indian communities was, then, largely decentralized and localized, along the lines of Saul Alinsky's community-organizing model that used grassroots, neighborhood approaches to effect substantive change.[45]

Although the AFSC understood Native Americans shared many of the same problems as African Americans—poverty, lack of educational opportunities, and discrimination—they also realized, quite early, that several things distinguished Indians from other minorities. A 1963 internal report from the Pacific Northwest Regional Office, for example, demonstrated a relatively sophisticated understanding of Indian affairs. First, the report acknowledged and applauded Native Americans' insistence on retaining their Indian identities. Although they knew some Americans, wedded to the melting pot concept, might find this troublesome, the AFSC fully supported Native American cultural persistence and promoted a national model of cultural pluralism. Second, they understood that many Native Americans had a special legal status as treaty tribes. These agreements were "the means by which the United States 'bought the country'" and explained why they received special exemptions from taxes on land, services, and rights to self-government. In addition, by mid-decade the AFSC clearly believed and publicly acknowledged that Indians should articulate their own goals and assume the public leadership roles regarding Native American affairs. AFSC's job was to take cues from Indians and help them achieve the goals they defined for themselves. As one AFSC staff member put it in 1966, "We need . . . to be careful not to appear to speak for Indians at a time when they should be and are speaking for themselves."[46]

AFSC's involvement in the Pacific Northwest first became formalized in 1957 with the establishment of an Indian Committee in Seattle. The Quaker group worked with the Klamath who faced termination and it also encouraged Tulalip and Muckleshoot young people to seek higher education. The staff assisted tribes in securing Office of Economic Opportunity and other government grants and helped with the formation of the Small Tribes of Western Washington (STOWW), a cooperative community-action program of seventeen tribes and groups. By the mid-1960s AFSC realized the brewing conflict over hunting and fishing treaty rights was heating up and concluded that this was the arena where they could make a difference, not only for local tribes but possibly also for many others. AFSC staffers had observed at close hand Washington State's efforts to restrict Muckleshoot, Puyallup, and Nisqually fishing and knew these tribes lacked adequate resources for legal defense. Moreover the Indians' side of the fishing controversy was inaccessible to non-Indians. The public had virtually no reliable sources for information on the history of fishing rights or the current situation.

So, in the winter of 1965, AFSC organized a study group to collect factual information about the controversies on the Nisqually, Puyallup, and Green rivers. The group included Walter Taylor, former AFSC National Indian Program Representative who had worked with the Senecas on the Kinzua Dam controversy; Bill Hanson, a former AFSC staff member turned Seattle attorney with deep interest in protecting treaty rights; and Mary Isely, chair of the AFSC Seattle Indian Education Committee. As the group's report came together during 1966 it offered several recommendations for AFSC action. Those included: continue to validate treaty rights, support fair judicial consideration, avoid making decisions for Indian people and groups while encouraging them to make decisions and support them when they do, and work for a better informed public. The last recommendation took material form when AFSC published the study group's *Uncommon Controversy*, which, in its first incarnation, appeared as a mimeographed publication with a run of 550 copies.[47]

The authors made clear from the outset that the fishing rights cases attracted the Quaker organization's interest because they had ramifications beyond Washington state. In a statement reminiscent of Kesey's Chief Bromden, *Uncommon Controversy* noted that Indians had come up against "the aggressive, development-oriented Western culture" and thus shared much with other peoples' struggles around the globe. For too long, and to the earth's detriment, Western civilization had imposed its values, religion, law, education, and technology on other cultures. But now, by recognizing the legitimacy of Northwest Indians as fishermen, people could also benefit "from the traditional conservation wisdom of Indians." Native Americans, the report explained, integrated work, play, and religion with the environment and could consequently "serve as a model for the survival of man suffering now from too much fragmentation and not enough community feeling." If Robby Stern stressed the Indians' oppression, the AFSC stressed their "ecological awareness of kinship with environment." Indians were not the ones who built the Grand Coulee Dam and destroyed fisheries. They did not dump sewage and atomic waste into rivers.[48]

Yet conservation was not the core issue. By adopting new values and attitudes, the book explained, Americans not only could increase the number of salmon in their rivers, they could simultaneously cultivate diversity and cross-cultural respect. The hostility toward Indians and their legal rights reflected fear of nonconformity and of cultural difference. The Quakers' concern was to stop imposing conformity and to encourage the kind of diversity necessary for a healthy society and planet. In fact, the AFSC concluded non-Indians needed to adopt a more Indian-like relationship with nature based on harmony rather than conquest. They also suggested a commission made up of Indians, sportsmen, and commercial fishermen to devise a fair allocation of fish. This was the right thing to do legally and morally.[49]

The Western Washington branch of AFSC hoped to capture not only local but also national attention with the book. Washington and Oregon newspapers carried stories about it, but efforts to attract Washington, D.C., and New York news outlets were "nil," as John Belindo, executive director of the NCAI, reported to the AFSC's Seattle office. Nevertheless, local and state coverage was widespread, including television and radio. In fact, Tandy Wilbur, president of the Western Washington Inter-Tribal Council, congratulated AFSC's Chuck McEvers after watching his television press conference regarding *Uncommon Controversy*. As he noted, "This is the first time that I know where [a] non-Indian entity publicly took a stand such as you described on T.V. last night and I am sure this will have an impact on the minds of many people." McEvers was probably relieved to get such a positive response since, as he told Wilbur, his greatest concern about the AFSC report was the tribes' reactions. He knew the topic was sensitive and that the tribes were not all in accord on the subject. He particularly feared being seen as a white man speaking for Indians. "We are anxious to support what Indians are saying themselves . . . and we certainly do not want to say anything that would undercut what Indians want said on this very important issue."[50] McEvers did not just make this point to Native Americans. When the largely non-Indian AFSC Indian Program staff met at an Indian Progress Roundup in Washington, May 2–4, 1967, they discussed a wide variety of issues and discovered they did not agree on many of them. But on one thing they found unanimity: commitment to Indian self-determination. McEvers summarized that conclusion, noting non-Indians should offer sympathetic encouragement, resources to help Native Americans do what they wanted to do, and "then, in Felix Cohen's words 'get out of the way.'"[51] (Felix Cohen was a federal Indian law expert and advocate of native sovereignty.)

AFSC distributed the first edition of *Uncommon Controversy* to all tribes in Washington and Oregon, the member tribes of NCAI, attorneys working on fishing rights cases, relevant state and federal government agencies, prominent sportsmen, federal legislators, various mass media outlets, and other national organizations committed to Indian affairs. Within a year the number of copies available dwindled to a mere dozen as requests arrived from tribes, libraries, students, attorneys, federal agencies, private organizations, and individuals from around the country. The goal to reach national audiences was realized, gradually. In 1968 the University of Washington Press asked to publish the book in paperback form because they believed it would sell as a case study with worldwide applications. Pleased with the partnership, AFSC set about raising the subvention the Press required. The AFSC, the Klamath Fund, Hogue Memorial Fund, NCAI Fund, American Indian Civil Liberties Trust, and the Harry Burks Memorial Fund all kicked in. Originally the UW Press planned to print 1,500 copies but before the presses rolled, orders for 3,000 had come in. So, they printed 5,500 in paperback, which sold for $2.50, and 500 in hardcover at $5.95. It is impossible to know how many people read this book, but it subsequently went into multiple printings and undoubtedly helped shaped the outcome of the fishing rights controversy. In fact, Vine Deloria Jr. said *Uncommon Controversy* was the most important thing AFSC had done for Indian people. When the fishing rights case was finally adjudicated and the tribes were victorious, a lawyer from the Native American Rights Fund wrote AFSC's Phillip Buskirk, "I hope you realize the contribution that American Friends Service Committee has made toward finding resolution to the overall fishing rights dispute ... especially by the publication of *Uncommon Controversy*."[52]

Not everyone on the Indian side of the dispute applauded the book, however. In the summer of 1970, Dee Linford Johnson, a member of Seattle's University [Quaker] Meeting and, according to an AFSC staff member, "an Indian. . . . closely involved with militant action including Fort Lawton and Puyallup" complained about the organization's role in Indian affairs. She believed *Uncommon Controversy* was "unfair" and, perhaps more important, the Quakers had no right to speak for Native Americans who could speak for themselves. Moreover, she thought they should be supporting the Puyallup fish-in on the ground. AFSC worker Arthur Dye discovered Johnson had not read the book, and so he gave her several copies. Although she cooled down, she remained extremely critical of AFSC. Interestingly, several days before this confrontation, a handful of AFSC staff members had visited the Puyallup fish-in camp, established in mid-August 1970. A non-Indian claiming to represent the Survival of American Indians Association called the AFSC office asking for donations of blankets, food, and medicine but the caller had not herself been to the camp and did not know the principal Native Americans involved. This made the AFSC staffers "nervous."

Using Muckleshoot tribal member and former AFSC staffer Leo LeClair as their conduit to the fish-in organizers, the AFSC group asked for an "invitation" to visit the camp. When they arrived two "white radical armed guards" met them. They saw about thirty or so people there, all of whom appeared to be non-Indians including a "girl with a rifle slung over her shoulder [who] scanned the sky with binoculars." They talked with camp leader Cyrus Cross, who had claimed the tribal chairmanship in a disputed election, and a woman he identified as Roberta Green. Cross made it clear they intended to fish once the salmon entered the river, expected state officials would attack the camp, and "were prepared to die because they had nothing to lose." When the AFSC representatives asked what they could do to help, Cross offered no answer. When asked if he needed legal help, he replied all lawyers were crooks and worked for the government. When asked if he wanted to speak with the governor, he said that would do no good. When asked if he had a copy of *Uncommon Controversy*, he said no "'and I wouldn't read it if I did.'" The AFSC representatives concluded they were dealing with a "thoroughly alienated man."[53]

Arthur Dye told Green that the presence of so many non-Indians–particularly armed non-Indians—would make it difficult for other Indians to support the Puyallup camp. She disagreed and told Dye that if he stayed overnight at the camp, not knowing when he might get "busted," he would appreciate "the white and black brothers who are protecting them." In the meantime, only Indians would fish and only Indians would guard the fishermen. Before leaving the camp, the AFSC delegation explained to Cross they did not want to interject themselves into a situation where they were not wanted, but they remained concerned and hoped a nonviolent solution would be found in order to eliminate the necessity of armed camps. They also offered to help generate an audience to whom the Puyallup could tell their side of the story. Clearly this kind of confrontational politics, with white radicals and weapons so visible, was antithetical to the Quaker approach. But they sympathized with the miserable conditions at Puyallup and believed that violence from the state side would lead to loss of life. On September 3, the AFSC received word the Muckleshoot Tribal Council had voted to support the Puyallups. Six days later, several hundred local police and Washington State troopers attacked the Puyallup fishing rights activists, arresting sixty of them. This became the triggering event that led the United States Justice Department, finally, to join the tribal suits against the State of Washington. Stanley Pitkin, a U.S. attorney, witnessed the assault on the fishing camp, the most violent and publicized to that point. Police used tear gas, the State Game Department officials wielded clubs, some Indians carried guns and knives, and one lobbed a firebomb. With tensions and violence mounting, Pitkin moved to support the Indians, end the bloodshed, and resolve the issue legally.[54]

This was the outcome the AFSC had hoped for. Much more comfortable with briefcase-toting lawyers than gun-toting white militants, they welcomed the federal involvement. They were less certain what their own future should be, however. The Seattle AFSC believed there was "considerable sympathy for the Indian situation in the non-Indian community and [hoped] . . . to provide a focus through which these non-Indians could assist" the tribes. Working with the Small Tribes Organization of Western Washington (STOWW) seemed one avenue. Helping interest foundations in providing grants to Indians was another. But even that could prove dicey. In fall 1970 AFSC Pacific Northwest Regional Office submitted a grant proposal to the Field Foundation asking for, among other things, $25,000 for the Native American Rights Fund's fishing rights related trial expenses. Arthur Dye consulted with Hank Adams about the grant. Dye told him three times he would not send it without Adams's support and three times, he claimed, Adams supported it. He went over the proposal line by line with Ramona Bennett and also with Tim Hansen of the Puget Sound Consortium, a loose support group for the Survival of American Indians Association.

After AFSC submitted the proposal, however, Adams called Vine Deloria to express unhappiness with the proposal and Deloria called the Field Foundation to complain about it. The Foundation did not care to be "involved . . . in an Indian War," and AFSC withdrew the application. They understood this seriously undercut the Field Foundation's confidence in AFSC but also concluded that "internal warfare [among Native Americans] is the name of the game and . . . we can't play without getting burned from time." Juggling relations with people such as Vine Deloria, who one AFSC staffer distrusted as a "prima donna" who could "blow hot and cold" and "move in and out of our region," Hank Adams, whose relations with Northwest tribal councils ranged "from bad to terrible;" and with tribal governments that were often in disagreement amongst themselves was a challenge indeed. Consequently, as the AFSC saw it, foundations understandably hesitated to fund Indian organizations. In comparison, the AFSC seemed better organized, respectable, responsible. Foundations were "not afraid of being involved in a controversial battle. . . . or of having the money used up in internal political squabbles" when they gave to the AFSC, Dye believed.[55]

Apparently part of Adams's problem with the Field Foundation grant proposal was its tribal approach. He favored, according to Dye, "an aboriginal Americans approach, outside the tribal structure." In spring 1971 Adams submitted, on behalf of the Survival of American Indians Association, his own proposal to the Field Foundation, asking for $100,000 to encourage intercommunity organization and cooperative development. In it, he made clear his distrust of tribal councils that "have in practice become isolated from the people" and whose disbursement of money only furthered the separation leaving communities "disoriented and unorganized." Adams believed his approach would take community organization out of the "realm of power politics" and would be free of "any imposition of personality controls." He had submitted this proposal without consulting AFSC, which did not particularly endear him to the Quaker group. Meanwhile the AFSC continued to maintain open lines of communication with and support STOWW, SAIA, and individual tribes—reminding all that it would assist them in any efforts *they* initiated and carried out through their own organizations. They also closely monitored the *U.S. v. Washington* lawsuit, which sought to affirm treaty rights once and for all, and worried that it would be a potential disaster because if it failed, "the Indian rights game will be over." And they felt cheered whenever evidence that tribes were using *Uncommon Controversy* came their way. In spring 1971, for example, AFSC learned that at state-held hearings on fishing rights, the Yakima Tribe showed up with a huge stack of the books and distributed them to everyone connected with state government and the legislature. At the hearing the director of the Department of Fisheries, Thor Tollefson, quoted from the book on several occasions. AFSC also was heartened to learn that it was being used in college courses.[56]

Trepidation about the lawsuit meanwhile remained palpable. In the summer of 1971, AFSC staffers feared things looked grim. They believed the Native Americans were divided not only on the issue but also on the legal strategies to pursue. The U.S. attorney was not experienced in fishing rights and was not consulting with Indians on how to handle the case. A united effort to garner public support and raise funds for an expanded informational campaign had not developed. Thus, in consultation with some of their Native American contacts and allies, they urged Robert Johnson, of the University of Washington Law School, to prepare an article on the case for the *University of Washington Law Review*. They knew he would seek considerable Indian input, define a legal strategy for the case that would unite different factions, bring the issue to a national audience, and increase the likelihood of additional government and foundation support. Johnson, an expert in both water and Indian law, had participated in a successful case which upheld Oregon Indian fishing treaty rights on the Columbia River. He agreed to write the article, receiving research support from the law school, the AFSC, and covering the remainder of expenses by himself.[57]

Eventually the controversy found resolution as attention and action turned from streamside demonstrations, with their potential violence and consequent publicity, to lawyers and the court system. Help came from the Seattle Legal Services, the Native American Rights Fund (NARF), and, as noted, most importantly the United States Justice Department. A 1969 legal victory in Oregon, *Sohappy v. Smith*, which acknowledged the right of several tribes to fish the Columbia River with minimal United States or local government regulation, was encouraging. And so by September 1970, when the Justice Department launched its case, *U.S. v. Washington*, most of the state's tribes joined the litigation. This, as it turned out, was a momentous turning point. The Indians now had the considerable power and resources of the federal government behind them. Finally, in February 1974, Judge George Boldt decided in favor of the tribes. It was an almost complete vindication of all the tribes had claimed as theirs. In a dramatic endorsement of treaty rights, Boldt supported the tribes on every major point. Moreover he boldly declared that the tribes' "fair share" of the salmon harvest constituted one-half of the fish and that the tribes had sovereign rights as governments to regulate their members' participation in that harvest. The federal court of appeals affirmed this decision in 1975 and the Supreme Court declined to hear an appeal one year later. *United States v. Washington*, according to attorney Charles Wilkinson, "carried a rare credibility. Minority rights, judicial courage, morality, generations of Native persistence, and the truth of history converged in the federal courthouse in Tacoma in 1974 to create the kind of elevated justice to which our system can sometimes rise." Ten months after first reporting on the Boldt decision, the *New York Times* claimed the ruling had already "made a dramatic difference for the better in the quality of [the tribes'] lives." For the first time in decades, they were becoming commercial fishermen again.[58]

Indians, of course, deserve the lion's share of credit and responsibility for this impressive victory. They fought long and hard to sustain treaty rights. They were the ones who consistently risked life and limb and livelihood, arrest and imprisonment. But they also won because they operated in a national climate that was growing more conducive to acknowledgement of treaty rights and the justice of Indians' positions. Counterculture and radical types, the NAACP and the ACLU, celebrities and students, Quakers and Episcopalians, African Americans and Mexican Americans were a "supporting cast" in all this—but an early, important, perhaps even crucial element. They did not represent a well-organized, disciplined, or regimented set of troops. They wandered in and out of Frank's Landing and other sites of contention. In some cases their attention and interest waned. But they shared the belief that the fishing rights issue represented America's legally sanctioned promise to a particular minority group. They also shared a commitment to the validity, viability, and perpetuation of various cultures within the nation. In their effort to redress America's imperialist past, as well as contemporary foreign interventions, these allies helped to capture the eyes, ears, and hearts of fellow citizens who, in the end, responded favorably to significant change. Hank Adams, STOWW, and tribal groups understood this at the time and used these groups for Indian purposes. But it was only a beginning.

2

The California Scene

California beckoned many of the nation's cultural and political cage-rattlers by the mid-1960s. Not all expressed an interest in Native Americans, but a number of the most prominent and thoughtful cultural leaders believed that in Indians they had found an important, American-based, alternative way of living; and images of Indians pervaded much of the California-based counterculture iconography. It is noteworthy that while the Pacific Northwest inspired Ken Kesey's *One Flew Over the Cuckoo's Nest,* he wrote the novel in California while enrolled in Stanford's creative writing program. Hippie entrepreneur and publisher of *The Whole Earth Catalog* Stewart Brand, actor Peter Coyote, and poet Gary Snyder were among others who found inspiration in Indianness, and made their claims from their own Golden State perches and perspectives. True, their reflections did not represent years of careful study or deep knowledge. These were, after all, young people just getting to know the world, seeking answers about how to live a life of substance and meaning. Their views of Indians had everything to do with their own yearnings and concerns.

Yet, these commentaries took root not simply in their own imaginations but in experience with actual Indian people, who either welcomed these youthful seekers into their communities or interacted with them when they appeared uninvited. In some respects there was little new in this phenomenon. For centuries Indians had seen Anglo American discontents wander into their camps, homes, and reservations or turn to their cultures. Outsiders with a genuine interest in Native American cultures found willing teachers. As the twentieth century went on, in some corners of the country, peyotists and their Native American Churches, in particular, welcomed non-Indian participants. Of course, not all knowledge was open to outsiders, and as the numbers of supplicants increased in the 1960s, often bringing with them drugs and sexual practices which did not adhere in reservation communities, the doors often closed. Yet, particularly early in the decade and in those places where non-Indian allies could prove useful allies in political controversies, the possibilities for communication and exchange were real.

What non-Indian sojourners learned was often limited. What made it significant, however, was the reach these non-Indians had in spreading their impressions and "understandings" of Indianness through the underground press, Gary Snyder's poetry and essays, and the best-selling *Whole Earth Catalog*. If alternative-seekers

Figure 2.1 Counterculture fascination with Indianness proved ubiquitous. This poster for the 1967 Be-In at San Francisco's Golden Gate Park typified "Indian" iconography.
Credit: Hoover Institution Archives, Stanford University, Stanford, California.

did not come to California with Indians on their minds, they could scarcely avoid them once they picked up the Haight-Ashbury based newspaper the *Oracle* or saw a poster advertising the February 1967 Be-In at San Francisco's Golden Gate Park, which featured a Plains Indian on horseback, guitar in one hand, blanket in the other (see figure 2.1). While for many, the more ephemeral images of Indians constituted the extent of their involvement, for others the encounter proved more probing and substantial. Whatever the level of engagement, one thing was clear: Indians were not only attractive symbols, but real people worthy of emulation and political support. They were not only historical figures of great dignity but contemporary human beings in distress. These developments in California—particularly the Bay Area—received widespread, national, and international coverage which, in turn, helped catapult these movements into broader significance. Media attention brought critics, but it also brought new converts. By the time Indian activism came to the Bay Area, in the form of a 1969 takeover of Alcatraz Island, many people had been culturally primed to hear their complaints with a sympathetic ear and to lend political and financial backing.

In the opening pages of Tom Wolfe's *Electric Kool-Aid Acid Test*, an account of Kesey and the Merry Pranksters' LSD-laced California experiences, the author careens down a San Francisco street in a truck with some Pranksters, including Stewart Brand and his "half Ottawa Indian" girlfriend Lois Jennings. The truck sports a bumper sticker that reads "Custer Died for Your Sins," and Brand and Jennings wear blazing disks on their foreheads. Brand, described as thin and blond, also wears a necktie made of Indian beads resting on his shirtless chest. They are on their way to the "Warehouse" where the Pranksters' bus "Further" is garaged and where they hope to reconnoiter with Kesey, who had been arrested as a fugitive after fleeing to, and returning from, Mexico in the wake of a marijuana possession charge.[1] Brand's claim to fame in this context was as creator, with San Francisco artist Ramon Sender, of the Trips Festival of January 21–23, 1966; a celebration designed to simulate an LSD experience without the LSD. Music and light shows would supposedly take its place. They hired impresario Bill Graham, a New Yorker and member of the San Francisco Mime Troupe, to help plan the event at the Longshoreman's Hall. The second night featured Kesey's and the Pranksters' "Acid Test"—a reference to an event the Pranksters had recently held at the Fillmore Auditorium where "hundreds of heads and bohos from all over the Bay Area turned out, zonked to the eyeballs." Kesey's arrest for marijuana possession two nights before the Trips Festival put something of a wrench in those plans, but the event went on with the arrest actually providing tremendous publicity. Thousands poured in, "even the first night," according to Wolfe, "which was mostly Indian night, a weird thing put on by Brand's America Needs Indians." But the biggest crowds came for the Acid Test on Saturday, many of them "bombed out of their gourds . . . coming out into the absolute open for the first time . . . heads from all over, in serapes and mandala beads and Indian headbands and Indians beads, the great era for all that."[2] Although Kesey would soon retreat to his farm in Oregon after serving six months in prison for drug possession, San Francisco and the nation would never be the same. The Trips Festival gave Brand an awareness—"a sudden, lucid awareness," as he later put it. "None of us knew that there were 10,000 of us outlaws until that weekend. That came as real news. Suddenly, overnight, it was 'Shit, we're not pathetic, we're powerful.'"[3] But how did "Indians" come to play such a prominent role in all this?

Stewart Brand, never more than a minor player in the Pranksters, was the one who was "into" Indians and the Trips Festival was something of a bridge from the Indian chapter of his life to the one that followed.[4] There was little in his background that would have suggested his turn to psychedelics . . . or Indians, for that matter. His road to Indians began during his army service on the East Coast. He found a community of artists in New York who stressed the importance of connection to the natural world and systems—an approach that seemed to mesh with his Stanford biology professor Paul Ehrlich's views. These artists created "happenings" where artists, their materials, and the audience together created an environment that eliminated boundaries between art and life. Excited by this idea, Brand searched for ways to participate more fully and joined an "art tribe" called The U.S. Company, or USCO, which added electronic technologies (strobe lights, multimedia slide shows, etc.), psychedelic drugs, and communal mystic togetherness to their counterculture gatherings. Brand contributed as a photographer.[5]

It was the camera that led him to Indians, as well. Returning to the Bay Area after his military stint, Brand not only continued contributing to USCO happenings but also studied design at the San Francisco Art Institute, photography at San Francisco State, and participated in a legal LSD study at Menlo Park's International Foundation for Advanced Study.[6] His experiences with Indians and the counterculture were about to begin. By May 1963 Brand landed a job taking photographs on the Warm Springs Reservation in Oregon. Up to that point, he had given Native Americans little thought other than noting in high school journals some thoughts on Indian views of nature and land. By the early 1960s he assumed they were noble, but dead . . . or drunk. What he discovered at Warm Springs was "a different America" and a "way more interesting reality" than his stereotypes had allowed. The Indian people he met were guarded, but friendly. When he began to take photographs without asking permission, they gently told him to ask before shooting. Otherwise, he found them "surprisingly forgiving" of a white man from Illinois.[7]

Brand's contact on the reservation was Delbert Frank, a member of the Confederated Tribes of Warm Springs (Warm Springs, Wasco, and Paiute tribes)

Tribal Council. Frank hoped to use Brand's photographs in a brochure about the reservation—a small tool in the tribes' long-term development plans. Frank, for one, hoped to pursue economic development wisely, knowledgeably, and with preservation at its core. Brand asked Frank to write down the messages he wanted the photographs to convey, and he would try to translate those same messages graphically or visually. Frank's intended audience was Congress, the public, and the Warm Springs people themselves. It was the latter which gave Brand pause. As he wrote in his journal at the time, "speaking to Indians about themselves, I've got to retool my mental camera . . . I need to know more about vocabulary of the audience. Emphasize, if I can inherent talents (often denied) to be with the land." Brand understood he was operating in a cultural context not his own. Meanwhile, he gained insight into the complexities of tribal politics. While doing his work on Warm Springs, Brand realized the reservation tribal council was divided about the nature of future economic development and about fishing rights in the Pacific Northwest.[8]

Coincidental to his time at Warm Springs, he read Kesey's *One Flew Over the Cuckoo's Nest* and thought the Oregonian had "got it right about Indians, a subject nobody was paying any attention to at the time." But beyond that, Kesey touched a chord deep within Brand. As he confided in his journal, he found the novel was "the answer to my dilemma between the revolution against the combine and preservation of things like old Indian ways . . . the battle of McMurphy versus Big Nurse is identical with Indians versus Dalles Dam or me versus the Army." The novel taught him any enemy of the Combine was a friend of his, and Brand considered Indians and LSD among such friends. So, what was he going to do about the destruction of his own civilization? What was he going to do photographically? The answer: expand beyond Warm Springs and bring the truth about Indians—particularly their ideas about land and nature—to the rest of the nation.[9] For the next several years Brand began showing up at reservations, camping out and taking pictures. "I was an early one," he explained, and so met no resistance to his presence. No one accused him of trespassing. Only later, say, when young people would barge into Oraibi on the Hopi Reservation after having read Frank Waters' *Book of the Hopi*, would such resistance become more common. But in the early 1960s, Brand was apparently tolerated and sometimes welcomed.[10]

Brand also contacted Kesey and showed him his Indian photographs. Kesey handed Brand a joint of marijuana—"not something you did to strangers then"—and before long, Brand became a "semi-Prankster," finding in Kesey's cohort "more stuff to tie into with his group that was genuinely original than there was anywhere else."[11] Of course, drugs constituted a mainstay of that new stuff. Both men had experimented with hallucinogens, including peyote. For Brand, the introduction to drugs started with friends in Big Sur and evolved into attending Native American Church meetings in Nevada, in part to have access to peyote. A handful of other non-Indians from the San Francisco area held an informal peyote meeting on Mount Tamalpais, in February 1962, marking a solar eclipse. By the following summer, they were attending peyote meetings with Paiutes, Washoes, and Bay Area Navajos. Eventually a core group moved first to Carson Valley, Nevada, and then, by 1965, to Santa Fe where they incorporated as The American Church of God. Under the leadership of people such as Rick Mallory, Jack Loeffler, and John Kimmey, the congregation of about two hundred consisted primarily of young whites mostly in their twenties, a handful of African Americans and Chicanos, and the rest Native Americans from across the Southwest, mostly in their fifties and sixties. Among the Native American teachers were Little Joe Gomez, Henry Gomez, John Gomez, and Tellus Good Morning (all of Taos Pueblo), John Pedro (Arapaho), Wilbur Doss (Navajo), Emerson Decora (Winnebago), and Paul Manarko (Jicarilla Apache).[12]

Brand himself "went up the cactus trail," participating in peyote meetings and sharing the other non-Indians' belief that in Indians they had found a genuine homegrown "counterculture" with "a mythic frame and depth that people were looking for" (see figure 2.2). Moreover, these were actual human beings who kept the whole experience from slipping into the purely romantic.[13] As Brand

Figure 2.2 Stewart Brand and Hola Tso, vice president of the Native American Church, near Sawmill, Arizona, on the Navajo Reservation, circa 1964. Credit: Stewart Brand.

saw it, the Native Americans gathered around a fire to eat peyote, sing and listen to "the voice of the Continent"—a voice that civilization's din had drowned out but which offered lessons on the "laws of harmony." Thomas Banyacya, David Monongye, John and Mina Lanza (all Hopi), Eddie Box (Southern Ute), Harvey Goodbear (Cheyenne-Arapaho), Oren Lyons (Onondaga), Mad Bear Anderson (Tuscarora), Rolling Thunder (Cherokee-Western Shoshone) and Larry Bird (Santo Domingo-Laguna) accepted the non-Indians' sincerity and willingly engaged with them.[14]

In Brand's excursions to reservations he began to observe rapid changes under way, with certain generational implications. As he saw it, the elders, spiritual practitioners in particular, sustained cultural traditions and received respect from the rest of the community for this. Middle-aged people seemed to be just trying to get by, survive, mostly by approximating white models. The youth seemed at a loss, not really listening to the elders until hippies came through and then they witnessed the "long hair convergence." At that point, some young Indians began to realize their identity provided automatic membership in an exclusive "club [to which] they already belonged." Out of the dominant society, which for so long had tried to extinguish Indian cultures, emerged children of privilege who completely reversed that impulse. Indianness was cool, something to be valued, preserved, and perpetuated.

But the non-Indians, including Brand, also learned some surprising things about Indians. First, they were funny. Expecting stoicism, they found instead a lively and often off-color sense of humor. Jokes about the color of vomit following a peyote meeting, for instance, caught Brand off-guard. Second, the patriotism exhibited by Indians was a revelation to him. The veneration of veterans confused Brand and created "major cognitive dissonance." To honor soldiers for military service in the context of the Vietnam War was anathema to the hippies, but to see Indians honoring them gave Brand and others a new perspective about something they had been absolutely certain about. It, in fact, took the "absolute" out of that certainty for Brand who did not change his opinion about the war in Vietnam, but did thereafter look at returning veterans with greater sympathy. Finally, he realized that the temptation to "get it wrong" with the environment was possible with anyone. Damage to the environment was everywhere and even Indians were capable of destroying the commons. He began to realize his notion of Indians as perfect environmentalists was overly simplistic.[15]

In 1966 Brand married Lois Jennings, a half-blood Ottawa woman raised in Washington, D.C. The marriage reinforced his involvement in things Indian. Through her, Brand witnessed tribal politics and became convinced they were a "contact sport"—something he wanted no part of. On the other hand, he observed Indian women speaking with authority and garnering genuine respect. He found that especially appealing and concluded: "this is the way it should be."[16]

Brand's visits to Indian communities and flirtations with peyote did not, in the end, satisfy him. His inclinations and ambitions were less inward and more outward. He wanted to take what he had learned from, and about, Indians to others. He seemed to feel a responsibility, in fact, to do so. As it turns out, the idea of publishing a photography book about Native Americans preceded his first step onto Warm Spring Reservation. The phrase "America Needs Indians" appeared in his journal by January 1964, and he intended to use it as the title of his book. Brand sought the advice of University of Chicago anthropologists Robert Thomas and Sol Tax as well as New York-based writer and historian of Native Americans, Alvin Josephy. But he probably found greater encouragement from his friend and fellow seeker Jack Loeffler at a midsummer 1964 peyote camp when Brand told him his vision for the work. Loeffler explained that he and others were also trying to look at America "straight like an Indian. And see what it is we can do." They believed Native Americans could teach them how to walk in beauty. The great issue now was to preserve the beauty of mountains and deserts on which to walk. Brand agreed it "has to come from within . . . when my world from without is in balance and harmony, as it is in these hills, in this desert, in this twilight with these stars. America needs Indians and America needs itself."[17]

Yet he knew that all was not well in Indian communities. That Native Americans sought out peyote "medicine" signaled some were experiencing sickness. On the other hand, they used it in a religious context and with discipline that indicated they were not as sick as white men. And, Brand believed, they neither feared nor competed with the land. Rather, their relationship was one of sustenance and love. He decided, then, that his book's full title would be "America Needs Indians: The Voice of the Continent." Brand was convinced the time had finally come for Americans to turn to Indians. People were beginning to learn to "be natives from the most native Americans . . . studying with the new clarity the ancient harmony of a shared land heritage."[18]

Brand's first step, then, was to create a multimedia show called "America Needs Indians." Inspired by his USCO connections, he displayed it at venues across the country, particularly colleges and community theatres. Using up to four slide projectors, movie projectors, music, and live performances, Brand considered it a "peyote meeting without peyote" and offered audiences a Trip Festival-like experience, several years before people were tripping. He juxtaposed white mythic imagery of Indians with photographs of actual Indian people, many from his own collections taken on Warm Springs, Blackfoot, Navajo, Hopi, Tohono Odham, and other Indian reservations. He used Edward Curtis photographs and live performances by Indian groups. Audiotapes played native music, storytelling, peyote songs and Navajo chanting. The message was simple: Indians are still here—an important and startling message for non-Indians to hear in the early 1960s—and have important lessons to teach, particularly regarding how to use the land, honor it, and maintain a continuity with it for decades.[19] The show was not scripted and constantly changed. More important, perhaps, than the message was simply the fact the show existed at all: that a non-Indian was traveling the country with a production featuring Indians and promoting them as worthy of consideration.

Of course the number of people who actually saw Brand's show was scant, but he made an effort to expand his influence. The content of his expanded project remained vague. In fact, the proposal Brand sent potential supporters spoke more about his burgeoning countercultural tendencies and interest in technology than Indians. It also smacked of a tendency to conflate Indianness with Americanness. As he explained his plan and its inspiration in 1964:

> The collision of the Indian and non-Indian cultures in America in the last ten years has dramatized the life and ideals of the Redman, so long neglected on his reservation. A mobile exhibit, in response to public interest, can display the best of his culture and ours. The format might combine the strength of the nineteenth-century Chataqua [sic] with the "son et lumiere" of modern electronics. It could be housed in an easily transported inflated dome—a product of our most advanced building technology and reminiscent of the highly mobile Plains Indian village. The exhibit as it travels through America can become a dramatization of our traditional faith in the future and of the sun, rain, wind, and land—a rediscovery of our national heritage.[20]

In a letter he sent to Alvin Josephy about his project, Brand included an architectural sketch of a Buckminster Fuller-like inflatable, sixty-foot dome with a tunnel entrance and exit on each side. He envisioned a translucent blue structure with balloons, flags, and feathers attached to attract attention. In the evening, as the show was about to begin, the dome would explode with the sounds and lights of a lightning storm. People would enter a tunnel lined with photographs, Cigar Store Indians, and a poster saying "America Needs You" before emerging into the central space with its maze of walls featuring photographs, drawings, paintings, and maps. Visitors would see slide shows and hear "pools of localized sound" or "a recorded sociological dialogue on the American Indian and the American non-Indian." At the center of the space would rest an unadorned and unlabeled circle—"a symbol of balance and resolution." A small door would usher visitors out through another tunnel and to a truck with an exhibit room-library for those who wanted more information on Indians. "The variety and richness possible in this exhibit are unlimited," Brand explained. "The great inflated hall filled with electronic light and sound, and graphic exhibits offers the opportunity for a presentation with no repetition. It can be as infinitely varied as the cultures it represents."[21]

Josephy kindly encouraged the young visionary. Moreover Brand informed Josephy that "America Needs Indians" had gained the status of photographic consultancy to Secretary of the Interior Stewart Udall, and that he had made arrangements with Macmillan Company and Grossman Publications to produce two books from the project. Now that Brand was approaching foundations and individuals for financial backing, he hoped Josephy would join Secretary Udall, photographer Ansel Adams, and others by writing a letter on behalf of "America Needs Indians." Josephy agreed, although the full-blown projects and books never materialized. Later that year, however, Josephy did see some of Brand's work in Carmel, California, and commented that Brand was on his way "to something new and very exciting."[22]

At this point, however, Brand was increasingly involved with Kesey and the Merry Pranksters. His transformation from Indian showman to environmental entrepreneur was under way. A boy who would become a San Jose, California, newspaperman heard Brand speak in the Bay Area around this time. Brand was "in his High Indian phase and showed up in top-to-toe full-fringed buckskin to tell us about Indian theology. Even to a middle-class 11 year old Mountain View [California] Boy Scout and Little Leaguer like myself, it was apparent after five minutes that this guy was a little light in his moccasins." But then Brand's "indifferent talk on Native American culture suddenly gave way to an animated exposition on how he had dropped acid on a North Beach rooftop and seen God." The reporter's father, a retired military officer and NASA security specialist also in attendance, at first "looked like he'd just been poleaxed in the forehead" until Brand got to his point. "Why haven't we seen a photograph of the whole earth yet?" In fact, Brand had lately been peddling, not the "America Needs Indians" show, but buttons which posed that very question. According to the reporter, his father's eyes lit up. He had heard of this guy—in fact, he had been looking for him! The father began a full-scale investigation on Brand, uncovering his Stanford education and military background, and concluded Brand probably was a crackpot. But his question remained a good one. Supposedly, the father's report on Brand to the director of the Ames Research Center accelerated NASA's production of excellent color photographs of earth from space, helping to usher in, simultaneously, the environmental movement of the late 1960s.[23] Even this whole earth concept, Brand later claimed, stemmed from his interest and interactions with Indians. His Indian wife liked outer space and "since I was being entranced by all of her premises as an Indian, I asked why she was interested in rockets. She said, 'each one of them gets us closer to home.'" Indians, Brand went on to explain, "are so planetary they also tend to be extra-planetary."[24]

Crackpot or not, Brand seemed to have a knack for finding a place on the leading edge of fashion and cultural change. Around the same time, March 1968, he was returning to California from his father's funeral in Illinois. Somewhere over Nebraska, he looked up from reading Barbara Ward's *Spaceship Earth*, and while looking out the window, mused about the people, some of them personal friends, who were "starting their own civilization hither and yon in the sticks" at counterculture communes. What could he do to help them? Where could they find windmills? Information on beekeeping? He decided to create an access to such services—first through a traveling truck store and eventually through a catalog of goods, dubbed *The Whole Earth Catalog*, a "counterculture Sears Catalog" or "a sort of Montgomery Ward for the hip movement." The first incarnation included a six-page preliminary booklist, including Reginald Laubin's *The Indian Tipi* (a hands-on description of tipi making and erecting). With samples of each book in their truck, Brand and Jennings headed out for the communes of New Mexico and Colorado. Although the couple realized only two hundred dollars in business that summer of 1968, they learned a great deal and returned to California ready to start production on the *Catalog*. By the next year, they produced supplements and suddenly caught the media's attention with stories in *Time*, *Vogue*, and *Esquire*. The *Catalog* became a cultural and publishing phenomenon reaching well beyond the initial market of hippie communards. In 1971 Brand had offers from Dutton and Random House to distribute the *Last Whole Earth Catalog* and Brand's reputation as entrepreneur-environmentalist and visionary was set. Not only did the catalog sell millions of copies, it also made money. For a counterculture capitalist, that posed a minor dilemma. What to do with the profits? In summer 1970 Brand decided to throw a party and give some of it away. The revelers themselves were to decide what to do with the money and at one point someone suggested: give it to any Indian who is here! There was an Ottawa tribal member in attendance—but it was Brand's wife, Lois Jennings, who declined. Eventually the guests narrowed the possibilities down to two: either donate it to a communications project or an Indian project. In the meantime, during the discussion, the money, which was in one hundred dollar denominations, had been passed around. Apparently some of the partygoers felt they were in need and helped themselves, because at the end of the event five thousand dollars was missing.[25]

The Whole Earth Catalogs were eclectic, offering information on items ranging from windmills and woodstoves to personal computers and geodesic domes. It represented one of the less-publicized, but perhaps more long-lasting, elements of the experimentation and alternative cultures brewing at the time: one that revered land, ecology, and technology. While it clearly idealized community, it did not eschew capitalism. It certainly celebrated the anti-authoritarian and the local.[26] Nor did Brand neglect his, by then, long-standing interest in things

Indian. Tucked in between geodesic domes and yurts, was a page in the 1971 edition that featured Reginald Laubin's book about tipi construction along with Brand's personal endorsement of tipi as living space. "To live in one," he wrote, "involves intimate familiarity with fire, earth, sky and roundness. The canvas is a shadow-play of branches by day, people by night. Depending on your body's attitude about weather, a tipi as dwelling is either a delight or a nuisance. Whichever, you can appreciate the elegant design of a tipi and the completeness of the culture that produced it." The *Catalog* also advertised Virgil J. Vogel's *American Indian Medicine* (along with the commentary that while Vogel looked at Indian medicine through Western anthropological and medicinal lenses, "weedmunchers could find no better guide"); George M. White's *Craft Manual of North American Indian Footwear*; Margaret M. Wheat's *Survival Arts of the Primitive Paiutes* (described as a book "about people living in equilibrium with their environment. They probably had no words for garbage or waste because they used everything"); W. Ben Hunt's *Indian Crafts and Lore*; and Andrew Hunter Whiteford's *North American Indian Arts*.[27]

In addition, the 1971 edition contained a two-page spread of Indian books that Brand recommended to his readership, again with his own commentary. He explained the list derived from two intense, though informal years (plus five slack ones) of hanging around reservations, Indians, anthropologists, and libraries. "Long may Indians, reservations, anthropologists thrive! They gave me more reliable information, and human warmth, than dope and college put together." Of course, he went on, books could never provide, by themselves, "The Native American Experience." For that people needed to immerse themselves in the land and make the acquaintance of some actual Indians. Nevertheless, these volumes offered an amazing amount of information. Among those Brand promoted was Frank Waters' *The Book of the Hopi*—"possibly the farthest out of the American Indians (in present times they are not as together as Zuni, or Taos, but they are larger and so is what they attempted) . . . Frank Waters' was perhaps too eager to write a Bible, but I can't blame him. It's that kind of knowledge." Brand also liked Gene Weltfish's *The Lost Universe*, which explained the Pawnee way of life "in a way that you could go now and live it. Here are old solutions to problems we consider unsolvable and new." *Black Elk Speaks*, by John Neihardt, demonstrated how Plains Indians' lives turned on visions—"solitary mystical whizbangs." This book not only offered Black Elk's accounts of Sioux life and historical people such as Crazy Horse, it also showed how an individual experienced his vision, was responsible for it, and revealed "the burden, joy and power of doing that."

On contemporary Indian affairs, he recommended Vine Deloria's 1969 *Custer Died For Your Sins*. Deloria, according to Brand, was "the perfect dude to write of current Indian politics." The son of a missionary but "enough Sioux to be Sioux," Deloria had long experience in National Indian Youth Council "stand-up-and-fight meetings" and as executive director of the National Congress of American Indians. Further, he was only thirty-five years old "and still funny." Deloria had what Alvin Josephy warned Brand about: "the traditional American Indian cut-throat zeal for politics." That, matched with his thoroughness and his humor, made him the ideal person to introduce readers to contemporary Indian affairs. Deloria's conclusion: land-based tribal identity was the best route for Indian survival. Since Deloria's primary intended audience was Indian people, Brand could not "resist a remark to young white Indian-savers: you can't help anybody by saving them; that's a self-defeat program. Relax and appreciate. Custer died for your sins. And your virtues." Brand had given up his efforts to convert Americans regarding Indians, so he looked to "a long-haired artist famous former-dope-fiend commune white person I know [who] is busy learning from his Indian friends at the Taos Pueblo: manners."[28] Sympathy and support was all to the good, but non-Indians should not interfere or assume too much with respect to Indian political affairs.

Just as he avoided personal involvement in Native American politics, so did Brand express little interest in Indian religion or spirituality—at least by *The Whole Earth Catalog* era. Still, he understood many other counterculture types were interested in religion and mysticism, and so the catalog included a section on that. In the company of books on Zen and Tantric Buddhism, Baba Ram Dass's (formerly Richard Alpert) *Be Here Now*, and *The I Ching*, Brand included Carlos Castaneda's *The Teachings of Don Juan: A Yaqui Way of Knowledge* (1968) and *A Separate Reality: Further Conversations With Don Juan*, noting "I don't have the words for the importance I consider these books to carry." Like so many other readers of his generation, Stewart Brand took Castaneda at his word, believing the University of California, Los Angeles anthropologist was indeed apprenticed to a Yaqui Indian man, the Don Juan of the title, who taught his student through various psycho-active plants including peyote and a mixture of psilocybin mushrooms.[29]

By publicizing Castaneda's books, as well as others on Indian-related matters, in *The Whole Earth Catalog*, Brand helped spread awareness of them to the far corners of the country. Like thousands of others, writer Gereth Branwyn discovered the *Catalog* when a friend's brother brought it home from college. She was then living "in a small redneck town in Virginia" and had never seen anything like it. No one around her hometown ever talked about whole systems, nomadics, Zen Buddhism—or, most likely, Indians.[30] In small towns and big cities all across the nation, counterculturalists and others found in the pages of this remarkable catalog the information they needed to pursue any of those topics and issues. Brand helped turn the countercultural into the everyday, the distant into the nearby, and the exotic into the attainable.

As Brand's interests evolved and expanded into other arenas—most notably computers and software, a 10,000 Year Clock and Library project, and an All Species Inventory—his involvement in things countercultural and Indian dissipated. His marriage to Lois Jennings ended in divorce in 1973. Brand, however, never renounced his connection to the sixties even though he recognized so much of it had been trivialized into fad or trend. "It was a lot better than that," he insisted. Some lasting and beneficial changes had emerged from that turbulent time. The sixties bunch had been "gutsy," trying "all kinds of stuff knowing that a lot of it wasn't going to work, but it was worth trying anyway... We knew it was historic... there was a great pushing of the edge.'"[31] For some, part of that edge was found in the company of Indian people. In the out-of-the-way places where some Indians lived, a few allowed Brand, and others, in. Consequently, "there was cultural mixing," he claimed. "Elderly traditional Indians could be seen engaged in uncharacteristic friendly hugs, direct eye contact with strangers, and language such as 'We knew there was a rip-off going down on Alcatraz long before the pigs came in.'" Indians provided the counterculture "with a living identity base." The counterculture, in turn, encouraged respect for Indian ways, particularly among younger Indians. "The longhair convergence was mutual reinforcement, a mutual loosening of dominant White strenuousness."[32]

Much of the relationship was ephemeral, overly romantic on the part of the counterculture, and shallow. Some of it became offensive and exploitive. Some *was* nothing more than passing fashion. But fashion can, and in this case most certainly did, affect culture and politics. When fashion connects to something important and substantive, it percolates down to the bedrock of change. Indianness may have been fashionable, but the core message at the heart of Brand's "America Needs Indians" and the collection of Indian books he peddled in *The Whole Earth Catalog*—that these are cultures worth studying and sustaining—stuck long after Brand himself shed his buckskins.

In 1971 poet Gary Snyder received an invitation to read his work at Indian high schools in the Southwest. At places such as the Navajo school in Fort Wingate, Arizona, student reaction divided between the "stomps," who preferred country and western music and a cowboy image, and the "cats," who leaned toward the beads and feather, rock and roll, hippie image. The cats liked Snyder's poetry and wanted to hear all they could from him about Chinese and Japanese culture. The stomps, apparently, were less impressed.[33] Most likely these young people knew little about Snyder—that he had been the inspiration for Jack Kerouac's character Japhy Ryder in *The Dharma Bums*, or that he had been one of the "elder statesmen" who presided over the 1967 San Francisco Be-In. They probably were not aware of his long-standing interest in American Indian cultures and his efforts to incorporate Indianness into his literary work. And it is highly unlikely any of the Navajo students had seen the issue of the San Francisco-based underground newspaper, the *Oracle*, which featured Snyder as one of the four "most respected voices in the Beat-Hippie-Psychedelic movement."[34] That February 1967 issue printed a complete transcript of an *Oracle*-sponsored Houseboat Summit Meeting that took place on Alan Watt's Sausalito houseboat. Watt was dean of San Francisco's Academy of Asian Studies and author of the best-selling *The Way of Zen*. Other participants included former Harvard professor and LSD-guru Timothy Leary, poet Alan Ginsberg, and Snyder. As these men wrestled with the conflicts between the antiwar movement in Berkeley and the psychedelic movement in Haight-Ashbury, between the spiritual seekers and the leftist-activists, they also addressed how to live in the world—whether to "drop out," as Leary suggested, or stay connected while simultaneously creating new social organizations, structures, and models. They addressed questions such as what kinds of practical advice could this assemblage provide? Should psychedelic drugs play a part in the new lives young people were attempting to create? As they formed new communities, should they legally incorporate to protect themselves? In the end, all four men agreed that going smaller, decentralizing, becoming "tribal" was the best strategy. Snyder, more than the others, attempted to root his comments in historical and anthropological reality. Time and again he turned to Indians to make his points.

Regarding people who sought an alternative "tribal" way, Snyder recommended they first decide *where* they wanted to live. Once they settled on a particular place, they needed to learn about the Indian culture that had preceded them—its mythologies, deities, and technologies. He assumed, of course, that in most places the local Indians would no longer be alive and that the "Indian culture" had been static, allowing for neither cultural change nor for the migrations of people in and out of an area. Non-Indian seekers of the 1960s, he explained, would have to find this Indian information in books and archaeological ruins. Further, they needed to understand the original ecology. Was it short- or long-grass prairie? What was the climate like? Finally, the best way to truly understand the place was simply to live on it—preferably in a tent that would expose them to the elements. They would then have to decide how to make a living on the land: would it be by farming? Hunting and gathering? In sum, take it back to the Indians, he urged. "You can do it in any part of this country today . . . cities and all . . . Find out what the Indians were doing in your own area whether it's Utah, or Kansas, or New Jersey" and approximate their approach. In response to this advice, Leary, who seemed to have no idea whatsoever what "dropping out" really meant or what it looked like, enthused: "That is a stroke of cellular revelation and genius, Gary. That's one of the wisest things I've heard anyone say in years. Exactly how it should be done."[35]

Snyder became increasingly fanciful in his comments about Indian-inspired familial and social structures, urging readers to break out of monogamous family organizations and create larger, clan structures. People should work at various jobs and pool their resources, he advised. They should not, however, bring their paychecks home to a tight, monogamous family, but rather to a larger unit where the sharing is greater. "The extended family leads to matrilineal descent and when we get matrilineal descent—then we'll have group marriage, and when we have group marriage we'll have the economy licked. Because with the group marriage . . . capitalism is doomed and civilization goes out." Although he claimed no particular Indian group as inspiration for his group-marriage idea, Snyder seemed to suggest it was native inspired. He also found attractive those elements of Indian cultures—as he presented them—that encouraged individuals to believe in themselves, seek out private visions, and thus gain personal power and knowledge through that experience. Maintaining some such cultures still existed, Snyder looked to the Comanche and Sioux who, he claimed, expected everybody in the community to seek out a vision at least once in his life. The idea was, "In other words, to leave the society to have some transcendental experience, to have a song and a totem come to him which he need tell no one—and then come back and live with this double knowledge in society." To this, Watts was particularly enthusiastic, hailing the "Indian system" as one which demonstrates to all that "the game rules of society are fundamentally an illusion." Snyder agreed and then concluded that this produced a particularly manly culture: "no one who ever came into contact with the Plains Indians did not think they were men!" The role and place of women, apparently, went unnoticed and unacknowledged.[36]

The summit-meeting conversation was freewheeling. It was not the best venue for Gary Snyder's ideas about Indians. For one thing, his efforts to explain the value of Indian models were continually interrupted by the others. But for readers of the *Oracle*, it was an important introduction to the man and his views of Indianness. And it certainly reached a much larger audience than any of Snyder's other work to date. Although the paper initially printed only about 3,000 copies, by the "Houseboat Summit" issue, the print run had jumped to about 125,000 copies and, according to one of its editors, five or more people read each copy, lifting circulation to over 500,000. Staff mailed *Oracles* to such far-flung places as New Zealand, India, and Vietnam. The publishers, in fact, claimed a worldwide subscription list with backpackers and other travelers buying as many as 100 copies and taking them home, as well.[37] The editors apparently found Snyder's commentary about Indians especially important because they illustrated the lengthy article with Native American-inspired imagery: thunderbirds, Plains Indians on horseback, a Navajo woman at a loom, totems, an Indian child in a cradleboard perched on a cornstalk, feathers, and headdresses. They also apparently believed that interest in things supposedly Indian was sufficiently strong because they devoted the next issue entirely to the subject. Meanwhile, Gary Snyder's name and association with counterculture and Indians was spreading.

Like Kesey, Snyder was a child of the far west—the Pacific Northwest. Although he was born in San Francisco in 1930, when he was two his parents moved to a small dairy farm near Lake City, Washington—north of Seattle. There Snyder's sensitivity and sympathy to the natural world, and the Indians who he associated with it, came to him as did an awareness that exploitation and despoliation characterized his own culture's treatment of the land. As a child, he watched the logging trucks roll by the family farm and became aware that some kind of violation of "the authenticity, completeness, and reality of the natural world" was under way. His sympathies were entirely with the place—with its views of stunning Mount Rainier to the east (at least on clear days) and the sight of the Olympic range to the west. These mountains were much more "real" to him than the city of Seattle, ten miles to the south. The two-acre Snyder farm was completely surrounded by woods, and by age nine his parents allowed him to camp there by himself. By age thirteen he was hiking in the Cascades, getting into "real wilderness." But Snyder was also aware others had preceded his family's presence in Washington. Without anyone pointing it out to him, he realized that Indians had lived—and continued to live—in the area. Once a month an old Salish man came to the Snyder farm, selling smoked salmon. He came from a small Salish settlement nestled on the Puget Sound shoreline a few miles away. "My childhood perception of the world," Snyder later explained, consisted of "white people, a few old Salish Indians, and this whole natural world that was half-intact and half-destroyed before my eyes."[38]

Eventually the Snyder family moved to Portland, where Gary attended high school, began to climb the region's mountain peaks, and attended Reed College. As a college student, he began to probe more consciously the contradictions of living in a society that seemed bent on self-destruction. He began a long process of analysis and study that led him, first, to Marxism and the belief that capitalism was at the crux of the problem. Then he turned to American Indian studies, "got close to some American Indian elders," and concluded "maybe it was all of Western culture that was off the track and not just capitalism—that there were certain self-destructive tendencies in our cultural tradition." For a Northwest boy, who grew up with Indians as neighbors, it was not such a leap, then, to turn in that direction. They were *of* North America. They had survived the onslaught of Western cultural and economic imperatives, against great odds. They clearly lived outside the mainstream and did not seem to participate in the destruction of the natural world. It was, in a way, a logical turn for the poet-in-the-making. Yet, he also discovered that, for the most part, Indian traditions were not available to him. "American Indian spiritual practice is very remote and extremely difficult to enter," he explained, "even though in one sense right next door, because it is a practice one has to be born into. Its intent is not cosmopolitan. Its content, perhaps, is universal, but you must be a Hopi to follow the Hopi way."[39]

This insight came later, however. While still a student at Reed College, Snyder joined a classmate on a field trip to the Warm Springs Reservation over Christmas 1949. There he collected a folktale and a fragment of a flood legend from an elderly Tsimshian and decided to write a paper on them. He also chose an Indian topic for his senior thesis, analyzing a Haida myth from anthropological, psychological, metaphysical, linguistic, literary, and functionalist points of view. What he concluded was that all people share a rich prehistoric lore, all groups have cultures until oppressed by invaders, and that indigenous people have the deepest insights into human nature and the best ways of life. He hoped others would share this insight before all indigenous people were destroyed. Once enrolled in an anthropology graduate program at Indiana University, Snyder quickly realized he was not meant to be a social scientist and left the academic arena. Snyder did not forsake Indians at this juncture; he just turned his interests offshore and became a "hemispheric traveler."[40]

Snyder moved to California where he began to hang out with poets and writers such as Allen Ginsberg and Jack Kerouac. He studied Eastern Asian languages at University of California, Berkeley. He had also studied Far Eastern cultures at Reed, reading Ezra Pound's and Arthur Waley's translations of Chinese poetry, some Confucius texts, and some classics of Buddhist literature. He was particularly taken with the Mahayana Buddhism traditions. So when he learned these traditions were still alive and well in Japan, Snyder decided to go there. He lived in Zen Temple Shokoku, studied Buddhism under Miura Issha Roshi, and began publishing poetry. In contrast to many North American Indian traditions, Buddhism presented itself as cosmopolitan and open to everyone, at least all males. "I knew that Zen monasteries in Japan would be more open to me than the old Paiute or Shoshone Indians in eastern Oregon, because they *have* to be open—that's what Mahayana Buddhism is all about." In short, Asia had a teaching tradition intact and available. Attractive traditions, teachers, and schools of wisdom existed in North America, "but unless you are born as a member of a certain Pueblo and have the right to enter a certain kiva, you can't get into these schools."[41]

From his first trip to Japan in 1956 through the 1960s, Snyder continued to visit Asia and study alternative traditions that inspired his poetry and, of course, his worldview. But he never forgot his interest in American Indians and often blended the Far Eastern and the North American because he saw them as ecologically and culturally enlightened religious and social forces. Describing himself as a "Buddhist-shamanist," he believed both Asian and Native American traditions offered a way to bind humans with the lives of magpies, beavers, and mountains ranges, and a way to intertwine the spiritual and the natural. Traditional Hinduism and Buddhism added an intellectual richness and complexity to Native American shamanistic and ritualistic ceremonial practices and community lifestyles. But

Indians had lived long and deeply in America and so, he explained in the 1970s, offered Americans the best models of how to live a full life, by developing a deep awareness—an organic, ecological, botanical, even geological understanding of place. And again, the best way to achieve that was by consulting Indian myth, ritual, and magic. Try to comprehend how they envisioned different animals and why they saw certain ones as especially powerful. "Why do the Winnebago see the hare as potent?" Move on to their economic uses of the land. What did they eat? How did they make clothes, medicine, and soap? Even if a person does not approximate these practices in his or her daily life, to know about them is to greatly extend one's awareness of region. The critical thing is belonging to the place. Understand what it means to live "carefully and wisely, delicately in a place, in such a way that you can live there adequately and comfortably. Also, your children and grandchildren and generations a thousand years in the future will still be able to live there. That's thinking as though you were a native. Thinking in terms of the whole fabric of living and life." That meant thinking like Native Americans, who had lived perhaps fifty thousand years in places such as California.[42]

To modern Americans who might look at, say, Paiute culture and conclude nothing was happening over all those years of living in the Great Basin, particularly regarding development of technology, Snyder argued that from a spiritual standpoint, a great deal was happening in "the evolution of consciousness." Intense meditations, over long periods of time, led to internal discoveries, "steady enactment and reenactment over and over again of basic psychological inner spiritual dramas." By focusing on "living harmoniously and righteously on the earth," these people achieved a condition of long-term stability. "I'm fascinated by that scale of time and by that scale of commitment, both to the land and to the process of evolution of consciousness. And I think the Indians have, thus, not only something to teach us about place and plants, and timber management, and game management, but also something to teach us about patience and long term commitment to a spiritual path." Of course, they did not realize their way of life without technology. Ishi, the so-called last Yahi, was a beautiful technician. But he used appropriate technology that accomplished just what he needed with materials readily available. Moreover, Indians did not need more sophisticated hunting tools, so they did not develop them. They hunted more with their minds than with weapons. They waited patiently for their quarry, acutely observing the animals they wanted, "entering into [the animal's] movement-consciousness-mind-presence" and demonstrating mastery of these things through ritual and ceremony. Most significantly, Snyder believed, they hunted for the animals that came to them. "When I was a boy I saw old Wishram Indians spearing salmon on the Columbia River, standing on a little plank out over a rushing waterfall. They could stand motionless for twenty to thirty minutes with a spear in their hands and suddenly—they'd have a salmon. That kind of patience!" In the end, what

Snyder learned from these examples was, "What it comes down to simply is this: If what the Hindus, the Buddhists, the Shoshone, the Hopi, the Christians are suggesting is true, then all of industrial/technological civilization is really on the wrong track, because its drive and energy are purely mechanical and self-serving—*real* values are somewhere else. The real values are within nature, family, mind, and into liberation. Implicit are the possibilities of a way of living and being which is dialectically harmonious and complexly simple, because that's the Way."[43] That, in sum, was the great achievement of many North American Indian cultures and the basis of their attraction to him.

If Snyder's views of Indians seemed to freeze Indians in time, or make them appear as historical rather than contemporary people, that was not his intention. He certainly understood Indian people had suffered, and lost a great deal, in the course of European conquest. Still, he knew they continued to live in North America. He hoped their period of greatest weakness was over. Whether these cultures could continue to survive was uncertain, but he thought those tribes with the largest populations stood the greatest chance. A major theme of human history had been the slow, steady destruction or absorption of "local, kin-based, or tribal populations by the Metropole." Although that dynamic was still under way, some cultures such as the Hopi and the Pueblos had shown an astonishing resilience. "I've often wondered what makes these societies so tough. And it may well be that they are close to an original source of integrity and health. Erasing all negative associations for the word 'primitive,' it means *primus* or 'first,' like 'original mind,' original human society, original way of being." They have reached a level of optimum stability and have demonstrated an incredible capacity to absorb all sorts of assaults and impacts. "Once they have reached maturity, they are almost indestructible."[44] But Snyder also understood their survival depended, at least in part, on political support, and so he fashioned himself a "spokesman for wild nature" and for the people who depended on it for their livelihood—the Paiutes, the Maidus, the Eskimos, the aborigines of New Guinea, the tribesmen of Tibet. He advocated more democracy, which meant the Navajo, Pine Ridge, and Rosebud reservations should be their own nations; the Indians of Puget Sound should have their fishing rights; and trees, rocks, and whales should be able to vote.[45] Clearly some of these ideas were more viable than others.

Perhaps nowhere did Snyder present his ideas about Indians more effectively and reach more readers than in his 1975 volume *Turtle Island*. The title, he explained in an introductory note, refers to "the old/new name for the [North American] continent, based on many creation myths of the people who have been living here for millennia, and reapplied by some of them to 'North America' in recent years. Also, an idea found world-wide, of the earth, or cosmos even, sustained by a great turtle or serpent-of-eternity." He chose the name as a way to help his readers see more accurately how they live on a continent of watersheds, plant zones, and culture areas. The poems are about the importance of place and the realization that the land itself is a living being. "Anglos, Black people, Chicanos, and others beached up on these shores all share such views at the deepest levels of their old cultural traditions—African, Asian, or European. Hark again to those roots, to see our ancient solidarity, and then to the work of being together on Turtle Island."[46] Some of the poems most pointedly reveal an "Indian" inspiration. "Prayer For the Great Family," for example, is patterned "after a Mohawk prayer":

> Gratitude to Mother Earth, sailing through night and day—
> and to her soil; rich, rare, and sweet
> *in our mind so be it . . .*
> Gratitude to Wild Beings, our brothers, teaching secrets,
> freedoms, and ways; who share with us their milk;.
> self-complete, brave, and aware
> *in our minds so be it . . .*[47]

Other poems such as "Control Burn," "Coyote Valley Spring," "Anasazi," "Mother Earth: Her Whales," and "Jemez Pueblo Ring" also speak to Snyder's Indian-related themes.

Winning the Pulitzer Prize for this collection greatly increased Snyder's readership and influence well beyond the Beats and hippies of San Francisco. Not all who read his work, however, were admiring. Some Indian authors, including Leslie Silko and Gerald Hobson, criticized him for "ripping off" Native American cultures. They believed that Snyder could not legitimately, authentically relate Indian ideas, views, and understandings and accused him of practicing cultural imperialism by adopting the persona of a shaman-healer. In the mid-1970s, characterized by a rising tide of ethnic politics and resentment toward people, particularly Anglos who claimed to speak for other ethnicities, this kind of criticism was not surprising. After so many centuries of non-Indians speaking for Indians, at a time when Native Americans themselves were finally finding publishers and being heard in their own right, it was understandable. But to these charges Snyder responded: shamanism was not solely an Indian thing. It was a worldwide phenomenon, and no one culture had proprietary control over it. Shamanism connected to the oldest, most fundamental of human religious practices. It informed the most basic folklore of cultures all across the planet, going back ten or thirteen thousand years, when all humans shared the same information and the same religious disciplines. He credited Native North Americans for keeping it alive and believed they were right to do so. For that reason, among others, everyone should work to keep Native American cultures and land bases intact. But that did not give his critics a monopoly, or sole control, over the concept.

True, he admitted, many people used the language of shamanism and wrote poetry about the natural and the wild, having had no actual experience with either. They had never seen the glint in an eagle's eye, a trout flipping its tail, or a bear backing up. "If you haven't seen these things," Snyder agreed, "you shouldn't write about them, whether you're an Indian or a white man. And there are a lot of contemporary urban Indians who haven't seen them either." But Snyder had experienced them. Moreover, "imperialism" was not an appropriate word to invoke in talking about poetry "because in poetry we all know we are free to lovingly use anything that's available." Nobody would tell a Shoshone poet that he could not write in English. No one would tell Kiowa novelist Scott Momaday he could not write like a Cambridge don, if he was so inclined. No one would say to him: "You're an Indian man, you should write like you wore buckskin." Just because Snyder's great-grandparents were Lutherans did not mean he could only write like a Lutheran. "That would really be tiresome. As artists we are all free to write about anything we like. And if it is inauthentic it will show up sooner or later. If it really works, then people will trust it." His own work, he explained, derived from many sources—from the many things he had learned over the course of his life. And it was "free and there for all of us. Just as Coyote is free for all of us. Coyote doesn't belong to anybody." As a trickster, Coyote is an archetype inside all people. Snyder simply meant to address certain universal "wholenesses" such as "oneness with nature, the oneness of mind and body, the oneness of conscious and unconscious, our oneness in society with each other. These are basic and ancient conditions from which we flourish." Interestingly, Momaday and Vine Deloria Jr. defended Snyder against the attacks of other Native American writers.[48]

Whether Snyder's self-defense satisfied his critics is unlikely, but it represented one of the more thoughtful, intelligent explanations of Indians' supposed attractions to a counterculture thinker. Undoubtedly some remained convinced Snyder *was* raiding other cultures for inspiration and that this represented yet another example of the dominant culture's ever-reaching, ever-grasping inclination to control and own everything. Snyder did not address the power whites had to decide which other cultures deserved respect. But in attempting to redirect his own culture's tendencies away from those very impulses, Snyder believed it was justifiable and appropriate to seek models outside Western European traditions and religions. To do so was to honor and respect those traditions, in the course of embracing them. To do so was to seek commonalities among human beings that transcended particular cultures and helped usher in a more healthful world for all.[49]

No one would claim Gary Snyder was a typical member of the 1960s counterculture. He represented the more sophisticated kind of thinking that emerged from the far West's version of that cultural phenomenon. His ideas rested on many years of study and contact with non-Anglo communities on both sides of the Pacific. Snyder cared about the political possibilities of tribalism for indigenous people rather than as a form of escapism for alienated youth. He was not seeking a native existence for himself, but rather a new way for all Americans to live in a post-frontier world—one based on ecological and anthropological sustainability and reciprocity. In a "movement" as diverse and diffuse as the counterculture, however, it is not difficult to find myriad examples of more superficial elucidations of Indianness. The pages of the *Oracle,* for one, provide an excellent place to find these more transitory and simplistic usages. The issue that followed the February 1967 "Houseboat Summit," in fact, was devoted to an Indian theme. The editors chose themes based on what they believed would interest the Haight-Ashbury community and what the editorial staff, writers, artists, secretaries, circulation people, invited friends, and "anyone who happened in the door" could agree on. The first thematic issue centered on "The Aquarian Age" and counterculture fascination with astrology. The Indian issue followed soon after.

As the editors later explained, the hippies' creation myth centered on the notion that they were reincarnated Indians who returned to earth with the intention of bringing the land and people back to traditional ways. They believed they shared a sense of cultural alienation with American Indians as well as a vision that earth and humanity could live harmoniously. The youthful dissidents thought that American Indian tribal life, before Europeans came, was the ideal expression of that harmony and that studying with, and about, Indians would be the best way to acquire such an existence. To prepare for this special edition, the *Oracle* sent a small group of artists and writers to the Hopi Reservation for inspiration. If the San Francisco-based hippies had a favorite tribe, it was the Hopi—likely reflecting that a few of them had read Frank Waters' *Book of the Hopi* and that some Hopi people willingly, at least initially, interacted with the Anglo-seekers. But little could be learned in a short visit, and the Indian issue revealed little evidence of Hopi, or any other tribe's, involvement.[50]

The Indian issue's cover featured an image of Nez Perce Chief Joseph's head floating above mountains. Flying saucers hover between Joseph and the peaks. On the bottom of each flying saucer appear the words "the," "city," and "of" and on the middle peak "San Francisco." The connection between Joseph and San Francisco is unclear (see figure 2.3). The issue's contents are equally diffuse and often puzzling. It includes an article titled "Tuwaqachi—The Fourth World," by Richard Grossinger, an utterly confusing, mostly incoherent essay; a piece called "Sun Bear Speaks" whose author identifies himself as "an Indian in blood and in spirit," who writes about the Indian sense of living and belonging with the land; an announcement of a new Haight-Ashbury tribe called Kiva; some songs identified as Sioux; and the remarks of Craig Carpenter, "messenger for the Hopi and other traditional Indian leaders." This last article, "Hopi Life Plan," explains the meaning

Figure 2.3 The *Oracle*, a Haight-Ashbury underground newspaper, frequently embellished its pages with fanciful Indian- and psychedelic-inspired imagery. This one blends a portrait of the Nez Perce leader Chief Joseph with flying saucers. Credit: Courtesy of the Bancroft Library, University of California, Berkeley.

of a petroglyph found near Old Oraibi that prophesied world destruction if the white man did not learn to respect the ways of nature, the earth, and Indian people.

The issue also included a poem by John Collier Jr., an anthropology teacher at San Francisco State College and son of the New Deal-era commissioner of Indian Affairs. In the poem, "Who Is An Indian," Collier takes on the voice of a Pueblo man who was "here before you came and, in spirit, will remain after you have gone . . . you white people of machines." White soldiers and missionaries fought and destroyed many Indians, but the Pueblos still existed. In fact, Indians did not perish but remained on earth "to be your teachers." Meanwhile white people helped remind Indians about the strengths of their cultures, particularly their relationship to nature and the value of the life-sustaining ceremonies and rituals to which they regularly returned. According to the poem, most whites, on the other hand, feared nature and destroyed it. But, Collier added as an "After Thought":

> I am the white man, the anthropologist.
> I listen to the Indian.
> His view of the white world IS true and historical.
> But I also see there is an Indian in all us,
> Submerged, but gnawing.
> We hurt in the same way the Indian does.
> Our bloods mingle in this hurt.
> You long-hair people, Beatniks, Hippies,
> call yourself what you will
> are you also living in an ancient memory,
> listening for a forgotten beat,
> listening for wind sounds and sea sounds?
> Aren't you seeking that paradise of forest stream and meadow?
> Have you not turned your back on the tumult, the speed
> the driven-ness of machines?
> You too stop time, in your own psychedelic way,
> to witness a flower,
> the brilliance of fire,
> the magic of the obscure and shadowed.
> You too yearn for the Eden of simplicity,
> of a life with urges, fulfillment and rhythms,
> You turn your face from the future.
> You seek the child within you . . .
> Nature people have this wholeness,
> And the wisdom that can only come from this self possession.
> You listen to be enlightened by the child's clear voice.
> The child within you IS the hunger for the Indian.[51]

Collier's image of the Pueblo here—as self-possessed, peaceful, content, childlike, deeply rooted in place, spiritually connected to the natural world—neatly summarized the appeal of Indianness to the "long-hair, Beatniks, and Hippies." The poem chastises whites for their destructive tendencies, the absence of harmony in their lives, and their lonely cities; but it also holds out the possibility that those attributes which Collier, and others, found so attractive and associated with Indians could be shared by whites—in fact, they already resided within those who sought it.

Throughout the issue, then, several images of Indians predominate. They are nature based and closer to the land. They have been victims of Europeans but somehow have managed to survive. And they are gentle and harmonious. But Gary Snyder's *Oracle* contribution, sent from Kyoto, Japan, called "A Curse on the Men in Washington, Pentagon," strikes a more discordant cord. The "Indian within," in Snyder's poem, is angry and given to violence, even murder. Anti–Vietnam War feelings clearly inspired it:

>As you shoot down the Vietnamese girls and men
>in their fields
>burning and chopping,
>poisoning and blighting,
>So surely I hunt the white man down
>in my heart....
>As I kill the white men,
>the "American"
>in me.
>And dance out the Ghost dance:
>To bring back America, the grass and the streams,
>To trample your throat in your dreams.
>This magic I work, this loving I give
>that my children may flourish
>And yours won't live.[52]

Whether or not to publish this angry poem sparked considerable debate among *Oracle* staffers. One photographer's father was an army captain who worked in the Pentagon and so the curse would have fallen upon him! After a vote, Snyder's verse narrowly made it into the issue, and the military son, along with several others, left the paper over the dispute. Snyder characterized such responses as "weird." "As I said to somebody," he wrote a friend, "telling the world to Love one Another is as dangerous and as big a responsibility as uttering a curse ... Especially when the curse is ... not aimed at people but at dangerous states of mind." After the first printing of thirty thousand copies, the editors received word from Snyder not to print the poem anymore because of a copyright dispute, and so they excluded it from other editions. But a rumor spread they had succumbed to political or spiritual pressure, and The Communications Company, the publishing arm of the San Francisco anarchist-oriented Diggers, mimeographed the poem and so continued to distribute it.[53]

One other piece spoke directly to political matters and indicated that even in Haight-Ashbury an awareness of practical, legal matters related to Native Americans attracted attention, at least occasionally. This article focused on the proposed Indian Resources Development Act of 1967, or Omnibus Bill, which the article characterized as a termination act. The legislation focused on ways to promote reservation economies through expansion of credit and creation of Indian corporations. One of the most controversial elements allowed tribes to sell or mortgage trust property. It also allowed Indians who wanted to withdraw voluntarily from their tribe to receive compensation. Participation in the program was to be voluntary and offered safeguards to prevent alienation of land. Tribal opposition was strong from the outset, not the least because Secretary of the Interior Stewart Udall had not consulted with tribes while formulating the legislation. Many of its provisions required the secretary's approval, thus extending the practice of paternalism in an age of rising demands for self-determination. Congress, in the end, did not support the bill, a major victory for Native Americans.[54]

The *Oracle* described the legislation as a thinly veiled scheme designed to acquire Indian land and destroy the last vestiges of tribal, communal life while presuming to usher Indians into the American melting pot. The ultimate outcome would be a weakening of Indian unity and a loss of resources. The article explained that American Indians were not "minorities" but rather "sovereign nations surrounded by Americans"; the author urged readers to help defeat the legislation. "Much of the reasoning behind the dissent that many Americans feel today towards war, American World Economic Dominance, and the insane consumption-oriented society can be extended to the Indian issue." Must these people, too, be forced into the American way "where trust and brotherhood are impossible, where anxiety, neurosis, conformity, and greed dominate all else in society? A society diametrically opposed to Indian Spirituality, Life and Community?" Indians needed help to save them from the corporations that will gobble their resources. "Many young people look towards the Indian for some spiritual guidance and for communal and ecological guidelines. This is not a free ride! If it is, then we are simply Ugly Americans stepping over poor dark foreigners. Americans are not Indians, cannot form a traditional Indian Tribe, but we can help each other and work toward a proper development of our respective karmas."[55]

Still, on the streets of San Francisco in 1967, the primary interest in Indians derived from what non-Indians thought they could acquire from them—rather than the help they could provide Indians. Some residents of Haight-Ashbury, in particular, envisioned the Hopi as the essence of tribe—a people who epitomized spirituality, peace, and love of earth (see figure 2.4). In an effort to create a communal center for the "tribes" of San Francisco, a "tribal council" formed to develop a "Kiva" in the neighborhood—a building that would serve as a place to teach, produce art, and encourage self-supporting rural communities. It would also be a meeting ground for the ten to two hundred thousand young people estimated to be heading to San Francisco in the summer of 1967. "The assumption is that new tribal forms are evolving and that this may be the time to venture a concrete manifestation of tribal existence." The Kiva secured a large vacant lot and created a tribal council of twelve men—not one of them Indian, let alone Hopi—that included Peter Cohon (better known today as actor Peter Coyote) and Emmett Grogan, both members of the Diggers.[56]

Peter Cohon moved to San Francisco in 1964 to pursue an M.A. in creative writing at San Francisco State College and to act with the Actors' Workshop. He rented an apartment in the Haight-Ashbury area and quickly found himself attracted to the San Francisco Mime Troupe, a leftist, anarchist-oriented theater. He joined the group and eventually participated in its street productions, as well

Figure 2.4 Pueblo and particularly Hopi cultures and spirituality attracted counterculture interest and imitation. This Haight-Ashbury neighborhood fence, decorated with kachina-inspired post-tops and the word KIVA, signals that fascination. Credit: Mary Anne Kramer and San Francisco History Center, San Francisco Public Library.

as traveling shows, put on primarily in college towns. Cohon, the son of a successful New York City investment banker and a mother who worked for civil rights, came West searching for an authentic life as an artist; looking for both personal freedom and liberating social structures; and trying to find solutions to the critical social problems of his day, ranging from racism to poverty to the Vietnam War. He was serious, intense, and like many people of his generation naive about the possibility for substantive change in American life. At a time when the civil rights movement and rising black consciousness "fused with a social upheaval," Cohon shared many youth's belief that society was "suddenly permeable and open to both self-investigation and change."[57] Solutions could be found in lots of places, including among Native American communities.

Cohon found his greatest expression of this political-cultural view through the Diggers—"a loose confederation of friends," including some from the Mime Troupe, who were dedicated to living out a genuinely alternative way of life. In particular they wanted to create "a society liberated from the carnivorous aspects of capitalism, a culture offering more enlightened possibilities for its members than the roles of *employee* or *victim*." All aspects of life came under scrutiny and challenge. Even theater was a commodity. What the Diggers attempted, then, was to use actors' skills in everyday life to construct events that were literally free and that would exist outside conventional expectations. They wanted to imagine their most authentic selves, act them out, make them real, and simultaneously engineer social change. Cohon later realized that he had begun this process of creating a new identity before he came to California—back as a student at Iowa's Grinnell College, when he and three friends ordered some peyote from a Texas mail-order source. When the peyote arrived, they did not know what to do with it. They went to the library and learned from an encyclopedia that the local Meskwaki (he called them Poweshiek) Indians had a peyote church. The students subsequently trekked to them for instruction on how to prepare and ingest the cactus. Some of the peyotists agreed to help and, before long, one of Cohon's friends noticed "his hands [were] dizzy." The young men went out into the starry, cold night and then dispersed. Cohon felt he had been transformed into a small wolf, "trotting effortlessly through the Iowa cornfields, following scents and colors, marveling at these newly heightened powers." At one place he stopped and saw dog tracks in the snow, where his footprints should have been. Later he saw a picture of coyote tracks and realized that the paw prints he saw on the ground were those of a coyote. When he eventually told Rolling Thunder, the Shoshone-Cherokee shaman who sent Joseph Quinones to Franks' Landing, about this experience the latter asked Cohon what he was going to do about it. Although uncertain what Rolling Thunder meant, Cohon decided he had received a special gift that he must honor. "Without fully understanding why, or what it might mean to me, but needing to mark the occasion somehow, I began using Coyote as a last name." It also became clear that Peter Coyote saw in Indian ways examples of how to live authentic, alternative lives. He likened the Diggers' attempt to realize their dreams in the flesh to the way Black Elk's village acted the shaman's dreams, by assuming roles and behaviors and costumes according to his direction.[58]

Adopting a name that smacks of Indianness was just one way Peter Coyote signaled a serious intention to incorporate Native American values, attitudes, and expectations into his life. He read books such as *Black Elk Speaks*, Mari Sandoz's *Cheyenne Autumn*, Vine Deloria's work, and ethnographic studies. But he was not satisfied with this kind of knowledge and sought out encounters with Indians, eventually "hanging out" with Rolling Thunder in Nevada, Hopis in Hotevilla, and Karuks in Northern California. He was "drawn into their humor, jealousies, practicality, sense of belonging and ritualizing of life" which "had a profound effect on [him]." He understood they were reserved and watchful, so in making his initial approaches, he imitated this same kind of behavior. He also made himself useful, helping repair cars, toilets, plumbing, and whatever else needed work. They drank together, hunted, and generally enjoyed themselves, but occasionally his Indian companions would punctuate the interaction with serious stories, or "teaching fables," as Coyote fashioned them. Although he gradually shed his identity as a "white man," he never pretended to be Indian. Yet often during this period he encountered hostility from Native Americans who thought he was "trying to 'cop their trip.'" However, "when they finally realized that I got my name from the same place their grandfather did, everything was cool, and Native people have appreciated my support and effort on their behalf over the years, and I've appreciated theirs."[59]

At the same time, Coyote understood that many other counterculture types did not interact with Indians but satisfied themselves with appropriating an idea of Indian "style." There was undoubtedly a lot of romantic claptrap circulating, and the idea of white people leading visions quests or sweat lodges was "revolting . . . as if you could simply extract one element from a vital, intricate, and profound culture, and market it as a commodity." Initially, there was "a natural interface" between hippies and Indians, but the hippie culture was "neither deep enough or profound enough, or disciplined enough to interest Native people too much." Many hippies, in their quest for an authentic life, allowed admiration of Indians to "get 'stylized' so that the buckskins, pig-tails, and feather obscured the honest moral quest underneath." He understood perfectly the Native American rejection of that. For their part, some Indians were ready to take advantage of non-Indians' interests. Some accepted the drugs, drink, and women that came along. "But basically, the hippies were not a culture; [they] were full of ideas and often half-baked sentiments and work ethics that left the natives uninterested in them long term."[60]

Perhaps the best example of this came with the proposed Hopi-Hippie Be-In—a plan hatched by Richard Alpert, who had taught at Harvard with Timothy Leary. He embraced the potential of hallucinogenic drugs to open avenues of consciousness and eventually went to India, found a guru, and became one himself. During spring 1967, while traveling in an old converted school bus, Alpert and a group of San Francisco and Los Angeles hippies stopped at Hotevilla for a meeting with elders to discuss the possibility of a Hopi-Hippie Be-In to be held at the Grand Canyon on the summer solstice. From Alpert's point of view, this would be mutually advantageous. He believed that American Indians were the hippies' spiritual fathers. Just at the time the Indians' own sons and daughters were going off to the cities and leaving their Indianness behind, "we had all these city boys, looking for spiritual relatives . . . if we could just get this thing put together, it would be a new statement of spiritual power in America." The event would simultaneously give a spiritual boost to Indians who were struggling with economic problems, alcoholism, and Bureau of Indian Affairs oppression. The unlikely assemblage at Hotevilla sat in a low-ceilinged adobe room. About twenty hippies ranging from ages sixteen to thirty-five, men and women, met with fifteen or so Hopi people. The Indian women and young men sat at one end of the room while the four elders, aged fifty to one hundred, Alpert estimated, sat at the kitchen table. Seated on the floor near the table, Alpert looked up at the elders: "These were the few men in whom the living God remained—for whom the myths were true prophecy—for whom the spirits were intimate associations, instead of abstractions! And under the table the gnarled hands and wrinkled arms, beringed and braceleted with turquoise, in poses of calm patient waiting; hands that still did the daily work and yet belonged to men firmly rooted in the spirit."[61]

Alpert understood he would have to offer something tangible to entice the Hopi to this "far-out" idea. He began by telling the Hopis that over 50 percent of the people in the United States were under the age of twenty-five and that in a few years, the youth would control the vote, the government, and consequently the Bureau of Indian Affairs. In the short term, people such as Secretary of the Interior Stewart Udall would never truly listen to the Hopis because they were committed to a value system that did not allow them to hear the Indians. Unlike *their* elders, non-Indian American youth did hear the Hopis' and other Indians' complaints. They were more responsive to their needs. Political support was on the way. In the meantime, America's youth needed the Indians' help even more because they lacked "spiritual sustenance" and direction on "how to carry out the tenets of a spiritually honest life." So far they had depended on chemicals, such as peyote, to break through, but this was merely a crutch. What they really needed were wise teachings and teachers, new myths, and places to flee from sick and decaying cities. Many young people were already migrating to rural places where they hoped to become farmers and raise families while living simply. Alpert claimed this was happening as if by some larger design, "as if a very large hand is guiding what is happening," and that part of the plan was for many to come together in the Grand Canyon—"a place where the spiritual feelings were pure enough and the closeness to the earth was direct enough so that people would trust the message that they would hear in their hearts." Thousands would come and he hoped the Hopi would participate too in a gathering that would benefit both, spiritually and politically.[62]

Alpert acknowledged Indians lived in a nation where the BIA still called the shots, and he did not want to involve the Hopi in anything that would harm them. He recognized that with thousands of people coming to the Southwest, even one miscreant could cause difficulties for the Indian hosts. At the same time, he urged them to "trust the process." He believed the youth who would come represented the "cream" of America. They will come with a "pureness of heart." At the same time, Alpert admitted he was ignorant about the region and that if the Hopi felt it was spiritually unwise for people to come together, at this time, at the Grand Canyon, he would call it off. Still, to disperse would only serve the interests of the government that wanted to keep the Hopis under the BIA and the hippies under the narcotics or health divisions. Divide and conquer remained the strategy. "Much of the power of your vision and our vision to the extent that it is a shared vision will come from the fact that we can make shared statements together, that we can make statements as human beings who say 'Enough!' We want to return to our humanity. So we want to reach in as deliberate a way as we can for the way in which the traditional Hopi and we can make statements together because that 'togetherness' is exactly what the government then must hear."[63]

Several Hopis responded, including Dan Chachunga and "Tomas." They did not speak directly to the invitation to join the hippies in the Grand Canyon. Their avoidance of the issue, in fact, makes clear they had no interest whatsoever in a be-in. Chachunga was gracious but urged the hippie assemblage to go back to their homes and be careful on the highway. He was old, needed his rest, and was going home himself. He thanked them for coming, meeting with them, learning from them, and hoped "we will continue to understand better each other, our ways and to work together so that we will preserve this land and life for all good people." Another Hopi man, identified as David, kept his reply short as well, explaining that the Hopi traditional religious leaders prayed for all people in this land "because we are caretakers of this land and everything in it." This was their duty even if some of their own Hopi people disregarded it. But other than that, he had no more to say.

Tomas's remarks were lengthier and focused entirely on practical, political problems the Hopi faced. He expressed disappointment that two attorneys had not shown up to address several specific problems plaguing the Hopi, including the tribal council's troubling relationship with the BIA and corruption on the reservation. The council was approving oil drilling and leasing programs against the wishes of traditional leaders and without the consent of the majority. Because so many of the Hopi were unaware of legal matters, they were at the mercy of the tribal council and its attorney. Further, BIA agency officials had recently physically abused an older Hopi man and tried to blame some Hopi boys for an automobile accident caused by the reservation superintendent. Tomas talked about the dispute with the Navajo over the joint occupation of land arising from an 1888 executive order and read a letter from the Seneca about the Kinzua Dam. In short, he talked politics and wanted help. The Hopi traditionals had tried everything and everyone they could think of: congressmen, senators, the president, members of different religious organizations such as the Quakers, and even the United Nations—all to no avail. But they had not given up. "I hope we can work out some way where we could get different leaders together here sometime and see if we can stop some of these things with your help or anyone with a good heart for the Indian people." It was a matter of survival for the Hopi. What they ultimately wanted was a life free of outside domination, a life free of pressure to conform to something they could never be, and a life that would allow them to keep their land and resources. "So I hope that your people think about these things and spread the word around so that maybe some proper one will come along . . . instead of asking questions he will go right into the proper place and see if they can straighten out this matter. The Hopi is still waiting for his true white brother." Tomas concluded by telling Alpert and his hippie cohorts the Indian hosts were happy they had come to meet with these Hopi leaders, hear their message, and see their village. "It is not much to look at but I believe that the Great Spirit has a purpose in bringing these people in this mesa . . . I have a great faith in them and I know that they . . . are concerned not only for their own people but for all people on this land with us." He urged them not to be afraid to approach the Hopi leadership. This was a time when they needed to work together.[64]

Alpert, however, was not particularly responsive to this appeal. Politics did not interest him. Thinking back on this encounter, a few years later, he characterized the Hopi synopsis of their problems this way:

> There, on that dry, dusty plateau in Arizona, I heard the statement [about the Indian boys' innocence regarding the automobile accident] in the presence of the living spirit . . . It was as if I was hearing from a bygone era, when a man's word was enough and his statement was truth. And it was these "savages" whom we had dispossessed and been systematically degrading. I felt a wave of nausea, and at the same moment, prayerful thanks to this man, still rooted in the Way, who spoke simply and without artifice, reminding me of how it used to be.[65]

Alpert could not see that what Tomas was talking about was not how it used to be, but rather, how it was.

The hippie interest in the Hopi did not go unnoticed elsewhere on the reservation. *The Hopi Action News*, a weekly publication out of Keams Canyon, commented in fall 1967 that hippies had "invaded" both Navajo and Hopi reservations and reported rumors they had come "to save the uncivilized Indians—(from what, we have not as yet been informed!)" Tongue-in-cheek, the author thought it unfair the Hopi leadership made them "officially unwelcome," claiming the locals had duplicated hippies' long hair for centuries (though they found growing beards more difficult) and that psychedelics were not new to the Navajo, especially peyote. In fact, the federal government should assign "our psychedelic brethren" to all reservations. Navajos could teach them about sweat baths and Sioux could use them as subjects in their "peculiar type of hair cutting." If all attempts to refine the "Hippy Way of Life" failed, they could always send the hippies to the Pueblos "as a last-ditch stand." The Pueblos would "throw the bearded society off the cliffs and mesas as they have historically done with unwanted missionaries." Hippies were not always a laughing matter, however, and at least some feared their impact on children. Joe Secakuku, a leader of the Hopi village Shipaulovi on Second Mesa, lamented that Hopi teenagers left for off-reservation boarding schools and returned home as hippies. They came back "worthless." This particularly upset parents who were fighting to maintain their way of life and culture.[66]

In the end, the Hopi-Hippie Be-In never happened. The Hopi had no interest. But some from the hippie side, notably Digger Emmett Grogan, also worked to kill the idea. Grogan himself was not particularly taken with Indians and Indianness, although, his self-aggrandizing autobiography does include an interlude when he goes to New Mexico with Larry Little Bird, from the Santo Domingo Pueblo, on a hunting expedition. The episode reads like "Brooklyn boy goes Leatherstocking." Once Grogan killed his deer, he immediately headed back to San Francisco. There he threw himself back into Digger activities, providing free food to the increasing number of Haight-Ashbury migrants.[67] He also attacked the Hopi-Hippie Be-In idea in a Communication Company broadside. Dated April 29, 1967, the sheet claimed the Hopis said no to the Be-In idea "because you mean well, but you are foolish. You are foolish because you don't think of the Indian. We are a small people—You [*sic*] fathers crush us—You are a tribe of strangers to yourselves not one with each other." Larry Little Bird had warned that the temperatures in the canyon could reach 120 degrees in the Grand Canyon, there was inadequate drinking water, and the Arizona police were already arresting 150 hitchhikers a week. Finally Grogan questioned the whole concept of the be-in. He thought the San Francisco Be-In was "a shuck! It was as empty as the news copy it engendered. It was removed from the people and organized by merchants." Young people could create their own celebrations. They did not need leaders to create them. Leave be-ins to college students and ad men.[68]

Grogan also claimed in his autobiography that a Hopi sheriff and his deputies threw Alpert's group off the reservation because they disrespected the land and the elders, stole sacred masks and exposed them to uninitiated children, copulated on ground the Indians considered holy, seduced Indian men and enraged their wives or fiancées, and gave marijuana and LSD to Hopi children. Although these charges were probably greatly exaggerated, Grogan's sense that most Hopis did not particularly welcome hippies was accurate. He believed his broadside, which was picked up and spread throughout the underground press, was enough to cancel "the shopkeepers' plans for a Grand Canyon blast."[69] The San Francisco *Oracle* editors agreed with Grogan about its colonialist implications and withdrew their support as well. The Hopi-Hippie Be-In idea died.

But critics could not kill the sentiments at the heart of the project. The cultural appeal of Indianness was just getting started. Further, the message that Indian people had significant political problems and needed allies was not ignored. In fact, much closer to the hippie homeland of San Francisco, something else was brewing—an episode on Alcatraz Island that allowed non-Indians of all sorts (hippies and housewives, movie stars and ministers)—to turn their romantic, inadequate, and flawed ideas about Indians into tangible and significant support for substantive political change.

3

Politics, Parks, and Alcatraz

In late summer 1965, the *Berkeley Barb* featured a story about Charlie Brown Artman, a young white man who had pitched a "wigwam" on the hills above Berkeley. Artman selected a magnificent site with a sweeping view of the entire Bay Area. The police did not look kindly upon this and within a day the tipi came down. The hill, the authorities told Artman, was public property and living on public property was forbidden. As it turned out, this was just one of many encounters Artman had with law enforcement from the mid to late 1960s, as he challenged policies ranging from drug possession to tipi erection. He believed himself to be a reincarnated Indian spiritually guided in this lifetime by the Native American Church. Because Native American Church members could lawfully use peyote for religious purposes, Artman maintained, as a fellow traveler he had the same right to use the hallucinogen. In 1963 he tested this theory in court, claiming religious immunity under an earlier ruling that acquitted a Navajo man who consumed peyote during a religious ritual. The court did not buy Artman's reincarnation story or his argument that he should have the same political rights as Indians and placed him on three years probation. But this did not discourage Artman, who continued to set up his tipi and partake of peyote rituals and determined that "This is the dawn of a new age."[1]

Artman, also known as Little Eagle, was the son of an Iowa minister. He not only lived in a tipi, had long hair, and dressed in a black cape with a peace symbol on the back, but also reportedly had "the power to provoke America's middle class to acts of violence."[2] This latter talent captured national attention when, on February 24, 1966, he picketed President Lyndon Johnson's appearance at New York City's Waldorf-Astoria Hotel and helped loft a banner urging Johnson's impeachment over his Vietnam War policies. As newspaper columnist Jimmy Breslin reported the next day, Little Eagle's sign attracted police attention and brutality, as a dozen men in blue waded into the crowd of "kids" with clubs flying. Not long after, Artman left New York City, concluding his plan to set up his tipi in Central Park "just wouldn't have worked out" and headed for Lander, Wyoming (near the Wind River Reservation, home to Shoshone and Arapahoe) where he hoped to establish a tipi city. Although some of his friends from the Lower East Side planned to rent a bus and help make this dream come true, winter in Wyoming is not the best time to attempt such a feat. Further, the local political climate would have been even less conducive than New York's. By spring Artman was back in Berkeley, crossing swords once again with local police, building inspectors, the district attorney, and the city council.[3]

The *Barb*, normally less sympathetic to wanna-be-Indian hippies than San Francisco's *Oracle*, took him seriously. Why? The reason was simple: Artman's playing Indian engaged him directly in political struggle. Of course the politics that mattered to him had nothing to do with Indians and everything to do with this Iowa migrant's quest for personal liberty. But he shared adversaries (presidents, narcotics detectives) with many others who lived on the east side of San Francisco Bay. And his Indian pantomime underscored a widely shared inclination to see Indians as historic resistors of all kinds of oppression. Turning to Indian symbolism followed. Berkeley radicals demonstrated a more acute interest and sophistication regarding matters of race than some Haight-Ashbury residents and revealed a greater sensitivity to those Indians who scorned hippies' claims to affinities and even identities with Indians. They were not, however, above exploiting Indianness for their own political purposes, plastering Geronimo's picture on posters designed to claim a park for "the people" and publicizing any individual Native American who resisted the military draft. They did not stop there. When Indians came to town with their political issues, Berkeley noticed. The takeover of Alcatraz, which began in the fall of 1969, for example, provided an immediate and dramatic opportunity to back up words with action. At the vanguard of support for the Alcatraz protest, hippies and leftists merely paved the way for many other non-Indians who agreed the time had come to realize Indian activists' demands for sovereignty, self-determination, and treaty rights. Just as with the Pacific Northwest fish-ins, celebrities and mainstream churches quickly stood behind the Alcatraz occupiers. This time sympathy and material aid went further: occupiers garnered support from rural, urban, wealthy, and working-class people. If such supporters' understanding of Indian issues was neither sophisticated nor deeply informed, it was nevertheless important. Never before in American history had Indians' claims to power and property received such widespread endorsement from non-Indian people.

Indians, then, found a prominent place on the pages of Berkeley's most famous underground paper. Scattered among articles on the anti–Vietnam War movement, farm workers' unionization efforts, black power, police repression, the John F. Kennedy assassination, and the incredible number of photographs and drawings of nude women (including women in bondage, frequently displayed on the cover) are stories about Indians. The tenor of the Indian-related articles was consistently political. And the interest was twofold: first, on how Indianness could promote non-Indians' political agendas; and second, on how non-Indians could assist Native Americans' struggles for political autonomy. To be sure, the inclination to use single-dimensional, even stereotypical, images of Indians as symbols of political resistance in a variety of issues was common. But so too was an acknowledgement that Native Americans had their own political struggles that deserved attention and help. Playing with Indian imagery was absolutely part of the repertoire of resistance. So too was acknowledging treaty rights, sovereignty, and the legitimacy of tribal claims to cultural and political power.

Sun Bear, for instance, warranted a lengthy interview in a 1967 issue of the *Berkeley Barb*. Identified as a "Chippewa" (today known more commonly as Ojibwa) who lived in Reno, Nevada, he published the magazine *Many Smokes*. He was also assistant editor of the *Native Nevadan*, a monthly newspaper devoted to Indian affairs. Sun Bear began the *Barb* interview with a pipe ritual. But the topics that engaged the reporter had little to do with spirituality, religion, or ritual. Rather the newsman asked Sun Bear about the Office of Equal Opportunity's (OEO) impact on Indians, the federal government's position on Indian land retention, and the legalization of peyote for members of the Native American Church. Sun Bear, in turn, talked about the grassroots interest on reservations in OEO programs and their consequent relative success, economic development initiatives, the dangers of termination policies, the trust status of reservation land, state efforts to interfere with the peyote religion, the importance of retaining tax-exempt status, and Indian self-government.

When the reporter turned to hippies' fascination with Indians, Sun Bear's response was generous: "more power to them. I feel that this is the start of something, that if people can come together and help each other to survive and improve things on this basis, then perhaps we are getting somewhere." His only advice was they needed to find an economic base for their new way of life and suggested poster art might be one of them. But otherwise he was neither offended nor dismissive of the hippie embrace of Indianness. In fact, he was happy to see them turn to Indians for answers. For their part, Native Americans did not mean "race" when they spoke of the "white man." Rather the term designated a way of life. When people of various races adopted Indians ways (which he said included values such as responsibility for the land and an ethic that promoted sharing) many tribes in America happily accepted non-Indians as brothers. As for Indians' futures, Sun Bear jokingly concluded the interview by suggesting the best way for them to secure a place in America was to convert "the palefaces to be Indians, and those that don't want to become Indians we could deport ... under the McCarren Act."[4]

Not all Indians who appeared in the pages of the *Barb* were as tolerant of hippie interest. Buffy Sainte-Marie, a Cree and Canadian folksinger, was simultaneously bemused but also decidedly dismissive and critical. "They'll never be Indians," she explained. "The white people never seem to realize they cannot suck the soul out of a race. The ones with the sweetest intentions are the worst soul suckers." Comparing this inclination to a weird, vampire-like impulse, Sainte-Marie placed the hippies who exhibited it in a historical tradition of people trying to identify with those they conquered. Reading books and eating mushrooms would help no one. Rather these youth needed to accept their whiteness, be "the best kind of white people they can be," and understand that there are some things white people will never have . . . or become. They should face their own history, accept what they have done, and then do something honorable as white people.[5]

The Berkeley paper also reported, rather gleefully, on the demise of the Hopi-Hippie Be-In, noting that the hippies' involvement offended the tribe by teaching Hare Krishna chants to children without the elders' permission, fornicating in the Grand Canyon, and dropping acid while running through a Hopi village in the nude shouting "We are free." It reported that the Native American Unity Caravan, which came to the Bay Area in September 1967 to increase awareness of the Omnibus Bill, declined an invitation from Ron Thelen, owner of the Psychedelic Shop in Haight-Ashbury, to discuss their religion, prophecies, and ways of life after which the hippies would present a two hour "'ritual film-sound statement' of who they are, and how they look at the world." The event, in other words, was designed as an opportunity for Indians to learn more about hippies. When the Caravan failed to show, Thelen attributed their absence to the media's negative image of hippies. The ubiquitous Rolling Thunder, however, did show up with "his Nevada delegation" of Shoshones and talked about the "Day of Purification" which was nearing—a time when Indians and their "true brothers throughout mankind, will return to the way of the Great Spirit."[6]

The *Barb* was not above jumping on Indian stories that fit *their* interests, however. Native American resistance to the draft was not a common event in 1967, yet this newspaper found several incidents to publicize. Richard Williams, a Western Shoshone ranch hand from Nevada, contested his induction into the army on the basis of an 1863 treaty between the United States and his tribe. Rolling Thunder, who was married to a Shoshone woman, endorsed Williams's resistance, claiming the treaty was an acknowledgment of peace and friendship, not surrender, and that it did not make Shoshone people into U.S. citizens, subject to the draft. Although Rolling Thunder was correct about the treaty, he apparently did not know about the American Indian Citizenship Act of 1924 which made all Indians citizens and thus Indian men draftable. Williams, meanwhile, had other grounds for protesting the draft. He had rheumatic fever and was financially supporting his disabled parents. But, according to Rolling Thunder, "they're drafting all Indian boys now . . . they take 'em if they're Indian and they can walk or crawl. I figure it's so the rich white ranchers' boys can stay out."[7]

Williams's saga included three trips to Salt Lake City, during which time his draft status evolved from 4-F (on the basis of health) to 1-Y (insufficiently educated), to 1-A (draftable). His local draft board in Battle Mountain, Nevada, told him he should have written a letter about his economic hardships. Unfortunately, his papers had already been forwarded to Salt Lake City, so he would have to go through basic training. But after that he would be able to leave the service—advice his lawyer later described as misleading. Instead, after completing basic training, the army sent Williams to Oakland to be processed for Vietnam. At that point, Williams, while on furlough, returned to Nevada, met with the tribal council, and asked for their support in helping him get out of the army. "As long as I'm living, they'll never get me over there," Williams told the *Barb*. "I think I've got a good chance of winning this." Meanwhile Rolling Thunder warned that white men must not upset the natural forces if they wanted peace and plenty. Indians lived in accord with these forces and understood earthquakes and floods could result from human actions. If the army convicted Williams of desertion, Rolling Thunder could not guarantee these disasters would not result.[8]

In August 1967, Williams's court martial assembled at the Presidio. In spite of the best efforts of Los Angeles attorney J. H. Teitz, who argued that the court martial lacked jurisdiction over the Western Shoshone because of the 1863 treaty, and Rolling Thunder, who warned that unless the white man changed his ways he would perish in a great fire, the court convicted Williams. It sentenced him to five years of hard labor, reduction in rank, loss of all pay, and a dishonorable discharge. The Traditional Indian Land and Life Committee of Los Angeles, which supported Williams's cause, announced their intention to help Williams appeal the court martial decision and contest the broader question of the federal government's power to draft Indians.[9] The issue, however, faded from the newspaper's columns. Although antiwar advocates expected to find Indian resistance to the draft—who else, but Indians, would be less patriotic, less inclined to put their lives on the line for a government that had treated their own people so shabbily?—they did not find many fellow-travelers after all. As Sun Bear explained, some Indians went into the military service willingly, others did not.[10] Native American resistance to the war in Vietnam or military service, as Stewart Brand had learned, was far from universal.

Still, the *Barb* and other Berkeley dissidents could not resist the inclination to use Indians as symbols of resistance, to subvert commonly used phrases and images for the purpose of creating arresting anti-images that fit their own purposes. A September 1967 political cartoon featured the caption "Let's Support Our Boys" in stars and stripes typeset. The accompanying image, however, presented not a group of soldiers, but a cluster of Indians including one dressed in a blanket, moccasins, and headband with feather; another wearing a cowboy hat and jeans; and a child peering from behind the blanketed man. The intended irony is clear. The boys in "uniform" that deserved Berkeley's support were not the army's, but the Indians'. A November 1968 cover featured a classic frontier image—Indians attacking white settlers outside their log cabin. Two men in headdresses raise their tomahawks above a woman shielding her child while another man, in the foreground, straddles the prone father-farmer with a knife pointed at his throat. The caption reads: "Thanx for what, paleface?" And a 1969 story chronicled a new organization, Committee of Concern for the Whiteman Problem in the Bay Area, which supported Indian claims to land bases and perpetuation of their cultural traditions. Playing off historical references to "the Indian Problem," this nascent organization urged the federal government to acknowledge Indian sovereignty. A spokesman indicated they did not expect "to define Indian traditional identity but to help it continue and grow stronger." They also stressed they would do nothing without the approval of Indian leaders. Among the Native Americans helping the organization get on its feet were: Rolling Thunder, Thomas Banyacya (Hopi), and Craig ("Mohawk Messenger").[11] Items on the agenda of an upcoming meeting included Donald Bitsie's (Navajo) refusal to be inducted into the army.[12]

The Berkeley issue that most evoked Indian imagery and its linkages to moral authority for resistance, however, was the controversy over the Peoples Park. In June 1968 the city demolished a boarding house on the corner of Dwight Way and Telegraph Avenue. Many interpreted this as an effort to force out undesirables by eliminating cheap housing. Some residents urged the University of California to lease the property for a park. When the university failed to react quickly, local activists, in an effort to rally both hippie and radical elements, urged people to take matters into their own hands and build the park themselves. Leftists divided over the controversy. Some thought the park issue was simply "bourgeois reformist." Others thought it could be a useful tool, appealing to hippie-idealists who, when crushed for their efforts, would then understand the realities of power and join radicals in political union. The idea captured many peoples' imaginations. As hippies, radicals, and activists descended upon the muddy lot to create their ideal park, the organizers quickly realized the absence of a park plan was leading to chaos.[13]

Even more importantly, they needed an intellectual justification for taking control of the property. The answer: the doctrine of users' rights which Europeans had utilized in justifying their claims for Native American land. If a claimant could show he was using the land more productively and wisely than its previous owner, he could have it. On posters with a bold headline: "WHO OWNS THE PARK?" and images of Indians—one version featured Geronimo holding a gun, another a generic Indian man—the Peoples Park advocates claimed affinity with the Costanoan Indians, pre-European occupants of the Berkeley area. That

Geronimo was a Chiricahua Apache and not a Costanoan was apparently of no concern to the poster designer. Recognizing that one day the university would insist on acknowledgment of its ownership, the poster presented a thumbnail sketch of the land's history, starting with the Costanoans who, the author presumed, had no concept of property ownership but believed those who used and lived on land were its guardians. These people lost control to Catholic missionaries who "ripped it off in the name of God." Next the Mexican government, with its guns and army, took it from the Catholic Church and then lost it to the United States which had an even stronger army. The Americans, in turn, sold the property to white settlers rather than to descendants of original Indian occupants who still lived in the area even though the "American army [had] killed most of them." Eventually the government sold the property to the University of California. At that point it "went the way of so much other land in America—it became a parking lot." Now, in the spirit of the Costanoan Indians, the activists were taking care of the land and guarding it. When the university arrived with its land title, "we will tell them: 'Your land title is covered with blood. We won't touch it. Your people ripped off the land from the Indians a long time ago. If you want it back now, you will have to fight for it again.'"[14] Of course there was no mention of restoring ownership to the Costanoans. The fight for control of the property was between non-Indians. Indian imagery and rhetoric was purely symbolic.

Meanwhile volunteers laid sod, planted trees, built a barbeque pit, and started a vegetable garden. University officials did not find the use rights claim valid, but did attempt some negotiations with the park builders and faculty members from the College of Environmental Design who wanted the site to be used an as experimental field station. Negotiations broke down. The Regents of the university demanded a resolution to the problem. California highway patrolmen evicted the park builders, constructed a fence around its perimeter, and secured university control. Thousands of students, hippies, and radicals marched on the park, but never arrived at the site. When protestors engaged in petty violence, the police reacted with tear gas and bird shot. Rioting broke out, police reacted with brutality, and Berkeley dissolved into turmoil. California Governor Ronald Reagan sent the National Guard, who occupied the town for seventeen days and upset people all across the political spectrum. Once the National Guard withdrew, the University Regents held firm against a park on the site, turning it into a parking lot (though no one ever parked there).[15] The Peoples Park initiative had failed.

Things turned out differently, several months later, when a handful of Native Americans occupied Alcatraz, an island in the San Francisco Bay. Counterculture types, radicals from the entire Bay Area, and eventually the nation took this cause to heart. Virtually overnight, Alcatraz became the national hotspot of

Indian activism, first among many Native American students and young people and eventually among non-Indians (see figure 3.1). If Indianness had proven useful to Berkeley radicals in their "struggles" then they, in turn, would try to be useful to Indians in their fight for political sovereignty, cultural survival, and land. Right in their front yard was an opportunity to demonstrate support.

Nearly two decades of social and political activism across the nation, ranging from the dramatic acts of the civil rights movement to demonstrations against the Vietnam War and the media attention such events elicited, provided useful models for the Indians who took over Alcatraz Island. That a handful of Native American college students, with the aid of some Bay Area Indian residents, chose to take on the federal government by seizing an abandoned federal prison and claiming it for themselves, at this particular moment in history and at this particular place, was not an accident or coincidence. What better locale for such an event than an island situated between San Francisco and Berkeley? What better time than the last year of a decade that was becoming synonymous with challenges to the status quo? The Indians who occupied Alcatraz Island meant to bring national attention to the special concerns and issues that engaged Native Americans. But the tactics they used were those of non-Indians. As one of the participants later explained, "Of course it was a stunt ... primarily to publicize a cause ... There was a lot of street theater in the Bay Area in those days, and this

Figure 3.1 A tipi, reportedly belonging to actor and activist Peter Coyote, symbolized the Indians of All Tribes takeover of Alcatraz Island, an occupation that lasted from November 1969 to June 1971. Credit: Courtesy of Golden Gate National Recreation Area Park Archives.

was another kind, one which was intended to put its message on a bigger stage via the media." And the methods proved spectacularly successful in attracting attention. They "changed the rules of Indian activism" and consequently garnered "more press attention than all the Indian struggles of the entire century," according to Comanche historian and museum curator Paul Chaat Smith. The Alcatraz takeover made Indian anger manifest and sparked rebellions and occupations across the country.[16]

The first effort to take Alcatraz for Indian people occurred in 1964 when a handful of Sioux claimed it on the basis of their 1868 treaty, which contained language regarding their right to the government's surplus land. The Federal Bureau of Prisons had abandoned the prison in 1963 and various ideas about new uses for the property circulated in the Bay Area, including turning it into a tourist and casino site funded by Texas oilman Lamar Hunt. The 1964 takeover garnered little attention, but the idea never completely disappeared. When the San Francisco Indian Center burned down in 1969 the United Bay Area Council of American Indian Affairs, as well as a group of Native American college students from San Francisco State University; University of California, Berkeley; and University of California, Los Angeles, joined forces and decided to take Alcatraz as a replacement site. As Adam Nordwall, or Fortunate Eagle, put it, when "1969 stomped past mid-year with riots in Berkeley and massive, electrifying anti-war protests in San Francisco, Council meetings began to find focus and energy from the restless spirit of more and more young people, many of them college students." Some council members worried they were "unrealistically riding a dangerous tide of the time," but the consensus was for Indian people to take Alcatraz.[17]

A coalition of student and urban Bay Area Indians consequently agreed that they would undertake this action using the name Indians of All Tribes, reflecting, in part, the tribal diversity of the participants but also representing their intention to address Indian issues well beyond the island in San Francisco Bay. They composed a clever proclamation, offering twenty-four dollars in trade goods for the island, a satirical reference to the bargain struck for Manhattan in the seventeenth century. The group thought Alcatraz particularly suitable for Indian land, noting with irony, that the island lacked fresh running water, adequate sanitation, health care facilities, and natural resources. Indians of All Tribes wanted to build a Center for Native American Studies, an American Indian Spiritual Center, an Indian Center of Ecology, and a training school on "The Rock."[18]

Success, of course, hinged on attracting non-Indian attention and the Indians of All Tribes found initial media support from Tim Findley, a young reporter for the *San Francisco Chronicle*. His beat included Native American issues, and he was a friend of Nordwall and other Bay Area Indians. Findley learned of the occupation plans at a Halloween party he hosted and then shared the tip with other reporters, who promised to keep the plans confidential.[19] The next and more significant takeover of Alcatraz began November 20, 1969. Media coverage materialized immediately. Indians occupied Alcatraz for the next nineteen months, until federal marshals removed the last occupiers on June 11, 1971.

Initially as important as garnering newspaper and television attention, however, was getting to the island. Here, too, non-Indians proved critical to the operation's success. Reporter Findley, a resident of Sausalito, connected the activists with sailor-bartender Peter Bowen of that little town's No Name Bar. Bowen, in turn, linked the Alcatraz-bound Indians to the "spirit of swashbuckling anarchy on the Sausalito waterfront" and with two other friends, "irreverent spirits," agreed to ferry about ninety Indians out to Alcatraz under cover of darkness.[20] Bowen and his sailor-friend, Brooks Townes, had not given Indian issues much thought before, although the latter, as a reporter, covered Dick Gregory's demonstration for Northwest Indian fishing rights several years earlier. Townes saw himself as one of the "can-do sorts unafraid to take on The Establishment . . . ready, willing and able to disturb a little shit anytime, anywhere any needed disturbing—always for a good cause, of course, especially if it might be a little fun."[21] Bowen was interested in annoying the Nixon White House and helping Indians. Family members had told him he was one-eighth "Algonquin" but more than that he wanted to "tie into the energy of protest that was endemic throughout the country at that time—to the Viet Nam war, to racism—and help an emerging dream amongst the youthful subculture of free love, communal living and just about anything but the Ozzie and Harriet/Father Knows Best world."[22] Bowen acknowledged he would never know how it felt to be terminated by the government. He had never been forcibly educated at "brutal boarding schools." He had never been the object of a policy designed to purposefully destroy his culture. But by joining this effort he wanted to demonstrate a measure of compassion for those who had experienced such things and he took pride in his small effort to redress "the genocide" his ancestors practiced. "It seemed we were doing something damned important. It was, of course," he added, seconding Townes, "also a lot of fun."[23]

Getting that first group of Indians over to Alcatraz turned out to be just the first step in an enormous demonstration of material and political support non-Indians devoted to the Alcatraz cause, which originally started in the Bay Area but quickly spread across the continent. It began in Sausalito—a bay village situated at the northern base of the Golden Gate Bridge that had long been an artist's community and by 1969 had become a refuge for counterculture types in flight from San Francisco. Some found in "The Gates" section of Sausalito the ruins of World War II shipyards and several surplus thirty-six-foot steel lifeboats that they converted into houseboats and "funky little yachts."[24] Among the residents was Candra Day, who had migrated from Massachusetts to Portland's

Reed College (for one year), then Berkeley, and finally San Francisco. Searching for a sense of community, Day found it in the Sausalito houseboat neighborhood where the boats were literally tied together. Sausalito was "an experiment in community living in freedom" and the symbolic importance of Indianness was there from the outset.[25] It was a conscious decision to embrace Indians, in part as a "style joke" with the "joke being on ourselves." Day and her compatriots certainly knew they were not Indians. But they consciously and deliberately made reference to Indianness because they wanted to refresh their relationship with the land, seek solidarity with "underdogs," support social justice, and express admiration for peoples whom they associated with visionary experiences and presumably more spiritual lives. Admittedly what they had in mind was an ideal linked to historical Indians, but they also knew Native Americans still existed and believed their reservations remained repositories of these ideas and life ways. For the most part, however, the connection with Indians "was all about symbols and metaphysics." Moreover, Day insisted, there was no confusing the white shamans of Sausalito and actual Indian people.

When the Native Americans heading for Alcatraz came to the Sausalito waterfront an enormous amount of communication and exchange took place (see figure 3.2).[26] The Sausalito-based counterculture, according to Day, saw the Indians' fights on reservations and on Alcatraz as "more legitimate than ours." Hippies had been driven out of San Francisco and other communities through repressive drug laws and other forms of political reaction. But their complaints paled in comparison to those of Indians. Their history of oppression was clearly much, much deeper and the Indians' needs more acute. When the moment arrived to act on these sensibilities, the Sausalito waterfront community's feelings of "cultural brotherhood" with Indians—those sensibilities epitomized in Indian iconography and dress—quickly transformed into political solidarity and action. That came through most dramatically in blockade-running to bring food and water to Alcatraz, circumventing a Coast Guard blockade to prevent such support. Brooks Townes participated in sailing hundreds of Indians over to Alcatraz and running the blockade for nine days after the initial landing. "For the first nine days, almost all [Indians headed for Alcatraz] were sent over to Sausalito with instructions to the find the 'Indian Navy'—which meant either me or Peter [Bowen] . . . We landed every Indian who wanted to go out there, and all of the stuff they brought plus goods increasingly donated by Bay Area citizens of all backgrounds."[27]

The opportunity to buttress the Indian occupation of Alcatraz and simultaneously engage in civil disobedience by running the Coast Guard blockade was highly appealing to hippies and political radicals on the Berkeley side of the Bay, as well. It joined their heart-felt politics with an opportunity to engage in heart-stopping action. The *Barb* excitedly reported that a "boatload of Berkeley street

Figure 3.2 In placing counterculture symbols, such as bell-bottom jeans, a peace sign, and long hair on an Indian activist, Alcatraz occupier Joe Morris's (Blackfeet) painting demonstrates the cross-cultural influences that characterized that event. Credit: Courtesy of Golden Gate National Recreation Area Park Archives.

fighters had set out for the Alcatraz [sic] on Friday only to be rammed by a Coast Guard boat and turned back." The *Berkeley Tribe*, another underground newspaper, took even greater interest in the occupation and filled its columns with stories about blockade-running and other measures of support. Staffers of this paper were idealistic and oriented toward radical politics, putting the paper out for practically nothing. They called themselves the Red Mountain Tribe and collectively created the paper in 1969, making editorial decisions on an "elective basis." Their greatest interest was in Bay Area community organization work, with particular focus on the Black Panthers, the Weathermen, and Chicano and Indian movements. According to one outside analysis, the paper opposed the military, the Vietnam War, and many government policies at home and abroad. It condoned soft drugs, including marijuana. And it did not carry the "sex ads" the staff objected to in the *Barb*.[28]

The *Tribe* reported exuberantly on the Alcatraz takeover. One issue's cover featured a drawing of Alcatraz Island with the San Francisco skyline in the background. Above the prison rose a huge cloud with an Indian man at its center, sunbeams emanating from behind him. The headline, which arched over it all like a rainbow, read: "Americans Recover the Rock." The main story, however, featured non-Indian efforts to bring Native Americans and supplies to the island. *Tribe* reporter Kathy Williams hitched a ride out to the Rock soon after the occupation began and noted that once they landed they were on Indian Territory. "We were their guests. Which is cool, because that's the way it should have been all along." She understood, and accepted, that Alcatraz was to be an Indian place for Indian people only. A Seminole man told her: "This is Indian property. Not white man's. We dig the support, we need the supplies, but the last thing we want is a lot of people coming here to hang around, even though they want to help. This is an Indian thing, and we want to be by ourselves and get down to making it into our center." She watched as sailboats and even a houseboat made their quick landings to unload milk, cheese, baked hams, and other supplies, and move on to avoid a Coast Guard confrontation.[29]

Her own boat was not as lucky. In an ancillary article headlined "Victory at Sea" Williams related her adventures on the thirty-foot long "good junk WOO" with "our hip skipper... Peter Jones." Fifteen people on board had set out from the San Francisco marina with several hundred pounds of food as well as the underground press reporters, who dubbed themselves the "underwater press" for this escapade. (The "straight press," she claimed, had hired oversized charter fishing boats that cost seventy-five dollars an afternoon.) As they neared Alcatraz, however, a forty-foot long Coast Guard boat rammed the *WOO*. Two Indian men on board jumped off while the rest of the passengers held on "for dear life." Meanwhile: "As the Coast Guard returned to engage us in battle we saw the Indians clutch the face of a rock and grab a lowered rope. They made it."

The federal marshals on the Coast Guard boat ordered their vessel closer to the *WOO* and landed a rope on one of its davits, allowing the authorities to tow the junk. A knife quickly materialized to sever that connection and the *WOO*'s occupants began shoveling the food supplies off board to the Indians on the dock. The Coast Guard rammed the boat again, so Jones decided to "get our asses OUT of here." With the military in pursuit of the junk, the Indians on Alcatraz "waved farewell and we gave them the clenched fist salute as someone lit up another joint." The *WOO* then limped back to its slip in the San Francisco marina, where Jones received a citation for reckless and negligent handling of a motorized vessel. He was uncertain where he would find the funds to fight the legal battle, let alone repair his boat. "But we won, of course," the reporter concluded. "We landed two Indians on their land, got a lot of food on shore and made it back to the dock in one piece after being attacked twice by the enemy. The revolution took to the seas and came out victorious"[30] (see figure 3.3).

The language of battle, revolution, and solidarity came easily to the *Tribe* reporter. It is notable, however, that the stories featured the reporters' experiences and escapades rather than the Indian occupiers'. The paper did not print the Indians of All Tribes' proclamation regarding Alcatraz or explain the Indians' motivations. In part, this reflects the reporter's fleeting experience on the island, but it also suggests the opportunity Alcatraz provided for radicals to demonstrate *their* commitment to and solidarity with Indian activists mattered more. About one month later, another *Tribe* reporter visited Alcatraz, expecting to find the ghosts of Edward G. Robinson and George Raft rattling their tin cups across prison bars to spark a revolt. Instead he "found the ghosts of Sitting Bull and Cochise ready to start a revolt of another kind." Although security was tight, he disembarked and while trudging up the stairs to the main cellblock encountered an Indian woman whose "attire showed that it is not as far from Telegraph Avenue to a Sioux reservation as I had thought. She wore the universal symbol of American youth, a psychedelic button. It read: 'Prevent Pregnancy, Have Oral Sex.'"

Admitting ignorance concerning much of contemporary Indian life, the reporter also noted many of the occupiers were uninformed about their own cultures, since many of them had been raised off-reservation. But, he thought, the occupiers' emphasis on cultural issues was a mistake anyway because it obscured the political realities they would soon face. "The real oppression of Indian people," he explained, "like blacks and Chicanos stems from unemployment, a racist education system, and a paternalistic, un-democratic government. The occupation of Alcatraz should be a first step in a fight for decent jobs, an educational system which teaches Indians how to organize their people for liberation, an abolition of the Bureau of Indian Affairs, and an end to drafting of Indian men to fight imperial wars. With these demands paramount, Indians can unite with other oppressed

Figure 3.3 Visitors to Alcatraz, during the occupation, learned when arriving at the island's dock they had reached "Indian land." Although the occupation did not lead to transfer of property ownership from the federal government to the Indians of All Tribes, it did bring national and international attention to Native American demands for policy reform. Credit: Courtesy of Golden Gate National Recreation Area Park Archives.

minorities inside the U.S. to fight for their freedom." He believed that most of the Indian occupiers were like the Greensboro lunch counter sit-in people: political liberals who believed the government, under pressure, would respond to their demands. They are suspicious of revolutionaries such as the Black Panthers.

> But as the struggle over Alcatraz continues and more importantly, as it spreads to the reservations—Indians will learn what black people know now. The full might of the capitalist state will fall on any group which demands significant reforms. The government will buy-off any Indian leaders it can—and jail the rest. Today the Coast Guard harasses the boats taking supplies to the island. Tomorrow the Federal Marshals may try to evict them. If their struggle continues, the armored cavalry may yet be called out for a second genocide of the Indian people. Today's Indians will learn, as their ancestors learned 100 years ago, that political power comes from the blade of a tomahawk.[31]

In some respects this column proved prescient. Eventually federal marshals did evict the occupiers. Several years later the armored cavalry did roll into Wounded

Knee and use its considerable firepower to ultimately dislodge AIM occupiers from their position.

The impulse to join, seemingly seamlessly, Indian issues with those of other "minorities," however, demonstrated an ignorance of Native Americans' particular position or special status as sovereign governments with treaty rights. The insistence that only armed resistance could be successful and the call to stop drafting Indian men for "imperial wars" spoke more to the *Tribe's* philosophical position and concerns than those of the occupiers. Still the newspaper's support is important, and its office remained a place where items such as warm clothes, firewood, blankets, food, toilet paper, Kotex and Tampax, and whatever else was necessary for survival was collected and delivered to Alcatraz.[32]

Furthermore, the paper remained concerned with the island occupation throughout the nineteen-month long experience, periodically reminding its readership of it while simultaneously using the subject for its own purposes (see figure 3.4). A spring 1970 issue printed a statement from the Seattle-based United Indians of All Tribes, however, that more clearly articulated Native groups' aims. The occupation of Alcatraz, it said, ignited the beginning of such unity, around the goals of meeting reservation and urban needs, returning treaty-guaranteed lands, and finding new ways of educating Indian youth. Meanwhile, genocide through termination, relocation, and assimilation continues. "Let yesterday's leaders be a source of wisdom and moral strength, but let youth be the fire of positive action in this new and lasting demand for self-determination. Let us also be sure that this fire is a steady, warming hearth, and never one of destruction."[33]

This time, then, the paper more accurately articulated Indian interests and issues, although the emphasis on nonviolence did not particularly appeal to the *Tribe*. The same edition also ran an article emphasizing the history of Indian resistance through warfare. "The white man came with his fucked-up European ideas" and encountered "a people that wore feathers and beads and no clothes at all when it was warm enough. A people who held sacred the forces in nature. A people that were unafraid to have visions and live by them. They were an ideal: a race of warrior-holy men." Popé, among the leaders of the Pueblo Revolt of 1680, and Crazy Horse, a Sioux man who fought Custer's Seventh Cavalry on the Little Bighorn River, exemplified the warrior-holy man ideal. "Most of what we're now seeking outside America is native to this land," the author explained. Neither Marx, nor Buddha nor other Eastern teachers could provide lessons that Indians did not already offer.

> And we don't need anybody to tell us to pick up the gun if we can see the righteousness of the Indian who fought to the death for his people... All of it pulses deep in the heart of the real America, of which the USA

Figure 3.4 The *Berkeley Tribe*, an underground newspaper, followed and supported the Alcatraz takeover for the duration of the occupation. Credit: Courtesy of the Bancroft Library, University of California, Berkeley.

where we live is only a perverted and deadly shadow. It was not a land where a man could say "I am a holy man, fuck war" because he would then be known as a traitor to his people. And it was not a place where a man could only be a warrior and scoff at things of the spirit, because then he would be known as less than a whole man. Today America is in deep need of that warrior-holy man. It is the only thing that will save her.[34]

Whatever the intentions of the Alcatraz Indians, their off-island, more radical supporters insisted on militarizing their cause.

That some occupiers were wary of too close an association with either hippies or radicals became clear in their response to Douglas Baker Jr. of the *Dallas Notes*, an underground newspaper from Texas. Baker informed the Indians of All Tribes that he would be in the San Francisco area in February 1970 and hoped to meet with them to further his support of their cause. In the meantime he sent them a copy of an "American freedom fighter poster" he and a friend had created of "TANTANKA YOTAKNA, Sitting Buffalo Bull," which featured their proclamation and "a rap by me" under his pen name Scott London. He promised one thousand posters for their use "because you're [sic] cause is righteous." He also enclosed three dollars to subscribe to their newsletter and hoped to visit the island in order to write an article on Alcatraz for the *Dallas Notes*' special Indian issue. He promised to bring his own food so he would not drain their resources and ended the letter with, "May the Almighty God watch over you and give you success in your undertaking." What is most interesting about the poster is the note written on it by Peter Blue Cloud and addressed to the Council on Alcatraz and Santee Sioux occupier and frequent Alcatraz spokesman John Trudell. The note indicated that Baker did indeed have one thousand posters for the Indians of All Tribes, but he also had four thousand more that he intended to sell at fifty cents each for his own profit. Baker was white. But most troubling to Blue Cloud, Baker appeared to be trying "to bring us into '3rd World Activists.' Also hints at hippiness. I personally think it puts us in bad light. Mr. [Aubrey] Grossman [their lawyer] should investigate." Blue Cloud then went on to highlight some statements from Baker's "rap" that especially concerned him: spelling Americans as "Amerikans," referencing "a coming together of the tribes" and "a gathering of the tribes," which harkened back to language associated with the 1967 San Francisco Be-In, and comparing Sitting Bull's death to the murders of Malcolm X and Black Panther Fred Hampton.[35] Clearly some members of the Alcatraz leadership did not want to be seen as partners with hippies, black nationalists, or the New Left. They did not, in other words, automatically see themselves as the natural allies of people such as Doug Baker a.k.a "Scott London."

But support from many other less radical individuals and groups were welcome, and the nature, diversity, and geographical reach of that non-Indian support was remarkable. What set Alcatraz apart from the Northwest fish-ins was the enormous volume of publicity and consequent aid it elicited. In terms of capturing national and even international attention, Alcatraz stands out as a critical turning point for Indian reform. It provided the opportunity and the focus for non-Indian supporters to find a place and a purpose to which they could contribute. Following a pattern established by Marlon Brando's support of Pacific Northwest fish-in demonstrations, movie stars, music personalities, and groups who visited Alcatraz during the occupation garnered the most press attention. Actor Anthony Quinn arrived at Alcatraz after spending the night at San Francisco's swank Mark Hopkins Hotel. He told the press the Indians had every right to the island noting, "Alcatraz is a small price for all the sins we committed and indignities we forced on the Indians." He said his support was unrelated to a film he had just completed in New Mexico entitled *Nobody Loves a Drunken Indian* and that Indians were reaching out for sympathy not only for themselves but for "Negroes, Mexicans, and other minorities." Explaining that his father was Irish but his mother was Mexican, Quinn promised financial support for the occupiers.[36]

Several months later Jane Fonda drove up from Los Angeles with her seventeen-month-old daughter, Vanessa Vadim, after reading an article in *Ramparts Magazine* about Indian issues. Staying in a San Francisco apartment normally occupied by New Left writer Todd Gitlin, she spent one night on Alcatraz with Grace Thorpe, daughter of Olympic athlete Jim Thorpe. According to one reporter, Fonda was "dressed for activism in a smartly tailored black leather midiskirt, black turtleneck sweater and black boots. Around her slim waist she wore a silver-and-turquoise Navajo belt." She wanted to do something for Indians, Fonda said, because they "have been oppressed and controlled for too long." She promised to drive across the country, devoting a month and a half to visiting reservations and talking to Indians. "The Indians need our help," she explained, "They're non-violent."[37] A few days later, Fonda moved on to the California State Assembly in Sacramento to urge the legislators to pass Democratic Assemblyman Jesse Unruh's resolution to Congress to give Alcatraz to the Indians for a cultural center. By the time she and a group of Alcatraz Indians arrived, the Rules Committee had approved the resolution, and Fonda and friends watched as the Assembly adopted it by a vote of 52–0. The Senate eventually defeated the resolution 16–14.[38]

A celebrity of a different stripe, Ethel Kennedy, widow of former New York senator and presidential candidate Robert F. Kennedy, also supported the takeover. She convinced National Football League Commissioner Pete Rozelle to encourage the Washington Redskins football team to donate a color television to Alcatraz. By the time the television arrived, in December 1970, the island had no electricity, and so it languished on San Francisco's Pier 40. Joe Morris, an Indian occupier, told a reporter, "We can't use the thing until we get some diesel oil to power the generator on the island. I wanted to get the Redskins to throw in 50 barrels of fuel, too, but no luck."[39] The Nixon White House seemed especially concerned about Kennedy's interest in Alcatraz, particularly when she threatened to take the Indians' case to the public unless the Nixon administration resupplied the island with water and power. Her concern with the situation sparked Washington attorney Edward Bennett Williams's agreement to serve as counsel in a lawsuit against the government designed to grant the Indians title to the property. Although White House staffer Leonard Garment doubted the lawsuit had any legal merit, he did fear a press conference on the suit would "feature some nasty remarks about White House 'cruelty' to the Alcatraz Indians in cutting off the water barge and the power-line." The public relations costs, in other words, were more threatening than the legal ones. But, he explained to Nixon aide John Ehrlichman, "we have bent over backwards with restraint and have no apologies to make on that score."[40]

Celebrities from the music world also threw their support behind the takeover of Alcatraz Island. The rock group Creedence Clearwater Revival donated ten thousand dollars that, among other things, purchased a boat to carry occupiers back and forth from the mainland.[41] Singer Gary Paxton informed John Trudell that he was sending out almost four thousand support letters along with a recording of his song, "Token: The Ballad of Alcatraz" to President Richard Nixon, Vice President Spiro Agnew, Secretary of the Interior Walter Hickel, all the nation's senators and governors, and many more. The song began:

> ... the white man came from far across the water
> And he brought with him his misery and his greed
> He drove us out and killed our red forefathers
> As he moved west his killing picked up speed.
> Yeah there were thousands of massacres and killings—
> And the white man took everything he could get his
> Hands on—Our land—Our food—Even our sons and
> Daughters—But not our heritage or our spirit—But
> Ooh he tried.

It concluded:

> Well it isn't much—just an old abandoned prison—Alcatraz
> But we'll proudly call it home—just one time white man—keep
> Your promise—give us back our home.
> Give us back our land, Ya don't want it anyway
> How long much we suffer, how long must we pay.

In his cover letter, Paxton explained he intended to use any profits he earned from this recording to support an Indian cultural center and to feed and educate poor Indian children. He promised John Trudell that he would not participate in any benefits that did not have the Alcatraz Indians' sanction. He apparently had already withdrawn from several events after learning that Trudell knew nothing about them because "if they were not on the level we didn't want to take a chance & ruin a possible friendship with all of you."[42]

Folksingers' support was quickly forthcoming. Berkeley's Malvina Reynolds wrote a song about Alcatraz a few days before the "invasion." The lyrics skewered Texas oilman Lamar Hunt's plans to develop the island:

> Alcatraz. We don't need that plastic jazz.
> Give us the island the way it was
> When the Indians had their day.
> Who needs an Astrodome in San Francisco Bay?

She promised to contribute one thousand dollars from its royalties to the San Francisco Indian Center and told a reporter she loved Indians and had all her life. Further, she believed they should not only own Alcatraz Island but also a huge chunk of California's Central Valley where they could work the land and be free of factories and tract housing. "Alcatraz isn't good enough for them," she claimed, "but it certainly is a first step."[43]

After the occupation began, Reynolds joined Buffy Sainte-Marie at a benefit for Alcatraz on December 12, 1969, at Stanford's Memorial Chapel. She added a new verse of her Alcatraz song for the event:

> Now the Indians hold the rock
> Just a grain of sand
> To the wilds we robbed them of their native lands
> Now they take their stand.
> Alcatraz. We don't need that plastic jazz
> Give us the island the way it was
> When the Indians have their day.
> We'll cheer those council fires in San Francisco Bay.[44]

Before an overwhelming non-Indian audience, she acknowledged she was "pale" in hair and skin compared to the others on the stage that night. She was, in fact, the only non-Indian speaker or performer. Ojibwa Adam Nordwall moderated the evening's affair; Mohawk Richard Oakes appeared briefly to present Sainte-Marie with a postconcert bouquet of flowers; and Winnebago Shirley Keith explained the goals of the occupation, promising several times, "We're not leaving." She told the predominantly white audience: "You can take credit for our being on Alcatraz because you and your government forced our backs against the wall. You're responsible. That's why we're there." If the audience was taken aback by this charge, Nordwall moved to soften it, indicating that Indians had always fought alone, but tonight they realized they no longer needed to do so because they now had friends. "There is a public that does give a damn." Keith did receive applause from the audience when she drew parallels between Indian policy and the war in Vietnam. Among other things, she said, "your government" has violated every treaty it ever made with Indians "just as it is violating the Geneva Accords of 1954 in Vietnam."[45]

Sainte-Marie was clearly the headliner that evening and sang some of her most powerful songs about Indian issues. Along with her better-known songs such as the antiwar anthem "Universal Soldier" and "Now That the Buffalo's Gone," she performed one in honor of the people fighting for their fishing rights in Washington state:

> My brave fishermen, by the river, by the sea
> Or on the shore by the nets keeping watch.
> By the nets, my heart is there with you.
> My brave little girl by the trestle in the cold
> Standing up to the sheriff and his guns
> By the nets, my heart is there with you.[46]

She remained cynical, however, about the long-term benefits of such concerts and doubted that her devoted fans actually moved from listening to music to political activism. Sainte-Marie explained to a newspaper columnist that although her music addressed real Indian issues and although it was fashionable to express support for Indian causes, she believed most people postured but did little. She herself had been guilty of inaction in the past. Now she was using her time and money to send several Indian people to law school and to start a program for supplementary training for teachers who wanted to work with Indians. "What I want to see is carpenters and bricklayers and guys who know how to dig wells and teachers who can teach an Indian things that are relevant to Indian life. People who know rudimentary Indian law and basic Indian history."[47]

If Sainte-Marie remained skeptical of non-Indian commitment, the Indians of All Tribes continued to welcome almost any kind of support and certainly sought out all favorable media attention. They jumped at the chance to begin broadcasting from the Pacifica Radio Network, a progressive radio group out of Los Angeles that carried the show via stations in Berkeley, Los Angeles, and New York. The broadcasts originated from the prison's main cellblock using equipment donated by employees of Berkeley's KPFA radio station. Station

Manager Al Silbowitz made clear the non-Indians simply provided the means for the broadcasts, but the content was "their thing—their voice . . . we're not telling them what to do. We want it to be their thing." Within a few months John Trudell and Silbowitz requested additional financial support from the San Francisco Cambrium Fund to continue the broadcasts. "These activities will, for the first time, give Native Americans an uncensored voice in the mass media (via the Pacifica Network) allowing urban and reservation Indians to communicate directly and regularly with one another," they explained in their grant request. The Cambrium Fund contributed $1200, about one-half that Trudell and Silbowitz requested, for general operating expenses. The Fund's David Fuller lauded them for their stance of nonviolence and believed that Indians deserved "equal access to the political and economic power which is justifiably" theirs.[48]

The occupation leadership labeled their broadcasts "Radio Free Alcatraz," a clear nod to the State Department's "Radio Free Europe," a Cold War era broadcast meant to reach people in the Soviet bloc about American-style democracy. The Alcatraz effort to capture international audiences worked, aided perhaps by the unfortunate coincidence that reportage of a U.S. Army massacre of nearly five hundred Vietnamese civilians at My Lai appeared simultaneously with news of the Alcatraz takeover. A tendency to join criticism of the Vietnam War, seen as an example of contemporary imperialism, with sympathy for American Indians, seen as victims of past imperialism, was becoming increasingly common. The massacre at My Lai, in particular, struck some as reminiscent of Indian massacres at nineteenth-century Western sites such as Sand Creek and Wounded Knee. The congruence of My Lai and Alcatraz, then, quickened off-shore interest in Indians, particularly in Europe. The *Times* of London editorialized that the only answer to the problems experienced by the "first Americans" was "some form of statehood conferring direct representation in Washington."[49]

Meanwhile, back home, additional support came from churches. It probably surprised no one that Haight-Ashbury's Glide Memorial Church hosted a poetry reading to benefit the American Indian Center and the Indians on Alcatraz in mid-December, 1969. Gregory Corso, Gary Snyder, Michael McClure, and Leonard Bruce were among the featured speakers and poets. The backing of the Palo Alto Society of Friends was also predictable. In their letter to Secretary of the Interior Walter Hickel they expanded the issue well beyond Alcatraz: "We believe that serious injustice has been done to these people since the day the White Man arrived on these shores. We ask that wherever treaties have been broken, restitution should be made and that in the future, all treaties be carefully honored." Indicative of the widening support these Native American activists received across the country were letters and financial contributions coming from: a group of students and faculty at the United Theological Seminary in the

Twin Cities area of Minnesota; the United Presbyterian Church's Board of National Missions (which sent a check after hearing Shoshone-Bannock and Alcatraz occupier LaNada Means speak); and the Scarsdale [New York] Congregational Church, which asked the Indians of All Tribes what they could do to help. It is noteworthy that these donations materialized about one year *after* the occupation began, belying the notion that support quickly evaporated as time went on.[50]

The relationship between Indian activists and mainstream churches could be rocky, however, as Browne Barr, pastor of Berkeley's First Congregational Church, learned when he came under attack from occupier Shirley Keith, for a sermon he gave on November 23, 1969, the Sunday after the initial occupation. He intended his message to be supportive, but Keith took Barr to task for being "more interested in a symbol of liberty than in a *realization* of liberty" and "for the pious tone emanating from" his pulpit. Barr responded that it was a bit strange for her to call a symbol "mere" when she and her compatriots were so busy creating a very effective one at Alcatraz. "Which do you think will have more power to change the Indians' lot, the center which you can develop there, or the symbol that you want it to become by holding up the Indians' rightful claim and judging the nation's shabby performance?" As for the distinction she made between symbol and realization of liberation, Barr believed they could not be separated and offered his own great-grandfather's experiences trudging through deep snow and weathering hot summers to bring medical care and a written language to the Dakota Indians of the Fort Snelling, Minnesota, area as someone whose actions served as "a symbol with far greater power than his person could deliver alone." Clearly stung by Keith's criticisms, Barr asked, "If you are so hard on your friends, what energy do you have left for your enemies?" But he concluded, "May you have speedy good luck and a widening group of supporters."[51]

Of course, many Indian groups endorsed the Alcatraz action. Among those who sent letters and telegrams of encouragement included Brooklyn's Indian League of the Americas, Inc.; Rochester, New York's North American Indian Club; the California Indian Education Association; Pyramid Lake Tribal Council; Winnebago Tribal Council; Inter-Tribal Council of Nevada,; the Denver Indian Center's Call of the Council Drums; Omaha Tribal Council; Phoenix Indian Center; the Native Alliance for Red Power of Vancouver, British Columbia; the Blackfeet Tribe; the Rincon Band of Mission Indians; the American Indian Council of Santa Clara Valley; and the Long Beach Indian Youth Council. Rodolfo Cortez Gonzales of Denver's Crusade for Justice also telegraphed the Indian of All Tribes: "Brothers, we fully support your noble and courageous stand by taking Alcatraz. The time has come for all the suppressed peoples to join together for our common liberation. The Crusade for Justice teaches the proud history of our mestizo, Indian blood, and offer whatever assistance we can give. Indian land to Indian people."⁵²

From the more conservative side of the political spectrum, Aran Ardaiz, of the American Indian State Council of the Republican State Central Committee of California, informed the Republican National Committee in early December 1969 that the Republicans were missing a tremendous opportunity to capitalize on the Alcatraz takeover and reform domestic Indian policy. Ardaiz had visited Alcatraz and concluded the occupiers would not relinquish it without giving the Nixon administration a "black eye." He believed the public overwhelmingly supported the takeover and that the Republicans could not stand much more negative publicity. "This is a *people issue* and our Interior Policy here can be most advantageous politically." The Nixon administration, then, should not hesitate to act positively by giving, or leasing, the island to the Indians.⁵³

It was, however, Democrats who moved quickly to endorse the occupier's position and goals. Jesse Unruh's resolution to the California Assembly was one example. George Brown, a Democratic congressman from Los Angeles, introduced a bill in the House of Representatives on December 23, 1969, calling on Nixon to give Alcatraz "back to the Indians" and directing him to begin negotiations. Co-sponsors of the bills included Democrats Shirley Chisholm and Allard Lowenstein of New York, Louis Stokes of Ohio, Edward Roybal of California, and Republican Ogden Reid from Illinois.⁵⁴ The bill did not pass, and Nixon took neither Ardaiz's nor Brown's advice regarding Alcatraz. California Republican Senator George Murphy proposed making Alcatraz a national park to honor all American Indians, but the Alcatraz occupiers quickly dismissed this idea because such a park would be run by the federal government.⁵⁵

Meanwhile organized labor joined the fight on the occupiers' side. Joe Morris, a Blackfeet, spearheaded the effort to engage union help. As a member of the International Longshoreman's and Warehouseman's Union, Local #10, this was his natural constituency. His appeal, addressed "TO ALL THE WORKING STIFFS," relied on sports imagery. While the politicians, "gambling czars," and others were "blowing hot air" about the island's future, "the American Indians decided to referee the bout. While the heavy sluggers were slugging it out, the Indians kayoed the hassle, by quietly taking the island." Now they asked the working class to help them by donating money for, among other things, automobile batteries, as well as the labor of volunteer electricians to help restore power and skilled plumbers to fix or replace old pipes. The Indians wanted to create a first-class museum and cultural center—a "monument to humanity." Lest his readers have doubts about the occupiers' patriotism, Morris assured them the occupiers wanted "to raise our heads again proudly and say not only '*I'm an Indian!* but *'I'm a U.S. Citizen*,' a full fledged American." Morris proved successful with his own local, whose executive board voted to donate $99.99 per week for ten weeks, a contribution that added up to one thousand dollars. But things did not stop there. San Francisco's Painter's Local Union #4 sent letters to President Nixon, Secretary Hickel, George Meany of the AFL-CIO, and S. Frank Rafferty of the Brotherhood of Painters, Decorators and Paperhangers of America, expressing their support for the Indians on Alcatraz and urging the national office to do likewise. The Ship Clerks' Association, Local #34 of the ILWU, donated one hundred dollars; the Federated Auxiliaries of ILWU, Northern California District Council gave ten dollars (the largest amount their regulations allowed them to donate to outside organizations); and the Millwright and Machine Erectors of Los Angeles sent a letter of solidarity.[56] In addition, the United Auto Workers Local #6 provided a Gestetner mimeograph machine so the Indians of All Tribes could print their newsletter. Other support came from the International Brotherhood of Boilermakers, Iron Ship Builders, Blacksmiths, Forgers and Helpers, of Local #6, San Francisco; ILWU, Local #14, Eureka, California; Supercargoes and Checkers Union, Local #40, Portland, Oregon; and ILWU locals from Oakland and North Bend, Oregon.[57]

As the occupation wore on, media attention began to wane and criticism of the occupiers picked up in San Francisco newspapers. Still, non-Indian support continued through 1970 and into 1971. Learning about the Alcatraz occupation from the *New York Times, Progressive* magazine, the *Nation*, the Dick Cavett and Merv Griffin television shows, correspondents' letters of affirmation poured in with messages:

"I wish I could do more for your people who are a living example of a people whose special spirit continues to exist despite the pressures and hostility of an alien culture."

"I believe the only hope for America is in the return to the values and beliefs of Native Americans."

"Don't surrender. Much public sympathy to your advantage."

"Give not one inch to the government. There shall be no more Sand Creeks or Wounded Knee Massacre's [sic]."

"You have a lot more support than you relize [sic], and you have the publicity no[w]. Strike while the iron is hot."[58]

The diversity of people who felt moved to write to the Alcatraz occupiers was remarkable. Women, some apparently elderly, from places such as Burlingame, California, and Hazel Park, Michigan, offered warm coats, a sewing machine, and material for clothing. Letters with checks ranging from one to one hundred dollars (some of them never cancelled) arrived from across the country: Washington, D.C.; McAllen, Texas; Cambridge, Massachusetts; Philadelphia, Pennsylvania; Hillsborough, California; Burley, Idaho; Olathe, Kansas; Maryland Heights, Missouri; Elkhart, Indiana; and Quinter, Kansas. The last was the home of Billie Flora, who described herself and her husband as "farmer-cow herd people struggling to stay on the land." They had just delivered a young heifer at two o'clock that morning. But Flora was moved to write after seeing Grace Thorpe on the *Merv Griffin Show*. "Our country is in such a sad stale-mate state," she wrote. "And we could have such a great life—loving and visiting people everywhere *if*. Love to you and Peace soon."[59] University of Chicago anthropologist Sol Tax, who was spending the academic year at Stanford's Center for Advanced Study in Behavioral Science, sent twenty dollars collected from two of his colleagues there. A single parent, recently divorced from her Seminole husband, sent one dollar—all she could afford since she had a three-year-old son to support. She offered to do all she could to help and asked to be kept informed on how things were going on Alcatraz. A man from San Francisco, who explained he was a member of the First Congregational Church in the city, sent one hundred dollars along with a troubling note: "I've always had great respect for the Indians, and am much more inclined to help them, than the Negroes." Jim Jones, pastor of the Integrated Peoples Temple in Redwood Valley, California, who eventually led his followers down to Guyana where they committed mass suicide in 1978, sent a check for seventy-five dollars from the church. The vast majority of correspondents who identified themselves by race indicated they were white. But a black, shoe salesman from Detroit, Michigan, penned a letter to "Richard the Loin Hearted" (presumably Richard Oakes) and described himself as "a *Black Freedom Fighter*." He sent five dollars but wished it was ten thousand. An Asian student from Los Angeles promised to get "some Asian brothers from 'AmerAsia'" to help out in the summer. A few supporters were Jewish, including one woman who made a donation to the Indians in honor of her cousin's bar mitzvah.

Some correspondence, deemed "nutmail," clearly came from people who were either mentally ill or under the influence of drugs. These letters were usually anonymous. One such letter, with its scathing criticism of the island takeover, was the exception to prove the rule. This writer urged the occupiers to "face reality ... If it hadn't been for the white man, you all would have liquidated each other long ago in your nomadic wanderings across the country, warring on different tribes." Ever since, white people have worked hard and paid taxes to support minorities who expected free handouts. "WE SAY, SINK ALCATRAZ! IF YOU NEED MORE MONEY, GET IT FROM AUBREY GROSSMAN, YOUR LOUD MOUTH MOUTHPIECE." Less poisonous, but perhaps equally unhelpful was the woman who wrote about her trip to Tiburon for dinner with her Bible class. As she sailed across the Bay, she thought about the Indians on Alcatraz and prayed that they would use the island "for the Lord Jesus Christ." They should repair the burnt building (referring to the warden's house that burned down during the occupation), transform it into a church, and name it "Lighthouse Church because Jesus is the 'Light of' the World."[60]

The vast majority of correspondents, however, not only understood the occupiers' position but fully supported it. The Alcatraz incident had clearly touched a nerve well beyond the confines of the "Left Coast." Sausalito counterculture types and Berkeley political radicals initiated non-Indian support, but it did not take long for similar sympathies to emerge across the nation and across political lines. The outpouring of such support also crossed racial, ethnic, and economic divisions. Who would have thought a San Francisco hippie would have anything in common with a farmer from Kansas? Who would have imagined an advocate of Berkeley's Peoples Park finding common cause with blue-collar unionists? But Alcatraz touched a chord, and for the first time in the twentieth century an incredible outpouring of favorable sentiment for a Native American protest, on a national scale, prompted people to express and demonstrate through their pens and pocketbooks encouragement and aid—and not only to the Alcatraz Indians (see figure 3.5).

The Nixon White House was well aware of this phenomenon. It, too, received letters from diverse constituents expressing sympathy for the occupiers and urging capitulation to their demands. Telegrams, petitions, and letters arrived at 1600 Pennsylvania Avenue calling on the president to "do something decent for a change" and give the Indians the island.[61] Six months into the occupation, the Interior Department informed the White House that Secretary of the Interior Hickel was receiving thirty to forty letters a day, with over 95 percent of them favoring to the Indians' demands.[62] The letters to the White House urged either giving or leasing the island to the Indian occupiers, and sometimes offered significant help. One man, whose fortune derived from Polaroid Land Camera Company, offered his seven-hundred-acre ranch in Marin County, near Muir Beach, as an alternative site for an Indian center. An Atherton, California, heiress wrote Nixon that he had "an impossible dream once and it became reality." Now he had the chance to make an impossible dream happen for Native Americans. She challenged him to sell Alcatraz to the Indians for twenty-four dollars as a way to match her own philanthropy. She intended to give 184 acres of San Jose, California, property to a new Indian group called "A Nation In One," "as a gesture of reparation . . . for the history of broken treaties and misunderstandings." She found the Indians of All Tribes' landing on Alcatraz to be a "brilliant coup . . . This is the best they can do without uniting into 'red power' and taking tomahawks to the whites as the blacks resorted to."[63]

A few people whose ties to Richard Nixon were even closer also wrote. One of his Whittier College history professors, who specialized in European History and self-published books about Indian folktales, sent a brochure about his latest offering to Nixon's personal secretary, Rose Mary Woods—perhaps in the hope of sensitizing his former student. Even Richard Nixon's "Aunt Ruth" Milhouse,

Figure 3.5 Harkening back to Stewart Brand's multimedia celebration of Native Americans, this poster repeats his refrain "America Needs Indians" as it encourages support for the Alcatraz action. Credit: San Francisco History Center, San Francisco Public Library.

from the Quaker side of his family, suggested he let the Indians have Alcatraz. We have too many taxes as it is, she explained, and more important needs than those of a park "many miles out in the ocean that only the very rich could ever visit." She did not want to see her nephew's administration "go down in history as another that dishonored our treaty with our Indians. There have been too many. Why not let the Indians pay the bills of rebuilding that old rock and win their real gratitude?" Believing she was speaking "for millions in America," Aunt

Ruth demonstrated neither mastery of California geography nor of fiscal affairs. Unfortunately, President Nixon's response is not in the file.[64]

Of course, the Indians on Alcatraz did not garner universal acclaim among Nixon's correspondents. One noteworthy voice of opposition came from the Bay Area-based Ohlone Indians who said if the land belonged to anyone, it was them. The people on Alcatraz, they complained, did not speak for any tribe, let alone for them. They had true historical claim to the property and if granted it, intended to make it into a wildlife refuge and way-station for navigators.[65] Another critic from Cornelia, Georgia, expressed disgust with this "Indian (savage) affair." Outraged that a young girl had been killed (Yvonne Oakes did indeed die early in the occupation—whether a victim of murder or accident remains unclear to this day), buildings burned, and law enforcement completely absent, he wanted to know what he could do, as a citizen, to "evick" them with the help of his attorney.[66]

Nixon's aides also collected news articles and editorial comments from across the country, again most of it supportive of the occupation. Among the clippings in their file was one from the *Palo Alto Times* which indicated former child-actress and Republican stalwart Shirley Temple Black was sympathetic to the takeover. Columnist Nicholas Van Hoffman's *Washington Post* piece compared historic treatment of Indians in places such as Sand Creek and Wounded Knee to events in Vietnam. Describing contemporary Indian policy as "genocidal" though carried out through starvation rather than sabers, Von Hoffman declared, "With the Indians and the Vietnamese many people want to know if extermination is the government's policy." The Indians on Alcatraz, he said, already knew the answer.[67]

The Nixon administration was taking hits from the right, as well. *San Francisco Business*, a publication of that city's Chamber of Commerce, criticized the White House for capitulating to the occupation, most recently by attempting to include the activists in plans for a national park that would incorporate Alcatraz. A May 1970 editorial from the *Hammond Times* of Indiana, on the other hand, urged the Indians of All Tribes to accept the national park option and the role of park developers and guides in partnership with the federal government. The paper understood the Indians' reluctance "to accept another white man's gift horse," but this one "could be the start of something big."[68] Meanwhile Nixon's aides collected whatever negative information they could find about the occupation. John Ehrlichman had a creepy fascination with a report of a young boy's alleged rape on the island.[69]

In-house records reveal that the White House never seriously considered meeting the Alcatraz occupiers' demands. Yet there is no doubt they understood the political climate demanded they move with caution and care. In January 1970 Leonard Garment, who had the title of special assistant to the president and served as point man on Indian affairs, informed Ehrlichman that he was not contemplating forcible removal of the Indians. "U.S. Marshalls chasing screaming Indians through the echoing halls and cell-blocks of the old prison would be too Kafka-esque to contemplate." It would also be political folly at a time when congressional and White House mail heavily favored turning Alcatraz over to the Indians. In the short term, Garment thought Ehrlichman should visit the island and thus demonstrate the president's interest in Indians' problems, particularly those of urban Indians.[70] By March 1970 Secretary of the Interior Hickel's patience with the White House strategy of delay wore thin. He fumed about the apparent tolerance of government trespass, feared it would only encourage similar actions elsewhere including Fort Lawton in Seattle, and urged public release of the government's intention to create Golden Gate National Recreation Area that would incorporate Alcatraz Island.[71]

Garment, a self-described "birthright Democrat and lifelong liberal" who ended up in Nixon's White House via their shared New York law-firm experience, continued to counsel restraint and patience through the summer of 1970. He believed Nixon supported this approach because the president empathized with Indians as "American homegrown victims, losers and survivors." Further, this particular occupation was particularly well-suited to confrontational politics: a supposedly good cause, a sympathetic public, a public relations-conscious group at its heart, and a visible piece of real estate in a major American city. With these factors in mind he cautioned, "we do not want a Kent State on Alcatraz," referring to the murder of four university students gunned down by Ohio National Guardsmen during a campus antiwar demonstration that spring. By fall Garment still argued against forced removal, claiming it could result in bloodshed—not a good idea at a time when college students were returning to their campuses, elections loomed, and the president's Indian legislative package was about to be aired in Congress.[72] Garment's policy of restraint prevailed until June 1971, when the White House concluded the time had come to force removal. As Garment saw it, the small numbers of Indians still living on the island, the significant decline of public support, and the long interval before the next election made the timing right.[73] On June 14, 1971, U.S. federal marshals escorted the last of the occupiers off the island and then released them.

While the mainstream presses around the Bay Area supported the move, the underground press did not.[74] The *Berkeley Tribe* remained particularly supportive of the occupation from beginning to end. On the one-year anniversary of the takeover they published a new manifesto from the Indians of All Tribes that pronounced they still held the rock, in part because of "our brothers and sisters of this earth who have lent support to our just cause" and reiterated their fundamental strategy of nonviolence. The group issued an invitation to all people in the Bay Area for a powwow at San Francisco's Pine Lake Park to commemorate "the first anniversary of the liberation of Alcatraz." They also requested volunteers to run supplies to the island. Among the items they still needed: oil, gasoline, firewood, tools, blankets, sleeping bags, and first aid materials. Meanwhile all Indians were invited to gather on the island to celebrate the "unity of All Tribes in the liberation struggle."[75] The *Berkeley Tribe* also printed a poem, by "coyote2," titled "Alcatraz Again":

> Smokey the bearing of ill will promises
> of maximal Indianniss [*sic*] upon the island rock,
> with end of trail statues fashioned in mental monstrosities
> Alcatraz, whose singing now is tribal youth,
> whose message to an insane world is courage,
> whose blood is the ancestor life stream
> singing and singing the ocean's tidal pull . . .
> political pollutions assembly-lined in the Madison Avenue
> of Nixonian nerve-gassed American atrocities, four score
> and seven million military massacres ago
> where pilgrims and pledges cannibalized a continent . . .[76]

The *Tribe*'s coverage of the end of the occupation also revealed their zeal for the action had not dimmed, characterizing the "pig marshals'" actions as "an invasion," disputing the "pig press'" descriptions of Alcatraz as filthy, and claiming the federal marshals were the ones who trashed the place (although its original condition at the time of the takeover was hardly pristine). The paper followed the case of three Alcatraz Indians charged with embezzlement and theft of government property for the copper cable they had removed from the island and sold to a metal company near Fisherman's Wharf—one of the few ways they supported the occupation. "The government chooses to prosecute them for using a bit of copper which was rightfully theirs, while a huge corporation like Kennicott Copper rapes the Indians' land in Arizona." This fight is "our fight too," the *Tribe* claimed. Six months later it covered the trial, giving special attention to the defendants' attorney, Don Jelinek, who described himself as a participant in the Alcatraz takeover since he had met with the Indians one night a week for a year and a half. The jury found the three men guilty, but the judge sentenced them to three years probation and admitted the federal government had acted in bad faith with the Alcatraz Indians. Finally, on the two-year anniversary of the occupation, the *Tribe*'s cover displayed a full-page, pen-and-ink drawing of Alcatraz, with San Francisco and the Golden Gate bridge in the background, an Indian man's head in the cloud above the island, and "ALCATRAZ Thanksgiving 1969" as the headline. The issue carried no Indian-related stories, however.[77]

The *Berkeley Barb*, which had not been as vigilant in covering Alcatraz as the *Tribe*, lived up to its name by criticizing the people who called themselves revolutionaries "by right of a single bust or be-in" but did little to help the Indians on Alcatraz. It blamed the Left for the occupation's ignominious end. "We bathed in the glory of their uprising while they were starving out there on the Rock." Where is the commitment to genuine change? The time had come to demonstrate an ability to build up as well as destroy, to "consolidate our gains and make them live for all to see. Had we helped the Red Man to create the community he dreamed of on Alcatraz . . . not the Coast Guard nor the army nor all the political power in America would have dared to intervene." The writer believed that America's conscience was at a turning point and all that radicals needed to do was demonstrate their ability to create a better society. He suggested everyone donate one dollar per month—a tax of sorts—to be given to various groups. The author promised to submit the first dollar and requested it "be belatedly given to the American Indian revolutionaries for the furtherance of their community goals."[78]

In the end, the Alcatraz occupation did not lead to the Indians of All Tribes obtaining title to Alcatraz or establishing an Indian cultural center there. Yet in terms of garnering tremendous attention to more general Indian claims and complaints, the effort was remarkably successful. Almost immediately it ignited similar acts of defiance by Indian activists across the country, publicizing a spectrum of issues that, in turn, inspired changes in attitudes and ultimately policies. Thirty years after the takeover, Adam Fortunate Eagle said, "We won the war—we just didn't know it at the time." John Trudell noted that even though they did not get what they wanted at Alcatraz, they raised issues of sovereignty to the nation and strengthened their own spirits.[79] Even at the time Richard Oakes understood an important page had been turned at Alcatraz. As he explained in 1972 *Ramparts Magazine* article:

> In many ways, the passing of Alcatraz marked an end to the era that had begun several years earlier with the fish-ins in Washington state, and had grown through the revolution of rising expectations fostered by the programs of the Great Society. Indians had in some sense suddenly ceased to be *chic*. Things had changed since the fact that they were captives inside white America had burst in upon the national conscience in the mid-60s, and as the war in Vietnam forced Americans to take a hard look at their history and understand that it was founded on a primal genocide against the red men.[80]

Americans had "rediscovered" Indians before "in a hot flash of guilt" and always the same things happened: some remedial legislation passed, people wrote a few books, and then concern about "the plight" of Indians faded.

But this time the rediscovery was not quickly eclipsed. Indian issues did not disappear. If the fishing rights campaign in the Pacific Northwest helped turn national attention to Indian affairs, Alcatraz secured it. San Francisco was a major American city with lots of media outlets and interest, much more so than Olympia, Washington. Alcatraz Island was familiar to many Americans and already had a national identity, unlike Frank's Landing or the Puyallup River. The Bay Area, with its history of tolerance for cultural difference and its more recent experience with political upheaval in places such as Berkeley, provided a solid base of support—both material and philosophical—for the Indians of All Tribes.

White House staff Leonard Garment certainly believed the Alcatraz occupation made a huge difference, proclaiming "it proved the catalyst for a historic change in American Indian life." In fact, he maintained, the enormous public sympathy and support made it possible for the White House to set in motion a series of proposals and legislative measures designed to address Native American demands for change. Nixon's Presidential Message on Indian affairs, delivered to the U.S. Congress on July 8, 1970, articulated the administration's dedication to self-determination and the end of termination. He called for the nation to break with the past and create conditions that would allow a new era in which Indians determined their own futures based on their own goals. He declared termination dead because it had abrogated the federal government's solemn treaty obligations that still carried "immense moral and legal force." The Nixon administration then followed the message with over twenty proposals for legislation including extension of the Indian Claims Commission, establishment of Navajo Community College, and the Alaska Native Claims Settlement Act. It was the 1975 Indian Self-Determination and Indian Education Act which crystallized and put into motion the centerpiece of Nixon's Indian policy. Unfortunately, Garment claimed, some of these reform plans became bogged down in congressional stalemate and the American Indian Movement's unrealistic demands.[81]

The symbolic force of occupying Alcatraz and mobilizing the general public also had its vulnerabilities as a strategy. As Vine Deloria Jr. put it, symbolic acts often "fail to articulate the necessity of specific action that can and must be taken by the government at the local, state and federal levels to alleviate the crisis." The fact of the matter was that Alcatraz occupiers had no legal claim to the island. There was no treaty or legal agreement upon which their demands rested—certainly nothing akin to the Northwest fishing tribes' Treaty of Medicine Creek. As Deloria saw it at the time, Alcatraz as public relations stunt had its greatest potential to bring about meaningful reform only if its occupiers called for a federal policy of land restoration, particularly for small reservations, and for restoration of original reservation boundaries to particular tribes. The occupiers themselves seemed satisfied with awakening the American public to the "plight of Indians," thus losing, according to Deloria, a great opportunity to change federal policy.[82] But Deloria underestimated the importance of awakening the American public—a necessary first step for changing hearts, minds, and policies. Awakening alone, of course, does not guarantee action. Appropriate action without awakening, however, is impossible. If the return of Blue Lake to the New Mexico Taos Pueblo in 1970 is any indication, the interplay between awareness, action, and change was critical.

Indian activism and counterculture support took root in the West Coast, but the seeds of both subsequently spread to rural America. Some hippies fled urban neighborhoods to begin new communities based on communal principles, and sometimes supposedly Indian models, in rural areas. In northern California and New Mexico, in particular, they found Indian people already in place. Some Indians served as mentors, reminding the non-Indians that going back to the land meant encounters with those who had never left it and who now needed their help to make—or remake—Indians' claims to it.

4

Back to the Land

A significant number of counterculture "tribal" members, who congregated in urban areas, eventually found conflicts with legal authorities and city life so oppressive they wanted to flee. Others wanted to establish land bases where they could put into practice their ideas about a new way of living and presumably become models for others. They wanted, as Peter Coyote put it, "to integrate ourselves into new communities, to expand our resources and our reach."[1] The migrants assumed rural life would provide sanctuary from legal repression, social stresses, and, alas, their own inadequacies. Some hoped Indians would help them carve out an alternative way of life. So, counterculture people left San Francisco for northern California, Big Sur, southern Colorado, and northern New Mexico, among other places. Eventually thousands of young people ventured into rural corners of the West, Northeast, Midwest—probably every state in the country, actually—in search of a supposedly simpler life: one "closer to nature," and one lived in community with those who shared their values, interests, and sensibilities.

Northern New Mexico, with its vast spaces and open skies, Indian occupants, and tradition as a mecca for artists, became a particularly potent magnet for counterculture communitarians from throughout the nation and even the world.[2] By the end of the decade, the Taos area alone witnessed the founding of more than a dozen communes and the migration of thousands of mostly young people. As Carol Hinton, who settled in a New Mexico commune put it, "What were they looking for? I don't think they really knew . . . something away from the city, back to the earth, the place where Indians live, where life is real."[3] For the more dedicated commune builders, the presence of Taos Pueblo and the opportunity to interact with actual Indian people proved to be one of the area's greatest attractions.

As it turned out, life in northern New Mexico was difficult, complicated by a four-centuries-old social and economic system that included Indians, Anglos, and Hispanos of various economic positions and political persuasions. Most of the commune builders came to the countryside with little in the way of practical skills for homebuilding or agriculture, let alone the skills for farming in the high, arid West. They quickly became drains on the more welcoming communes. Few communes lasted. Moreover, the "hippie invasion" reignited deep conflicts within the Taos community and violence broke out, particularly between Hispano youths and counterculture types. While the counterculture interest in Indians was sincere, though often thin, the number of Taos Pueblo people who publicly responded to the hippies' presence, and engaged with them, remained small. Meanwhile the contemporary political issue that should have garnered the greatest support from the youthful newcomers—the return of Blue Lake to Taos Pueblo—actually generated very little direct help from them. In part, the communitarians had their own, often overwhelming, problems to resolve. But by the late 1960s, the issue had also become wrapped up in the legal and political intricacies of congressional legislation—something better left to the Pueblo tribal council, the National Congress of American Indians, and the more formally constituted, long-term non-Indian allies such as the Association on American Indian Affairs, the National Council of Churches, and the National Committee for Restoration of the Blue Lake Lands to the Taos Pueblo. That this most prominent New Mexico Indian issue found resolution at the height of hippie activity in the Southwest was not coincidence, however. Counterculture interest in Indians received widespread media coverage and, consequently, helped create a growing national consciousness about Indians and their political concerns. As the Nixon administration looked for a symbolic issue that would appease Indians and supporters, Taos Pueblo benefited.

Meanwhile, interest in Native Americans remained an important cultural component in the lives New Mexico communitarians were building for themselves. Places such as the successful, long-lasting New Buffalo and Lama communes, in particular, sought out the counsel and advice of Taos Pueblo people and, at least for a time, found a handful of Indian mentors who taught lessons on subjects ranging from construction of adobe bricks to peyote-meeting rituals. The distinctive element of the New Mexico experience, one that separates it from the Pacific Northwest or the Bay Area of San Francisco, is people went there to build lasting communities inspired, in part, by what they imagined Indian communities to be. Some arrived with the expectation that they would transform vague dreams of "living like the Indians" into reality. They meant to put into practice what were undoubtedly innocent and unrealistic notions of "tribal life." The presence of Pueblo people throughout northern New Mexico, and Navajos and Hopis not far to the west in Arizona, meant that the opportunities to engage with actual Indian people, in their homelands, increased. So too did the likelihood of unwanted intrusion and violation of local norms and values. Yet, the opportunities to learn about Indian affairs, on the ground and with reservation communities, also increased and some of the newcomers became involved in constructive ways. By moving into the figurative front yards of reservation-based Indians, counterculture types came to live cheek-by-jowl with people who had forged tribal cultures over hundreds, even thousands of years—sometimes in those very spots. Most of the hippie migrants did not comprehend that such cultures could not be adopted (or co-opted) overnight. They did not understand such ways of life evolved out of centuries-long experiences. Only later, upon reflection and with the benefit of hindsight, did some realize, as Iris Keltz put it, "We mimicked the ways of Native Americans without admitting to the waves of generations behind their traditions."[4]

Although many non-Indian interactions with Indians were fleeting and ephemeral, others proved lasting. If at the height of the commune "craze," the New Mexico–based hippies could realistically offer little in the way of practical political support to Indian political causes, in the long term counterculture migrants who remained in northern New Mexico sustained a lasting interest in Indians and Indian affairs. Some stayed and eventually supported tribes regarding cultural, political, and economic issues. Further, the symbolic message remained: Indian ways had value and deserved recognition, even emulation. Just as the "gathering of the tribes" in San Francisco captured media attention, so too did the communes of New Mexico and the drumbeat of adulation for Indianness found yet another outlet. Were the counterculture communitarians part of the imperialist, colonizing process? Did they attempt to appropriate aspects of Native American cultures despite little deep understanding or sensitivity? Did they disrupt the daily life of Taoseños and create conflicts between people and within families? Absolutely. But they also helped push into the nation's consciousness an awareness of Indians as living people who had still vital cultures and political claims that deserved recognition, widespread support, and legal sanction.

There were many roads to Taos by the late 1960s. For decades Anglo artists and seekers of various sorts had been making their way to the little northern New Mexico town. Some stayed and recorded the place and its Indian inhabitants on canvas. Others wrote about it. Beginning in the early 1900s, starting with the Taos Society of Artists and followed by individuals such as Mabel Dodge Luhan and writer Frank Waters, northern New Mexico had its advocates, boosters even, who captured through paintbrushes or prose the place's attractions. This had the consequence of encouraging even more people to come.[5] By the late 1960s, that flow turned into a flood. The motives propelling the sixties Bohemians to New Mexico were inevitably diverse. Some would claim they did not choose Taos, it chose them, maintaining that it had always been a holy place, a center of spiritual power that inevitably drew those who were open to its vibrations. As the *Sage*, a Santa Fe–based alternative newspaper wrote, "hippies or long-hairs have been sent or drawn to New Mexico by spiritual forces and beings for important spiritual, intellectual and physical work." The newcomers had much to learn because they were only at the beginning of their task, which had as its ultimate goal replacement of "the old system of exploitation of nature, man's work, and the people's art and crafts with a true union of people." Barbara Garson of San Francisco opined in the *Sage's* pages that New Mexico and New Orleans would have been the spiritual and metropolitan centers of the continent, the Mesopotamia and Greece of North America, if "an artificial European thing hadn't been deposited on each coast." In California, she sat on the periphery. New Mexicans constituted the center.[6]

For others, the spiritual allure resided in the Southwestern connection to the peyote religion and the possibility of linking with the Native American Church, which maintained its association with this region. As early as 1960, Jack Loeffler, who did not join a commune or consider himself a "hippie," yet participated in the "hip scene," attended a peyote meeting on the Nevada-California border. He learned that his Indian hosts used peyote to "cleanse themselves from working in the Oakland shipyards" and began to realize the harm "western monoculture was wreaking on traditional cultures." Around the same time, Loeffler met Stewart Brand and became acquainted with his "America Needs Indians" project (see figure 4.1). Although he worked with Brand for a time, Loeffler was more interested in the mythic than the media aspect of Brand's work and moved into a Navajo hogan near Navajo Mountain, "the most remote part of the United States at the time." Eventually he received a Ford Foundation grant to create a traveling exhibit on Navajo history for Navajo schoolchildren. In time he became an ethnomusicologist and recorded native songs throughout the Southwest and Mexico and learned that his "deeply felt intuition that Native American cultures, any traditional culture that stays in the same place—that is indigenous to place—has a reciprocal relationship to that place" was, in fact, borne out.[7] Peyote, of course, remained important. On July 4, 1965, Loeffler hosted a peyote gathering at a fire-lookout spot where he spent the summer. Stewart Brand and Lois Jennings attended. So too did New Yorkers Steve and Barbara Durkee, who went on to found Lama, and Max Feinstein, who was instrumental in the founding and naming of New Buffalo—both communes in the Taos area. "A lot of actions emerged from that peyote bash," Loeffler remembered.[8]

Others, including those who became more directly involved in the commune movement, also found Indian ceremonialism, including the peyote religion, to be a crucial connection with Indian people. John Kimmey, whose move to the Southwest preceded the major hippie migration, represented this element. Living and working as a mason in Nevada in 1965, Kimmey, a former cultural anthropology student, became involved with Washoe Indians and the ceremonial aspects of their lives. While participating in a ceremony, he had a vision that consisted of two words: "Taos" and "Oraibi." He hitchhiked first to Oraibi, on

Figure 4.1 Stewart Brand (*right*) with Jack and Jean Loeffler, circa 1963. Loeffler worked for a time with Brand on the "America Needs Indians" project but discovered he was more interested in the mythic than the media aspect of Brand's work and moved to a remote corner of the Navajo Reservation. He eventually became an ethnomusicologist, recording native songs, and became politically active in the Black Mesa Defense Foundation. Credit: Stewart Brand.

the Hopi Reservation, where an old man told him that he must have a purpose among the Hopi, but that he needed to complete his journey first. So he went on to Taos. The first person he met there was Little Joe Gomez. According to Kimmey, Gomez's father had told Gomez of his own vision: when Little Joe became older, "grandchildren" not of his race would become his primary students while his own grandchildren were off learning the white man's ways. When Gomez met Kimmey, he said: "you must be the ones." Two years later Kimmey moved to Taos and spent eight "intense" years learning from Little Joe Gomez (see figure 4.2). He eventually worked as a tribal planner at Taos Pueblo and taught at a contract school at Hotevilla on the Hopi Reservation.[9] Peter Rabbit, whose birth name was Peter Douthit and who first lived at the commune Drop City near Trinidad, Colorado, visited Taos in 1959, at the suggestion of poet Max Feinstein. Eventually Rabbit moved to Taos, drawn by the Pueblo which he once described as "the most interesting community that I've ever seen" and "the most successful commune in the country." He added that hippies came to Taos "because of strange old men that lived out there at the village. Specifically, for me, it was Little Joe Gomez, who was the only fully realized human being that I've ever met in my life."[10]

Bill Gersh migrated to New Mexico in 1968, driving a 1948 Dodge out of Berkeley, California, where he was "burned out . . . and wanted to get into the rural, Aquarian involvement." The attraction of New Mexico for him derived from the nexus of Native American presence, the spiritual power of the place,

Figure 4.2 John Kimmey moved to Taos in the 1960s and became a student and friend of Taos Pueblo Little Joe Gomez. Credit: Lisa Law.

and psychedelics. Everybody had taken the latter, he explained, but they felt the need for a concrete identity

> and maybe the natives served that function for them . . . coming to a place like Taos would give more of a spiritual backbone. A place that had been going for a long time [rather] than taking acid in Cambridge or taking acid in Berkeley and having this hallucinatory experience on the streets of Telegraph Avenue. Here you could come out and see . . . yeah, you'd go to a pueblo and you'd see a pulse. You meet an Indian on the street and you start talking to him and you know something ancient was here . . . There was something special in this area. More so than in Boulder, Colorado. More so than in upstate New York. More so than in the Napa Valley or Sonoma. This was like the suction cup of energy.[11]

But if Gersh was drawn to Taos' energy and Indians, he was also pushed out of California by the increasingly tense racial politics of Berkeley. He had supported black power but felt that as that movement became increasingly nationalistic, there was no longer a place for him in it. He wanted to help, rather than fight, the Black Panthers but the "tension had become a real pain in the ass for me." So in flight, Gersh decided to live in a rural place and ended up in Taos. "This was the real focus point... if you were crazy enough, you ended up in Taos" because even then Santa Fe was "chi-chi" and Albuquerque "a cow town." For a time he lived at Reality Construction Company in Arroyo Hondo (also started by Max Feinstein) with Jewish girls from Brooklyn, blacks from the South, Puerto Ricans, and Dominicans, "a quasi-radical inter-racial nuthouse [that thought it was] going to save the world with anarchistic philosophy." By 1971 he had fled to the Magic Tortoise Foundation, which he helped found, near Questa, New Mexico.[12]

If an Indian presence did not originally lure Lisa Law to New Mexico, it was the "vibration of Indian people" that kept her there (see figure 4.3). She moved from California in 1967 to give birth to her first child at Santa Fe's Catholic Maternity Institute for Natural Childbirth. Lisa and her husband, Tom Law, who had been road manager for the folk musicians Peter, Paul and Mary, were already living in a tipi in California. When they arrived in New Mexico, they set up the tipi at the New Buffalo commune in Arroyo Hondo, north of Taos. The Laws stayed only for a few weeks to get to know the residents and help build the main house. Ultimately they moved on to Santa Fe where they could be close to the birthing center. They also lived with the Jook Savages, a musical group that operated more as an extended family than a commune, in La Puebla and Abiquiu. Eventually the couple put down roots in a farm near Truchas, purchased by actor John Philip Law, Tom's brother. Their interactions with Hispanic neighbors were not always harmonious because the locals had never seen anything like them before. But the Taos Pueblo clearly continued to be an attraction, particularly the peyote clan, the dances, and the more welcoming tribal members such as Little Joe Gomez, Teles Goodmorning, and Joe Sun Hawk Sandoval. The Indians' commitment to a presumably simpler life and connection to nature and the earth appealed to Lisa Law. "We were into the Indian culture, going to ceremonies, and really believing in Mother Earth and Father Sky."[13] She settled in New Mexico permanently, where she gave birth to three more children, making sure each had contact with Indian cultures, spirituality, and appreciation of the natural world while they were growing up.

Even communitarians who did not establish homes in the Southwest found the Indians of the region an attraction and source of wisdom. In 1969, San Francisco-based Digger Peter Coyote took a road trip from Olema, a commune on the foggy coast of Northern California, to consult with the Hopis. The turn to Indian advisors was not a new idea. Earlier, while living at Black Bear Ranch, one of the "Free

Figure 4.3 Lisa Law moved to New Mexico in 1967 just in time to witness and photograph the hippie presence and the commune movement. She also became well acquainted with New Mexico's Hispano and Indian people and eventually joined the fight to end the Navajo relocation that resulted from the Navajo-Hopi Land Settlement Act of 1974. Credit: Lisa Law.

Family camps" located in the Trinity-Siskiyou Wilderness, Coyote and others interacted with the local Karoks, Yuroks, and Hoopas. The Native Americans, he believed, were attracted to the "zany community with its bare-breasted women and the copious amounts of elderberry wine we made." The Indians brought fresh salmon to trade and showed the Black Bear Ranch occupants how to properly smoke it. On one occasion some local Indians carried in a dead cougar which they said was illegal to possess and did not want to be caught with the carcass. Commune members ate it. The hippies also consulted with some Karok people on the best way to discourage the visits of a black bear marauding the ranch. One old man suggested a shotgun shell filled with rock salt and directed toward the bear's hind quarters. By the time Coyote returned to the ranch with the suggestion, someone had killed the bear—an outcome that devastated Coyote.[14]

The Indians of the Southwest, and the Hopis in particular, seemed a more appropriate source of wisdom and direction to Coyote. Although Olema was an anarchic social experiment where people could be and do what they wanted, Coyote found that community members expected him and Nick Fosmo, Rolling Thunder's foster son, to provide direction as informal leaders. Seeking guidance for this role, the two embarked on a road trip to the Southwest in the summer of 1969. Their itinerary included a tour of communes and a visit with David Monongye, a Hopi priest. Stops at the Disciples of Thunder commune near Rolling Thunder's home in Elko, Nevada; Libre and the Red Rockers' place in southern Colorado; and Placitas in New Mexico provided neither lofty models nor encouragement. Even the Indians they encountered were dispiriting. The Santo Domingo Pueblos, according to Coyote, hustled the tourists in Santa Fe. The Indians in Gallup ("the toughest town I've ever been in. Indians here so fucked up and over they'll kick anyone's ass for a drink," he wrote in his diary) did not appeal to them either. But the Hopi seemed different. "The Hopis live a monastic, worshipful life," Coyote recorded in his journal, "and Fosmo and I believe that if anyone knows about communal living outside the premises of the industrial paradigm, these people might." Somehow they managed to secure an introduction to David Monongye, a tribal elder who had interacted with other young Anglo seekers including John Kimmey. They arrived on Monongye's doorstep having followed the blacktop up the mesa to Hotevilla; past the small gardens of corn, beans, and squash; and by the children who yelled as they passed: "Hippieeees."[15]

At Monongye's house Coyote and Fosmo found a cluster of young "rodeo-riding Indian dudes, tough and dusty, close-cropped black hair, high cheekbones, pitiless eyes." Their presence signaled a message: act appropriately in the presence of the Hopi elder, or else. Monongye was in his 90s, slight, sophisticated, and cheerful. Coyote was immediately struck by the differences between "our two cultures (if I could risk calling our Olema prototype a culture)." Coyote and Fosmo presented a gift of a tie-dyed sheet, which they immediately realized was inappropriate, "gaudy, defiant, ebullient, confident, and vain." The Hopi's home was made of bare plaster and its objects consisted of a basket, a rattle, a feathered prayer stick, and small bundles tucked here and there in the rafters. Everything had its place and its function, yet Coyote believed that "some invisible spiritual treasure permeates every inch of this couple and their home." After a meal of red beans, tortillas, and coffee with milk and sugar, Monongye asked why they had come.

Daunted by the Hopi elder's "genuine authority," Coyote did his best to explain Olema's experiment in living, their point of view, their trials and errors. He openly revealed their failures, both collective and personal, and asked for "something of worth [to take] back to my own people." Describing the experience as being akin to that of a psychiatrist's office where one's own articulation of the problem is the first step toward understanding, Coyote noted that Monongye listened without judgment before talking with the young Anglo men about Hopi mythology. He talked about "'the last days,' the period when a world dizzy with incoherence and indulgence was about to disintegrate." He did not, apparently, offer any advice on the Olema experiment or commentary on the hippie phenomenon. The Hopi couple then invited their guests to spend the night, which surprised Coyote and Fosmo since they had been warned white people were not allowed to spend the night at Hotevilla.[16]

When they awoke the next morning, they found the Monongye home filled with old men having a meeting of some kind—some dozing, some attentive to whoever was speaking. No one paid attention to the hippie guests. Coyote was struck, again, at the contrast. "How different it is from the chaos of our communal life. Children line the walls in respectful silence. When they get restless, they rise and slip outside like shadows, and only after the door closes quietly behind them do you hear the cries and screams of play . . . I am chastened and amazed. Steady parents raise steady children." They spent a few more days with their Hopi hosts, listening to Monongye's songs and his good-natured teasing about Anglo music which, he claimed, was only about love whereas the Hopi have many songs about water—something rare and precious. He wondered, "with feigned innocence," whether white people sang about love because it was equally rare in their world. Monongye sang parodies of cowboy songs and encouraged Coyote's efforts to honor owls and other forms of life in his original songs. As they left, the Hopi gave him their blessings. In retrospect, he wrote:

> I realize that the most important gift we received [w]as the opportunity to witness and participate in an ancient, ordered spiritual life, for our bodies to experience what such an existence felt like. We were afforded a glimpse into a self-sufficient system that had taken thousands of years to develop. The lightness of their personal lives, the absence of the demands they made on the environment and each other was chastening and elevating. For all its hard lessons and physical difficulties, the trip had succeeded. We had a high water mark to aspire to, and I returned to California with that fixed as firmly in mind as mine could fix anything then.[17]

Although Coyote's powers of expression, and understanding that such a life reflected thousands of years of development, exceeded that of most hippies, this perception of Hopi life and its presumptive value as a model was typical and representative of the time. Of course, Coyote's Olema and the other communal experiments of the late 1960s did not have the Hopis' deeply rooted history and heritage. Nor did its experiment in social anarchy lend itself to such long-range commitments and permanence. If their intention was "to be in continuity with indigenous people who centuries earlier had lived where [they] were living," the day-to-day realities of life at Olema and other communal experiments mitigated against long-term success.[18]

Yet in the early days of this back-to-the-land movement, few participants anticipated defeat. The innocence with which these people threw themselves into their experimental communities and their naiveté regarding the anticipated locals' response was breathtaking. As an August 1969 article entitled "Why Taos?" in the alternative newspaper *Fountain of Light* explained, nothing less than the future of America was coming to Taos and the new generation pouring into the place should be seen as the "highest compliment" to Taoseños—Indians, Spanish, and Anglos alike. This generation was seeking new values and "an honest land on which to nurture tender shoots." They sought a certain quality of life which, they believed, already existed in Taos. It was a tribute to Taos, the article explained, that the latest newcomers wanted to live there. Hippies were coming not to change Taos culture, but to learn from it and become a part of it. Just like the conquistadors, mountain men, and artists of the past who came with their own dress and outlooks, so too did the hippies. Yet all of these groups "made contributions, left their marks." Many of the hippies were well educated, talented, and accomplished, but they came humbly, asking questions and searching for "individual expression and the sanctity of life." Printed in both English and Spanish, the piece ended: "We earnestly pray that the good people of Taos will open their hearts and minds and find the wisdom to give the right answer. All America Waits."[19]

Among the problems with this appeal was its assumption that Taos spoke with one voice, that the Indians, Hispanos, and Anglos saw things the same way. There were, in fact, many fissures in the community—some based on ethnicity and race, others based on class, and still others on generation. The article also failed to acknowledge the legacy, and perpetuation, of colonialism, most dramatically represented by Spanish conquistadors but also exemplified by mountain men, traders, twentieth-century artists, and the 1960s migrants themselves. These people "contributed," but their presence also carried terrible costs for both Indians and Hispanos.[20] Finally the enormous numbers of newcomers who poured into Taos County by the end of the decade overwhelmed residents—including the hippies and communitarians already there. Perhaps the wonder is not that the locals did not welcome the migrants, but rather that the reaction was not more severe.

If the New Mexico communes' interest in Indianness had a prototype, northern California's Morning Star was the closest. One of the earliest sixties communes, it became the seedbed for a New Mexico-based community, a spin-off named Morning Star East. The desire for Native American connections, at least symbolically, had its first expression here. Many of the community's inclinations, challenges, and problems reemerged in the Southwest, as well. It is important to note that the New Mexican communes' founders came to that state from the west and the east to create these experiments in living. They did not spring up from New Mexican soil under the direction of locals who had, presumably, grown up in the neighborhood of Indian people all their lives.

Lou Gottlieb, organizer and musical director of The Limelighters folk-singing group, owned the thirty-one acre ranch in Sonoma County that became Morning Star. Its purpose was to challenge American assumptions about private property and exclusive relationships between people. In the end drugs, nudity, uninhibited sex, poor sanitation, and building-code violations alarmed the ranch's rural neighbors and led the local law enforcement to ultimately shut it down. Its origins stemmed from the January 1966 Trips Festival in San Francisco that featured Stewart Brand's "America Needs Indians" show. There, Gottlieb met Ramon Sender and they talked about community and rural living. By May 1966, Sender took up residence on Gottlieb's ranch property and the next month, Gottlieb and others arrived. In November, the first seven young refugees from Haight-Ashbury arrived and the following January, the ranch experienced its first visit by a county narcotics officer. That spring, Diggers filled up the place. They came to tend to the orchard, start a garden, and grow food to give away in San Francisco.[21]

From old correspondence found on the ranch, Gottlieb discovered that the place already had a name: Morning Star. Sender then found what he identified as an "American Indian symbol," though the tribal derivation remained unspecified, of a morning star: an eight-pointed star with a circle in the middle which, in turn, contained a heart and within that, a cross. Although Gottlieb compared his ranch to historic intentional communities such as Brook Farm, Oneida, and New Harmony, there were several aspects which clearly signaled this was a sixties commune: the use of illegal drugs, the regular practice of free love, and the identification with supposed Native American symbols and ideas. Morning Star's statement of faith reads like a combination yoga and faux Indian "Earth Mother" creed. The commune's purposes, according to "Morning Star Faith and Thy Community Church of the Order," included "the living of a primitive life of harmony with revealed Divine Law" and "the teaching by example of the 4 beliefs, the 4 missions of planetary purity, the 4 elemental yogas, [and] the 7 Divine Laws." The four missions of planetary purity were "open earth, open air, open fire, open water" and the prayers which addressed those missions included

"Earth: O Earth, be fruitful. Thou art our own Mother's breast. I share you with all life." And "Air: O Air, scented with early mists, Thou art our Mother's breath-aura. O wind in the trees, Only thou, Only thou." The four elemental yogas of voluntary primitivism include this advice: "*Shitting*: Find a patch of garden-ground that needs enriching [*sic*]. Open the earth gently, squat, relax, breathe deeply six times, let it happen—don't push. Feel the Earth accept your offering." Other recommended yogas included nasal douching and nude sunbathing.[22]

If most of this seemed flaky and had no connection to any practicing Native American culture or tradition, the Morning Star Ranch inhabitants did not seem to care. In fact, they added to the mixture elements of Buddhism, Judaism, Christianity, Sufi Muslim, and Hindu religions. This veritable hodgepodge of ideas, most of them superficially understood at best, characterized the community's creed. But its foundational ideas remained focused on Voluntary Primitivism, which included renunciation of both carbon-combustion engines and exclusive ownership of land which constituted, according to a Morning Star postcard dated 1968, the Original Sin. Man commits it "when he slices up his Mother Earth's 'sweet flowing breast' in order to buy and sell the pieces." "No Trespassing" signs cause "war, racial strife and marital unhappiness." But if you placed a morning star symbol in your window and opened your door to everyone, then you would find peace in your heart, your life would improve immensely, "sex [would] become the healing ecstasy it's spozed [*sic*] to be and you'll be living in the Kingdom of God." Although they philosophically denounced internal-combustion engines, commune members did not completely eschew technology, using automobiles, for instance. They understood their experiment could only prevail in an economy of abundance, the kind that characterized the 1960s United States, and they proposed a synthesis of sophisticated technology "with a voluntary return to the ancient, tested ways—living close to God's Nature and in harmony with the elements."[23]

The Morning Star commune garnered some favorable press, including a *Time* magazine article that applauded their garden and its consequent "new-found trip of work and responsibility." But most public comment on the experiment was negative. And the closer people lived to the commune, the more likely they abhorred it. One neighbor began a petition drive to demand the county enforce laws to reduce the commune's fire hazards, traffic, and public nudity. It did not take local officers long to respond. In summer 1967 about thirty county officials and two FBI agents began plastering signs on the habitations (mostly tipis and lean-tos) indicating they were unfit for human habitation. When the chief probation officer's assistant asked Gottlieb to tell his estimated fifty "guests" to vacate the area, Gottlieb reached for an Indian analogy to explain why he could not do that. "I have never denied anyone access to this land," he told a reporter. "It's like the Indians—land held in trust for all to enjoy." When brought to court by the county, the musician again turned to Indian imagery and symbolism, explaining that he held the land "in the tradition of the American Indian, in trust for the Great Spirit." But the court was not convinced, and as the lines hardened between the "straights" and the "freaks," some commune inhabitants fled to Bill Wheeler's ranch ten miles west of Morning Star while other "warriors remain[ed] for rearguard action." Still others left for New Mexico where they established Morning Star East.[24] Legal hassles continued until May 1971 when county bulldozers tore down all structures except Lou Gottlieb's cabin, a one-room former egg-shack, effectively ending that communal experiment.[25]

Morning Star's spiritual eclecticism lived on in many of the New Mexican communes. Lama blended Sufi, Buddhist, Hindu, Jewish, Islamic, Christian, and Native American elements with the LSD experimentation begun at Timothy Leary's Millbrook community.[26] The Durkees, who migrated from New York to California to New Mexico, originally intended to build a "spiritual dude ranch"—a large community complex with space for about one dozen "tribes." As Barbara Durkee later explained their vision, it was to be "like a pueblo—only bigger." On entering the central building, one would see representations of tarot cards on the walls and a ladder leading up to a meditation hall designed along the lines of an ashram in India. Pie-shaped apartments would then lead out from the center, each housing a different orientation or type. While the Durkee's friend, Richard Alpert, went off to India for enlightenment, they went to New Mexico to look for land. They spent a year, renting a house at Nambe Pueblo before finding the property that became Lama.[27]

The end result was a bit simpler than their original spiritual dude ranch, but it certainly represented their religious orientation As Lama increasingly emphasized metaphysics and Asian religions, Steve Durkee took a different direction, changing his name to Nurideen, starting the Islamic center, Dar al-Islam, on the Chama River near Abiquiu. Meanwhile, the Jook Savages, a loose hippie group of several couples with links to Los Angeles' music world, encouraged Sikhs from California to establish an ashram and community near Espanola. Yogi Bhajan, who altered Sikh traditions to fit American culture when he immigrated in 1967, captured the interest of the Jook Savages at the East-West Center in Los Angeles where he taught yoga. Tom Law, one of the Savages, became something of a front man for Yogi Bhajan, inviting him to teach yoga at the Jook Savage's Summer Solstice Celebration on Tesuque Pueblo land in 1969. Law went on to teach yoga on the stage at Woodstock.[28]

But it was New Buffalo, described by Lois Rudnick as "the archetypal hippie commune" and publicized nationwide when Dennis Hopper and Peter Fonda filmed a section of the quintessential sixties film *Easy Rider* there, that found its inspiration primarily in Native American practices. Of course, the Indian inspirations were random and diffuse. Max Feinstein, one of the founders, selected the New Buffalo moniker as a nod to one of nature's providers—"the sacred part of nature that nurtures us all"—though it was a subsistence connected more to eighteenth- and nineteenth-century Plains Indians than Southwestern ones.[29] New Buffalo's earliest inhabitants pitched tipis while they learned the art of adobe construction (see figure 4.4). They quickly built a kiva and by the summer of 1968 had planted a garden of corn, beans, and squash. New Buffalo's Indian inclinations attracted the attention of a *Playboy* magazine reporter. In his 1970 account of the New Mexico communes, the reporter emphasized the "intensive fascination with the Indian roots of the American experience among the turned-on youth" over the other religious and cultural inspirations and influences at work. Having rejected their parents' ways, he explained, the young people still required teachers and so they turned to the Indians, who were supposedly experts at "how to live in the raw" having been "out there in the wilds a long time existing quite well without benefits of industrial civilization." Giving no indication of having actually interviewed any Indian people, the reporter explained that the Pueblos lived much as they had when Spanish explorer Vasquez de Coronado came to New Mexico in 1540. They never accepted notions of private property. They idealized peace and order. They lived in close relationship to nature and willingly subordinated themselves to the group. They were, as the young American newcomers put it, "the original hippies."[30]

Figure 4.4 Tipis, long a symbol of Indianness to non-Indians, popped up at the New Buffalo commune, near Taos, in 1967 even though Pueblos and other indigenous people of the area did not use them. Credit: Lisa Law.

It is noteworthy that a few of the Taos Pueblo people willingly interacted with the New Buffalo commune. According to Rick Klein, who used part of his inheritance to purchase the land for the commune, "Teachers appeared to us... when we got here," from the Pueblo. "I don't know what it is about the people from Taos Pueblo," he said, "but I've been around a lot of different tribes and stuff and somehow the people from Taos Pueblo just have an incredible heart." Later, several of them told Klein, perhaps partly in jest, they helped the communards because they took pity on them. Clearly these youths, whether migrating from New York's Lower East Side or California's Los Angeles basin, understood nothing about carving out a living from the New Mexico soil. But "they knew our hearts were in the right place and their hearts were in the right place too to come and help us." Individuals such as Little Joe Gomez, John Gomez, Henry Gomez, Joe Sunhawk, Tellus Good Morning, and Frank Samora—"we're not going to see their kind again"—came to New Buffalo and showed the newcomers how to build adobe bricks, garden in the desert, follow the appropriate ritual celebrations related to the changing seasons, and practice the peyote religion (see figure 4.5).[31] Several Taos Pueblo men, in particular, mentored the New Buffalo all-night meetings of the Native American Church.[32]

One description of a peyote ceremony at Morning Star typified these events. In this case, Little Joe Gomez presided over the ceremony. He spoke in imperfect English as he saw to it that participants followed correct ritual procedures.

Figure 4.5 With the help of some locals, including Taos Pueblo people, New Buffalo commune members learned to make adobe bricks. Credit: Lisa Law.

The ceremony took place inside a tipi, facing east. As people entered, they moved around the circumference of the tipi, going from east to west and circling the central fire. Adjacent to the fire, a peyote button rested on an earthen altar. "A gourd rattle, a water drum and Little Joe's singing started the nightlong ceremony. The sounds merged like the wind, rain and lightening during a storm and became the heartbeat of the world," according to Iris Keltz. "Little Joe's attempt to teach transplanted dropouts of an urban materialistic society to pray and to revere the natural world was nothing less than noble." Less dignified, however, was the common reaction to ingesting the peyote. Many of the celebrants vomited. Even Gomez left the tipi to throw up in a nearby arroyo. After the drum and rattle passed around the circle for the last time, a woman representing Earth Mother entered, carrying a pail of water on her head and praying. As the sun gradually rose and the participants began to look, once again, "more human, less mythic," people brought breakfast into the tipi, and after the closing song, peyote fans and gourd rattles went back into their cedar boxes. A group then went to the Black Rock hot springs for a soak.[33]

New Buffalo began with a peyote meeting, and people periodically sponsored them, either for an individual or family or on behalf of the entire commune. On Thanksgiving Day 1971, for instance, a woman sponsored a peyote meeting for the entire New Buffalo commune. Frank Samora, Joe Sunhawk and Joe Gomez, participated with Samora leading the rituals. But local Taos Pueblo people came to New Buffalo on other occasions, including a party on the night of a full moon in the spring of 1972 when Joseph Cruz and others joined "long-haired hippies, dark-skinned gypsies and big-chested, long-legged dancing girls getting it on in the front yard" singing "their ancient songs." More rarely, New Buffalo people visited the Pueblo at an Indian's invitation. Joe Concho invited some of the commune's residents to help with his corn harvest, offering them some corn for their help.[34] The Taos Pueblo people who visited New Buffalo apparently acted entirely on their own and did not represent the Pueblo in any official capacity. In fact, the Pueblo made no official pronouncement about the newcomers or the communards who found Taos Indians so attractive.

It is rather difficult, then, to discern from contemporary sources how most Taos Pueblo people felt about the hippie influx and its consequent adulation of Indians and Indianness. A rare newspaper statement from tribal leader Tony Reyna indicated officials had difficulty with some of the newcomers who wanted to "go Indian." "They have come out here with their hair in braids and wearing beaded head-bands and expected to move right into the pueblo," he told a reporter. "We have had to call the police to evict them."[35] Reyna, a World War II veteran, businessman, and chairman of the Taos police commission, claimed the only Indians the hippies met were "the winos who stagger around Taos Plaza." Those on the reservation were too busy working to get involved with them.

Anglos used to call Indians "dirty and savage, but it's the other way around now. Those hippies are so filthy I won't let them try on moccasins at my shop." Their efforts to copy Indian dress were actually insulting, he said. Indians believed they must work and contribute to their community. "The hippies don't contribute anything, they just want to mooch."[36]

Scholar Lois Rudnick more recently suggested that Taos Pueblo people looked at "the hippie invasion with bemusement and tolerance because the hippies did not interfere with their land and practices, were enamored of the way they lived, and sought them out as mentors."[37] A story that apparently circulated at the time claimed that this bemusement could take the form of rather outrageous practical joking. In one case, a young hippie man sought Indian advice on butchering a deer. They told him, "Be very careful and never let the anus touch the ground. That's the most sacred part of the animal." Later, at the feast, they ceremoniously served the hippie the "sautéed sacred sphincter while [they] struggled to keep a straight face."[38]

That such joking took place is likely. But to characterize Indian reaction as bemusement, as Tony Reyna's example indicates, understates the hostility. One Anglo resident of Arroyo Seco, who moved to northern New Mexico in the early 1960s, lived near New Buffalo and was not enamored with the counterculture invasion. He offered his own view of hippie-Taos Pueblo interactions in a fictional short story. In this tale, hippies, who had already insulted the local Spanish population by rejecting the middle-class life to which they aspired and by running naked in the fields, also disrespected the Indians. True, they found the Pueblo and the beautiful mountain that loomed above it attractive. They revered the Indians for preserving their own way of life, "remote and inviolate," for themselves alone. Yet the hippies wanted to live on the mountain and learn its secrets. So, when a Pueblo leader refused their request and ordered them to remain outside reservation lands, they snuck past the Pueblo at night and headed up the mountain. For eight days the trespassers eluded the Pueblo trackers. Finally the Indians caught the hippies and marched them down to the Pueblo where a group of Indian men chastised them. One old man told them: "You should not be here; you don't belong here. We should not have to see you or hear you or smell you. You are not here to us." The hippies replied that no one owned the mountain and that they had every right to enjoy the natural world too. Another Pueblo man acknowledged that while they did not own the mountain, they were its guardians and in trespassing on the property, the hippies had "trespassed on our hearts." Rather than admitting their error and offering an apology, the intruders became more belligerent in their own defense and just as it appeared Indians and hippies would come to blows, a woman arrived on the scene, demanding her husband return home. This interruption broke the tension, a Taos Pueblo man began to laugh, others joined him, and they freed their prisoners with the warning, "Now! Be quick or you might not have another chance to get out of here alive." This piece of fiction reflects the author's belief, based on personal experience, that the hippies displayed insensitivity toward not only Hispanos, but Indians, as well. Consequently, the Pueblo insisted that the newcomers, like all outsiders, keep their distance.[39]

Of course, Taos Pueblo was not the only New Mexican Indian community to encounter the counterculture communards. Tesuque and Santa Clara Pueblos had their own close encounters of the counter-kind, particularly with a group out of California known as the Hog Farm. Member Wavy Gravy, also known as Hugh Romney, described the group as an "expanded family, a mobile hallucination, a sociological experiment, an army of clowns." It consisted of about fifty people and their pet pig, Pigasus. The group originated in the San Fernando Valley, when Wavy Gravy, his wife Bonnie Jean, and several others, rented a farmhouse for free in exchange for feeding the farm's forty pigs. Wavy, once described as the "court jester of the counterculture" and "holy house clown of the cosmos," had been part of Ken Kesey's Merry Pranksters. The group regularly hosted Sunday events at the farm and put on light shows at rock concerts. Eventually they took to the road, coming to New Mexico in 1968, at the encouragement of Tom Law. At the 1968 summer solstice celebration on Tesuque Pueblo lands, Law introduced Wavy Gravy to the sweat lodge, encouraging him to alternate between it and a frigid mountain stream. "After about four times around I had a vision," Wavy quipped. "I don't remember what it was but it's the first time a bathtub ever got me high." On July 4th they joined a celebration at El Rito where the "Spanish-American natives . . . ringed the scene wide-eyed and clung to their cool, belting beers. Only their children were super free. They joined in the music and dance." The humor that Wavy believed so essential to a celebration of life, however, could sound flippant and even disrespectful to Indians. As they prepared for an event near Los Alamos ("death merchant Americana"), he remarked, "The *kachina* mask of the Hopi molds the dancer into the God he represents. Believe in your clothes. It works if you work."[40]

The following summer the Hog Farm returned to New Mexico, this time leasing land from the Santa Clara Pueblo. Once the entourage arrived in their buses, however, the Pueblo apparently had a change of heart. Wavy Gravy had spent the first night up on a mesa, away from the group. Upon joining the group the following morning, members of the Hog Farm informed him that Santa Clara Pueblo people intended to evict them. When the Indians arrived at the Hog Farm camp with guns to reinforce their message, Wavy Gravy decided to retreat. As he related it:

> Up come these Indians, riding their guns, not just Indians, but these spacific [*sic*] Indians. They ain't Hopi Indians and they ain't Taos

Indians. I mean I just don't wanna put them in a bag . . . 'cause that's some kinda mental murder, baggin' a guy . . . But these Indians, it seems they all wanna grow up and be dentists, which is a problem with a lot of people who never had much. So we start to talk to these Indian guys and I say, "Red man speaks with forked tongue," and they get an attitude and say, "Leave," and I say, "We wanna clean the place up, lots of cigarette butts," so they gave us a day to *clean up and clear out*.[41]

The Hog Farm moved on to Llano, where they leased land from a Hispano and every Sunday hosted locals, including Anglos, Indians, Hispanos, and other "freaks," for dinner and beer. Wavy Gravy's irreverence toward everything, however, did not mean indifference to Indian political issues, and the Hog Farm eventually provided material support at sites of Native American political protest in California and Washington, D.C.

In the end, whether tribal governments ignored the hippies' presence or encouraged them to move along, individual Indian people decided for themselves whether to interact. There were so many youthful spiritual seekers around, they were impossible to avoid. Hot springs were one place where hippies and Indians encountered one another. According to Joe Sando, hippies bathed nude in a spring east of Battleship Rock, so Jemez Pueblo people stopped frequenting it until the local sheriff cleared the hippies out. Other local Native Americans allowed and even joined hippies at area hot springs.[42] Plus, Pueblos permitted non-Indians to attend public ceremonies and feast days—open to everyone. Initially, the counterculturists' appearance—dressing "like Indians," having long hair and beards—did not cause alarm. In 1967, an interviewer attempted to provoke Porfiero Montoya, of Santa Ana Pueblo, into a condemnation of hippies, but Montoya remained neutral. "I think we haven't heard enough yet to talk about it," he explained. "They [Indian people] might heard about that word hippie, but we just don't discuss it or they haven't said anything about it yet . . . As long as nothing happens why, maybe one come to the village and visit with them, well they don't pay too much attention yet." But eventually things did happen. At the Santa Ana Pueblo feast day in July, during the late 1960s, hippies brought paper bags, filled them with food, and carried them away. This behavior regarding food, intended for guests to eat at the ceremony, greatly offended the people of Santa Ana. The same thing occurred at Zuni's Shalako ceremony, so the Zuni closed the ceremony to all non-Indians for about twenty years.[43]

The counterculture interest in drugs further distressed some Indian people, particularly parents of adolescent children. First, not all Indians were peyotists. Further, not all hippies limited their drug ingestion to peyote. Marijuana and LSD would have come to New Mexico with or without the hippies, but in the late 1960s that group was most closely associated with these "new" drugs. In

1967, Porfiero Montoya knew little about LSD—only what he had read in his son's copy of *Life* magazine. "But, from what I gather," he told an interviewer, "I don't believe it is anything good . . . whoever takes it . . . He hurts himself and his brain . . . his life is gone you know. Just like if you take marijuana or whatever that is, or an alcoholic." Even if the person had a dream while under the influence of LSD, Montoya did not believe it was a legitimate dream or vision: "He is not dreaming it normal, he is getting that drug till it give him that kine [sic] of a dream." Such dreams would do a person no good. Finally, because LSD and marijuana were, he presumed, habit-forming and harmful, he thought they should be outlawed. Joe Sando believed that the hippies' primary long-term legacy to New Mexico was the negative impact of the drugs they brought and encouraged other young people to try. Indian parents, like parents all across the country, feared for their children's health and well-being when these new recreational drugs came to town.[44]

Some of those Indian children, however, found the hippies interesting. Diane Reyna, of Taos Pueblo and daughter of Tony Reyna, was in her midteens when the hippie invasion hit her hometown. She understood the influx caused concern and even fear among some elders. They got into a "reactive state" and although the Pueblo made no official response, the reservation itself offered a major boundary. Hippies could visit during the day but had to be out by nightfall. Besides concerns about drugs, disheveled appearances, and sanitation, some Indians—particularly World War II veterans—were deeply disturbed by the antiwar element, underscoring the differences between generations. Diane Reyna's own reaction was more benign. She found they had "an air of innocence." They seemed playful, circus-like. But she did not connect with their interest in becoming Indian-like. That impulse toward supposed Indianness "didn't register" because it was "not like us . . . There was no way they could be. There was no way they could have any idea what it really meant to be Indians." The hippies' use of Indian imagery, then, was neither a threat nor a compliment. Its superficiality and their apparent lack of pride in themselves made such inclinations meaningless.[45] Yet some Taos youngsters, Indians and non-Indians, found the pull of hippies and communes seductive. Taos, which had been a sleepy little community before the invasion, suddenly found itself a center of national media attention. Some of the kids, naturally, wanted to be a part of it. Although Reyna did not interact with them, others did. There was cross-cultural emulation of hippies with their beads, incense, and head shops. And some local kids, as their parents feared, succumbed to the drugs.

Meanwhile, by 1968 the massive influx sparked tensions and overwhelmed the town. Diane Reyna remembered one schoolmate telling classmates that he wanted to beat up a hippie just because he had long hair. The teacher used the comment as a "teaching moment," asking him to think a bit about his feelings and to see the connection between social difference and the potential for violence. Of course these kinds of tensions percolated all across the nation, but in Taos it took on greater immediacy as the town struggled to cope with thousands of transients. The incident "taught me a lot," Diane Reyna claimed, including not to judge people solely on the basis of physical appearance and not to fear people who look different. She believed other Taos adolescents learned the same thing. But over the long-term, the hippie invasion ran its course, the fad faded, and life at Taos Pueblo remained essentially unaffected. A few marriages came out of it. Some of the counterculture-communitarians settled permanently in northern New Mexico, but overall, there was no long-term impact on the Pueblo. As for politics, Reyna acknowledged, the Pueblo reached out for non-Indian support wherever they could find it.[46]

Although in 1967, the Taos community seemed fairly relaxed regarding rumors of a twenty thousand person be-in supposedly slated for Taos (it never happened), hints of anxieties to come appeared. Concerns about drugs and news stories about locals dying in Vietnam, often young men with Hispanic surnames, suggest two of the potential sources of conflict. Nevertheless, comparing this new generation of seekers to D. H. Lawrence (an analogy the writer probably would not have welcomed), the *Taos News* urged its readers to put aside their fears and welcome them to the spacious Taos Valley, which had enough room for all.[47] By 1968, however, things were rapidly turning ugly. Anti-hippie letters began to appear in the paper. Police raids on hippie households yielded stashes of marijuana. The town enacted new laws against hitchhiking, and the newspaper again felt it necessary to publish an editorial reminding Taos residents that hippies had civil liberties too. In the same issue, the paper announced filmmakers were coming to Taos to shoot the movie *Easy Rider*.[48]

Some residents rose to the counterculture's defense. Writer and editor Spud Johnson, who had come to Taos in the 1920s as part of Mabel Dodge Luhan's circle, dedicated one of his regular columns to the Lama Foundation, which had begun building its center north of Taos on Lobo Mountain. Although a year before, Johnson had doubted rumors of such a community springing up, by summer 1968 the place was under construction, including a kiva, a Buckminster Fuller-inspired geodesic dome, and a collection of A-frame buildings for living. Johnson was impressed with "these idealistic young people" who had "actually done it"—that is, begun to realize their dream. He assured his readers the Lama community eschewed drugs and alcohol and one of the residents was a professor from a western university, while Steve and Barbara Durkee, the leaders of the group, were also experienced teachers. "In short," he concluded, "there was nothing remotely 'hippie' and certainly nothing phony about this community of hard working young people who . . . are dissident and revolutionary only in that they are convincingly devoted to a new way of life."[49]

Others also counseled tolerance; although, they could not quiet rising fears. As the numbers of migrants increased and the health, social, and political problems escalated, violence broke out. The tensions and problems were complicated and diverse. Meanwhile stories about the return of Blue Lake, water rights issues, and Indian civil rights accompanied those regarding the brewing crisis of a hippie invasion in 1969 and 1970. Operating on parallel tracks, an accelerated Indian rights movement and the heightened hippie migration coincided. Businessmen and chamber of commerce types mostly feared the latter, worrying that the publicity about hippies in Taos (generated by national media outlets ranging from the *New York Times, Los Angeles Times*, NBC, CBS, to *Playboy*) would only encourage more to come and simultaneously kill their summer tourist business. Others feared the health consequences of presumably dirty young people, whose communes, they believed, became breeding camps for hepatitis, drug use, addiction, licentiousness, and, of course, disrespect for parents and other authorities. The thought of thousands of privileged young people, mostly Anglo, throwing off the trappings of affluence annoyed, even angered, some Taoseños striving for a better standard of living. Perhaps no issue angered the local populace more than those educated, healthy young people applying for food stamps. To be "poor by choice" and refuse to work was unthinkable. To stress a system in a region and state that was extremely poor was outrageous. New Mexico was the third-poorest state in the nation and one-third to one-half of Taos, Rio Arriba, and Mora counties' population (not including the recent migrants) collected welfare. Furthermore, the handful of wealthy hippies who bought large tracts of land inflated real estate values. Others took jobs away from locals. And the contrast between the youthful migrants and many of their contemporaries from Taos who were serving and dying in Vietnam angered many.[50] Perhaps inevitably, then, violence broke out, sometimes initiated by locals against hippies; sometimes the other way around.[51]

Not all the counterculture people were indifferent or insensitive to their impact on northern New Mexico. Some joined locals in their concerns, particularly regarding a fresh deluge of hippie migrants. The *Astral Projection*, an Albuquerque underground newspaper, strongly discouraged newcomers. It presented a dismal view of the situation in a 1969 article entitled "Coming to Nuevo Mexico? Read This First." Taos County had a per capita income of $1,392, lower than Mississippi ($2,081), the poorest state in the nation. It was also a harsh climate, beautiful but difficult. The artists who came earlier in the century found acceptance. But the hip people found turmoil and resentment "created in no small way by their disregard of the laws of nature and lack of respect for other people and other customs." They understood that in a place where 44 percent of the population received some kind of social service, people who arrived without income, and then abused the food stamp program, were "justifiably viewed as a burden." Moreover, diseases did pose enormous problems. Hippies in Taos County were suffering from tuberculosis, an alarmingly high rate of hepatitis (due to lack of sanitation in the communes), dysentery, venereal disease, and even a few cases of bubonic plague near Albuquerque. Most of the young newcomers were raised in cities or suburbs and had no idea how to live in the country. For all of these reasons, then, to some, the message was clear: don't come to Taos![52]

But the messages were mixed. That summer the same paper published conflicting views of New Mexico as destination. A report on the Hog Farm's Summer Solstice celebration on Tesuque Pueblo and U.S. Forest Service land emphasized the positive, describing the event as a "religious education, carnival, celebration of life, week-end picnic and important spiritual celebration all rolled into one." Ken Kesey's bus "Further" was there and "tribal entertainment" included school bus races, a light show, and rock music. Tourists, Indians, "chicanos," and others stopped by out of curiosity but became swept up into the spirit of human warmth and fellowship. The same issue, however, carried another story announcing New Mexico was "NOT a Mecca on the Mesa—it's the Ghetto of Mecca." This account emphasized the persecution of hippies though it also acknowledged the latter shared a portion of blame for the problem. Too often they desecrated the lands and traditions of the Indian and Chicano people. Some of this stemmed from insensitivity and lack of awareness. "The Chicano culture here is in many ways quite closed and *very* repressed and incidents of public nudity and balling upset some people, not to mention more extreme cultural transgressions such as freaks, allegedly, breaking into two *kivas* (sacred places) at the Taos Indian Pueblo, reportedly setting one on fire." People in Truchas were very upset with hippies who washed their clothes and bathed in the community's drinking water. Others feared the "longhairs" competition for the few available jobs. Still others reasonably resented the new influx of Anglos coming in and buying property the Hispanos felt to be theirs but were unable to acquire. If you're going to buy land, the authors advised, find out how the locals feel about your presence first. Do not move in, like so many Anglos before you, flashing your money and remaining indifferent to your new neighbors. In fact, before coming, read about the place's history, understand that it is not "bourgeois America," but rather "this is one of America's colonies" and learn "about the 120 year struggle by Chicanos and even older struggle by Indians to get back millions of acres stolen by Anglo ranchers and their Anglo law buddies." Alas, so far, hippies were making the same mistakes they had made in Haight-Ashbury and on the Lower East Side. They did not bother to get to know their neighbors or give them a chance to get to know them. The only hope for hip people in New Mexico: "Get ourselves together and get together with the other embattled and oppressed people, or get blown away."[53]

Some locals recognized the growing divisions apparent on both sides of the hip-straight divide and sponsored community meetings to discuss the problems. Ministers, teachers, and representatives of the newcomers participated. At one of these meetings, a participant told the assemblage that the hippies did not create the tensions, they merely brought them to the surface. An underlying resentment between ethnic groups had long been part of Taos social life and this latest influx merely served as a catalyst. Another cautioned that Taos was not as sophisticated as it thought it was. It "remains basically a provincial town with people who are not used to confronting the problems of big cities." The *Taos News* agreed: "Spanish Americans don't like anglos, anglos don't like hippies and hippies don't really like anybody but other hippies"—an interesting triptych of Taos types that completely ignored the Native American residents. Reminding readers that for more than four centuries Taos had endured newcomers it did not initially welcome, the paper claimed that after each "new culture" arrived, with the passage of time, "each of these ways of doing things rubbed and bounded against one another until the friction created caused them to melt and fuse together and mold what is today's Taoseno; a unique type. Not Spanish, but with some Spanish characteristics. Not Indian, but with some Indian characteristics. Not Anglo, but with some Anglo characteristics." The new hippie would eventually be tempered, as well. Some representatives would work hard and become valuable members of the community. Others would "eventually blow away like chaff, just as did some Spaniards, some Anglos and some artists." In the meantime, everyone needed to practice brotherhood. Clearly, this assessment of Taos as a melting pot owed more to fantasy than reality.[54]

Still, at least one resident of Taos, Gerald Ortiz y Pino, argued that hippies and Hispanos had something in common: both suffered at the hands of the tourist-oriented business interests. Now the latter were trying to expel "middle class anglos who reject the values that have been shoved down people's throats in New Mexico in the name of acculturation." The civic leaders had cleverly managed to incite Hispanos into attacking hippies. "Let's stop being used," Ortiz y Pino argued. "We don't have to prove our manhood, our machismo by beating up hippies. Leave that to the impotent Anglo businessman." Speaking for the counterculture communards, Bill Quinn urged the community to "cool it" and remember that the hippies, like early Spanish settlers before them, came to Taos for its space and freedom but also because of its "still living Spanish and Indian cultural richness." The solution was fair and equitable justice to all, regardless of skin color or hair length.[55]

Of course, northern New Mexico offered an array of social and political issues that could have encouraged a coalition of Anglo, Indian, and Hispano. If such cross-cultural and ethnic cooperation were possible, surely here it could be realized. Some of the counterculture newcomers did want to join ranks with

Chicano activists who demanded the return of lost Spanish land grants to Hispanic villagers. When such demands to the governor of New Mexico brought no response, members of the newly created La Alianza Federal de Los Pueblos Libres, under the leadership of Reies Lopez Tijerina, demonstrated at the Tierra Amarilla Courthouse. Officials arrested them. On the day of their arraignment, about twenty armed Hispanos organized a "citizen's arrest" of the district attorney at the Rio Arriba Courthouse. A shootout followed and the National Guard moved in to reassert control. Tijerina, in fact, envisioned a movement supported by Pueblos, Hispanics, and hippies. Meanwhile, in an attempt to encourage cross-ethnic understanding, the Chicano newspaper, *El Grito*, explained to the Anglo newcomers why they might be perceived as "gringos" in light of 120 years of land loss to Anglo ranchers and their lawyers. It urged them to think about their impact on land values, the welfare system, water resources, and Hispanos' sense of propriety and culture. "It cannot be said too often: there is a long, hard political and economic struggle in these beautiful mountains, a struggle for land and justice. That struggle calls for fighters and supporters, not refugees with their own set of problems. You may see the scenery and relief from an oppressive America. We see a battleground against oppression." The paper's advice: don't come to New Mexico, at least not now. "And when you do come, come as a revolutionary."[56] Under the circumstances of the so-called hippie invasion, the likelihood of such an alliance working was slim, and the effort to create it only served to reinforce nonmilitant Hispanos' suspicions of the whole movement. The majority wanted nothing to do with radical politics, hippie allies, or the label of "Chicano."[57]

That the Anglos did not completely understand the land issues was evident at a January 31, 1970, meeting when about 120 men, women, and children congregated at the Reality Construction Company commune to discuss a plan to purchase one hundred thousand acres of land in northern New Mexico for an "Earth Peoples Park." Here people would practice organic farming, live close to the land, and "learn from the natives." The origin of the idea is a bit obscure, but Berkeley's Peoples Park imbroglio probably partially inspired it, while the Woodstock music festival experience of the previous August, a Hunger Festival in northern California, a Winter Solstice celebration in San Francisco, and a conversation at Jemez Hot Springs were credited with promoting the concept. Committees were set up in Los Angeles, San Francisco, Seattle, and New York to raise money for the project; and Gilberto Romero and other Chicanos from "La Raza" "rapped" about the idea at this Taos area meeting. La Raza members were particularly interested in where this land would come from. Might it be acquired in contested Spanish land grant acreage? When cautioned that residents would see this as "just more Anglos moving in and taking over," one participant insisted they were not all Anglos, but rather a mixed group including Mexicans and Indians. They were brothers who shared the experience of being oppressed. To the latter point, another presumably non-Hispanic said, "Yes, but we chose our lifestyle. They didn't."⁵⁸

The La Raza people were not convinced. One suggested if the hippies wanted to do some good, they should go to the South, buy land, and turn it over to African Americans. Further, there were no Indians present to speak for themselves. "Most of them were killed by your ancestors on the way over." But the main points the Hispanos made were that no one should buy or sell New Mexico lands and that the majority of "Chicanos" simply did not trust the newcomers because they had been robbed and pushed around too long by Anglos. "I consider every man my brother," one Chicano participant, said, "but there are differences. There is a ruling class and a minority group. You just want to live like the Chicano, like the Indian. Don't get land in Taos County, or even in northern New Mexico. There isn't enough water here." Moreover, Hispanos make a living here only by going to Wyoming in the summer to herd sheep or to Colorado to pick crops.⁵⁹

After listening to these charges, the group agreed that once they had raised the requisite one million dollars, they would buy smaller pieces of property up and down the Rockies, creating a chain of small villages rather than one big park. "That way you're not zapping on the local population," one person noted. They expected to raise the money by asking every person who was at Woodstock, in person or in spirit, to contribute one dollar. "Rich kids buying land is a dead idea." However, when one "cat" wrote out a check for $3,500 for Earth Peoples Park, the coordinator accepted it. With that unrealistic scenario settled, the group went outside, stood in a circle, held hands, and feeling "the Kachinas on the mountains watching us, the circle whooped and ran into the center, and we were really together." After "an old hippie ritual" of lighting a joint of marijuana, which disappeared into the crowd, they agreed to meet again in one month, and in the meantime to go into the community and talk with locals about whether they would like to have the hippies as neighbors.⁶⁰

Not surprisingly, Earth Peoples Park never materialized. But the communards learned, at least, something about the political complexities of land-holding and stake-making in New Mexico from this exchange. The underground press subsequently reported and widely disseminated the lessons learned. Nevertheless, increased awareness of ethnic and racial differences did not translate into a universal rapprochement between the hippies and the Hispano population.⁶¹

The Taos Pueblo, meanwhile, seemed more open to support from any quarter regarding its major concern of the day: the return of Blue Lake, a sacred site, to tribal control. Ever since the Taos Pueblo people had established their village in its current place, circa 1300, they considered Blue Lake part of their territory. Spanish, Mexican, and American rule acknowledged that "ownership" until 1906 when President Theodore Roosevelt created Kit Carson National Forest and appropriated Blue Lake within its boundary, offering no compensation. The Pueblo, however, did not want compensation. It wanted the federal government, and non-Indians, out of this holy place. For over sixty years the tribe fought to reclaim it. In a complicated process that involved the Pueblo Lands Board, the Senate Indian Affairs Committee, the Indian Claims Commission, and the National Congress of American Indians Executive Committee, Taos Pueblo unwaveringly made clear what it wanted: title to the land. Opposition from New Mexico Senator Clinton P. Anderson, the Taos County Commissioners, the Forest Service, cattlemen, timber interests, the National Wildlife Federation, the Wilderness Society, and hunting and fishing interests consistently killed efforts to return the land.

After the Indian Claims Commission finally determined in 1965 that the government unjustly took the area, Representative James Haley, chairman of the Subcommittee on Indian Affairs, introduced a bill in 1968 to restore it to the Pueblo. It died in the Senate. Meanwhile, Taos Pueblo astutely sought favorable publicity from newspapers across the country and participated in a television documentary about the issue. They garnered additional support from a panoply of Anglo-dominated organizations and individuals including the Association on American Indian Affairs(AAIA), the American Civil Liberties Union (ACLU), the National Council of Churches (NCC), the archbishop of Santa Fe, former secretary of the interior Stewart Udall, the Eastern Association on Indian Affairs, American Friends Service Committee, the Sierra Club, and the National Committee for Restoration of the Blue Lake to the Taos Indians—all groups or people with extraordinary financial resources and/or political experience and sophistication. This non-Indian support, particularly from churchmen and women who argued that Blue Lake represented Taos Pueblo's church and that access to it was an issue of religious freedom, proved crucial in swaying political figures, outside of New Mexico, to back restoration. This was the first, though not the last, Indian religious claim handled by the National Council of Churches, the most influential and credible organization in the nation on such issues.[62]

The issue also received attention from the underground press—certainly more than any connected to La Raza or Rieis Tijerina. In the end, Indians were the greater attraction, offered the presumably greater example of an authentic life and relationship with nature, and so elicited the strongest political support.[63] But by the time counterculture types and communitarians began settling into northern New Mexico, the Taos Pueblo's decades-long efforts on this issue were finally coming to a satisfactory end. As part of his new Indian policy emphasizing tribal self-determination, President Richard Nixon threw his support behind Representative James Haley's 1970 bill to grant trust title to forty-eight thousand acres of the national forest, including Blue Lake and access routes from the Pueblo. It also granted an exclusive-use area of 1,640 acres around the lake itself, although without exclusive access thereto. It was not exactly what the Taos Pueblo wanted, but it was certainly a compromise they could live with. On December 15, 1970, President Nixon signed the bill into law.[64]

Hippies and commune dwellers may have been supportive, but they wielded none of the tools the Pueblo's more politically savvy and powerful Anglo allies such as the AAIA, ACLU, and NCC had at their disposal. Still, their role was not irrelevant. In fact, it was probably crucial in explaining the timing of the Blue Lake's resolution. According to historian R. C. Gordon-McCutchan, "A sympathetic climate of opinion was created for Blue Lake by the surging counterculture . . . While few of them voted or wrote to their congressmen, nonetheless they were expressing an appreciation of and respect for Indian values." Furthermore, the tribe's strategy of matching a call for religious freedom with reverence for the land also fit with "the spirit of the times . . . Those who were seeking a renewed relationship to the land and who were concerned with ecology naturally rallied to the cause of an Indian tribe with a centuries-old tradition of worshiping nature, and who also were fighting to protect their wilderness from the depradations [sic] of timbering and poisonous sprays."[65] The counterculture communards of New Mexico consistently articulated these sensibilities, and if they did not marshal much in the way of political skills, they attracted considerable media attention and became, perhaps unwittingly, part of the tribe's public relations support system.

Further, in a moment of intense national turmoil, President Nixon needed an issue that would mitigate the political fallout from some of his other policies. Indian affairs became the nexus for a more liberal stance on at least one element of domestic policy. Nixon's willingness to respond to Indian demands for greater power over their own affairs and greater sensitivity to their cultures and religious traditions stemmed, in part, from his friendship with his Whittier College football coach who was Native American. It was also politically expedient.[66] The Taos Blue Lake issue came along just as events were playing out at Alcatraz Island, with no end or satisfactory solution in sight. Unlike Alcatraz, where Indians had only the most tenuous legal claim to the place, Taos Pueblo's legal claim to Blue Lake rested on much more solid ground. Public support was much broader and deeper. It consequently offered the Nixon administration a chance to respond favorably to an Indian demand and perhaps garner political support from those who normally opposed Nixon. It worked. The *New York Times* praised the new policy on the front page, and letters flooded into the White House from across the country commending the president.[67] The White House also encouraged, with apparent Taos Pueblo support, media coverage of a

July 25, 1970, visit to the Pueblo and Blue Lake by Kim Agnew, fourteen-year-old daughter of Vice President Spiro Agnew (who was chairman of the National Council on Indian Opportunity); Leonard Garment, special consultant to the president and point man on Indian issues; and others. Miss Agnew presented a ceremonial cane to tribal Governor Querino Romero, similar to those presented to the tribe by Charles V of Spain in the sixteenth century and President Abraham Lincoln in the nineteenth, even though Leonard Garment had been advised that the Taos Pueblo, which recognized he was among "the real movers" on the Blue Lake issue, would prefer that a man present the cane. Kim Agnew also made a private visit, escorted by tribal leaders, via horseback to Blue Lake.[68]

As the Blue Lake fight was coming to an end, the Hopi imbroglio over the Black Mesa strip coal mine also attracted significant counterculture support. Of course, the Hopi had long been among the hip peoples' favorite tribes, but this case involved a complicated and powerful set of adversaries—those hippies shared with Hopis. As the *Astral Projection* explained, this battle pitted the Hopi against the federal government, corporations, state and local governments, and a puppet tribal government that rubber stamped BIA decisions. This included the lease arrangement that allowed Peabody Coal Company to mine coal on Hopi and Navajo lands. Between the strip mines and the water-slurry pipelines designed to move the coal to power plants, threatening underground water tables, crops, and livelihoods, this economic activity endangered not only sacred lands but the entire Hopi way of life. To counter this disastrous scenario, the paper urged readers to send money to the Hopi Fund in San Francisco or the Committee for Traditional Indian Land and Life in Los Angeles.[69]

Others, closer to the Southwest, also mobilized to support those Hopi people who opposed the mining operation. In February 1970, for example, Jack Loeffler and a handful of others started a Central Clearing House in Santa Fe to gather and disseminate information on environmental matters affecting the Southwest, including the activities at Black Mesa. Working with people such as David Monongye of Hotevilla and traveling the country with Thomas Banyacya talking about the issue, Loeffler helped start the Black Mesa Defense Fund to educate the public and hopefully stop the project. They carried on a public relations campaign and initiated six lawsuits, but to no avail. Perhaps the culminating moment for Loeffler came at the 1972 United Nations Stockholm Conference that he attended, along with four Hopis and two Navajos. Thanks to the efforts of Stewart Brand and anthropologist Margaret Mead, who rented a gallery which became "3rd World Central," people from all over the globe gathered and shared their stories. In this way, the Defense Fund managed to get the Black Mesa issue before a world body but that, too, failed to change anything. The adversaries were too powerful; the solutions too complicated. Discouraged by their inability to alter activities at Black Mesa, the group finally gave up, raised enough money to retire its debt, and closed its door.⁷⁰ Even though they failed, Loeffler believed "the Black Mesa scene brought a large number of people who had been communal hippies back into activism."⁷¹

By 1971, Taos fever appeared to have dissipated among the counterculture migrants. Perhaps it was stories of violence directed toward hippies that warned prospective communards off. Perhaps it was the difficulties of life in a high mountain valley that encouraged many to leave. Perhaps it was the contrast between their naive expectations and the realities of Taos life that led to the relatively quick demise of many of the communal experiments.⁷² But not all folded. New Buffalo continued into the 1980s, eventually becoming the home base of the Sustainable Native Agricultural Center, a nonprofit group dedicated to preserving native seeds, and then a bed and breakfast designed to attract tourists interested in Taos' counterculture past.⁷³ The Lama Foundation still operates.

Through all the turmoil of the "hippie invasion," Taos Pueblo and other New Mexico Native American communities quietly carried on. For a time they found themselves, no doubt reluctantly for the most part, the inspiration for a youth movement hungry for new models. They weathered that moment and even benefited politically from it. Never before in American history had so many non-Indians sought out interaction with Indian people for the purpose of learning from them, attempting to approximate elements of native life, and supporting the political demands of these communities. The mostly young people were largely unwelcome. They were undoubtedly naive. They ruffled many feathers. But running through this move "to the Indians" was something genuinely distinctive in American culture. There had been, since colonial days, a few non-Indians drawn into Indian country. What was different now was the scale and, consequently, the political significance of the idea that Indian cultures were attractive, and worth venerating and, certainly, preserving. This represented the absolute antithesis of the assimilation and acculturation models that had prevailed for centuries.

Where hippie alternative communities popped up, the national media followed and in describing the hip interest in Indians, unwittingly spread the message far beyond New Mexico and the Southwest. Reporters appeared to accept the counterculture image of Indianness, neither ridiculing nor dismissing it. Consequently the celebration of Indian ways continued to seep into the national consciousness, finding receptive audiences not only among the liberal, progressive churches that had joined forces with tribes, such as the Taos Pueblo, many years before, but also among people who had never previously given Indians a thought.

By the early 1970s, then, interest in things Indian shifted away from the Southwest to flashpoints across the nation where more radical Native Americans, mostly young, ratcheted up the pressure to acknowledge Indian grievances and demand not only attention but also significant political reform. The American Indian Movement, in particular, captured the interest and support of America's New Left and politically oriented counterculture. Along for the ride were many mainstream organizations. Even the president of the United States and at least some of his men were paying attention.

5

From Coast to Coast

In the early 1970s, interest in Indians spread far beyond the American West that spawned it. Native American activists took tactics put into practice at Alcatraz and fish-ins to the opposite end of the continent, even penetrating the heart of the nation's capital. For the first time in the twentieth century, Indian affairs grabbed headlines nationwide as activists "invaded" or occupied patches of real estate from coast to coast and held demonstrations to call attention to issues ranging from land claims and treaty rights to sovereignty and self-determination. Furthermore, interest in Indians was no longer limited to the counterculture, radical fringe groups, or Protestant progressive groups. Indians became the subjects of influential, best-selling books such as *Bury My Heart at Wounded Knee* by Anglo librarian and writer Dee Brown and Vine Deloria Jr.'s *Custer Died For Your Sins*. Even Hollywood turned its attention to Native Americans, producing new kinds of Westerns with late twentieth-century political sensibilities. Films such as *Soldier Blue* and *Little Big Man* reversed the standard roles for Indian characters—cavalrymen played the villains to Native American heroes.

Through these mediums, people received new messages about Indians in a milieu of social, cultural, and political turmoil. Complaints about injustice from African Americans, Mexican Americans, and Native Americans gathered force and sometimes generated negative backlash. Overlaying it all was the deeply divisive war in Vietnam. The global implications of Americans' treatment of minorities, particularly Indians, did not escape readers or moviegoers who understood they criticized not only the United States' past imperialism but its current foreign policy, as well.

The books, the movies, the takeovers, or attempted takeovers, of Seattle's Fort Lawton, Mount Rushmore, the Statue of Liberty, and the Bureau of Indian Affairs Building in Washington, D.C., came in a torrent. In fact, Paul Chaat Smith and Robert Warrior have adroitly characterized the period of Indian activism between Alcatraz and Wounded Knee as hurricane-like.[1] Indian people were at the heart of the storm, providing its genesis, motivation, and energy. Non-Indians were swept up in the winds of change, drawing them into the currents, sometimes attracting and encouraging support, sometimes repelling. The Nixon White House could not ignore the tempest either—particularly when it touched down in Washington, D.C., in the fall of 1972, just days before the presidential election. Out of this confluence of forces came substantive change.

That change permanently put to rest termination of tribal governments and the trust relationship between them and the federal government, and helped advance the realignment of federal policy in a radically different direction. The Justice Department began to defend Indian treaty rights. Further, some demonstrations ended in remarkable victory. In Seattle, for instance, the United Indians of All Tribes (UIAT) succeeded where the Alcatraz occupiers failed. They received a lease to a chunk of the recently abandoned Fort Lawton military base and established an Indian cultural center, which exists to this day. Victory was not guaranteed, however. The Pit River Tribe, located in an isolated patch of northern California, did not prevail in their efforts to regain land. Their distance from a sympathetic non-Indian audience and from media centers undoubtedly played a role. So too did the greater complexity of their case and the greater power of their adversaries: federal agencies and major corporations who used and owned the disputed land. In a confrontation related to that effort, an Anglo property caretaker murdered Richard Oakes, a key figure in the early days of the Alcatraz takeover and supporter of Pit River activists.

The murder went unpunished and the rage provoked by this miscarriage of justice helped inspire the Trail of Broken Treaties caravan to Washington, D.C. The ensuing takeover, and trashing, of the BIA headquarters ended in a standoff with the federal government ultimately granting what was essentially amnesty for destruction and theft of government property. It also provided over sixty thousand dollars to send the activists home. In a different era, such large-scale law breaking would have met with an iron hand of punishment and repression. In the nineteenth century much less dramatic episodes of resistance meant death. But by the end of 1972, although some criticized the Nixon administration's handling of the Trail of Broken Treaties and BIA takeover (and there had been those in the government who advocated use of force against the occupiers), it is difficult to see its immediate reaction as anything but moderate. Such restraint would change with the occupation of Wounded Knee, South Dakota, in 1973; but, in the meantime, many of the Trail of Broken Treaties participants themselves interpreted the federal response as a victory. Rather than turn the tide of public sympathy against them, such episodes, with their calls for justice, continued to generate goodwill and sympathy. By bringing these issues to the doorstep of the White House and Congress, activists thrust them deeper into national consciousness and revealed a greater willingness among non-Indians to, if not sanction threats of violence as a political tool, forgive them and take seriously the necessity of instituting genuine reform in Indian affairs.

In spring 1972 Vine Deloria Jr. was disgusted. From the mid-1960s through the publication of his own highly successful book, *Custer Died for Your Sins*, in 1969, it appeared that Indians' contemporary problems had finally arrived on the national agenda. Not so long before, termination threatened Native Americans' well being. But various media outlets had finally picked up on contemporary Indian problems. Even *Time* magazine covered stories on native activist groups and sponsored a conference for Indian scholars in order to lay groundwork for a presentation of Indian issues to the American reading public. Alcatraz, of course, had captured national, even international, attention. And then, "as if the whole thing were too much for America to understand," Deloria wrote, "we were buried by the phantoms of the past—the Indians that white America likes much better": dead ones. To his mind, the reading public preferred to read *Bury My Heart at Wounded Knee*, Dee Brown's blockbuster saga about the post–Civil War Indian Wars, to Deloria's book on contemporary Indian politics. Brown's was a good book, Deloria allowed, but hardly anything new. More frustrating, it diverted attention away from present-day problems. "So the American public felt sorry as hell about Chief Joseph and Dull Knife being mistreated while the Washington state game wardens stalked 17 year old Allison Bridges [Al and Masile Bridges' daughter, who participated in the Frank's Landing fish-in activity] with their telescopic rifle sights, and white vigilantes shot Hank Adams in the stomach while he slept in his car." Rather than shedding light on these atrocities, Brown's book instead "spawned a number of sickening visitations to the romantic past."[2]

Bury My Heart at Wounded Knee: An Indian History of the American West arrived at bookstores at just the right moment. Published in 1970, it rode the wave of Indian interest and helped propel it. Brown—whose former books ran to more traditional fare regarding Western history with titles such as *Fort Phil Kearny: An American Saga*; *The Gentle Tamers* (about white women in the West); and *The Galvanized Yankees* (Confederate prisoners of war sent out West for the duration)—decided to offer a "new" perspective. Rather than celebrate America's movement west, Brown looked at expansion from the perspective of Indian people and thus critiqued it. He intended "a narrative of the conquest . . . as the victims experienced it," which encapsulates the tone of the book. It was a eulogy for a vanquished people. Even though they "have vanished from the earth," their words lived on in the transcripts of treaty councils and formal messages. Brown presented the story of westward expansion by facing east and offering the viewpoint of those who suffered its consequences. He believed "the culture and civilization of the American Indian was destroyed" but the stories that lay behind that tragedy still needed to be told.[3] Such a comment not only collapsed multiple Indian cultures into one, but also mistakenly assumed their demise. It denied their rich diversities and capacities to survive while adapting to change. But it also brought Indian historical experiences to new and broader audiences. It gave an uninformed reading public a historical perspective they lacked otherwise. It provided a flawed, but still useful, context to those very much alive Indian people demanding restitution for past injustices, those who appeared in newscasts and in the morning newspapers' headlines.

The episodes Brown featured are now familiar to many non-Indians but were less so at the time: the Navajo's Long Walk to the Bosque Redondo Reservation and back, the Sand Creek Massacre, miners' and the army's invasion of the Powder River Country, the Seventh Cavalry's slaughter of Cheyenne people on the Washita River, the defeat of the Comanches and Kiowas in Palo Duro Canyon, the Nez Perce War, the pursuit of the Chiricahua Apaches into Mexico, the Modoc War, and of course the massacre at Wounded Knee in 1890. The text, which did not claim to offer a "balanced" view, emphasized white treachery and brutality. For instance, while admitting Sioux and Cheyenne men had mutilated Lieutenant William Fetterman and his men after a battle near Fort Phil Kearny in 1866, Brown noted these were merely the "same mutilations—committed upon Indians by Colonel Chivington's soldiers" at Sand Creek two years before. "The Indians who ambushed Fetterman were only imitating their enemies, a practice which in warfare, as in civilian life, is said to be the sincerest form of flattery."[4] The implication was Indians did not mutilate enemies before they learned the practice from white people. Throughout the book readers found not one photograph of a white person. They would look in vain for an image of Lieutenant Colonel George Armstrong Custer, General Phil Sheridan, or even Colonel John Chivington. Instead Brown used only Native American portraits which emphasized their individual personalities, dignity, and humanity.

The cumulative effect was dramatic, devastating, and quite moving to a reading public. Much of this material was new to non-Indians. At this time only a handful of universities responded to Native American students' demands that they teach Indian history or offer Indian Studies courses. Secondary and elementary school curriculums lagged even further behind. Just as Helen Hunt Jackson's *A Century of Dishonor* shaped late nineteenth-century sensibilities about Indian affairs and led to policy reform, so did Brown's *Bury My Heart at Wounded Knee* appear poised to play the same role in the late twentieth.[5] None other than Vine Deloria Jr., clearly in a more generous mood than he would be a year later, thought so, noting in a 1971 review that the book "may well dominate the next century of literature dealing with American Indians." It was, he went on to say, "THE book that many young Indians have wanted written for a long, long time" and the book he wished he had written. Kiowa novelist M. Scott Momaday also found Brown's book "extraordinary" and a narrative of "singular integrity" that made it difficult to put down. It satisfied peoples' new-found interest in "the underside of American history," a dimension of the past which was richly documented, though relatively unknown. Brown's book, Momaday asserted, provided "a better understanding of what it is that nags at the American conscience at times (to our everlasting credit) and of that morality which informs and fuses events so far apart in time and space as the massacres at Wounded Knee and My Lai," a village in Vietnam where American soldiers killed hundreds of Vietnamese noncombatants.[6]

One week after this review appeared in print, *Bury My Heart* debuted at number ten on the *New York Times* best-seller list. Over the next several weeks, it crept up the list, vying with Charles Reich's book about the counterculture, *The Greening of America*, and Alvin Toeffler's *Future Shock*. By June 6, 1971, Brown's book captured the number one spot on the best-seller list and stayed there. It remained on the list for fifty-seven weeks until April 1972 and eventually sold more than five million copies.[7]

Such sales certainly superseded those of Deloria's *Custer Died For Your Sins* or his 1970 follow-up book, *We Talk, You Listen*. The former, with its catchy title, nevertheless, found a wide readership and catapulted the author to national fame. *Custer Died For Your Sins* did not trade in sentimentalism or nostalgia, nor did it dwell on the past. Deloria's Indians were neither vanquished nor vanished. It was, as one reviewer noted, "a bitter, searing, intransigent indictment of all of white America's dealing with the Indians" that fastened its sights on twentieth-century anthropologists and political liberals who believed they knew what was best for today's Indians and would force their will, whether Indians wanted it or not. It was a book of fierce attack and "icy anger."[8] Perhaps that tone, as much as the topic, made Deloria's work less popular.

Nor did non-Indian writers completely ignore contemporary issues in Indian country. Freelance writer Stan Steiner published *The New Indians* in 1968. Focusing on the new generation of college-educated Indians who supported renewed tribalism, sovereignty, treaty rights, and cultural resurgence, Steiner featured people such as "the young and brilliant" Deloria. Based on many years travel in the West and informed conversation with Indian people, Steiner's book explored contemporary organizations such as the National Indian Youth Council and issues such as fishing rights. The modern renaissance of tribalism, he explained, "was uniquely Indian" in that it included "respect for the elders by the youth; the recognition of the youth by the elders." It blended the old with the new, the historic with the modern. The following year, in 1969, the Washington, D.C., Citizens Advocacy Group published *Our Brother's Keeper: The Indian in White America*, a scorching critique of government policy and the Bureau of Indian Affairs, in particular. It billed itself as a "report on the status of these conquered people living among us" and was less interested in the past ("We shrug off history") than the present.[9]

Still, Deloria's charge that Americans found dead Indians more interesting and sympathetic than live ones gives pause. And Brown's message that Indian cultures were dead and gone was not only profoundly inaccurate but deeply troubling and counterproductive to Indian people who were fighting hard to perpetuate their cultures. For his part, Brown did not completely ignore the contemporary situation. He ended his introduction with the comment that if readers should ever visit a modern Indian reservation and see the poverty, squalor, and hopelessness there, his book might begin to help them understand what they were witnessing.[10] But he offered no comment on contemporary issues. That he preferred to tell stories about the past rather than the present cannot be denied.

A sense of that past, however, proved crucial in shaping non-Indian perceptions' of current affairs. Treaties, as living documents with contemporary meaning and even power, could not be understood without some grounding in the historical experiences and relationships that created them. Once readers understood treaties' genesis, as well as the long history of their abuse and misuse, they were more likely to accept their present-day relevance. History was neither a smokescreen nor a distraction. It was an inevitable element of contemporary relationships of power. The effect of Brown's book was to remind non-Indians of America's shameful past regarding treaty violations and thus provide contemporary Indians with the moral force to match the legal standing with which to legitimize their claims. Some might call the Anglo reaction "guilt" or see it as fleeting and superficial. But it was a crucial component of American Indians' appeal to the nation's conscience and to the political effort to legislate change. Such reform included realizing past promises codified in historic treaties still had legal legitimacy. Fifteen-year-old Deborah Sue Brown, from Cherry Hill, New Jersey, was sufficiently moved after reading *Bury My Heart at Wounded Knee* to write to President Nixon that the book made her realize how "horrible the Indians are being treated."[11] It was, in fact, the combination of Deloria's emphasis on the present and Brown's on the past that proved a powerful one-two punch in shaping the interested public's perceptions of Indians and encouraging sympathy for their current demands. Brown's book reminded them of the nation's perfidy. Deloria's suggested ways to remedy it.

From the perspective of 1972, however, Vine Deloria did not see things this way. He told Indian audiences that whites did not "give a damn about Indians because the only Indian they will accept is the barefoot child of nature who makes dramatic speeches as recorded by Dee Brown and others." He blamed Native Americans as much as non-Indians. There were too many national Indian organizations, creating confusion and making it easier to co-opt a handful of leaders here and another handful there. Indians needed to unite, concentrate on shared goals, and consolidate the gains they had made. They should stop "being America's favorite media clowns" and approximate the experiences of blacks and Chicanos who had "made a dent on contemporary society." Native Americans needed to develop strong alliances, including with non-Indians and regain credibility with government foundations, churches, and the general public. And they should use the media more sparingly. "The once intense interest in Indians is now on the downswing because even Chief Joseph gets boring after a while and nobody knows about the modern issues that are really important." He went on:

> The heart of America is hard as granite. We have fooled ourselves if we are thinking that the events of recent years have educated the American public as to Indian problems. We have simply overwhelmed the media with trivia and it has fled into the past toward uncomplicated Indians and taken us with it. If we are to return to modern America, we had better get it together and start acting as if we really were real.[12]

The test of Deloria's pessimism came in events and actions on the ground. Did public attention prove fleeting? Had nothing of substance come from the growing demand for meaningful change in the way the United States interacted with, and treated, Indian people?

In the months following the initial takeover of Alcatraz, similar actions sprang up across the nation. Native Americans in New York attempted to "liberate" the Statue of Liberty, while others in South Dakota briefly occupied Mount Rushmore and Badlands National Monument. On Thanksgiving Day 1970, John Trudell, who had temporarily left Alcatraz, and some leaders of the recently established American Indian Movement (AIM), such as Russell Means and Dennis Banks, joined local Wampanoag activists in disrupting a recreation of the first Thanksgiving at Plymouth Rock, Massachusetts. They buried the "rock" in sand and spit on it and then briefly occupied a newly constructed replica of *The Mayflower*, which they considered burning, but ultimately refrained from that level of destruction. After the "Pilgrims" invited them for dinner, the Indians turned over the turkey-laden tables, sending people screaming toward the doors. The demonstrators reportedly salvaged four turkeys for themselves, however. The Twin Cities Naval Station in Minneapolis; and Nike missile bases in Milwaukee, Chicago, and the San Francisco Bay Area experienced brief takeovers. Bureau of Indian Affairs offices in Cleveland and Denver became targets of Indian demonstrators. Participants, often veterans of Alcatraz, selected sites that met several criteria: they were federally owned and recently abandoned or likely to encourage media coverage, given their particular historical or symbolic resonance.[13] The episode at Plymouth, for instance, led to no Indian arrests. The lesson there seemed clear: the time had come to express Indian complaints and America seemed willing not only to bear such disruptions but also to listen. No doubt these events alienated some. But they seemed to attract attention and sympathy from far more.

In keeping with patterns found among the Pacific Northwest tribes, not all Native Americans supported these events or welcomed the media coverage. The Inter-Tribal Sioux Association, for example, assured Secretary of the Interior Walter Hickel they did not condone those Indians who conducted the sit-in at Mount Rushmore, which the association members referred to as the "Shrine of Democracy." They expressed concern about possible damage to Mount Rushmore and to the Indian people who lived in the area. The occupation was straining race relations because whites blamed "all Indians for this flaunting of the law." The association believed the activists, who were not from South Dakota, should take their grievances to Congress and the college students among them, particularly those receiving BIA scholarships, should go back to school rather than demonstrate. The Inter-Tribal Sioux Association also forwarded a copy of their resolution on the topic, requesting that the federal government, state, and local law enforcement officers remove the militants "who do not represent the Sioux of South Dakota." The Park Service initially intended to allow the activists, camped illegally on the slopes of the monument, to stay. They assumed that once the activists' initial enthusiasm had subsided, and fall came and the weather turned cooler, they would leave on their own accord. The demonstrators had not interrupted the public's use of Mount Rushmore nor had they done any damage to it. But the letter from the Inter-Tribal Sioux Association convinced the Park Service that measures should be taken to remove them.[14]

Increasing numbers of non-Indians, however, sympathized with the growing flurry of takeovers. Ranks of supporters received new recruits from across the country, demonstrating growing continental consciousness about Indian discontent and activism. One of the more intriguing groups to reach out to Indians was the Interreligious Foundation for Community Organization (IFCO), an interdenominational "parachurch" agency, headquartered in New York City and established in 1966 to create lines of communication between mainstream American churches and minority communities. IFCO's involvement in Indian affairs not only underscored the national scope of support but also brought more African American and Native American activists together. The relationship was not always smooth.

The initiative for IFCO came from the Board of National Missions of the United Presbyterian Church, which wanted to join forces with other denominations in training organizers and supporting local community projects. A veritable who's who of the nation's religious establishments signed on, including the American Baptist Home Mission Societies, American Jewish Committee, Board of Missions of the United Methodist Church, General Board of Christian Social Concerns of the United Methodist Church, Catholic Committee for Urban Ministries, Executive Council of the Episcopal Church, Board of Homeland Ministries of the United Church of Christ, the Lutheran Church in America,

National Catholic Conference for Interracial Justice, and the Foundation for Voluntary Service. At first IFCO focused primarily on projects within African American communities. But in 1969 the board reached out to Native Americans as well. Through grants it supported community-action projects related to voter education, community-owned cooperatives, job training, urban planning, and tenants rights; but it did not shy away from funding groups engaged in protest activities some would characterize as radical or "militant." Grant recipients included the American Indian Movement (AIM) and Cesar Chavez's United Farm Workers.[15]

Under the leadership of the first executive director and Baptist clergyman Reverend Lucius Walker, IFCO expanded funding and service to Indian communities. The motivation came in response to proposals from Indian groups, such as the National Indian Youth Council. Uncertain how to evaluate these proposals and yet anxious to incorporate Indians into the process, IFCO invited a collection of Native American leaders to two "Indian-American Task Force" meetings in Chicago in March and May 1969. Among the participants in the May meeting were Jess Sixkiller, director of American Indian United; Elizabeth Locklear, Baltimore Indian Center; Al Elgin, Inter-Tribal Friendship House in Oakland, California; Sydney Beane, Arizona Indian Association; Joe Muskrat, Adlai E. Stevenson Institute of Indian Affairs; and Mel Thom, founder of the National Indian Youth Council.[16]

One invitee who chose not to participate was Vine Deloria Jr., who had sharply criticized churches in his recent *Custer Died For Your Sins*. Deloria told Walker he did not see how IFCO, which he described as "an organization in search of meaning," could have "any significant relationship" with Indians in small communities. For some time, he told Walker, who was African American, whites had handpicked their favorite "Indian leaders," who had no time to truly understand the peoples' problems because they spent so much time, at churches' expense, flying from one meeting to another. The gap in time between the articulation of ideas and concerns in communities and the churches' efforts to keep up was unbridgeable. Deloria suggested IFCO "forgo expedition into the mists of Indian Affairs and concentrate on the New York situation." Indian people at the local and regional levels needed to solve their problems themselves. He then finished with a flourish: "I have always fought against white paternalism . . . But I am not about to substitute white paternalism for black paternalism and fight the old fight of the last decade over again."[17]

Walker apparently did not reply to these charges. Instead, he simply sent Deloria another invitation for another task force meeting. He reiterated IFCO's interest in promoting Indian self-determination through a Native American advisory committee of six people plus two board members, and Indian consultants for field visits to projects. This time, Deloria—undoubtedly frustrated by the lack of response to his initial charges about black paternalism—went ballistic. "HOW FORTUNATE THAT INDIANS SPONTANEOUSLY CAME TOGETHER, SET UP A REPRESENTATIVE BOARD AND THEN APPLIED TO JOIN 'IFCO.' And how DOUBLY fortunate that IFCO voted to accept them!!!... Seriously, man. You spades do your thing and us savages will do ours." Deloria recommended that Walker attend a traditionalist meeting on the Onondaga Reservation in central New York state, if he truly wanted to understand what was going on in Indian communities. "Except that white eyes and spades are banned. (Also 'breeds' like myself)." Then Deloria softened a bit, telling Walker he was coming to New York to publicize his book and seek a contract for his next project, *God is Red*. He welcomed the opportunity to meet unofficially with Walker on a "hombre-hombre basis" and discuss what their respective communities could do "with the proper catalytic agents working behind the scenes." He warned that he was not going to be "a friendly Indian companion like Tonto and Mel Thom" and added: "I will not ask you to eat dog soup if you don't serve me watermelon. In the meantime, try and be a credit to your race."[18]

If Deloria meant the last comment to be a joke, it did not translate well. He knew that such humor often did not work across racial lines. In *Custer Died For Your Sins*, Deloria noted there was little Indian-black communication to begin with and that jokes were especially dangerous because they could be easily misunderstood. Blacks, he offered as an example, did not appreciate or understand cards some Native Americans had printed with the statement, "We Shall Overrun," a reference to the civil rights anthem, "We Shall Overcome." The Indian version humorously harkened back to Hollywood images of Indians attacking wagon trains and pioneer settlements. On several occasions, "there was a tense situation until the card was explained."[19] This time his letter elicited an immediate, sharp response from Walker who stated he did not intend to "be as judgemental [sic], presumptuous, egotistical, and uncouth as you seem imminently [sic] capable of being." Until he had evidence to the contrary, in fact, these were the qualities "this 'spade'" now attributed to Deloria. Walker, meantime, saw himself as someone who was trying to rise above divisiveness, self-interest, "and the racism which both Blacks and Indians have learned from the white man." Still, he hoped to find ways to get beyond this "senseless sparring" and encouraged Deloria to visit him "when you arrive in New York to put the legal finishes to your current pimping activities." Walker realized that by writing so frankly in reply to Deloria, he risked becoming the subject of his next exposé. He valued the opportunity to meet Deloria; although, "I still don't believe that you're so important that I should spend time fighting with you." Apparently, Deloria did not become formally connected with IFCO, but Deloria, Walker, and Marilyn Clement, who was primarily responsible for the organization's relations with Native Americans, did meet and share ideas.[20]

This exchange signaled that a coalition between African American and Native American activists could prove bumpy. Deloria's hesitations about IFCO seemingly derived more from doubts about church-based paternalism than race. Other invitees to the task force meetings, however, expressed concerns about allying with black people. In the May 1969 American-Indian Task Force meeting, one participant admitted to his colleagues, "I know a lot of people that I've talked to don't particularly care to be associated with Negro people." Another expressed concern about IFCO's support of black power. "I don't think we want to march. We don't really want to be like black power." A Mrs. Warren concurred that most Indians did not support demonstrations such as the fish-ins in Washington state, because they did not believe such demonstrations were "Indian." Consequently the activists "have had to get hippies and anybody they could." Nevertheless, she admitted, it had "taken a great deal of guts and determination for these people [demonstrators] to keep fighting."[21]

The task force group, then, confronted Walker with their concerns about joining IFCO. Among them: "Would we be jeopardizing our very precious Indian image?" and "Do we want to be associated with Negro people?" "Are we going to be caught between a white funding agency—and a Black funding agency?" Walker responded that IFCO truly wanted to become representative of all people engaged in community development, including Indians, Puerto Ricans, Chicanos (a term he had to define for the group), blacks, and poor whites. To reach Indian communities, IFCO knew they needed Indian participation, particularly in getting the word out about IFCO's existence and helping IFCO evaluate proposals. Walker admitted that some invitees to the task force had declined attending, saying Indians did not like blacks or there was nothing IFCO could do for Indians. If task force members agreed, then he needed to know that. "Perhaps there's so much anti-Black feeling that Indians just don't want to be related to IFCO." Nor did he deny that some IFCO-funded projects were radical. "You know, that's our bias. There aren't that many good radical action projects in the country, however . . . we are not exclusively funding radical action projects." Their primary goals remained organizing the minority poor, encouraging them to speak for themselves, and taking action as they wished. Walker told the task force members:

> It's not a black thing. It's not an Indian thing, it's a white thing that keeps us apart. We learn how to hate from them. And we perpetuate that hate at our mutual disadvantage . . . We need to find some way to cut into that . . . You've got to have that [racial pride and consciousness] to stand up against the man in order to be a man in today's world . . . So that's where we are. We need to be very clear on that and if that's too hard, too way out for Indians to buy there shouldn't be any strain but you should make a decision that you're not ready to go that way yet.[22]

It surprised him to hear some Indians say they had not been treated unfairly, yet it was not his place to speak for Indians. Maybe Indians did not want to march or demonstrate. Maybe they did not want to use rough language or push too hard. "That's okay," he told them. "But we need to know what is important in the Indian community so we know what to plan."[23] In the end, the task force members voted to encourage Indian involvement with IFCO, naming Mel Thom and Al Elgin as task force representatives to the IFCO board and another six people to serve as an advisory committee. They urged IFCO to hire American Indians as staff members and reserved the right to determine their own "unique and indigenous methods in affecting social change in American Indian Affairs."[24] In the years to follow, AIM, in particular, received a number of grants from IFCO.

Meanwhile, other non-Indian sympathizers scrambled to keep up with and provide material support at new takeover hotspots. Often the episodes ended before such support could be mobilized. At the vanguard was, once again, the left-leaning underground press. Just days after federal marshals removed the last of the Alcatraz occupiers in June 1971, the *Berkeley Tribe* announced the takeover of an abandoned Nike Missile Base near Tilden Park, California. "The move was brilliant, instantaneous, catching the pigs completely off-guard," the paper crowed. It was "a great victory for the people." When the convoy of nine cars arrived at the base, in the wee hours of the morning, the armed security guards laughed at the Indians' intentions, not taking the threat seriously. Nevertheless, the property soon became "liberated territory." Photographed next to a sign that read "Alcatraz Still Lives On," Alcatraz occupation veteran John Trudell urged readers to donate bedding, water containers, water, food, flashlights, radios, tools, sledgehammers, first aid supplies, and can openers. He also encouraged people to organize demonstrations as a show of support. But before help could be marshaled, army police regained control of the Nike base and, with the help of Richmond and Contra Costa County officials, removed the occupiers. According to the *Berkeley Tribe* reporter, the army "invasion" began at four a.m. when their trucks crossed the Richmond Bridge and headed for the base. By eight a.m. the occupiers had been removed. Officials arrested twenty and released them by 11:30 a.m. "The Indians have been attacked by the government twice in the last two days," the paper declared. "It is up to us all to make the next move. LET'S GET TOGETHER AND GET IT ON. The struggle of the Indian is the struggle of ALL PEOPLE. ALL POWER TO THE INDIANS OF ALL TRIBES!"[25]

Other occupations proved more successful, and non-Indian support moved beyond sympathetic media coverage in the underground press and short-term material support from leftist sympathizers to friendly mainstream coverage and, remarkably, government acquiescence to activists' demands for property. While the Alcatraz occupation failed to acquire real estate for Indian purposes, several other actions led to land transfers for a pan-Indian university, in one place, and an Indian cultural center, in another. Both of these goals were among the stated intentions of the Alcatraz occupation. That they failed in San Francisco Bay but were realized elsewhere is seldom remembered.

One of these cases began on November 3, 1970, when eighty Indians occupied an abandoned Strategic Air Command military base near Davis, California. The group eventually secured it as an Indian-run college called Deganawida-Quetzalcoatl University. The genesis of this idea actually preceded the Alcatraz action. University of California, Davis professor Jack Forbes, who was Powhatan and Lenape, knew the 640-acre facility was to become surplus property. Since the early 1960s, Forbes and founders of the American Indian College Committee had been developing proposals for an indigenous university, with input from other Indian people. Alcatraz, Forbes believed, was not an appropriate site for a college given that it was damp, inaccessible, and lacked suitable buildings. The Davis site, on the other hand, offered usable structures, good agricultural land, and views of sacred Pupunia (Mount Diablo), Maidu Buttes (Three Peaks), and the Sierras to the east. Thus, he and others organized a board of trustees for D-Q University, followed federal procedures, and applied for the property. The federal government, however, awarded the land to the University of California, Davis, instead.

In response, UC Davis Indian students and some Alcatraz veterans climbed the property fence and began a peaceful occupation, with Chicano students and people from Alcatraz providing logistical support. The university's name reflected the Native American-Chicano partnership (Deganawida was an Iroquois or Six Nations prophet and leader; Quetzalcoatl, an Aztec), and the founders planned to inaugurate both Native American and Chicano studies programs as part of the curriculum. The *Berkeley Tribe* explained to its readers, "a strong sense of unity [exists between Native Americans and] Chicano people who the Indians view as being primarily Indian culturally and racially." Not only Chicano students but also Asian students, farmworkers, and Indian prisoners at Vacaville prison lent support to the occupation. The latter donated $123 to the "defense fund, which is a lot of money at prison wages." Between the occupation of the site and obtaining an injunction to prevent UC Davis from seeking control, advocates of D-Q University ultimately prevailed, and the trustees received the deed to the site in April 1971. The project quickly received funding from the Ford Foundation and federal grants, and classes began that July. The White House hoped D-Q University would satisfy the Alcatraz occupiers' demand for an Indian university. It continued to operate for nearly thirty-five years.[26]

The other remarkable West Coast victory occurred in Seattle. Although the episode has garnered little attention, the takeover of Fort Lawton resulted in a clear-cut victory for its occupiers. While the United Indians of All Tribes did not receive title to the disputed property, they obtained a ninety-nine-year lease to part of the abandoned military post, renewable for two more hundred-year terms and rented at one dollar per year. The Indian group created the Daybreak Star Center within Seattle's Discovery Park, which still operates. In this case, the surplus federal land at stake was an abandoned army post located within Seattle city limits, part of it adjacent to the residential Magnolia neighborhood, part of it ending in a bluff overlooking Puget Sound. Washington senator Henry "Scoop" Jackson had sponsored a bill in the Senate to sell surplus federal lands at low cost to cities for public parks, including the fort property to Seattle. Indians in the city, inspired by the Alcatraz occupation, had a different idea. They wanted a portion of the 1,100-acre Fort Lawton (named for an army officer who fought in the Indian Wars, captured Geronimo in Mexico, and died in the Spanish-American War) set aside for an Indian and Alaska native cultural center, an ecology center, and maybe a restaurant.

On March 8, 1970, carrying sandwiches, potato chips, sleeping bags, and cooking utensils, between seventy and one hundred Native Americans "invaded" the site. Some climbed the bluff, others scaled fences, and still others attempted to breach two heavily guarded gates. A group of about thirty managed to erect a tipi on the military grounds and began setting up camp before the 392nd Military Police Company, armed with riot gear, rounded them up and carted them away. Bob Satiacum, the Puyallup man who had many years' experience with fish-ins, attempted to read a proclamation of the occupiers' intentions, a variation of the Alcatraz manifesto that emphasized how much like an Indian reservation the abandoned prison appeared. In this case, Satiacum noted, "this place does *not* [my emphasis] resemble most Indian reservations. It has potential for modern facilities, adequate sanitation facilities, health care facilities, fresh running water, educational facilities, fisheries research facilities and transportation facilities." But military police bullhorns drowned out his message. Meanwhile, throughout the grounds, army MPs and Indians "acted out a Keystone Kop comedy" as the police chased occupiers here and there. Reporters followed the demonstrators, most of who went peacefully to jail. While the scene was chaotic and children were crying, observers witnessed little violence against the Indians—a claim some Indian participants later disputed. Of particular interest to the journalists was Grace Thorpe, Sac and Fox daughter of Olympic athlete Jim Thorpe, who had come from Alcatraz to lend a helping hand.[27]

Perhaps conditioned by earlier fish-in celebrity sightings, the mainstream journalists paid particular attention to actress Jane Fonda's brief appearance and expulsion from Fort Lawton. She was in the Seattle area to speak with soldiers at Fort Lewis about her opposition to the war in Vietnam. The army expelled Fonda from that fort, as well. Noting that Bob Hope could "come onto a base and glamorize war and make it funny," she thought it noteworthy that someone who wanted to "speak out of concern for the G.I.s—their opposition to the war and their fight for democratic rights—is banned." In a standing-room-only news conference, Fonda explained that she had not been invited to Seattle to participate in the Indians' demonstration. She simply went to Fort Lawton on hearing about the action and intended to be "an observer," assuming that her presence "might decrease the likelihood of brutality against the Indians." Surrounding her at the table sat a cluster of young Indian men including Bernie Whitebear, son of a Colville Confederated Tribe mother and Filipino father, and Sid Mills, a Yakima currently living at Frank's Landing. They wore slings on their arms, nursing injuries they received while incarcerated. Whitebear had spent his early years on the Colville Reservation, attended the University of Washington, served in the United States Army (reportedly as a Green Beret), and began organizing events to make Native Americans more visible in Seattle as early as 1961. He spent some time at Alcatraz during that occupation and returned to Seattle willing to employ similar tactics there. Whitebear emerged as the primary leader of the Fort Lawton takeover.[28]

Elsewhere that day ninety people, about half of who were Indian and half non-Indian, picketed the U.S. courthouse before moving to Fort Lawton where they demonstrated outside the gate carrying signs such as "Custer wore Arrow shirts," "Custer had it coming," and "Custer died for your sins" (see figure 5.1). Satiacum believed the demonstrations would be productive. "I think we have many friends—non-Indian friends—who support us." When a spokesman for the radical Seattle Liberation Front offered assistance, however, Bernie Whitebear told him they could provide food and financial help, but the Indians did not need "physical support." The Seattle Liberation Front would have to remain mostly out of sight. The demonstrations were "almost festive," and reporters favorably contrasted the Indians in native garb to "beefy MPs." Moreover, word reached beyond Seattle. "You can't imagine how fascinating this kind of story is in Europe," a representative from an Italian news agency told the *Seattle Times*. A *London Daily Express* reporter, however, seemed more interested in Fonda than the Indians, describing her as "new at this protest thing. Sort of like a third-rate Vanessa Redgrave." Occupier and Colville Tribe member Randy Lewis, however, later concluded that Fonda's presence guaranteed them important press coverage. "She broadcast that face and that Barbarella body," he later recalled, "which granted the [public relations] foothold occupiers needed." Enough information regarding the demonstrators' cause reached the outside that, by March 12, Bernie Whitebear enthused about the tremendous support and money pouring in from all over the nation. The United Indians of all Tribes deposited the funds in an account at Seattle First National Bank.[29]

Figure 5.1 Although not as well known as the Alcatraz occupation, the 1970 demonstrations at Fort Lawton, Seattle, proved more effective in some ways. The city of Seattle agreed to lease sixteen acres of Discovery Park (which Fort Lawton became on federal evacuation) to the Indians of All Tribes. An Indian cultural center remains there to this day. Credit: Museum of History & Industry, Seattle, Washington.

On March 15 a second "invasion" of Fort Lawton took place. The intention this time was to let President Richard Nixon know they were serious about the demand for land and wanted him to appoint a representative to negotiate. Bernie Whitebear led seventy-seven men, women, and children onto the military reservation. Post commander Colonel Stuart Palos ordered the military to arrest them, and once they were in the stockade, fed them noodle soup and bologna sandwiches before releasing them. Fifty-two men, twenty-four women, and one fifteen-year-old boy were "processed" (their names and fingerprints taken). This time they lodged no charges of brutality, and a representative from the Seattle Human Rights Commission observed the proceedings, as well. Jane Fonda briefly visited the Indians picketing outside Fort Lawton's gates and also made an appearance at the next day's demonstration at the U.S. courthouse where sixteen of the detainees faced arraignment. Fonda told reporters her presence was probably not helping her career, particularly among conservative people in Hollywood, but the Indians' cause was just and worth the professional risk.

Among those brought before the court were fish-in veterans such as Alison and Valerie Bridges, Robert Satiacum, and Sid Mills, as well as Grace Thorpe, Bernie Whitebear, and Leonard Peltier, an Ojibwa-Cree, who would later become well known among leftist Indian sympathizers when the federal government charged and convicted him of murdering an FBI agent on the Pine Ridge Reservation. The only negative notes: two dozen residents of the Fort Lawton neighborhood signed a petition demanding "some action be taken to stop the noise and stupid acts that occur." And the Seattle Park Board went on record as wanting complete control of the surplus property, something they had been working on for six years. They resented the fact that only now were Indians stepping up and risking the entire project. One board member noted the fort could only provide about four hundred acres of parkland. Meanwhile, Indians had millions of acres of reservation land where they could develop cultural centers, offering the Yakima Tribes' 180-square-mile reservation as one example.[30]

Once again, several Northwest tribal leaders criticized the demonstrations and takeovers. Glen F. Galbraith, executive secretary of the Spokane Tribal Council, and Oswald C. George, chairman of the Coeur D'Alene Tribal Council, dismissed the demonstrators as mere publicity seekers. They charged the activists with destroying the "true image of the American Indian." Galbraith characterized complaints that reservation conditions were deplorable as "boring" and maintained that the Spokane Reservation had law, order, educational facilities, sanitation, and health clinics. George acknowledged the activists *were* Indians, but they did not represent their tribes. Neither Satiacum's Puyallup Tribal Council nor the Small Tribes Organization of Western Washington endorsed the Fort Lawton demonstration. An officer of the Northwest Indian Economic Development Association assured Senator Jackson that group supported his position on Fort Lawton. Moreover, Bernie Whitebear did not represent them or any major urban Indian organizations in King County. "We take a dim view of his conduct and attitude on the matter," he wrote, "and we do not condone his actions as well as the over militant and activist attitudes of restless and self-appointed leaders." The Northwest Affiliated Tribes organization, the governor's Indian Advisory Committee for the state, and the National Congress of American Indians headed by Makah Bruce Wilkie of Neah Bay, Washington, all remained silent about the Seattle events. The Seattle Indian Center did not participate and the action alienated the American Indian Women's Service League. Only two local, urban Indian organizations, Kinatechitapi and Northwest Indians, Inc., lent food, office space, telephones, and transportation. Meanwhile the Seattle Liberation Front and the Black Panthers continued to offer support and "clout"—something Whitebear again resisted, stating, "We have been able to control the real firebloods among us but if the city is forcing us into a confrontation the city will be the loser."[31] Perhaps he had noticed such alliances did not particularly endear fish-ins activists to the general public or other Indian people. Yet the threat to mobilize them could prove useful.

For the most part, though, Whitebear and others wanted to use a lighter touch (see figure 5.2). They believed such tactics were more likely to encourage

Figure 5.2 Bernie Whitebear, of the Colville Confederated Tribe, emerged as an effective leader of the Fort Lawton occupations. Credit: Museum of History & Industry, Seattle, Washington.

support and promote education. Outside Fort Lawton's gates Indian and non-Indian supporters assembled a vigil and remained for three weeks. The group became known as Resurrection City, a reference to the 1968 Poor People's march and encampment in Washington, D.C. Among their more playful planned activities, the United Indians of All Tribes engaged a retired Lakota ranch hand and rodeo rider named Frank White Buffalo, purported grandson of Sitting Bull, to conduct a ceremony. He smoked a buffalo horn pipe, dusted the ground with an eagle feather, spoke in Lakota, and lifted his arms skyward. Within twenty minutes the words "A New Day" and "Fort, Give up. . . . Fort, Surrender" appeared overhead, courtesy of skywriter Art Bell of Bell Air Service. When asked if the whole event wasn't just a bit hokey, White Buffalo agreed it was. Colonel Palos then invited White Buffalo into the fort and the latter gave the army commander an honorary title, Kangee-Saihe, or Crow Foot. Yet, such stunts kept the reporters coming, and they published Whitebear's messages about Seattle Indians' unemployment rates (37 percent compared with non-Indians' 7 percent); average life span (sixty-four years for white Americans, forty-four for Indians); homicide and suicides rates among Indians (triple the national rates); and illiteracy rates (seventy-five thousand Indians were functionally illiterate); as well as explanations of how the Indians would use the land if ceded to them.[32]

By the end of March, the United Indians of All Tribes decided to take down Resurrection City's tipis. About fifty people rushed past the guards for a final "takeover." But the leadership agreed to pursue legal channels to secure the property, and thus tactics shifted from direct action to negotiation. They elected a seven-member council, which Whitebear chaired, and met with the Economic Development Administration (EDA) that had an Indian desk and enjoyed greater credibility among Native Americans than other federal agencies, such as the Bureau of Indian Affairs. The two groups discussed petitioning the General Services Administration (GSA), which gave federal agencies thirty days after land became surplus to file for use of the land. They thought the land could possibly be put in trust status under the EDA. Fort Lawton's Colonel Palos was among those supporters who thought such a plan "legitimate." A delegation to Washington, D.C., also testified before a hearing of a House Interior subcommittee considering bills related to the disposal of surplus federal lands. The congressmen sympathized with Indians but did not seem particularly convinced that giving them surplus lands would solve their problems.[33]

Meanwhile, Senator Jackson urged the House to act rapidly on his bill allowing sale of surplus lands to cities for parks. He had already fended off efforts to construct an anti-ballistic missile base at Fort Lawton and saw his bill as a way to cement his own conservation bona fides. The Sierra Club, Federation of Western Outdoor Clubs, Washington Alpine Club, Audubon Society, Isaak Walton League, Seattle Junior League, and League of Women Voters counted themselves among Jackson's most vocal supporters of this legislation. Although several constituents feared the park would end up harboring hippies and fostering crime, Jackson's mail overwhelmingly supported his park plan—*until* the Indian takeover. And then the tide turned, not against the park but toward incorporating Native American interests and demands into the final plans. "Why not give the Indians a portion of Ft. Lawton," one correspondent self-identified as Grandma wrote, "and *without* a big hassle." F. P. Hartnett agreed: "We should give them back Ft. Lawton & for once do a just & right thing. . . . Just about everyone in Seattle agrees with me." Another correspondent nodded to the Alcatraz takeover which she thought was "simply wonderful," adding "Everyone talks about [the] black minority—their troubles. What about the American? We acquired lands from them but what have the blacks given? They only ask. The Indians are the true America and to say the least they have been treated most shabbily." Jackson remained reluctant to take up the Indians' cause.[34]

In the face of the senator's resistance, the United Indians of All Tribes delegation appealed to Commissioner of Indian Affairs Louis Bruce, to support their plan for an "urban Indian endeavor." In 1970, they claimed, the only government-supported Indian program in the city, a local Office of Economic Opportunity-CAP project, had a budget of about twenty-seven thousand dollars. Meanwhile, Seattle budgeted over fifty thousand dollars in retainer fees alone for a park-development consultant to help them with plans for Fort

Lawton. Clearly priorities were askew. Intervention from the BIA could make all the difference. Bruce responded by temporarily placing a hold on Fort Lawton lands but the Interior Department quickly put a stop to that, most likely under political pressure from Senator Jackson and Seattle Mayor Wes Uhlman. Uhlman informed Indian department officials that the people of Seattle would be outraged if the BIA intervened and stopped the park. A little over one week later Assistant Secretary of the Interior Harrison Loesch assured Jackson the BIA had no intention of requesting the property.[35]

In the end, the General Services Administration granted the property to the city of Seattle, transforming the problem, overnight, from a federal dilemma to a municipal one. Seattle, however, proved amenable to working with the United Indians of All Tribes. Perhaps the overwhelming number of letters supporting the Indian activists' demands encouraged such an outcome. From the city's point of view, setting aside some of the property for an Indian cultural center was fine as long as it remained open to the public. As Mayor Uhlman later explained, "We just felt it was the right thing to do." The takeover had dramatized UIAT's desire to be involved, and he agreed they had every right to participate. As the youngest person ever elected to the mayor's office, Uhlman supported civil rights, protected the Seattle Black Panthers from an FBI raid, and declared a César Chávez Day and Gay Pride Week during his two terms in office. A willingness to work with UIAT fit the pattern. Even before the property changed hands, the mayor's office began talking to Whitebear and others about an Indian cultural center in the park. A public hearing revealed tremendous support for the idea. According to Whitebear, forty non-Indian community organizations backed it. "It was all rhetoric until then," he acknowledged. "Now we showed some muscle." Letters from constituents to Jackson and Uhlman continued to pour in supporting Indian demands. And perhaps most important, the UIAT applied for, and received, a grant for the center from the federal Health, Education and Welfare Department.[36]

Finally in November 1971, Seattle Mayor Wes Uhlman, Senator Jackson, and Bernie Whitebear announced the terms of the new agreement. The nonprofit United Indians of All Tribes Foundation received a lease to sixteen acres of parkland, at the cost of one dollar per year. The lease could be renewed for up to 297 years. The city also provided funds for a Native American social-services center, located elsewhere and operated under contract by the American Indians Women's Service League. The only matter of continued dispute was what to call the new agreement. Whitebear insisted on "treaty." Senator Jackson labeled it an "agreement," and Deputy Mayor John Chambers called it "a sort of hybrid treaty." Whitebear came around, admitting, "The white man doesn't keep treaties. It's a legal, binding agreement." Whatever its appellation, the moment surely represented a significant victory. The *Seattle Post-Intelligencer* editorialized that both sides acted wisely and responsibly. In particular, Whitebear, "a latter day Metternich," showed great restraint, the paper claimed, in refusing Black Panther and SDS support, which would have "polarized beyond redemption" the issue. The photograph that accompanied the *Seattle Times* story about the agreement showed a relaxed, happy crowd standing behind Jackson, Whitebear, and Uhlman at the public announcement.[37]

Five months after the rather ignominious end of the Alcatraz occupation, the Seattle demonstrators could claim a remarkable victory. True, they did not receive all 1,100 acres of Fort Lawton surplus lands, and their tactics and methods caused divisions within Washington's and Seattle's Indian populations, generally along generational lines. But something tangible—land and a cultural center—came of it. How do we explain their success? Their techniques included: demonstrate to attract attention, but stop when it appears publicity might turn negative. Avoid violence, if possible. Keep more radical allies at arms' length, but welcome support behind the scenes, as well as from celebrities. Continue to negotiate with authorities. Be willing to accept a compromise that honors the original intention, even if it is not total victory. The United Indians of All Tribes had two more factors working in their favor. They operated in an urban environment, where they could count on not only a relatively favorable press but also a generally favorable sympathetic, liberal public. As Bernie Whitebear's brother Lawney Reyes put it, "We had a lot of white, Asian, black and Mexican support."[38] Finally, they also demanded public lands deemed "surplus" and thus available.

Activists who demonstrated in rural areas and who challenged the federal government's and/or corporations' use of federal lands that were not deemed "surplus" faced a much more difficult climate and challenge. The odds, in fact, proved overwhelmingly against them.[39] The Pit River Indians' efforts to regain property in northern California demonstrated the tremendous difficulties tribes continued to face. Their failure underscored the amazing success at Fort Lawton. It also revealed there were limits to the value of direct action and the reach of non-Indian support. The episode began when some tribal members refused an Indian Claims Commission (ICC) settlement for lands taken illegally in the 1850s. Led by Chief Ray Johnson, they turned down their share of $29.1 million in claims money, which the ICC awarded in 1964, and continued to demand the return of 3.5 million acres that overlapped parts of Shasta, Lassen, and Modoc counties. The Pit River Tribe made little headway, however, and in June 1970, inspired by the direct protests sprouting up across the country, tribal Chairman Mickey Gimmell and about two hundred Indians decided to occupy Mount Lassen National Park. When armed federal marshals met the demonstrators at park gates, they avoided confrontation and moved to a Pacific Gas and Electric (PG&E) camp about eighty miles away. Richard Oakes joined the action as did other Alcatraz veterans and about thirty members of the counterculture group the Hog Farm. This time the contested territory was not "surplus property." Much of it was not even federal land. Major corporations including PG&E, Southern Pacific Railroad, Pacific Telephone and Telegraph, Hearst Publications, United Fruit Growers, U.S. Plywood, and Publishers Forest Products (a subsidiary of the *Los Angeles Times*) owned it—a veritable who's who of California's major economic and political powers. Moreover, the fifteen directors who sat on PG&E's board included the chair of Levi Strauss Company; the vice president of Stanford Research Institute; and the president of the Bank of California, who also sat on the boards of Shell Oil Company, Safeway Stores, and Western Union. If ever there was an American David and Goliath story, the Pit River Tribes' claim on Northern California was it. This was not simply Indians versus the federal government. It was Indians versus American corporate power.[40]

That, of course, made the confrontation even more exciting for Berkeley-based radicals and reporters at the *Berkeley Tribe*. The *San Francisco Chronicle* also covered the story, acknowledging that the property was the original home of the Pit River Indians "from whom the Government has conceded the land was stolen in 1853." Unlike Alcatraz, in fact, the paper noted *this* land claim hinged upon legitimate rights, as determined by the 1959 Indian Claims Commission decision. The problem was the government refused to return the property and insisted that the tribe had agreed to relinquish all rights to it in exchange for a portion of the million-dollar settlement (which came out to a payment of about forty-five cents an acre).

When the demonstrators first arrived at the entrance to Lassen Volcanic National Park, the park superintendent sympathized, telling Gimmell—who had announced the land belonged to his tribe—"you are a luckless people." He did not, however, intend to let them into the park; and after a tense standoff with the helmeted, armed marshals, the occupiers settled in at the PG&E camp. The site included cabins with refrigerators, stoves, and three or four bedrooms; a swimming pool; running water; and indoor plumbing. The Pit Rivers and their allies started a bonfire in the meadow, drummed, and sang. Gimmell read a proclamation that denounced the termination policy, refused the ICC settlement, demanded the return of all government and corporate lands ("with the exception of that 'owned' by private individuals"), along with all the profits they made on the resources since 1853. He also insisted on reparations for all California Indians who had died, suffered, or experienced poverty over the last century and called on the government and corporations to repair the damage they had done to the land.

In addition, Gimmell's statement called for Indian religious and cultural freedom, the institution of Indian studies programs across the nation, and instruction in schools about "the true story of the Indians." One tribal councilman then told the assemblage, "Don't feel you're a stranger here. This is your land. This is my land. This is Indian country. My ancestors lived here ... Feel welcome. Let your spirit be free!" The *San Francisco Chronicle* reporter contrasted the scene with "bleak Alcatraz where the sordid recent past hung like a ghost in the fog. The mood in the still warm pre-dawn hours in the wild unsullied country of Shasta County was one that brought back memories of the Pit River people's ancestors at harmony with their home." Finally, at around 4:30 a.m. the occupiers went to sleep.[41]

The next morning they enjoyed the camp amenities, including swimming in the pool and catching trout in the nearby stream. The idyll, of course, could not last. Responding to a PG&E request for help, on June 7, 1970, sheriffs, marshals, highway patrolmen, and, reportedly, FBI detectives arrived at the camp and "linked up in a campus-unrest cordon, their long riot clubs poised. It was the rustic and the urban facing each other." But the arrests commenced peacefully, with only Grace Thorpe resisting arrest by going limp and requiring four men to carry her away. Wavy Gravy and about thirty Hog Farm members were also there, having come up after hearing Richard Oakes speak about the Pit River situation in the Bay Area. They responded to Oakes's call "for back-up from friendly freaks or anyone else who wanted to help." Although the occupation would be conducted solely by Indian people, the "mostly white middle class madmen" of the Hog Farm intended to provide necessary background support—the sort of thing other non-Indians had offered at Frank's Landing and Fort Lawton. When they arrived, the Hog Farmers met a mixed reaction from the Indian activists—some wanted them to leave, others encouraged them to stay. But the Hog Farm and its bus, called Asp, accompanied the caravan to Lassen National Volcanic Park and on to the PG&E grounds. When the Hog Farmers started cavorting in the nude in a nearby waterfall some of the Indian women became upset. But Wavy Gravy and the rest understood the problem and thereafter refrained from further objectionable behavior. "We were guests on their turf and must go by the rules of the ground. Right on, grandmother earth!"[42]

When the law enforcement officers arrived, however, they arrested only the Indians and several European filmmakers. "Freaks were weirdly ignored," according to Wavy Gravy, so he and the other hippies collected the children, put them into the Hog Farm bus, and kept them fed and cared for until authorities released their parents from jail. Between their own supplies and venison provided by some Native Americans, the hippies prepared "hot dinner delivered in moonbeams." That night the occupiers and their Anglo allies gathered around another campfire. Gimmell spoke: "It's as if the Indians have been standing amid the ashes for a long time ... Now, after many years, a flame has been kindled which continues to burn." He believed the fire was burning bright now "because for the first time we are being supported by our friends. Friends around us here tonight who are not even Indians and friends who are not even from the American continent," referring to R. Giuseppe Slater and Gloria Laskowich, who were filming a documentary about the Pit River action and who had also been arrested that day. "I believe the fire burns here tonight because these friends have helped keep it alive." Acknowledging that he spoke only for himself (and perhaps implying not all would agree with him), he turned to the Hog Farmers and said, "I welcome you all as friends . . . and as brothers." Buffy Sainte-Marie sang at the campfire, as she had earlier in the day outside the jail. Some of the men invited a Hog Farmer named Fred to join them on a deer hunt and Wavy Gravy concluded "that was the moment of breakthrough. Through the thin red line. The next morning it became official. The Hog Farm became honorary members of the Pitt [sic] River Tribe. The Pitt River Earth People tribe."[43]

Meanwhile PG&E announced that it would drop all charges against those who had trespassed at the camp. About seventy-five Pit Rivers and friends returned the next night, actively seeking arrest and a consequent day in court when they could establish the defense that they could not be trespassing on their own land. PG&E decided to prosecute the second time, and the Pit River Indians at the camp announced they would, in turn, arrest S. L. Sibley, president of PG&E, for trespassing. The Hog Farm returned to San Francisco and, in partnership with the Native American studies program at the University of California, organized a Summer Solstice fundraiser for the Pit River defendants. The Grateful Dead, the New Riders of the Purple Sage, Osceola, and a new band called Indian Puddin' and Pipe provided free entertainment. On "Summer Solstice evening," Wavy Gravy later remembered, "it seemed all San Francisco was there, movin' perfectly, flowin' like water." A light-show and a door prize (an actual decorated door) kept the crowd engaged and, in between musical acts, Pit River council members explained their grievances. Most of the proceeds went to the Pit River arrestees' defense and some went to the family of Richard Oakes, who had been badly beaten in an Oakland bar a few days before the concert. Doctors had given up hope for his recovery; but Mad Bear Anderson, a Tuscarora, came out to California from New York when he heard Oakes was hospitalized and, many believed, healed him.[44]

Non-Indian support and interest in the Pit River case remained relatively small and localized. Further, neither the Hog Farm fundraiser nor Mad Bear Anderson could, in the end, protect and defend either the Pit River Tribe or Richard Oakes. In October 1970 Pit River Indians and other Indian supporters occupied a site at the Four Corners area in Burney, California, protesting logging operations in the area. As the demonstrators began felling trees to build structures for their own use, about eighty federal officers and sheriff's deputies, carrying mace, clubs, and guns, surrounded the camp. Some of the Indian men and boys picked up sticks and pieces of lumber to defend themselves and, according to one source, "all hell broke loose." Indian occupants were clubbed, sprayed with mace, and arrested. PG&E, the federal government, other corporations, and even the workers who lost wages when Pit River actions stopped logging operations, had no intention of responding to the occupiers' demands. The Indian Claims Commission case, they argued, settled their legal (and moral) obligations once and for all. Two years later, in 1972, a caretaker at a YMCA camp in Mendocino County, California, located about one hour north of San Francisco, shot and killed Richard Oakes during an altercation over Indian boys borrowing the camp's horses without permission. A jury subsequently found Oakes's assailant innocent of involuntary manslaughter.[45]

Although activists attempted to interest media in these events, and thus elicit public sympathy, they were not nearly as successful as the Fort Lawton or Alcatraz occupiers. As months turned to years, the novelty of confrontation politics paled and public interest dropped off. Perhaps most significantly, the Nixon White House made it clear—by the end of 1972—that such tactics would no longer work. The Pit River Tribe would have to find redress either in the court system or through Congress.

San Francisco–based attorney Aubrey Grossman, who had worked as an Alcatraz lawyer and offered his service pro bono to the Pit River Tribe tried to change White House officials' minds. Encouraged by the president's 1970 message to Congress confirming self-determination and other reforms, as well as the return of Blue Lake to the Taos Pueblo and some land to the Yakima Tribe, Grossman hoped President Nixon might consider a Presidential Proclamation in favor of Pit River claims or use his power to transform the Indian Claims Commission award from cash to land. In a series of lengthy letters and telegrams from tribal leaders as well as Grossman, the Pit River Tribe laid out their case and concerns, making an appeal based on Nixon's new policy initiative. "Some in the Tribe were skeptical and cynical about your Message. However, you were so direct and strong in your criticism of what has been done that they felt you were saying that you would do something, however small, to correct [past injustices]," Grossman wrote. Blending compliments on the president's basic policy stance with implied threats to Nixon's reputation should he fail to respond to their pleas for help, the tribal chairman warned the president that he would ultimately be judged on what he did, rather than what he said. There were men in his administration who were threatening to kill the Pit River people and if they did so blood would be on Nixon's hands. "We know you would not like history to record that the first Indian massacre in almost 100 years took place in your administration and when the Indians were simply doing what unions do thousands of times every year." The tribe intended to do everything possible to protect its members from a massacre and believed that media exposure of the current threats would protect them. Meanwhile, the important first step for President Nixon to take would be direct communication with the tribe. "If you can go to China to talk to Mao Tse Tung why cannot someone of importance in your administration talk to us?"[46]

Actually, the White House's Bradley Patterson had been in touch with Ross Montgomery, chief of the Pit River Tribe. He also talked with Forest Service people. But Patterson was not sympathetic to the Pit River case, claiming its leaders were "well known as confrontationists." In early December 1972, he told Montgomery the tribe would have to get the issue into a court of law. "I went further," Patterson reported to fellow White House staffer Leonard Garment, "and told Montgomery that there wasn't an official in the city of Washington who wasn't damn sick and tired of Indian confrontation tactics by this point, and there was absolutely no sympathy for his cause if he handled it that way." Patterson told the same thing to attorney Grossman "in stronger language" and believed the lawyer had gotten the message. The Pit River Tribe's only hope was either through the courts or through Congress. Garment then followed up with a letter to Grossman reinforcing the White House impatience with takeovers and occupations, noting that only recently they had witnessed first-hand the "folly" of such an approach in Washington, D.C., with the Trail of Broken Treaties events. "Confrontation, threats and worse will only turn the nation's sympathies away from helping to meet the needs of Indian people, and I say this to you," Garment cautioned, "as a member of an Administration which has taken the lead to meet these needs through both administrative and legislative proposals."[47]

Grossman and the Pit River Tribe, who had been fighting for nearly a decade, were not easily dissuaded. In lengthy letters to the White House, Grossman continued to recount the history of the Pit River Tribe's case, believing that no one in the federal government truly understood it. They wanted to reopen the claims case, but when they tried to file a legal case, the Department of Justice would not to allow it. The only way they could ever get their foot into a courtroom, Grossman believed and advised the tribe, was through so-called confrontation politics. Only by breaking laws would they then have access to juries who would decide in their favor. That outcome would be "of great public relations significance" even though it would not actually return the land to them.

Grossman held out hope the Nixon White House would open negotiations with the tribe, making legal action unnecessary, and providing them with a land base of, say, 10,000 acres (of the 3,500,000 stolen from them in the nineteenth century). There *was* a great deal of white support for the tribe, the lawyer insisted. Plus the overwhelming moral right was on their side. The Tribal Council deserved, at the very least, an opportunity to speak with the president as he had with the leaders of Taos Pueblo.[48]

The White House did not budge, taking the position that in the absence of action from Congress, there was nothing the executive branch could do.[49]

Unfortunately the Pit Rivers had neither Taos Pueblo's decades-long experience of lobbying Congress nor, Grossman's claims notwithstanding, Taos' significant non-Indian support behind their demand for Blue Lake. Neither the courts nor Congress held much promise for the California tribe. Although confrontation tactics were not swaying the White House, the tribe continued their on-the-ground resistance, interfering with timber sale operations a year after the Grossman-Garment correspondence had yielded no change in official policy. That, too, altered nothing.[50]

One year before, tribal Chairman Ross Montgomery told reporters, "We have found that large numbers of white people, when they hear the truth will support our struggle to get back our land." But by 1973, it had been four years since the Alcatraz takeover, and Indian occupations no longer seemed to attract the same level of attention from non-Indians. Moreover, the Pit River case was geographically remote and politically complicated. Few Americans knew about the Indian Claims Commission and even fewer probably understood the Pit River complaints about the award. Perhaps the greatest impediment the tribe had to face by 1973, however, was fallout from the Trail of Broken Treaties and the takeover of the Bureau of Indian Affairs Building in Washington, D.C., as well as the occupation at Wounded Knee on the Pine Ridge Reservation. The first set of events, which took place in November 1972, brought Indian activists into the very heart of the nation. It tested the limits of national sympathies and revealed that even large-scale devastation of government property did not necessarily discourage support. The Wounded Knee occupation, which began in February 1973, showed the federal government could, and would, turn to repressive violence to stop such actions, taking some risk, but believing the nation's patience with takeover tactics had ended. Officials were wrong. Once again significant numbers of non-Indians heard Indian activists' complaints, sympathized, and supported them.

The Trail of Broken Treaties episode revealed even the federal government's willingness to listen to and negotiate with activists had not yet been entirely spent. In fact, the White House ultimately provided amnesty and travel funds to a group of Native Americans who did enormous damage to the BIA Building and stole literally tons of documents from it. However justified the latter may have felt regarding these actions, there is no denying that vandalism and theft of federal property of this order would not be treated so lightly today. Yet, in the climate of the early 1970s, after a decade of demonstrations marked by violence such as those (most recently) at Kent State University and Attica prison, the occupation attracted relatively little negative attention. Nixon's advisors believed the president had more to lose by using violence against the protestors than by negotiating. Further, media coverage was not highly critical of the BIA Building occupation, and the White House continued to receive letters and telegrams supportive of the Indians throughout the ordeal. To be sure, some (including tribal leaders) criticized the White House's handling of the affair for its leniency, but for the most part the public remained sympathetic to Indians and their demands for change. Importantly, the Nixon administration did not use the occupation and its aftermath as an occasion to reconsider its fundamental commitment to the principles of self-determination, treaty rights, renewed tribalism, and other reforms.

The Trail of Broken Treaties had its genesis in August 1972 at the Rosebud Sioux Reservation fair. Robert Burnette, former tribal chairman of the Rosebud Sioux, and the American Indian Movement's Dennis Banks hatched the plan for an Indian march on Washington, something along the lines of the 1963 march on Washington or the Poor People's march of 1968. It would take place in the days leading up to the presidential election; timing that proved less than fortuitous because President Richard Nixon was out of town campaigning and the nation was preoccupied. Nevertheless, the expectation was this pan-Indian march would catapult AIM into national prominence and generate greater public attention than their earlier, small-scale demonstrations. Other organizations participated in the plans, including the Survival of American Indians Association (SAIS). The plan might not have gone beyond the conceptual phase, however, had Richard Oakes's murder in California not enraged West Coast Indian activists. That event, on September 21, 1972, provided the necessary spark for the cross-continental demonstration.

Disparate Indian groups, with AIM clearly dominating, met in Denver in late September to strategize and finalize plans. From Frank's Landing, Hank Adams issued a Survival of American Indians Association statement about the Trail of Broken Treaties, articulating its purpose: "To seek common understanding may seem trite—but to establish a meaning for the unbroken chronicle of broken treaties, and unbreached [sic] infamy visited upon Indian people by unquestioning majorities of White America, taxes all abilities for rational understanding... Therefore, we begin our respective journeys with a question... 'Why, America???'; and propose to return with answers of what must be done by ourselves and all others... in order that our children might be ensured their future." Adams made clear they would rely on news media to explain their purpose and progress, and depend upon support from Christian churches at both the national and state levels. It remained to be seen if local churches and denominational laities would provide help along the way. Paradoxically, he noted, official tribal leaders denounced them even though many tribal members sympathized and supported the caravans. The Ecumenical Metropolitan Ministry (E.M.M.) of Seattle issued an Information Sheet asking churches to coordinate support for the caravan as it moved through their areas. Among the things they could offer: food, gasoline money, emergency medical care, places to sleep, and church visibility at press conferences. The E.M.M. would also serve as a communications and resource base for the caravans, collecting money from donors and passing it along to the Indians. Among the gifts they forwarded to the Trail of Broken Treaties caravan was a five thousand dollar contribution from the National Committee on Indian Work of the Protestant Episcopal Church. This money came in response to a SAIS proposal for funds to collect data about Indians, provide information to Indian communities that emerged from the caravan, "keep the caravan rolling," and draft new legislation.[51]

In October 1972, three strands of caravans began their cross-continental trek to the nation's capitol. AIM co-founder Russell Means took charge of the group from Seattle, Dennis Banks the San Francisco group, and George Martin the Los Angeles group. Each traveled east along a circuitous route through reservation communities, where they gathered new recruits and also new critics. Younger Indians were particularly excited by the caravans. Tribal leaders often did not share their enthusiasm. According to Ted Rising Sun, a Northern Cheyenne, when they came to Busby, Montana, and attended a Cheyenne dance, "They didn't mix well because they didn't know any Indian songs, they didn't know the dances, they didn't know any Cheyenne. They were rather frightening to some of the people here. I tried to point out they were scaring people . . . They were more of a disturbance than anything. People told them to leave." But if the activists alienated many of the older Cheyenne people, they excited many of the younger ones, who literally leaped out of their school's windows to greet the caravan and hear its message.[52]

At first the caravans' purpose was not particularly well-defined. The leaders wanted to highlight treaty rights, educate the public about tribal self-determination, and emphasize Indian grievances. They also wanted the trip and related events to be nonviolent and cautioned all participants against drinking and drug use. They were to be on their best behavior, as they depended on Indian and non-Indian supporters to provide food, housing, and money for gasoline along the way. The American Friends Service Committee (AFSC), which had worked hard on behalf of Pacific Northwest fishing rights, was less enthusiastic about the Trail of Broken Treaties (TBT). An internal memo from the Pacific Northwest regional office to Philadelphia headquarters revealed the AFSC's involvement was minimal and the groups' Indian Committee did not particularly want to encourage the Washington march. By the time the caravan from Seattle reached Minneapolis in late October, the AFSC had learned the TBT was "beset with problems." It looked like no housing had been secured at their Washington destination and that the participants lacked money and provisions to get back home. The AFSC Middle Atlantic Region attempted to line up stand-by resources and tried to alleviate the hardships of the families involved, as did Washington, D.C., area Friends from the Florida Avenue meeting, Quaker House, William Penn House, and David House.[53]

Meanwhile as they moved across the country, TBT travelers spoke in churches where they solicited donations and places to stay along their routes. The northern-most group found considerable support from the churches in Mankato, Minnesota—site of a mass hanging of thirty-eight Sioux in 1862. Vernon Bellecourt collected about one thousand dollars worth of gas and food from Mormons in Utah, even though he was removed from one church in Salt Lake City for his aggressive style of fund-raising. Participants believed colleges, universities, and reservations were also excellent places to raise funds and enlist additional Indian recruits to the project.[54]

Once the caravans converged on St. Paul, Minnesota, on October 23, they organized workshops to further refine their purpose. Hank Adams crystallized the critical issues in a document named the Twenty Points. "I learned then that [Adams] is a genius at analyzing problems and interpreting the Indian outlook vis-à-vis the Eurocentric male worldview," Means later wrote. The Twenty Points called for a variety of things, some more politically realistic than others. Among the less realistic were demands that the treaty-making process be revived and that historic unratified treaties, such as those made in California in the 1850s, be resubmitted to Congress. Other points called for restoration of a 110-million-acre native land base, abolition of the Bureau of Indian Affairs, restoration of tribal rights to Indians who had been terminated, Indian commerce and tax immunities, and an opportunity to address a joint session of Congress and the American public. At its core was a call for recognition of treaty rights, tribal sovereignty, an enhanced land base for Indian people, and a new way of conducting Indian affairs in this country—one that placed much greater power into the hands of Indian people.[55]

According to Russell Means, the group intended to present the Twenty Points to officials in Washington along with a timetable for realizing these demands. Dennis Banks wrote a letter to President Nixon in early October, alerting him to the caravan's plans to come to Washington with one hundred thousand people and asking for a meeting. Leonard Garment, special assistant to the president, answered Banks that the president's schedule precluded such a meeting but that arrangements would be made for them to meet with an administration representative. Other planned activities included construction of tipis and sweat lodges in West Potomac Park, spiritual services at Arlington National Cemetery and the Iwo Jima Memorial (to honor Pima World War II hero Ira Hayes), and public discussions of the Twenty Points.

All plans were scrapped, however, when the several hundred Trail of Broken Treaties Indians arrived in Washington and found the only housing available for them was one church's basement. The Saint Stephens and the Incarnation Episcopal Church turned out to be too small and reportedly rat infested. Robert Burnette, charged to find housing for the caravaners, had failed to find sufficient accommodations. He blamed Assistant Secretary of the Interior Harrison Loesch, who had issued an October memo directing BIA employees to refrain from assisting trail participants. But the Trail of Broken Treaties had not requested help from the BIA, so if Loesch's memo was not helpful, it also could not be considered responsible for the breakdown in planning and preparation. Plus the National Congress of American Indians (NCAI), the largest Indian organization headquartered in Washington, shared the BIA's stance on the TBT and also declined the caravan's appeal for support. Angry and frustrated with conditions at the church, Trail leaders who had been meeting in the BIA auditorium nevertheless decided to make the BIA the scapegoat and so took over the agency's building. This was neither an abandoned prison nor a soon to be decommissioned military post but an important, active federal office building. This occupation represented an altogether different category of challenge to authorities and consequently raised the stakes considerably. Several hundred Indians barricaded themselves inside and demanded negotiations regarding the Twenty Points. Over the next five days, tensions escalated. The occupiers proceeded to trash the building and its furniture, art work, and documents. At least part of the destruction derived from reaction to a General Services Administration police force, which at one point entered the building in riot gear and ordered the occupants out. A fight broke out before the police retreated.

Miscommunication among federal officials and between Indians and officials only made matters worse. Tensions reached a fever pitch on November 6 when police prepared to enforce a court-ordered eviction while occupiers prepared to burn down the building. The seemingly ubiquitous Wavy Gravy and the Hog Farmers, who happened to be in Washington, D.C., at the time, presented a short-course to the occupiers on how to use a video camera so they could photograph the police when they stormed the building. Black power advocate Stokely Carmichael and the famous pediatrician and author Dr. Benjamin Spock visited the building and lent their moral support to the Indians. So too did local black leader Marion Berry, "raising the specter," according to White House staffer Bradley Patterson, "of the Washington black community's making common cause with the Indian occupiers" (see figure 5.3). Before any more lines could be drawn, Garment called off the police and made a final offer to negotiate. Memory of the deaths of the college students at Kent State and the political consequences of that bungle continued to hover over the White House. Everyone, including Nixon and John Erlichman, agreed on the folly of force in the TBT situation.

The occupiers chose Hank Adams to lead their negotiating team. Garment found him highly intelligent and sophisticated but "nervously tentative." In the resulting deal, the federal representatives agreed to form a task force that would review federal Indian policy, analyze and respond to the Twenty Points, and recommend against prosecution for the seizure and occupation of the BIA Building.

Figure 5.3 Indian activism drew from a wide spectrum of non-Indian support. Although most came from progressive and left-leaning groups and individuals, here evangelist and anticommunist Carl McIntire joined American Indian Movement (AIM) leader Dennis Banks at the Trail of Broken Treaties demonstration, Washington, D.C., November 1972. Credit: Corbis/Bettman.

Although not part of the formally written agreement, the federal representatives also provided $66,650 in travel funds to help the occupiers return home. This money came from the Office of Economic Opportunity's budget. By November 9 all Indian occupiers had dispersed. As the clean up began, workers found documents soaked in gasoline littering the floor. Other documents went missing: Trail participants took an estimated twelve tons of paper from the BIA, records relating to property ownership, trust accounts, and water rights. Russell Means later declared victory. "We had taken over the alleged nerve center of the BIA for seven days and had trashed it so thoroughly that it would be more than six weeks before operations could resume—and no one missed it! We had confiscated tons of documents, had been paid to leave town—and no one had been arrested. I felt the growing force of our convictions and knew that spiritual power was our greatest strength." Hank Adams, apparently, felt otherwise, "anguished at this failed attempt to push an aggressive policy agenda in a nonviolent manner . . . Indian people had attained no victory, not even a scent of it."[56]

How did these events affect the growing demand for a national reconsideration of Indian affairs? President Nixon momentarily soured on Indian issues, but his staff, particularly Brad Patterson and Leonard Garment, did not. Although Garment believed the Trail of Broken Treaties episode lost the activists support from previously sympathetic editorial writers and federal officials, he still thought progress on Nixon's comprehensive Indian reforms possible. In fact, he and others continued pursuing them, with emphasis on making self-determination meaningful, in the company of tribal leaders and more mainstream national Indian organizations—a strategy in place since 1970. They did, however, take a harder line regarding the Twenty Points and the issue of stolen documents. In their cover letter accompanying the official response to the Twenty Points, addressed to Hank Adams, Leonard Garment, and Deputy Director of the Office of Management and Budget Frank Carlucci hoped "the wanton destruction in the Bureau of Indian Affairs building and the theft of many of its contents by members of the Trail of Broken Treaties will be seen as the distracting and divisive act that it was—an act which served only to impede the progress already being achieved by the combined efforts of the Administration and the responsible Indian community." The document then went on to reject the idea of restoring the treaty-making process. Governments make treaties with foreign nations, not its own citizens. Meanwhile, ratified treaties were still in force and would be respected while national Indian organizations and tribal governments represented Indians' interests. The Indian Claims Commission existed to settle legal and moral obligations to Indians. No new commission to review treaty commitments was needed. It also rejected the call for a national federal Indian grand jury, arguing such an institution would "subdivide our American system of justice into ethnic slices, each skewed to give special attention on a racial basis." The executive branch's responsibility was to ensure the judicial system operate free of considerations of race, creed, or culture. In short, the White House refused to consider the most sweeping calls for change (such as restoration of total sovereignty and treaty making, and the return of vast lands to Indian people). It emphasized realism—the kind of constitutionally possible changes that might be made and the legislative proposals Congress was currently considering.[57]

Not surprisingly, the Trail of Broken Treaties leadership was not pleased. Hank Adams issued a press statement characterizing the White House response as "virtually devoid of positive content" and reflecting "the hostile attitude which federal agencies and officials have maintained against independent and creative Indian thought, expressions and proposals, and most Indian people— even before initiation of the TBT and occurrence of the BIA November occupation." Adams went on to claim that Brad Patterson warned him the FBI was going "to get as many of you guys as we can." Just after the end of the takeover, in fact, Patterson had cancelled a meeting with Adams and announced there would be no further discussions between the federal representatives and TBT people until they returned all records and properties removed from the BIA. They would have to work through the FBI until that time. To Adams this represented "the first betrayal of the commitments" made during the BIA occupation. Rather than help Adams return the documents, this new stance would only increase "fear and apprehension generated by random police searches or harassment and other exercises of police authority against Indian people, wholly innocent or otherwise." Adams had been working with TBT leaders across the country to return the documents, but people needed reassurance that merely knowing about their location would not be a basis for criminal prosecution. Now, it appeared to him, the government was more interested in pursuing prosecutions than receiving returned records. The White House's pledge of amnesty, he charged, was "in the pattern of deceit which this Nation followed in using amnesty and truce promises for securing the prolonged imprisonment of Sitting Bull and the deaths by execution of Osceola and Leschi, among other famous Indian leaders across this country."[58]

The White House stance revealed pressure from other quarters within the federal government to harden its stance. If Adams and AIM leaders were not particularly happy with Garment's and Carlucci's responses, they would have found other elements of the executive branch even less amenable to their goals. The Federal Bureau of Investigation was particularly hostile. The FBI had been collecting information on Hank Adams, Clyde Bellecourt, Vernon Bellecourt, Sid Mills, and Russell Means, among others, for some time. Sid Mills's file, originally classified by W. Mark Felt (the informant "Deep Throat" of the Watergate era) provides some insight into the Bureau's interests. The report listed Mills's participation in the BIA takeover, demonstrations at Fort Lawton and Fort Lewis, and fishing rights protests along the Puyallup River in August and September 1970. In spring 1969 he spoke on behalf of fishing rights at an "anti-establishment" coffee house in Tacoma, which catered to military personnel, and spoke at a teach-in in that same city protesting the court martial of the Presidio 27—soldiers charged with mutiny. Leaflets distributed at the GI-Civilian Alliance for Peace at Seattle, in February 1969, indicated Mills had served two years and four months in the army, including time in Vietnam where he was wounded. He had been confined in the Fort Lewis stockade for being AWOL and had been arrested for fishing illegally in Thurston County. More recently, Mills had joined twenty-five other people, the United States Solidarity Delegation with the Chinese People, on a thirty-five-day visit to the People's Republic of China. Other participants included James Forman, leader of the International Black Workers Congress, and students who hoped to "build unity among the Revolutionary Third World Forces." While in China, Mills showed a film about the Indian occupation of Alcatraz and spoke about the struggle against imperialism. According to the FBI file, Mills told the audience that he hoped to learn much from them and welcome them to the United States on May Day. He called

Indians "political prisoners" of the commissioner of Indian Affairs and said they would continue their fight against the capitalist system. The FBI's informant described Mills as "violence-prone" and a "good talker."[59]

Further evidence that the activists were being scrutinized is provided by the Department of Justice's *Civil Disturbance Information* booklet that monitored the Trail of Broken Treaties' progress across the continent. After the takeover, the FBI claimed in its "Summary of Extremist Activities," that AIM was training five-man guerrilla cells in explosives and demolitions in order to engage in sabotage and ultimately create a separate Indian nation. Meanwhile AIM was reportedly traveling the country armed with rifles and pistols supplied by "black groups." They also supposedly planned future burglaries of National Guard armories to enhance their own arsenals. Clearly, from the FBI's standpoint AIM and the Trail of Broken Treaties participants were radical, armed, and dangerous. Nowhere in this documentation did the FBI acknowledge the support offered by the nation's progressive church organizations or local parishes.[60]

If the FBI seemed particularly alarmed and ready to assume the worst of the TBT caravaners, the rest of the country seemed comparatively calm and almost sanguine about the takeover. A few individuals expressed indignation regarding seizure of the BIA in letters to President Nixon. A dozen or so people from Ponca City, Oklahoma, for instance, asked the president to prosecute "those miserable misfits that willfully damage our government property." They particularly wanted to discredit TBT participants Carter Camp and Martha Grass, who claimed to be from Ponca City but who were "just agitators—representing no one but themselves and other dissidents." On the other hand, a group from Baltimore, participants in John Hopkins University Chaplain's Sunday Experience Program, sent a message of "wholehearted support" to the Indian activists. A more nuanced and ambivalent response, however, came from Charles Trimble, executive director of the National Congress of American Indians, who expressed abhorrence at the destruction of the BIA building and particularly at the loss of records. But he then went on to say that "we thread common paths with the leaders of the organizations which comprised the Trail of Broken Treaties March" and that after studying the Twenty Points, it was very likely NCAI would support many of the same positions. Further, "the bond of Indian blood, Indian brotherhood, is strong." Trimble criticized the federal government for negotiating with the marchers while simultaneously planning repressive police measures against them. "Such two-faced action only lend credence to the strong accusations made by the activists." As it turned out, the Nixon administration's handling of the occupation attracted more criticism than the takeover itself.[61]

The same inclination to criticize the Nixon administration's actions during the BIA occupation rather than the Indians' typified the right-leaning media. The *Wall Street Journal* dubbed the decision to "hand over more than $60,000 to the militants with only a perfunctory accounting... incredible." It looked like an attempt to buy "pre-election calm." The *Arizona Republic* charged the White House with being paralyzed by fear and choosing "to ransom the American government from the hands of small-bore despots." A commentator with CBS radio thought the vandals should be prosecuted and officials who advised appeasement fired, while a commentator for the *Los Angeles Times* doubted that Ku Klux Klan members or "right-wing motorcycle thugs" would have gotten away scot-free from prosecution with traveling money, to boot. The paper concluded Nixon administration officials "should be red-faced over their mistakes with the redskins." Perhaps most outraged were conservative columnists Rowland Evans and Robert Novak, who characterized the Nixon administration's reaction to the BIA events as "shocking... the worst permissiveness he has so harshly decried in his political opponents." While high-level Interior Department officials wanted to evict the Indians, who were "violence-prone hoodlums, with no claims to legitimacy," the White House overruled them. Patterson and Garment were in-house "liberals" and by delegating responsibility for the situation to them, the president signaled he preferred appeasement to firmness. "The White House did not move against the invasion," the columnists claimed, "because it feared public support for the Indians."[62]

More sympathetic to the administration was the *Washington Post*. It found the White House's reaction "a responsible way to defuse a powder keg and yet to address the serious grievances underneath." Rather than inviting another Attica, Nixon's men found a more peaceful alternative. "How ironic that the President's own strictures against 'permissiveness' should now be thrown back at him, from the political right." Although the *Post* did encourage prosecution of some of the Indians, they also thought sacking the BIA paled in comparison to the damage European settlers had done to the sackers' ancestors. The newspaper believed Nixon was on the right track in pursuing justice for Indians and concluded: "Though the Indians' protest in Washington may have awakened some of their fellow Americans, and turned off others, their quest to reclaim their property and dignity is making some progress: not nearly enough to discharge the settlers' awesome debt to the first American but enough to provide a basis for hope of more."[63]

The *New York Times* echoed a similar assessment. The paper called Garment's readiness to negotiate "sensitive" and acknowledged that the negotiations to follow could affect all future relations between Indians and the federal government. An article published the week after the occupation ended reminded readers of Indians' "long list of grievances" and indicated that many were choosing to seek redress through the courts rather than on the streets. The Ford Foundation had recently granted $1.2 million to the Native American Rights Fund, a legal services group. "The question raised by the 'Trail of Broken Treaties' protest is whether Indians—by reputation a patient race—will be content to wait while the wheels of justice slowly turn; or will they, as they did last week, rush to the barricades?" Liberal columnist Jack Anderson nearly celebrated the spiriting of BIA documents out of Washington, D.C., ridiculing the police's unwitting role as accomplice as they escorted the TBT participants and their booty out of town. When Anderson's assistant, Les Whitten, looked at some of the stolen papers in Phoenix and another location, he emphasized their revelation of the sordid picture of U.S.-Indian relations rather than their theft, dubbing them "Broken Treaties Papers."[64] Far from a ringing indictment of the Trail of Broken Treaties, these kinds of reactions stopped just short of inviting more of the same.

The Trail of Broken Treaties did one more significant thing: it attracted congressional attention, albeit more as a platform to investigate and criticize the Nixon administration's handling of the incident than to chastise Indian participants or begin a serious soul-searching study of Indian affairs. Only a few days after the episode concluded, Representative Wayne Aspinall, chairman of the House Committee on Interior and Insular Affairs, scheduled hearings before the Subcommittee on Indian Affairs regarding the seizure and occupation of the BIA Building. Among those Aspinall most wanted to publically question were John Ehrlichman, Leonard Garment, Egil Krogh, Bradley Patterson, and John W. Dean, as well as Secretary of the Interior Rogers Morton, Assistant Secretary of the Interior Harrison Loesch, and Commissioner of Indian Affairs Louis Bruce. Clearly Aspinall, a Democrat from Colorado, intended to target the Nixon administration's handling of the episode. In a move that would anticipate the White House response to Congress' attempts to investigate Watergate, John Dean initially informed Congressman Aspinall that the president's staff, as a matter of well-established principle and precedent, did not testify in Congress about their performance of duties on the president's behalf. Within the increasingly beleaguered White House, Frank Carlucci warned Garment and others the hearings were intended to embarrass the administration and discredit the president's policy.[65]

In the end, Morton, Loesch, Bruce, and Frank Carlucci appeared before the subcommittee. Bruce and Carlucci emphasized the incendiary situation within the building and while, Carlucci said, they were "mindful of the need not to mollycoddle lawbreakers," the options at the time were seriously limited. The TBT leaders, he claimed, were "overwrought . . . emotional to the apparent point of irrationality" and willing to martyr themselves. Firm and immediate action can lead to tragedy, such as that at Kent State University in 1970. Their bullets took down some innocent bystanders, as well. Instead of going that route, "We had substituted conversation for confrontation, something that perhaps ought to have been done a century earlier." Meanwhile the White House expected to pursue issues related to the theft of documents and had already arrested several people. At the same time, they had no intention of penalizing all Indians for the misdeeds of a few. Rather, they intended to continue implementation of the president's July 1970 Indian message to Congress which emphasized self-determination and socioeconomic progress.[66] The only immediate change was a serious one: Secretary Morton fired Harrison Loesch, Louis Bruce, and John O. Crow, deputy Indian commissioner. Otherwise, the Nixon administration went on record as staying the course regarding Indian reform.

Among the non-Indians who applauded the Nixon administration for its restraint at the BIA Building was the American Friends Service Committee (AFSC). Clearly concerned about the TBT's lack of solid organization and planning from the outset, the chaos at the BIA Building represented the AFSC's worst nightmare. Yet, it too kept its faith in Native American activism, although preferring negotiation and litigation as tactics over occupation and threats to property and of violence. The rage and destruction exhibited in Washington did not turn them away. One week after the episode ended and the TBT marchers disbanded, the chair of the AFSC's Community Relations Committee sent Nixon a letter of appreciation for his administration's willingness to negotiate with the hundreds of Native Americans who had borne a long and frustrating experience to get to Washington in the first place. Plus, the Twenty Points, the AFSC believed, made legitimate claims for self-determination and adequate land and economic resources "based upon recognized treaties with the United States." Now that the building occupation was a thing of the past, the Quaker organization hoped these legitimate demands would still receive "careful and respectful consideration." Early in his presidency, Nixon articulated a policy that was both sensitive and encouraging. He followed it with the support of Blue Lake restoration to the Taos Pueblo and the Alaskan Native Land Claims Settlement Act. The TBT's Twenty Points offered yet another opportunity, the AFSC explained, to show good faith.[67]

In the meantime, Dennis Banks, Russell Means, and other AIM members returned to the West where, within a few months, they would again attract the nation's attention—this time at Wounded Knee.

6

On to Wounded Knee

The Trail of Broken Treaties caravans brought Native Americans from west to east in an effort to secure national attention regarding treaty rights and tribal sovereignty. In the immediate aftermath, participants dispersed in various directions—some heading to cities, others to reservations. Those who returned to reservations, however, were not universally welcomed, particularly by tribal leaders who preferred less confrontational methods. Perhaps no community reflected these deep divisions over political power, strategies, and goals more than Pine Ridge Reservation in southwestern South Dakota, home to the Oglala Sioux, or Lakota. There, in a hamlet called Wounded Knee, the forces of established power, a partnership between tribal and federal authorities, came into conflict with tribal members who felt oppressed by the BIA-supported reservation government. Some of the Pine Ridge dissidents invited AIM to help them push back. The upshot was a "takeover" of the Wounded Knee general store and church in February 1973 followed by a seventy-one-day siege. Before it ended, several occupiers died; federal forces marshaled weaponry akin to a small-scale war, including seventeen armored personnel carriers (APCs) and phantom jets. The Justice Department arrested 562 people on charges related to the siege. Even as violence escalated, supporters remained steadfast. Once again an enormous outpouring of sympathy from non-Indians for the occupiers manifested itself in tangible support—both during and after the occupation. Mainstream and progressive churches, liberal lawyers, leftist organizations, African Americans and Chicanos, hippies, college students, movie stars, and housewives rallied to the cause. The backing was constant and the long-term consequences profound.

The occupation of Wounded Knee became the last major showdown of the 1970s. Nearly one decade after they had first mobilized for treaty rights in the Pacific Northwest, Hank Adams and his Survival of American Indians Association, Dick Gregory, Ralph Abernathy, the Crusade for Justice, Marlon Brando, and the American Friends Service Committee weighed in. Other veteran supporters such as the National Council of Churches, Dee Brown, the underground press, and the mainstream press played a role. New organizations also emerged, most notably the Wounded Knee Legal Defense/Offense Committee and its successor the Native American Solidarity Committee. Although the initial spark for the conflict revolved around internal tribal politics and the troubled, complicated issues of reservation governance, AIM leadership worked hard to make the episode about broader issues. The confrontation at Wounded Knee proved complex; the issues at stake thorny. But it also provided another opportunity to teach national and international audiences about treaty rights, sovereignty, tribalism, self-determination, and justice and to convince non-Indians that political reform was not only overdue but necessary.

If the Trail of Broken Treaties ended ambiguously, at best, and ignominiously, at worst, Wounded Knee in some respects proved even more disastrous. The White House brought enormous firepower down upon the occupiers—something the Nixon administration hesitated to do in major urban centers such as San Francisco Bay or Washington, D.C. Remote South Dakota was another matter. Further, once the occupation ended, it was clear the federal government was in a punitive mood, intending to prosecute all participants to the fullest extent of the law. Most of the top leadership eventually escaped conviction and jail sentences for the Wounded Knee occupation, but the same was not true of lesser known defendants; and the leadership faced convictions for actions they had taken elsewhere. Moreover, after the occupation, the tribal government intensified its repression and violence broke out again on Pine Ridge.

To the extent the purpose of the occupation was to convince the nation that Native Americans continued to suffer and that treaties must be acknowledged, Wounded Knee proved powerful. People paid attention. It penetrated the national consciousness in a way no other protest had. According to historians Paul Chaat Smith and Robert Allen Warrior, "Wounded Knee received more attention during its first week than the entire previous decade of Indian activism combined." White House staffer Leonard Garment believed the longer the occupation dragged on, the more sympathy it generated. He concluded AIM achieved its objective, deeming it "another brilliantly cinematic news event, this time in the . . . vast natural stage where the great moral dramas of nineteenth-century U.S.-Indian history had been played out."[1] On the issues of Indian self-determination, treaties, and native power, the corner had been turned. More and more non-Indians finally understood that the days of non-Indians dictating to Indians had ended. Resistance to Indian power would continue but the future for Native American people, their cultures, their tribes, and their potential to exercise power at least over their own tribal members would become more secure than it had been in over a century. A significant number of non-Indians finally understood Indians had a right not only to exist but to control their own lives.

In a now-commonplace pattern, the majority of Native Americans distanced themselves from the events at Wounded Knee. The more politically oriented of them continued to opt for moderate, mainstream strategies such as battling through the courts and working the halls of Congress; places where they would achieve some successes in the years to come. But those kinds of tactics—important and necessary as they were—simply failed to command or secure the attention of most non-Indians. The drama associated with fish-ins, Alcatraz, and the occupation of Wounded Knee captured non-Indians' interest. The slow, compromise-laden legislative and legal processes did not. Substantive change required a spectrum of strategies and all necessitated non-Indian cooperation. Native American leaders of the staged events continued to welcome non-Indians into their fights, albeit intending them to stay in the background. They needed non-Indian support, resources, and expertise. In part, because they often had no tribally based, "legitimate" political authority, they had to seek support wherever they could find it. But more than that, they understood change would come only through cooperation. They could not do it alone.

The episode at Wounded Knee in 1973 was many years in the making. Ever since the Pine Ridge people voted to accept the 1934 Indian Reorganization Act with its council system of government elected by tribal members, dissatisfaction with these newly created governments was common. By 1973 tribal Chairman Dick Wilson's rule had offended so-called traditionals who believed Wilson favored mixed-blood over full-blood Oglala for reservation-based employment and essentially barred his political opponents not only from jobs but also services. Wilson organized a tribal security force, dubbed "goons" by his opponents, to enforce order and beat up AIM supporters. (His police embraced the sobriquet, claiming the letters stood for Guardians of the Oglala Nation.) Things really heated up when Wilson welcomed federal military and law enforcement, including about seventy-five members of an elite U.S. Marshals' Special Operations Group, to protect against any AIM efforts to take over federal buildings on the reservation. Government officials even mounted a machine gun on the Pine Ridge BIA building.[2]

Wilson's opponents were not cowed. First, they created an organization called Oglala Sioux Civil Rights Organization (OSCRO) and then attempted to impeach him. When that effort failed, one of the dissidents, Ellen Moves Camp, suggested AIM be invited to Pine Ridge. Meanwhile, AIM's successful efforts to shed public light on racism and injustices related to murders of several Lakota people, including Raymond Yellow Thunder, in recent months, had attracted some positive attention from dissident Pine Ridge residents. In a meeting at Calico, on February 27, 1973, Russell Means, who was Oglala Sioux but had not grown up on the reservation; Dennis Banks, Ojibwa from Minnesota; and other

AIM activists including some from Pine Ridge, listened to the complaints from OSCRO members. As the assemblage deliberated its options, taking over Wilson's offices in Pine Ridge or the BIA Building seemed suicidal. Finally, Frank Fools Crow, speaking in Lakota (and thus requiring translation for Means and others) urged AIM to go to Wounded Knee and "make your stand there." The choice was inspired. Dee Brown's recent best seller, *Bury My Heart at Wounded Knee*, had made the place nearly a household name. Many Americans—probably for the first time in the twentieth century—now knew this was a place where something had gone terribly wrong eighty years before. What better symbol for Indian distress and what better place to make the case for redress? OSCRO members hoped AIM's takeover of Wounded Knee would shine a spotlight on reservation corruption and help them oust Wilson. The AIM leadership's goals were more complicated. They expected the episode would provide them greater legitimacy. After all, here at Pine Ridge, members of a reservation community had sought them out, including elders and spiritual leaders with deep cultural knowledge, something many of the younger activists lacked. On the other hand, they had valuable experience in political action, not to mention contacts with powerful media and sympathetic lawyers. It was a partnership that transcended generation and tribe. AIM, then, hoped to use the episode to raise issues regarding sovereignty and self-determination while, at the same time, strengthening their own legitimacy.[3]

Dennis Banks and Frank Fools Crow led fifty-four vehicles out of Calico through Pine Ridge, surprising the tribal police and U.S. Marshals who had expected a confrontation there. From there they went on "toward deep history, toward Wounded Knee." Some of the spiritual and political leaders stopped at the burial site of the 1890 massacre victims. Others went on to the Gildersleeves' trading post where they seized guns, ammunition, food and clothing, and ransacked the place. Still others occupied the white-steepled Sacred Heart Catholic Church. The church's priest and the Gildersleeves became hostages. The occupiers put together a list of demands and announced that they were operating under the provisions of the 1868 Sioux Treaty. They wanted Senator William Fulbright to convene Senate Foreign Relations Committee hearings on Indian treaties, Senator Edward Kennedy to investigate the Bureau of Indian Affairs including all reservation offices, and South Dakota Senator James Abourezk to investigate all Sioux reservations in the state. Demands changed over the next days, including removal of Wilson as tribal chair, complete overhaul of the reservation government, and protection of all Indians' legal rights. Occupiers maintained that the United States had only two options: negotiate the demands or kill all the men, women, and children who took over Wounded Knee.[4]

White House officials—particularly Brad Patterson and Leonard Garment—were on the frontlines once again. As Smith and Warrior put it, these men had been relatively successful with past occupations "because they followed one rule above all others, and that rule boiled down to this: no Wounded Knees (referring to the 1890 massacre at the Pine Ridge site). Now they had to prevent a Wounded Knee at Wounded Knee." Beyond this, federal officials did not agree on strategy. Some members of the Nixon administration wanted a quick, military solution. The U.S. Marshals' Special Operational Group was already in place. They, the FBI, and other elements of the Justice Department chafed at restraint, and within the White House a constant debate took place on whether to use force to expel the occupiers. Not until Colonel Volney F. Warner explained what a military assault would mean in terms of money, manpower, and lives lost did the assault advocates back down. Meanwhile Garment and Patterson advocated "an alternative to a military-like option which ha[d] almost unthinkable consequences," one that acknowledged the legitimacy of Indian grievances, even if AIM was not the proper representative with whom to deal. Further supporting this position was the weight of public opinion. The majority of letters coming into the White House urged Nixon to tread lightly and recognize Indians' rights. Patterson understood that many Americans, sympathetic to Indians in general, did not differentiate between AIM and other Indian groups. And Leonard Garment saw the four thousand people who attended a special mass on behalf of Native Americans at New York's Episcopal Cathedral of St. John the Divine in late March, 1973, as just one example of "what we're up against in dealing with Wounded Knee." *New York Times* coverage of the mass underscored its significance.[5]

Even with the moderated response, the combined federal-state-tribal military arsenal brought to bear at Wounded Knee was truly astonishing. Over the course of the occupation, various law enforcement agencies mobilized phantom jets, 17 armored personnel carriers, M-16 rifles with 50,000 rounds of ammunition, 11,760 rounds of M-16 tracer ammunition, 8,200 rounds of M-1 ball ammunition, 20 sniper rifles, 2,500 star parachute flares, M-79 tear-gas grenade launchers, and infrared lights.[6] They set up roadblocks and attempted to blockade the AIM-occupied town. For their part, the ragtag "guerilla army" had a few automatic rifles and the weapons and ammunition from the trading post, plus the makings of Molotov cocktails. In terms of firepower, there was no comparison.

But the occupiers had other "weapons"; most critically, favorable public opinion and media interest. National and international media provided far more coverage than Alcatraz or the Trail of Broken Treaties had received. A Harris poll indicated 93 percent of its participants had heard of the Wounded Knee occupation and 51 percent sympathized with the occupiers (as opposed to 21 percent who sided with the government). At the height of the occupation, the *New York Times Magazine* printed a lengthy article by writer Alvin M. Josephy Jr. that clearly favored the occupiers. Deeply sympathetic to the protestors, Josephy explained their demands to manage their own reservation affairs, protect their natural resources from non-Indian exploitation, overthrow corrupt tribal governments, protect treaty rights, and end poverty. He provided historical context and explained new frustrations in the wake of the Trail of Broken Treaties debacle and consequent doubts about the Nixon administration's sincerity regarding government policy reform. The shooting of Hank Adams and murders of Raymond Yellow Thunder and Richard Oakes underscored the prejudices, atrocities, and injustices that continued to plague Indian people. Josephy's article was detailed, learned, and sophisticated. It ended with a call for Nixon to renew his dedication to tribal self-determination. Josephy supported immediate observance of treaty rights and federal trustee obligations to assure protection from non-Indians. Finally, Josephy recommended a massive public works program to employ Indians and end their poverty. Would, he asked, "the Administration listen to the Indians and respond wisely to their new crisis?"[7]

President Nixon's reaction to Wounded Knee was ambivalent, criticizing the tactics but supporting the goals. During the early days of the occupation, then, his message was twofold: AIM had no political legitimacy but Indians' grievances were real. As Nixon explained in a press conference, "The lawlessness has got to stop—if it does not stop in South Dakota it will not stop anywhere. But the [government] inaction has also got to stop—the lack of progress on our legislation, the inadequate organization of Indian programs."[8]

Meanwhile, in what was now becoming a common pattern, the first non-Indians to enlist in the Wounded Knee campaign were college students, leftists, and counterculture types from Berkeley to the Twin Cities to Washington, D.C. By 1973 the organizations and methods for sharing information about "the action" on Pine Ridge and for marshalling material support were well-established. AIM was particularly effective in tapping into this ready-made constituency, making common cause with antiwar, Chicano, and African American activists. They knew the "lingo," they had the rhetorical skills, and they had the underground newspaper and campus connections.

A pamphlet entitled "Wounded Knee, 1973," for example, circulated in progressive and radical circles. Published during the siege, its intention was to educate people about the situation in South Dakota and to counter government and "established media" representations. Rather than merely articulate complaints against Dick Wilson, it connected the current crisis to nearly two centuries of federal policy that wiped out tribes, broke treaties, and left Indian people in wretched conditions. Now, the Oglala Sioux Civil Rights Organization and AIM had created something new: the Independent Oglala Sioux Nation which, the pamphlet claimed, like the Provisional Revolutionary Government of South Vietnam, set up a temporary form of government until the people of the community could establish a more permanent structure. This new nation sounded more like a multiracial commune than a Native American community: "communal living is being reestablished inside the new nation. People are working together in close groups who have come from different tribes and different parts of America. They are teaching and using individual skills to build community strength." No one locked doors. Everyone shared food. And "all receive what they need." Residents shared the work, dividing it into areas such as maintenance, food, clothing, border security, and the hospital. People from around the nation who arrived for short periods of time, for instance, proved particularly helpful in staffing the medical aid station. Leonard Crow Dog taught them Indian medicine, but they also used Chinese and Western medicine.[9]

Wounded Knee looked to Crow Dog for its spiritual leadership (he was from Rosebud Reservation but joined the AIM effort on Pine Ridge because he believed they were trying "to get back to a true life"). His message, however, transcended the Lakota to include whites, blacks, and Mexican Americans. As the pamphlet presented it, Crow Dog's vision was one of racial cooperation. He taught the best way to survive was to live "in harmony with the earth, all the Great Spirit's creatures, the sun, the moon and the fire"—but also with other races. Crow Dog explained that at one time all people made up one tribe, but then they had dispersed in Four Directions: "The white man went North, the black man went South, Yellow man went East, Red man went West." The white man, in particular, had strayed from living in accord with the Great Spirit's creatures. The time for the Four Directions to reunite had come and Wounded Knee was the place. "The Indian people, Black people, Chicano people as well as national minorities have gone through a cultural awareness awakening. Inside Wounded Knee the fighting spirit is guided by a spiritual way of life that appeals to all enslaved people to join together and become free by any means necessary." It was essential that Native Americans, Chicanos, blacks, Asians, and poor whites, who had been taught to fear and despise one another, come back together. One of the most important consequences of the creation of Oglala Independent Nation would be the unity between "the Red man and the Brown man's struggles. The nation of Aztlan must always relate to and support the struggles of the Indian people, and accept the fact that the Chicano people came from the Indian race. This is the unity of the Chicanos and Indians inside of Wounded Knee."[10]

The new Oglala nation also acknowledged the importance of women and hinted that the feminist revolution, just beginning in mainstream America, was also penetrating South Dakota. As the pamphlet explained it, women's "traditional role" was to run the home and care for their families while men hunted and protected the home. At Wounded Knee women did the cooking and cleaning. Although some might see this as perpetuating oppressive roles, Indian people respected running a household as necessary for survival. Of course, giving birth to future generations gave women a particularly treasured place in the community. Some women transcended traditional roles, helping with security and defending borders. They "have been part of the militant Indian struggles of the last four years and are therefore very skilled and able to help to defend the nation." Men who condescended to women would be criticized.[11]

If part of the pamphlet meant to convey a sense of Wounded Knee as a multicultural, countercultural mecca, the rest reinforced the message that this was a war zone. Loaded with photographs of Native American occupiers wielding guns, it reminded readers that the community was surrounded by a determined, deadly enemy. Although a restraining order from the U.S. District Court of the western district of South Dakota meant some food, medicine, and cooking fuel could get through the blockade, those who tried to bring in supplies overland became targets. It was so dangerous that the route they took into Wounded Knee was dubbed the "Ho Chi Minh Trail," reaching to the readily available nomenclature of the Vietnam War. Wounded Knee had become a "free fire zone" where anything that moved would be shot. In fact, the pamphlet claimed, "The scene is very much like Vietnam, the same tactics and the same weapons." Federal officials were even teaching the BIA tribal police how to use the armored personnel carriers. Although the weaponry was updated, there was nothing new about the government's basic tactic of using Indian against Indian. It was BIA police who killed Sitting Bull and Crazy Horse in the nineteenth century. "And analogously to the Indochinese strategy [where] the U.S. trained Vietnamese to kill Vietnamese, things are coming full circle." In fact, what was happening at Wounded Knee was "very similar to revolutionary fights that have gone down in other countries." At this point the situation was more a stalemate than a full-fledged war, however, with one nation asserting its sovereign rights, already negotiated and upheld by the United States, and the other revoking those rights by military force.[12]

To help, the pamphlet recommended sympathizers should stop viewing their struggles as separate and begin to support one another. Whites, in particular, must support national-liberation struggles "by any means necessary." They should demand that media tell the truth about what is going on in South Dakota. Further, all progressive people should donate food, warm clothing, blankets, fuel, military aid, farm equipment, media equipment, and, of course, money for legal expenses and land purchases around Wounded Knee. Supporters could take these donations to their local AIM chapter or to one of the national coordinating centers including the Wounded Knee Support and Communications Center in Rapid City or the Wounded Knee Legal Defense/Offense Committee or to its lawyers, including Mark Lane and William Kuntsler, of New York.[13]

Clearly the pitch to multicultural, antiwar, and counterculture types paid dividends. It is no surprise that groups in the San Francisco Bay Area, for instance, mobilized. On March 9, 1973, University of California, Berkeley students organized a "U.S. Hands Off Wounded Knee!" rally in Sproul Plaza. Speakers included Roxanne Jackson, identified as an eyewitness at Wounded Knee; Adam Nordwell, of Alcatraz fame; Ken Miliner, from the Young Socialist Alliance; Magdaleno Mora, of El Movimiento Estudiantil Chicano de Aztlan (MEChA); and a speaker from Students for a Democratic Society (SDS). On March 14, Vernon Bellecourt, executive director of AIM, spoke about Wounded Knee on the Berkeley campus. One week later "United People for Wounded Knee" rallied on the steps of a San Francisco federal building to support AIM, the demands of the Trail of Broken Treaties, and "the pan-American quest for justice."[14]

Underground presses leapt at the story, sending reporters to South Dakota to cover a homegrown "revolutionary" movement. Wounded Knee offered not only the chance to support Native American rights, but also to make common cause with all oppressed people and remind readers of connections between domestic issues and Vietnam. It also offered the chance to participate in something radical, righteous . . . and real. That was the appeal for Marcus Dinsmore, sent to South Dakota by the Unicorn News Radio Network to report on the occupation. The righteousness came from the justice of their claim: "This is their country." The reality was, as Black Panther Party leader Stokely Carmichael explained when he came to Rapid City to talk with AIM leaders, the government was caught in a dilemma. It could not move against the occupiers, because it knew the land rightly belonged to the Indians. Yet, the government *had* to move against them, in order to keep what they had taken. Moreover, reporter Dinsmore mused on the juxtaposition between his pre-Wounded Knee romantic visions of "sitting around some unspecified hills with our black berets, our AK-47's flown in from China and the spirit of Che Guevara guiding us in a down to earth, stoned out war," and the *actual* experience of being totally lost as he tried to make his way into the Wounded Knee compound, laying face-down in the mud with a fifty-pound pack on his back, while automatic weapons fire rained down around him. At that moment, "all those fantasies of revolutionary war crumbled away." Until going to Pine Ridge, he had never thought of Indians as equivalent to Vietnamese peasants or—for that matter— as living, defiant people whose cultures had survived. This was the first inkling he—and many others—had that the last warrior had *not* been killed at the end of the nineteenth century. And he learned, during his two months there, that this was not a one-shot effort by an "Indian Weatherman cadre . . . [but] the opening (or reopening) of war to defend the culture and religion of nearly one million human beings trapped inside the United States." AIM, he insisted, had enormous support on Pine Ridge and so had something no other "revolutionary nationalist group" in the U.S. had: "a mass base of MATERIAL support and a land base."[15]

Wounded Knee, however, had additional significance for the white people who took part in it. Many radicals, Dinsmore claimed, had forgotten the meaning of sacrifice. At this place they learned, perhaps for the first time, to risk their lives. The nature of that sacrifice took different forms for different people. "It was a difficult thing for many of my strong white sisters, who have struggled so rightfully for the last several years to break down roles, to be told by a young Indian male to go wash the dishes and put down the gun and to understand that it was neither their place, nor the right time to say, 'no.'" That they did so, he claimed, was a "sacrifice of their principles, so hard fought over in the past" and so an "incredibly beautiful sign of strength and political love." Other dramatic challenges came in encounters with Native American religion. This not only tested Dinsmore's agnosticism, but also his manhood. When John Strike, an Oglala, invited him to take part in a yuwipi sweat lodge ceremony, he found the heat torturous and had to leave before it was over. "I felt miserable and white. I felt as though I had failed to prove myself, to prove my courage in my ability to stand near the heat." Strike reassured Dinsmore that it was not a test of courage and that Indians simply had more experience in sweat lodge ceremonies. White people were just beginning to learn, but they would eventually master it. Feeling better, the reporter concluded, "It was a cleansing thing to hear. It summed up all the lessons that I had learned from Wounded Knee. We as white people have much to learn from the Indian War."[16]

Some reporters associated the struggle at Wounded Knee with other so-called revolutionary fights. The *Berkeley Barb*'s "Sgt. Pepper," for instance, lumped AIM's struggle for lands with those of Black Septemberists in Sudan, American blacks in Brooklyn, the Palestinians, the Irish Republican Army, and, of course, the Viet Cong. Others, however, took care to distinguish the particular issues at stake in Wounded Knee, including Dick Wilson's regime and the deeper question of Native American land and rights restitution through treaties.[17]

Many articles provided information on individuals and groups providing material support to the occupation as well as information on where readers could offer their help. A group called Venceremos and the Peoples' Medical Center in Redwood City organized a speakers' bureau to educate people about Wounded Knee and put together a caravan of medical supplies. The National Free Clinic Council, representing 350 free clinics across the nation, unanimously voted to send food, medicine, and medical personnel to the occupation site. African American actor/singer Sammy Davis Jr. put up bail for those arrested during an attempt to deliver medical supplies to Wounded Knee from Los Angeles. Marlon Brando refused to accept the Academy Award that March, citing Hollywood's treatment of Indians in movies and television, and was rumored to be on his way to Wounded Knee, attracting much favorable underground press coverage. A committee of rock and roll stars organized to raise money "for the Indian movement." Dickie Betts of the Allman Brothers initiated this effort with the support of Alice Cooper, The Band, and The Grateful Dead. The East [San Francisco] Bay Chapter of Vietnam Veterans Against the War sponsored a benefit to raise money for Wounded Knee, and San Francisco's Glide Memorial Church organized demonstrations. One reporter wrote about a "Trail of Broken Treaties" festival that took place in Oakland, describing his discomfort with the dances the Native Americans performed there. "I can't help feeling that they are performing, putting on a Sunday show for a predominantly white audience, however sympathetic to the cause." But he reconciled himself to the situation by reminding himself that "if the Indian people need allies in this country, and they obviously need them, this is one of the ways of generating sympathy, understanding, and a bit of needed money for the Wounded Knee adventure." Finally, in early April, the *Berkeley Barb* encouraged people to participate in a massive march to Wounded Knee during Easter weekend. The plan was to walk through the government roadblocks, break the stalemate between sides, and "compare the negotiations going on, or not going on, about Wounded Knee to the Paris negotiations about Vietnam." Some people showed up, but the supporters did not breach the roadblocks and officials arrested nineteen of them.[18]

Wounded Knee provided the Denver-based Chicano organization Crusade for Justice another opportunity to lend support to Indian activists, as well. According to Crusade member Ernesto Vigil, the Chicano group endorsed native peoples' struggles in part because their "mixed bloodlines" predisposed them to look favorably upon Indian demands for self-determination. The Crusade dedicated one and one-half pages of its April 1973 newspaper, *El Gallo*, to Wounded Knee, floating such headlines as "Hands Off Wounded Knee" and "Support Indian Rights." The Crusade also tried to monitor media coverage and the federal government's maneuvers, as well as provide cash and supplies to those headed to Pine Ridge to join the occupation. But its most dramatic action came in the organization, with the Denver AIM chapter, of a march on the downtown Denver federal building on March 6, 1973. As opposed to the 1,200 participants AIM and the Crusade claimed, the local FBI report counted 400–500. Even so, this was an impressive turnout. FBI reports also suspected the Crusade made a deal to provide AIM with machine guns manufactured in Mexico. Vigil found the idea laughable. No such guns existed and roadblocks effectively kept most Chicano supporters out of Wounded Knee.[19]

Other non-Indian supporters, however, did break through the government blockade. Some did so via a dramatic airdrop on April 17, 1973. William Zimmerman, an anti-Vietnam War activist from Boston, conceived the plan and carried it out with the help of eight other men; three rented Piper Cherokees; and dozens of others who raised money, bought the food, coordinated publicity, and prepared the legal work for the operation. Not unlike the "Sausalito Indian

Navy," the Anglo sailors who provided critical support to the Alcatraz takeover, the Wounded Knee airlift brought together an informal, ultimately ephemeral group whose motivations ranged from the political to the personal. Zimmerman saw Wounded Knee as an event that crystallized "America's countless crimes against the Indian people" but also epitomized the nation's crimes against the people of Indochina. "As Americans, as people who worked in opposition to the Viet Nam War," he wrote a few years later, "we felt close to the struggle at Wounded Knee and believed that we had a stake in its outcome." Not all shared such sentiments. One young recruit admitted, "I don't know shit about Viet Nam. I don't think I'm even that concerned about the Indians. I just want some free flyin' time, man; I'm just after the hours." Still, Zimmerman believed that airlift symbolized the nation's most privileged and free opponents of its political system reaching across class and racial barriers to help the least privileged and "the ever-present possibility of acts of solidarity."[20]

Those living within the Wounded Knee compound were appreciative. The airlift came at the right time and represented essential material, not simply symbolic, support. As Dennis Banks remembered it, they were starving, the federal noose was tightening, and backpackers faced increasing difficulties getting into the compound. The seven duffel bags that floated down on parachutes brought not only much needed food, but also the unspoken message, as Banks put it, that "Goddamn! Somebody *cares*! They *care* if we survive or not, and they knew how to deliver this manna from heaven! Plus, the planes were called 'Cherokees!'" Each bundle also contained a printed message declaring: "Your struggle for freedom and justice is our struggle . . . This is a fight against an unyielding and brutal government that makes the poor people of the world its victims in its search for power and profit." Banks choked up when reading the message aloud as the assemblage cried and embraced. Zimmerman declared the airlift a clear victory, allowing the occupation to continue for three additional weeks. Banks, while grateful for the food and emotional lift, believed the federal government's frustration over this breach in its blockade led to "a full-blown attack of unleashed fury and the death, later that night of an Apache man, Frank Clearwater, who had arrived only the day before to support the occupation."[21]

That AIM received support from antiwar groups, Black Panthers, Chicanos, and political radicals came as no surprise to the Nixon White House. An investigation of AIM noted that the organization had joined with Chicano groups "for disruptive activities." Although there was no evidence of close cooperation with radical black groups, meetings between AIM and black nationalist Stokely Carmichael were noted. Supposedly a member of the Omaha, Nebraska, "Mau Maus" donated thirty rifles to the occupants, while undesignated southwestern-based "Chicanos" provided forty to sixty semi-automatic weapons and Mexican-manufactured ammunition. The White House claimed it had evidence of support from leftist individuals and groups such as the Students for a Democratic Society, Peoples Coalition for Peace and Justice, Youth International Party, Revolutionary Union, and Vietnam Veterans Against the War (VVAW)—all of whom had been involved in AIM activities in the past. Black Communist Party member Angela Davis, radical attorney William Kunstler, and VVAW lawyer Mark Lane had either visited—or tried to visit—Wounded Knee in March. The report maintained that white radicals left when they learned they were not welcomed by Indian leadership. Supposedly the only white sympathizers encouraged to stay were the Vietnam Veterans Against the War—"probably because of the more practical nature of VVAW's help—in obtaining supplies and in providing military knowledge and experience."[22]

What was surprising to the White House officials, however, was AIM's support from mainstream churches and even from other branches of the federal government. They seemed unaware that churches and religious groups had been supporting Native American activist agendas, including that of AIM, for years. Their commitment had been clear well before the crisis at Wounded Knee. Mainstream progressive church groups particularly jumped at the opportunity to fund projects related to Indian education, poverty, and racial discrimination. AIM, which began in 1969 as a Minneapolis-St. Paul organization dedicated to ending police brutality against Indians, evolved into other social justice issues and spread nationally. Its charismatic leadership and eagerness to seek grants from church groups made it a natural recipient for support. The Roman Catholic Church's Campaign for Human Development gave AIM $40,000 in 1971; the Episcopal Church donated $10,000; and the United Methodist Church $4,500 for the Trail of Broken Treaties. Further, AIM schools in Cleveland, Milwaukee, and Minneapolis had received federal funds.[23]

AIM also received a number of grants, starting as early 1969, from the African American dominated Interreligious Foundation for Community Organization (IFCO), an organization sponsored by the National Council of Churches (NCC). AIM and IFCO were a natural match. The latter's interest in funding community-based organizations, including those that did not shy away from radical language and tactics, certainly helped. In fact, IFCO staff believed AIM was the group "most nearly aligned with a mass-base of Indian people working together on a wide range of problems" in the Minneapolis-St. Paul area. For its part, AIM was happy to receive whatever funds came its way and welcomed grants from IFCO to support "survival schools" and AIM's "Red School House," a Twins City-based alternative school designed for American Indian children. But the relationship was not always a smooth one. Frustrations with communication, particularly follow-up reports regarding accountability, ruffled feathers back in New York. More frustrating were the public, political swipes AIM took at

IFCO, just at the moment they were accepting the organization's funding. IFCO Executive Director Lucius Walker chided Clyde Bellecourt for an AIM 1969 Annual Report which claimed IFCO was "another Black oriented program which seems to be taking pre-designated Indian funds and using them for Black programs instead." Stunned by this complaint, coming as it did in the wake of an IFCO grant of $15,000 to AIM, Walker informed Bellecourt that such untrue comments seriously undermined IFCO's credibility and ability to fund future Indian projects. Given "the kinds of murder, repression, harassment and exploitation which both of our peoples have faced and are facing in this country," Walker wrote, "I would like to think that we could work together in development of a common strategy against a common enemy. If that is possible, please let me know." Bellecourt apparently did. Two years later an internal IFCO evaluation cited AIM as "an IFCO model project," one that was transitioning from a regional to a national coalition which, the evaluator believed, would have a huge impact on Indians everywhere. Even when by 1974, in the wake of the Wounded Knee trials, IFCO sensed AIM was going to take a less visible national role and reemphasize community development at the local chapter level, they continued their support.[24]

AIM simultaneously sought, and received, support from other church-based groups, including those for whom the tag "radical" was anathema. It is an interesting commentary on the times and AIM's cachet that church-based organizations not only listened to its complaints about Christian activities among Indians but also invited them to their meetings, handed them microphones and speaking spots, and followed up with support. Just at the moment Lucius Walker was courting Native Americans for IFCO, AIM emissaries engaged a variety of other religious organizations with the intention of restructuring church boards, commissions, and missions to better serve Indians. For centuries, they argued, churches had established missions among Native Americans, but the latter had not necessarily benefited from such efforts. AIM believed that only "with full control over all programs related to the Indian community locally, regionally, and nationally by the Churches, will the American Indian be able to lift himself from the depth of poverty." Churches needed, then, to support Indian organizations that stressed self-determination, and Indians needed to control all church programs designed to benefit Native Americans.[25]

To further these goals, AIM took its "Challenges to the Churches" to the Lutheran Council in the U.S.A. Indian Ministry Conference, which was meeting with the Annual Assembly of Lutheran Church and Indian People in Sioux Falls, South Dakota, in July 1969. Reverend W. Walter Weber, National Indian Ministry Consultant for the Lutheran Church-Missouri Synod, began the conference by acknowledging the church's past failings and inviting Indian participants to suggest ways to reform. A Minneapolis delegation took up this offer, introducing

Clyde Bellecourt and Dennis Banks. Their highly charged speeches changed the nature of the meeting as they stated that "350 years have been wasted by the churches through indoctrination that the white people were our saviors." They aired, in particular, the grievances of urban Indians, criticized Lutherans for "foist[ing] their ideas and ways on Indian people to the detriment and degradation of Indian people" while doing nothing to truly help them, and presented a "Challenge to the Churches" that they wanted the assembly to endorse.[26]

The "Challenge" called for a national board with 75 percent Indian membership and an Indian chair, support for Indian groups to determine their own needs and actions, condemnation of the Bureau of Indian Affairs' "criminal actions" and demand for its reform, commitment to spend one dollar per year on services for every Native American for the next ten years (originally one thousand dollars per year), and agreement to make available at no charge church properties for use by all minority groups. AIM's presentation electrified the meeting. The participants suspended the remainder of the agenda and devoted themselves to discussing the "Challenge to the Churches." Banks meanwhile informed them that the Lutherans were in "very grave trouble," but the Indians at this conference would try to help them.[27] In the end, the conference participants unanimously supported the "Challenge." What is more, they offered the following:

> We would ask forgiveness of our Indian brothers and sisters and hereby publicly acknowledge our personal and corporate sins of racism, greed, insensitivity, dehumanization, robbery, assault, haughtiness, apathy and other overt and covert injustices and inhumanities... Our political and ecclesiastical systems have fostered second-class citizenship where rules are written to play a white man's game. The beauty, depth, and sensitivity to the rhythm and wholeness of life in the Indian community has been methodically obliterated from the American scene. We are less human; our nation is poorer; the family of God in Jesus Christ is hurting because of the continuing anguish which is carried by Indian people.[28]

Although they did not endorse AIM itself, it was clear that AIM had achieved a major victory here.

The following year, when the conference reconvened in Sioux Falls, participants established the National Indian Lutheran Board consisting of eighteen Indian and six non-Indian members. AIM believed they had made great progress in implementing their "Challenge to the Churches." And the effort did not end there. In August, 1970, AIM presented the Challenge to the Walther League Youth Conference in Rosebud, South Dakota, where attendees endorsed it. That same month, Clyde Bellecourt spoke at Madison Square Garden in New York before the American Lutheran Church National Luther League Conference where twenty-four thousand Lutheran youth in attendance also endorsed the Challenge. And in November the National Conference of the American Lutheran Church declared March 14, 1971, as Indian Concern Sunday. Offerings collected that day would be forwarded to the National Indian Lutheran Board which, in turn, would use the funds to implement the "Challenge to the Churches."[29]

AIM leadership moved to other denominations, as well. The National Council of Churches invited Bellecourt and Dennis Banks to attend their meeting in Detroit in December 1969. Presenting the same Challenge to this group, all thirty-three denominations within the NCC endorsed it. According to Russell Means's account, however, the AIM leadership had to force its way onto the program of the plenary session. After interpreting promises that they would be allowed to speak as empty, Means claimed that Bellecourt grabbed a microphone and began addressing the thousands of people assembled in an enormous auditorium. Someone turned off the microphone, but Bellecourt kept talking. People on the floor demanded the microphone be turned back on, Bellecourt had his say, and the NCC (which included mainline denominations such as the United Church of Christ, Methodists, Episcopalians, Presbyterians, and Quakers) voted on a formal resolution accepting AIM's demands. Within the year, Bellecourt also spoke at the National Conference of Catholic Charities held in Washington, D.C.—the first time the organization had ever invited an Indian to address it.[30]

All of this, of course, preceded the events at Wounded Knee. In the midst of that episode, and when occupiers faced multiple trials and court appearances, AIM discovered that churches would not abandon them. The NCC, from the outset, sent a telegram to Nixon, the U.S. attorney general, director of the BIA, South Dakota congressional delegation, and tribal Chair Dick Wilson expressing its deep concern that the occupation be resolved through peaceful negotiation. Moreover the crisis at Wounded Knee brought into "sharp focus our awareness of the violation of our intra-national treaties for which we all share responsibility." Churches, in fact, had been partners in the creation of the crisis, the NCC claimed. Beyond letter writing, the NCC board authorized material support to the occupiers and personnel to deliver food, medical and sanitation supplies, and to monitor events on the ground while encouraging a negotiated settlement.[31]

John P. Adams of the United Methodist Church's Board of Church and Society took the most active role of Anglo church people and the NCC, moving back and forth between occupiers and federal agencies to keep the lines of communication open during the early days of the crisis. In one of the more interesting partnerships that arose out of this tangled and volatile web, he transported Survival of American Indians national director and fish-in activist Hank Adams into the village. Adams then served for a time as mediator between the occupiers and the Nixon White House.³² John Adams also carried AIM's invitation to Rev. Ralph Abernathy, African American civil rights leader of the Southern Christian Leadership Council, to come to South Dakota and accompanied Abernathy on his visit to Wounded Knee. There, Abernathy told the occupiers, "I have made a pilgrimage from the tomb of Dr. Martin Luther King, Jr. to Wounded Knee. This is a great symbol, I believe. It ought to express to the American people that two great peoples who have suffered separately in the past are committed to seeking justice together in the future" (see figure 6.1). John Adams's activities were sufficiently effective to earn the enmity of tribal Chair Wilson who successfully ejected NCC from the reservation. Yet, the NCC remained actively involved from off-reservation office-trailers; they continued to monitor and encourage negotiations, paid for AIM leadership expenses to Washington, covered the funeral costs for two occupiers killed during the siege, and provided transportation for occupiers who left South Dakota when the episode ended.³³

Support did not conclude there. After the siege, the executive secretary of the American Baptist Churches U.S.A. wrote to the U.S. district judge in Sioux Falls, South Dakota, in January 1974, to urge that the 129 Indians being held on Wounded Knee–related charges, be tried instead in St. Paul where they would receive a fairer trial. "The rights of Indian people have been denied far too long,"

Figure 6.1 Civil rights leader Ralph Abernathy (*left*) traveled to Wounded Knee during the 1973 occupation to show his support for AIM's demands, joining Dennis Banks (*right*) and Russell Means (*center*) at a press conference. Credit: Corbis/Bettman.

he claimed, "and their pleas for justice too long ignored." The NCC donated fifty thousand dollars in bonding notes during the consequent trials. And while the justice system churned slowly, church interest did not fade away. In 1976 the National Council of Churches pleaded with President Gerald Ford to commute Leonard Crow Dog's various sentences, stating, "The Governing Board of the National Council of Churches is deeply concerned over what seems to be a pattern of continuing oppression and exploitation of Indians with federal complicity."[34]

Such expressions and material manifestations of support, while undoubtedly welcome, did not solve all occupiers' pressing legal needs. Yet as the Wounded Knee occupants fast became defendants in need of legal help, additional legal aid rapidly materialized. In fact, it did so even before the occupation at Pine Ridge ended. While earlier actions in the Pacific Northwest and Alcatraz had attracted a handful of sympathetic lawyers, Wounded Knee was remarkable for the scores of lawyers and legal aid workers, not to mention students and nonprofessional volunteers, who offered their help, if only for a few weeks or months. On March 22, 1973, about one month into the occupation, AIM general counsel, Ramon Roubideaux, announced at a press conference the formation of a Wounded Knee Legal Defense/Offense Committee (WKLDOC). Beverly Axelrod, a California attorney who had taken on Black Panther cases, and Mark Lane, perhaps best known for his book *Rush To Judgment*, which challenged the Warren Commission report's conclusion regarding the John F. Kennedy assassination, appeared with Roubideaux. The organization first sought a temporary restraining order against the Department of Justice, U.S. Marshals Service, FBI, and others who, they argued, were depriving Wounded Knee residents of their civil rights. WKLDOC intended to pursue these legal tactics until South Dakota "begins to look more like America and less like war-torn Southeast Asia."[35] A few weeks later, they filed two suits. One asked for a temporary injunction against the federal government in order to allow food and supplies into the compound. The other sought a temporary injunction against Dick Wilson, charging him with terrorizing, harassing, and assaulting those who supported AIM or simply opposed him. U.S. District Judge Andrew Bogue denied both motions.[36]

WKLDOC's legal efforts accelerated after May 8 when the protestors left Wounded Knee and law enforcement withdrew their weapons. Several weeks later, over Memorial Day weekend, a group of lawyers and legal workers congregated in Rapid City, South Dakota. They met with representatives from AIM and OSCRO to plan their legal defense and their upcoming discussion with the Nixon White House representatives regarding treaty rights. Fifty-four people participated, from sixteen cities in eleven states. The majority were not locals, but rather legal professionals who came to South Dakota, and eventually

Nebraska and Minnesota, offering their expertise to the many Native Americans facing Wounded Knee and other AIM-related prosecutions. Some attorneys had been inside Wounded Knee during the occupation, but most came after—responding to recruitment appeals from the National Lawyers Guild (NLG) and the ACLU, or on their own initiative. William Kuntsler, famous as the defense attorney for antiwar defendants such as the Chicago Seven and the Berrigan brothers, as well as for civil rights defendants Stokely Carmichael and Dr. Martin Luther King, came at the invitation of the defendants. NLG took perhaps the most prominent role. Founded in 1936 to defend the New Deal from American Bar Association attacks, the organization had evolved over the decades, defending clients such as the "Hollywood Ten" who appeared before the House Committee on Un-American Activities; the Mississippi Freedom Democratic Party; and people associated with the anti–Vietnam War, civil rights, and Black Power movements. With about five thousand members nationwide, NLG had appealed to its membership as early as March for short-term commitments to the Wounded Knee defense. Soon, lawyers from Denver, Minneapolis, Berkeley, New York, Boston, and Madison, Wisconsin, showed up in South Dakota or offered their services from their homes. Beyond lawyers, many law students and others who had no legal training whatsoever joined WKLDOC's efforts, often just for a short period of time. Paul Chaat Smith, son of a Comanche mother and self-described "suburban Indian" from Shaker Heights, Ohio, dropped out of college and drifted off to the WKLDOC Sioux Falls, South Dakota, office in August 1974. "It was a glorious mess," Smith later claimed, "and a logistical nightmare . . . Legal workers were oppressed by the lawyers. White people ran everything . . . Paranoia was rampant, and completely deserved because security was both a constant obsession and almost nonexistent. Drinking was banned, and practiced frequently." Many of these volunteers knew little about Indian law let alone Indian affairs, tribes, or people. And the relationships among Native American activists and lawyers were not always simpatico. The turnover was significant but so too was the enthusiasm. For all the chaos, WKLDOC won most of the cases and, Smith admitted, "I loved it." He spent the next five years bouncing around the movement.[37]

    Not all legal volunteers came from the left. The National Association of Criminal Defense Lawyers (NACDL)—an organization not known for radical politics—contributed the second-largest number of attorneys to the Wounded Knee defense. Joe Beeler, a former Chicago-based public defender and member of NACDL, recruited among this group at their August 1973 annual meeting. The association responded by sending a delegation to South Dakota and pledging to help out. Soon, thirty-five NACDL lawyers offered their services to WKLDOC. Some of the volunteers never came to South Dakota, but not all of the legal tasks required their on-the-spot presence. Beeler and Mark Tilsen, an attorney from

St. Paul who decided to take a year off from his own practice, oversaw the assignment of duties to the volunteers. Tilsen also served as day-to-day coordinator for all criminal and civil cases, while Beeler coordinated all of the so-called nonleadership cases. Lane accepted responsibility for evidence gathering and for the Custer, South Dakota, cases. Len Cavise, a Washington, D.C.–based lawyer from the NLG national office, contributed organizational skills.[38]

The Memorial Day weekend meeting revealed that the partnership between non-Indian lawyers, legal workers, and law students, on the one hand, and Native American defendants and supporters, on the other, would pose special challenges. Carter Camp, an AIM leader and defendant, along with Wallace Black Elk, a Lakota spiritual leader, believed the entire process had to begin with educating the non-Indians on Indian culture and spirituality. Some non-Indians balked, doubting this was the best use of precious time. Yet other non-Indians who agreed that respect for Indian values was crucial to the defense itself prevailed. The debate over whether to handle the cases by committee, under the Indian defendants' direction, or to parcel out individual cases to individual lawyers, tilted toward the former. The lawyers also agreed to volunteer their time. All money raised for the defense, therefore, would go to pay for bail or material resources necessary for the defense.[39]

Articulating the Wounded Knee occupation's central purpose to non-Indians would be crucial to fundraising. AIM leaders, in particular, spent much of the summer of 1973 raising money. Vernon Bellecourt traveled to Europe, setting up support committees in Belgium, Denmark, Germany, France, Britain, Sweden, and Italy. He received more sympathy than hard cash, however. At home, Dennis Banks, Russell Means, and Clyde Bellecourt hit the lecture circuit. Dick Gregory and Noam Chomsky helped raise money for legal defense of Wounded Knee defendants. WKLDOC began producing materials including booklets, press releases, and newsletters to convey the message to a largely non-Indian audience.[40] The "Wounded Knee Information Booklet" included a statement from AIM that ignored the complexities of Pine Ridge's reservation politics and emphasized treaty rights. The Oglala Sioux, it explained, had a treaty that was 105 years old but it had been continually violated. The time had come for the United States to live up to that agreement and the other 370 treaties it had signed. Quoting from a statement attributed to AIM, it went on:

> We are the landlords of this country and at Wounded Knee we showed up to collect. These treaties supersede any state laws and, in fact, prevail over federal law. If the country is going to live up to its constitution, then in fact it must live up to its treaty commitments. We still have to go to court to ascertain our treaty rights. Once again we have to rely on the White Man and wait for him to give us the right we already have. If he

goes against his constitution and convicts us, we will prove to the world that this is really a police state instead of a free country. The Wounded Knee trials are the most important of the century. They will expose how America practices its founding philosophy.[41]

In other words, Indians depended upon the "White Man's" constitution, courts, opinions, and willingness to live up to the nation's political values and philosophy. Ultimate power rested not with Native Americans but with their treaties and the government that signed them. Clearly, dependence on non-Indians doing the right thing was central to resolving the problems of Indian country.

These issues would be worked out, however, through the legal prosecutions of individuals who faced serious prison terms if convicted. To raise money, the lawyers had to "put a face" on the cases (see figure 6.2). As they explained it, WKLDOC took on all defendants in the federal Wounded Knee cases; those in the tribal cases; and those resulting from a protest at Custer, South Dakota, which preceded the Wounded Knee occupation. The cases covered civil, criminal, and tribal charges. The Wounded Knee defendants included the "leadership trials" of people such as Dennis Banks and Russell Means (whose joint trial would garner the most publicity) but also 123 other men and women arrested for "making their first political stand for the civil rights of Indian people" by bringing food, medicine, and clothing to the Wounded Knee area. The nineteen Custer defendants faced indictment for a demonstration outside a courthouse in South Dakota after the white murderer of Wesley Bad Heart Bull, an Oglala Sioux from Pine Ridge, received a two-month suspended sentence. One unsuccessful government case involved Dr. Paul Boe, director of social services for the American Lutheran Church, who refused to testify before a grand jury about events inside Wounded Knee he had witnessed as a negotiator and mediator. When Boe invoked a clergyman's privilege, the court held him in contempt. Within hours of beginning his sentence, the Eighth Circuit Court of Appeals overturned the contempt finding. Boe resigned from his position with the American Lutheran Church and indicated he would begin immediately to work for justice for Indian people.[42]

The financial resources of the government prosecutors were daunting. According to one WKLDOC fundraising document, the U.S. government spent between five and six million dollars on the seventy-one day siege alone. The subsequent court actions would require millions more, with the St. Paul leadership trials costing taxpayers five thousand dollars per week. Even though the Indian defendants' lawyers and other legal aid workers accepted no salaries, they still needed housing, food, and, of course, telephones, office supplies, and transportation, not to mention resources for research related to the long, complicated cases. Plus the cases were being tried in various venues, so WKLDOC

204　HIPPIES, INDIANS, AND THE FIGHT FOR RED POWER

Figure 6.2 Part of "putting a face" on the Wounded Knee defendants' cases, including harkening to the past. Evoking historical Indians, in this case Lakota leader Red Cloud, to raise support for contemporary Indians typified poster art of the 1960s and 1970s. Credit: Minnesota Historical Society's Wounded Knee Legal Defense/Offense Collection.

established offices in Rapid City, Sioux Falls, St. Paul, Porcupine (South Dakota), and Lincoln in an effort to provide sufficient support.

The fundraising effort was as wide-ranging as was the response. The skill and energy of WKLDOC volunteers to compose fundraising letters and the geographical reach of the contributors was much more impressive than that of

Alcatraz. Furthermore, AIM's more radical rhetoric and willingness to brandish weapons, things that did not occur among the Alcatraz occupiers, did not discourage sympathies. The international donations were noteworthy. Letters of support and financial contributions (many of them small) came in from the United Kingdom, Canada, Poland, Costa Rica, Brazil, the Netherlands, Belgium, Australia, Switzerland, and Germany. A contribution for fifty-five dollars came from the German American Indian Group in Stuttgart, to benefit the children of Wounded Knee defendants, and a group called KIVA from the Netherlands sent one hundred dollars. The extent to which supporters understood the situation is uncertain and the letters suggest critics of capitalism, American consumerism, and U.S. foreign policy found in the Wounded Knee case a cause to which they could attach their anti-Americanism. H. Marius Spanier wrote from Hanover, West Germany, "I was very delighted to hear that A.I.M. leaders do not want an integration in an American way of life or any other technical system . . . You are living in a land, which belongs not only to the most capitalistic, imperialistic states on earth, but also to the most technical infected [sic] nations. Indians of Northamerica [sic] have my full sympathy, cause they fighted [sic] through to many years against the rotten consume-society of U.S.A." A self-described Rastafarian from Essex, England, sent along with his small contribution the statement, "I personally despise capitalism." Others understood the events as part of the problems facing many of the world's indigenous people. From Sao Paulo, Dagomir Marquezi wrote, 'We have, in South America, the same problem: the unrespect to the Indian rights. Wounded Knee is an exemple [sic]: let's divulge it." Sean O. Cionnaith, Director of the Irish Republican Movement, expressed a keen interest in Indians' struggles to "own their own country" and wished WKLDOC well "in your just struggle against those who have stolen your lands for their own benefit," obviously assuming the organization consisted primarily of Native Americans. He thought his organization could raise some funds and publicize the cause, making good on the offer a few months later when he sent a twelve pound contribution to the WKLDOC office in Sioux Falls.[43]

The support from domestic sources was equally eclectic. A correspondents' file from people whose last names begin with the letter "A" revealed a range of backers. Arline Abdalian promised to sign and circulate a petition WKLDOC sent to her union, the General Council of Stewards, District 65 (Distributive Workers of America). A graduate of Barnard, Abdalian worked for the college as a secretary and also promised to help raise funds. She believed trade union support could be a determinative factor for the Wounded Knee defendants and found her own District 65, which had supported the United Farm Workers, Farah Strikers, and the Angela Davis defense fund, to be particularly progressive. "I know of no other groups who have suffered such massive attacks nor endless reprisals than the Indians and the workers," she wrote. Emilio Alvarez Jr. believed that the Wounded Knee defendants' legal problems were emblematic of those many minorities had suffered. That the government censured AIM and fabricated charges against the leadership was not surprising. If they succeeded in convicting leaders such as Banks and Means, this would represent an "enormous setback for all minorities as well as Indian people." And Jean Allen, a seventy-nine-year-old woman from Bakersfield, California, expressed her anger toward the role U.S. Marshals and other government officials played at Wounded Knee. She thought their behavior was much worse than that of the Indians. She did not have much money to donate, "But I have a big mouth."[44]

Among the hundreds of letters WKLDOC received, New Yorker Gwenne Ellen Freiman's was particularly heartfelt, focused, and articulate. She probably represented many in the sentiments that accompanied her "small but deeply felt contribution toward the restoration of human pride and dignity in America as expressed by the activities at Wounded Knee."

> My empathy for the Native American is very real . . . as a Jew I am no stranger to what violence fear and greed can provoke in others; in those who view themselves as the majority and claim criminal, often murderous "majority rights" against those who live differently and want only to be permitted to live in their own personal relationship with God and their land . . . because I know I live and prosper on stolen land under the yoke of "benevolent oppression" by the government, I am sending this check, which I know will be microfilmed by the FBI, as a refusal . . . as a denial of complicity . . . and as a simple affirmation of the spiritual and emotional rights of men. When liberty is denied and internal freedom lost in the noise of false, superficial sentimentality, a crime has been committed for which there is no possible reparation . . . the destruction of the human soul.[45]

In its absence of commentary regarding issues such as treaty rights or self-determination, sovereignty or reservation governance, this letter is typical. Among the hundreds of letters WKLDOC received, most correspondents lacked precision on the nature of the political struggle, but expressed goodwill toward Native Americans, in general, and AIM, in particular. The overwhelming message was one of sympathy and encouragement.[46]

It is also noteworthy that political opponents' efforts to present AIM and the Wounded Knee occupation as violence-prone did not seem to faze letter writers. WKLDOC, in fact, did not shy away from gun imagery in its fundraising. In fact, they wanted an image that included weapons. One poster, designed by Joe Jaqua, a Mission Indian who offered his skills as an artist, depicted the Oglalas defending their land with guns. They were willing to kill or be killed to protect their sovereign nation. "We are tired of our people being depicted as passive. The poster must be a picture of pride, force and militancy."[47]

AIM's willingness to meet violence with violence gave some supporters pause, however, particularly church-based supporters. But they found ways to justify and explain it away. Paul Boe, of the American Lutheran Church's Division of Social Service, addressed this issue in a letter to his board and the acting president of the American Lutheran Church. He acknowledged that "the question always comes up, 'How can we support an organization—such as AIM—when so often its activities end in violence and destruction of property?'" Boe admitted he struggled with this question. Yet, he reminded his board that when the American Lutheran Church approved a document called "Decision in a Time of National Crises," which stated the church must be willing to match proclamations for justice with actions, it committed itself to a "readiness to experiment and a willingness to take risks." Supporting AIM, a group that advocated justice for American Indians, represented just that kind of risk. True, the church deplored violence and destruction of property but it also supported justice and equality. For years others had tried, with little success, to combat the racism, segregation, and poverty endemic in Indian country. "If justice is to be achieved some group or groups with the courage to press their point persistently will have to be supported. Forces against change are strong." AIM had, he seemed to be suggesting, the determination to "press the point" and had little alternative to meeting force with force.[48]

John P. Adams saw his role in the African American civil rights movement and at Wounded Knee as one of conflict resolution. To avoid violence through negotiation and communication was his goal. Yet he had learned by watching northern cities blow up in the riots of summer 1967 and in the wake of Martin Luther King's assassination in 1968, that sometimes violence could not be contained. He believed the church's first priority was to make certain it did not "sanction the forces of repression . . . the church must not bless the violence of repression." Its proper role was to listen to those who suffered injustice and to use its resources to transmit their complaints to the more privileged. In violent incidents, listening should be even more intense. While he did not condone AIM militancy, neither did he condemn it.[49]

Given the Quaker antipathy toward violence and commitment to pacifism, how did the American Friends Service Committee reconcile this most fundamental ethic with AIM's willingness to make guns a central feature of their public image and return force with force? One Friend, Alfred Ames, asked this very question of the AFSC's central office in Philadelphia, clearly doubting the soundness of AFSC's support of AIM during the takeover of the BIA Building and its public statements regarding the affair at Wounded Knee. He cautioned AFSC Executive Secretary Bronson Clark that the government would not tolerate "armed insurrection within its borders." While the federal response to the BIA takeover was "craven" and its actions at Wounded Knee were "dubious," a government trying to sustain a "credible stance in a global balance of terror with the Communist dictatorships" would not brook violence from a small group of "erratic individuals." Ames believed AIM's "antics" were counterproductive and absolutely incompatible with Friends' principles.[50]

J. Philip Buskirk, National Representative of the AFSC American Indian Program, replied to Ames's challenge by explaining the AFSC's roots regarding native issues ran very deep, based on much experience in the field, thought, and respect for the dignity and rights of Indian people. Nearly all the program staff and many program committee members were Native American, he claimed, and the AFSC was absolutely committed to the "powerful and widespread move among Indian people to assert their historic rights and cultural identity." Sidestepping the philosophical issue Ames raised (much as Boe did with the Lutherans), he insisted the Trail of Broken Treaties had been a "sincere and spontaneous" attempt to bring federal attention to long-standing grievances. That the episode ended in the unfortunate wreckage of the BIA Building mattered less than the government officials' failure to respond to the need for review and genuine discussion. Therein lay the tragedy. As for Wounded Knee, Buskirk argued, the AFSC's role was assuring medical services were available for the people in the compound and urging negotiation of the issues rather than violence. "Our statements were aimed primarily at government officials," Buskirk explained, "because theirs is the overwhelming power." He felt certain that if the government showed restraint in confronting "a small group of determined men [alas, ignoring the many women involved in the occupation] at the site where a bloody massacre once occurred [that would] result in far more credit and credibility for the whole United States than would the crushing of that group by sheer force."[51] In short, Buskirk evaded the fundamental question.

Still, AIM's controversial profile, both among Indians and non-Indians, remained an issue for the AFSC. During the winter of 1974, a report from the field to the North Central Regional Office in Des Moines, Iowa, reassured the organization that there was "little or no romanticizing of violence and guns" among AIM people on Pine Ridge. Rather, they saw guns as necessary tools for self defense. Otherwise they neither promulgated a rhetoric of violence nor had illusions about violence being a means to achieve their goals. Instead, AIM was working hard to meet its ends and restore human dignity in a way that ultimately reduced violence.[52]

The AFSC moved somewhat guardedly with respect to Wounded Knee, however. Its many years of experience with tribal leaders and with the sometimes tortured entanglements of tribal politics led them to avoid getting caught in *those* crossfires. Yet, the organization did not hesitate to criticize the federal government. One of its first actions was to call upon the U.S. government to renounce the use of force at Wounded Knee. In a telegram sent to the U.S. Attorney General Richard Kleindienst and Secretary of the Interior Rogers Morton, AFSC pointed out the government could not possibly justify the use of "death dealing force" against a small armed band whose hostages willingly stayed after being offered the opportunity to leave. Violence would not only injure those actually hit by the gunfire but would destroy hope for justice and reconciliation. They also called for an impartial study of Indians' oil, timber, fishing, and other treaty rights, and right to a decent education and health care. As Quakers who had worked for years with Native Americans, they had often observed the serious violations of rights and were not surprised by the demonstration at Wounded Knee. The group consequently called for the withdrawal of federal marshals and the immediate instigation of an impartial investigation of Indian rights violations. Further, AFSC worked to assure medical personnel and supplies as well as food moved into the occupation site in the early weeks, continued to pressure the Justice Department to avoid ultimatums and other "truculent action," contacted key senators and congressmen to reinforce the need for genuine negotiation regarding the Twenty Points from the Trail of Broken Treaties, and sent staff and volunteers from their regional offices to monitor checkpoints at the blocked perimeter of Wounded Knee.

AFSC did not, however, send staffers to Pine Ridge and advised all staff to stay away. So, Ben Richmond, a member of the Portland staff, submitted his resignation in order to go to South Dakota in March 1973. He and other Portlanders (part of an informal group that called themselves the Main Street Gathering) intended to bring food to Wounded Knee. The FBI stopped and arrested them before they even left Oregon; a violation of civil liberties that deeply offended Richmond. Meanwhile, by the third week of March, the AFSC decided there was no useful action for them to take on-site at Pine Ridge or Wounded Knee. Their role would be to call attention to the grievances expressed first at the Trail of Broken Treaties and now in South Dakota—to educate, not agitate. And their emphasis would remain on national grievances rather than local ones. To the AFSC, the central issues at stake at Wounded Knee and throughout the nation were sovereignty under treaty provisions, Indian land and its management, control over natural resources, and new relationships with the federal and state governments. The Friends group understood Wounded Knee was a "highly symbolic" place to make a stand and the people there were among those who preferred "quick death to creeping oblivion." The occupiers "know we have in our hands the instruments to deal death, yet hope we might have in our hearts the will to seek with them justice and peace."[53]

Once the trials for Wounded Knee defendants began, AFSC maintained its relatively conservative involvement. Its Minnesota Community Relations Task

Force recommended the AFSC not attempt to influence the court's decisions, serve as fundraisers for the defense, or defend specific actions of AIM in Wounded Knee. Instead they encouraged the group to keep all AFSC offices informed about the trial, monitor the trials to assure fairness, support treaty rights as relevant to the trial, express dismay that the government had already reneged on an agreement signed at the end of the occupation, and urge the government and all Americans to confront and begin to resolve the real grievances and needs of all Indian people. Although the AFSC would not send money to the defense efforts, they would recommend others contribute to WKLDOC. In the end, they did not want to be unduly associated with AIM, preferring to stress the rights of all Indians. If they took a strong pro-AIM posture, they feared, they would lose a great deal of Native American support. And they wanted to maintain a consistent message about the larger issue of treaty rights and sovereignty over individual trials and defense cases.

The one exception to this strategy came after federal Judge Fred Nichol dismissed five of the charges, and eventually the entire case, against AIM leaders Dennis Banks and Russell Means due to misconduct and deception on the part of the federal government. After that trial ended, twelve jurors and an alternate sent a letter to Attorney General William Saxbe urging him to drop all charges against all other Wounded Knee defendants. This group then formed, with the help of WKLDOC attorney Mark Lane, an organization called Jurors and Others for Reconciliation. Their goal was to meet with Saxbe and encourage him not only to drop federal charges but also to pressure South Dakota and Nebraska to drop theirs and begin an era of reconciliation by taking treaty rights seriously and reducing BIA control over Indians' lives. AFSC joined the jurors, Lane, and representatives from a variety of legal and church organizations (including United Methodist Church, American Lutheran Church, United Church of Christ, Episcopal Church, Unitarian Universalist, and the National Council of Churches) in a November 1974 meeting at the Justice Department. They received a respectable, if ineffective, hearing. This outcome did not surprise an AFSC staff participant who admitted they never really had much hope for turning the Justice Department around. But he found it a useful opportunity to press the larger issue of treaty rights and thought it remarkable that this group of citizens—"coming from the most unlikely place"—that is, the upper Midwest—wanted to help keep these issues alive.[54]

Meanwhile the AFSC celebrated a victory for themselves and, of course, the Native American tribes whose interests rested at the heart of the fishing rights controversies. Just as the confrontational tactics of AIM were meeting with a devastating federal response, the more mainstream approach of seeking justice through legal means was proving effective. Events seemed to be coming full circle. Just as the action on the barricades at Wounded Knee subsided, a federal judge in Washington state announced his decision on a case prompted by the fish-ins of the previous decade. January 11, 1974, three days after the Means-Banks trial opened in St. Paul, Judge George H. Boldt affirmed the Indian right to fish outside reservation boundaries on the basis of a 120-year-old treaty and allocated 50 percent of the catch to the treaty signatories. The decision known as *United States v. Washington* was, according to a Native American Rights Fund lawyer, the most emphatic affirmation of treaty rights ever issued by a federal court. In a letter addressed to the AFSC's Philip Buskirk, the attorney noted: "A decision like this makes the endless days of research, writing, preparation, haggling with the government, and trying to translate the entire matter into an understandable dispute for the public and the court seem very worthwhile. I hope you realize the contribution that American Friends Service Committee has made toward finding resolutions to the overall fishing rights dispute (which, of course, is not totally resolved), especially by the publication of *Uncommon Controversy*." Buskirk was overjoyed not only over the fishing rights victory, but because he now believed the decision would have far-reaching influence on the validity of all treaty rights and help Indian nations protect land, water, and other natural resources.[55]

As for the outcome at Wounded Knee, little change seemed imminent in the short run. Wilson did not step down from power on Pine Ridge, although Russell Means nearly defeated him in a 1974 election for tribal chair. The White House paid little attention to the specific grievances against Wilson, the 1868 treaty, the Twenty Points, or other issues. They insisted, in fact, that matters regarding treaties rested with Congress not the executive branch. Instead the Department of Justice arrested hundreds of occupiers, held them under high bail, and multiplied the charges against them. Although the government's conviction rate was less than 10 percent, the constant pressure took its toll. As one scholar of the trials put it, "Virtually every AIM leader in the country would be either in jail, dead, or driven underground within the two years following the occupation of Wounded Knee."[56] Ironically the executive branch itself was under increased scrutiny as the corruption associated with Watergate unfolded. This affected AIM's cause. Government misconduct during Wounded Knee, for example, helped free Dennis Banks and Russell Means from successful prosecution. The Nixon presidency soon collapsed.

If AIM came out of Wounded Knee seriously weakened, the process of educating non-Indians about self-determination and treaty rights continued and began to translate into substantive change. Nixon aid Leonard Garment believed that one of the many unfortunate outcomes of Watergate was it dissipated the administration's ability to pursue its Indian reform initiatives. What he failed to understand was this movement was bigger—much bigger—than Nixon, or AIM for that matter. It could go on without both. And it did. Garment himself, unwittingly, demonstrated that very thing by acknowledging the Supreme Court's 1980 decision that the United States had violated the 1868 Treaty of Fort Laramie and must pay fair compensation for unlawfully taking that land. The Sioux litigants refused the cash and insisted on the land. While the nature of compensation remains to this day unresolved, there is no doubt the Sioux won the battle.[57]

Of course the people involved in the Black Hills and the Pacific Northwest fishing rights cases knew these outcomes represented not ends, but beginnings. Still, they were momentous victories that offered a moment to pause and acknowledge the collective efforts of Indian and non-Indian people who helped achieve these landmark decisions. They had been a long time coming, but there was still far to go.

Epilogue

In 1973, just as the Wounded Knee Legal Defense/Offense Committee began organizing for the trials that followed the occupation, about fifteen WKLDOC volunteers traveled to Omaha to hear Angela Davis speak. She talked about the "Founding Conference for a National Defense Organization Against Racist and Political Repression" that had been held that May in Chicago. Other speakers at the Omaha event included Dolores Huerta who spoke about farmworkers, Jose Che Velasquez who addressed concerns of Puerto Ricans, and Anthony Russo (co-defendant with Daniel Ellsberg) on the Pentagon Papers case. Davis was the most expansive in her remarks—noting that racist and political repression in America was more conspicuous than ever and required not only a vigorous countermovement but one that crossed racial and ethnic lines. All contemporary progressive movements faced similar threats. "Black liberation struggles are under attack; liberation movements of Chicanos, Puerto Ricans, Latinos and Asians are being violated." But she did not stop there. "And today," she said "we must be especially conscious of the government's attempts to disrupt and destroy the Indian people's just struggles for independence and sovereignty."[1]

Davis pointed to police actions in African American ghettos, Latino barrios, and on Indian reservations as examples of what she meant. Prisons and court systems only reinforced police repression, which she knew firsthand. But the latest example came from Wounded Knee where the federal government had arrested and charged hundreds of people, using what she called the "Rap Brown Anti-Riot Act" on a massive scale. People in many states faced arrest simply because officials believed they were on their way to Wounded Knee or because they were Native American and *might* be on their way. Photographers faced arrest for attempting to record events at the occupation site. Not only were participants or potential participants' rights violated, but so was the public's right to know.[2]

In other words, everyone suffered under a racially and politically oppressive system, so everyone must share in the process of fighting back. Most of the repression, Davis acknowledged, fell upon people of color. But white people who fought the existing economic and social system were also targets of the officially sanctioned tyranny. She reminded her audience about the historical tradition of white people who participated in the nineteenth-century abolition of slavery movement, resisted the Indian wars, criticized the war against Mexico, organized labor guilds and unions, fought for woman suffrage, and "resisted the imperialist aims of the first world war." White people, too, had fought battles and left a legacy of struggle to their children who, in turn, had also been jailed, beaten, and even killed.[3]

The Omaha assemblage agreed the solution to oppression was solidarity and it welcomed everyone who shared a commitment to justice. As an example of what an organization such as the National Defense Organization Against Racist and Political Repression could do, Davis asked her audience to consider Wounded Knee. According to opinion polls and official surveys, the occupation in South Dakota revealed tremendous support for Indians' struggles throughout the nation. But that support could not be effectively funneled into action because no national movement or group existed to organize and lead such efforts. If "we had already established our organization we would have been able to call for a nationwide demonstration in solidarity with our struggling Indian sisters and brothers. If we had openly and massively displayed our resistance and solidarity, perhaps we could have averted the murders of our brothers Frank Clearwater and Lawrence Lamont," two occupation participants who died at Wounded Knee.[4] She saluted the many "brilliant and courageous lawyers" who carried the fight into courtrooms and knew the strength of their position rested on the strength of the people. The key, however, remained cross-community, cross-racial cooperation. What Davis and the others wanted, in short, was a national organization to systematize the kind of informal, disparate, and even chaotic support politically progressive people and groups had been providing for over a decade.

Something along those lines did materialize in 1975. This group's focus, however, centered on Indian issues, and thus it was not as all-encompassing as the organization Davis and others envisioned. The Native American Solidarity Committee (NASC) formed in St. Paul, Minnesota, and was an outgrowth of the Wounded Knee Legal Defense/Offense Committee. Its mission was to create a broad-based coalition of groups and individuals who would move beyond legal defense and trials and toward a broader support for "the struggles of Native American people for self-determination, independence and sovereignty." NASC chose "solidarity" in its title because it did not intend simply to organize support, but rather to organize "in solidarity *with* Native American people . . . [to] stand beside them in struggle together for freedom and self-determination against a common enemy."[5] The group's first newsletter noted six chapters—in the Twin Cities, Washington, D.C., New York, Philadelphia, Boston-Cambridge, and San Francisco. It hoped to attract supporters from a wide variety of groups. The Philadelphia chapter, for instance, included representatives from the Black Panther Party, Prairie Fire Organizing Committee, American Friends Service Committee, Puerto Rican Socialist Party, and National Coalition for Social Change. Within a short time, NASC claimed additional chapters in Amherst, Atlanta, Chicago, Yellow Springs (Ohio), Portland, Seattle, St. Louis, and Barre, Vermont.[6] It saw itself as the logical outgrowth of the decade-long resistance that began with Pacific Northwest fishing rights and grew with the occupations at Alcatraz, the BIA Building, and Wounded Knee. These events not only politicized Native Americans, the group claimed, but taught all Americans about their shared struggle against imperialism. As the nation approached its bicentennial, it must demand a celebration "without colonies! We must demand sovereign rights be restored to native peoples!" Although the rhetoric was vigorous, membership was not. Almost from the start, the San Francisco chapter suffered from "diminishing membership."[7]

NASC struggled to establish a permanent presence just as the fever pitch of direct action had peaked and began a precipitous decline. It never became a significant force in American politics. The organization nevertheless serves as a fitting conclusion to this study because it represented an effort to formalize the informal coming together of like-minded people working to promote civil rights, civil liberties, farmworkers' rights, and Native American treaty rights, which typified the years leading up to the bicentennial. From the Quakers to the Lutherans, from the San Francisco-based counterculture to the housewives of Burlingame, from local labor union organizations to movie stars such as Marlon Brando and Jane Fonda, a wide variety of individuals and groups took action in these dramatic times. They supported with their words, deeds, and wallets the nation's movement toward economic, political, and social justice.

By tracing the moments of cooperation among such unlikely partners, this book offers an alternative perspective on the amorphous cultural changes reverberating across the continent that led, in time, to political and economic reform, if not revolution. The starting point for understanding such change must be with the Native American people, tribes, and leaders who survived the termination era and continued to insist on their treaty rights, sovereignty, and cultural survival. But they knew they could not do it alone. There were simply not enough of them. The levers of power rested in non-Indian hands. By the early 1960s, a disparate collection of liberal, progressive, and radical organizations; churches; and individuals of various races and ethnicities stepped up to support them. As the example of Native American rights demonstrates, such coalitions were fraught with difficulties, frustrations, and challenges. Tribes divided. Native Americans were not of one mind regarding the proper tactics and methods to achieve justice. Generations split. Historic antipathies remained. Sometimes new enemies materialized. Misunderstandings and missed opportunities abounded. Racism was so pervasive in the United States that few could claim to be free of its effects. Native Americans' suspicions of African Americans sometimes worked against cooperation, and African Americans' unfamiliarity with the distinctive nature of Native Americans' legal status as treaty tribes only served to make that relationship more challenging.

By the end of the 1960s, both Native American and African American groups shared an antipathy to Anglo American prominence within their organizations and made it clear that, if whites wanted to join them, they would have to take background positions. Anglo financial and legal help was welcomed, but black nationalists and Native American "militants" demanded the public leadership roles. They would no longer allow others to speak for them. White supporters usually understood and accepted that, but some did not and left. Church-based organizations, such as the American Friends Service Committee, had to hedge basic core principles—such as commitment to nonviolence—in the course of supporting the American Indian Movement (AIM). At times, Native Americans had to put aside antipathies toward Anglo "hippies," counterculture types, and political radicals because they needed their bodies at streamside or statehouse demonstrations. Anglo counterculture types often had little more than superficial understandings of, and commitment to, the political issues at stake in places such as Frank's Landing, and their involvement proved fleeting.

These are just some of the internal tensions affecting such coalitions. Added to this were outside forces, such as the federal government intent on suppressing radicalism, and even reform, through systematic surveillance, arrests, and costly prosecutions—the political repression Angela Davis talked about in Omaha. The rising prominence and power of law-and-order advocates and conservative officeholders initiated a dramatic turn away from progressive change and toward retrenchment. Finally, the war in Vietnam, a critical backdrop to these events, gradually wound down as did the accompanying domestic dissent. Dissidents seemed increasingly less inclined to take to the streets for any purpose.

In looking back at the period between the early 1960s and the mid-1970s, all the reasons cooperation should *not* have happened make the occasions when it did occur all the more significant. Moreover, this joint activity encouraged a significant push toward making real—in the case of Native American concerns—centuries-old promises of property rights to natural resources, sovereignty, and self-determination. The greatest achievement was bringing to the nation's attention the deep problems that existed in Indian country. But activists also pointed out ways to achieve recovery and restitution, through realization of treaty rights, for instance, or legislation designed to address and remedy past injustices. Consciousness was raised, to use a phrase of the time—a necessary first step. Practice changed too, though not always immediately and, of course, quite simply—not always. In the short term, the Indians of All Tribes failed to acquire Alcatraz property, but scored a piece of Fort Lawton. Taos Pueblo and other tribes regained control of sacred spaces. In the long term, the fundamental turn toward the spirit, if not the letter, of Hank Adams's and the Trail of Broken Treaties' Twenty Points has prevailed.

Just as the moments of cooperation came in fits and starts, and at disparate places such as the Nisqually River, Alcatraz, Taos, Washington, and Pine Ridge, so too did the pro-reform legislation and court cases that materialized following the most publicized spectacles of protest. These laws and decisions demonstrated that indeed something dramatically different was happening in Indian affairs. Most of the tangible results occurred in local communities and in tribal settings far from national media coverage. The improvements in tribal life were often more piecemeal than transformational. But taken together, they add up to a clear commitment to new national priorities, understandings, and obligations. The American people and the federal government, it now became clear, had embraced Stewart Brand's mantra of the early 1960s: "America Needs Indians" and took positive action to assure their permanence in the nation.[8]

In the aftermath of the most contentious years of protests and demonstrations, the United States Congress and courts acquiesced to Indian demands for more power over their lives and resources. As legal scholar Charles Wilkinson put it, by the mid-1970s, tribal action on many fronts "had fundamentally reshaped the circumstances that held sway just a generation before. Congress jettisoned termination, advanced a new policy of self-determination, and began to give relief to terminated tribes."[9] More specifically, Congress launched a series of laws that underscored a decisive turn toward restoration of tribal power and perpetuation of native cultures. It started in 1970 with President Richard Nixon's administration, which made self-determination the cornerstone of his formal Indian policy. Five years later, in 1975, the year of Nixon's impeachment and withdrawal from office, as Wounded Knee defendants continued to be prosecuted and jailed, Congress passed the Indian Self-Determination and Education Assistance Act. This legislation directed the BIA and Indian Health Service to contract with tribes for federal programs rather than depend on federal agencies to do the work. Reform oriented, rather than revolutionary, the act nevertheless meant steadily increasing tribal control in the years to follow. It helped develop tribal infrastructures, leadership opportunities, and lifted morale.[10]

Other legislation came through the congressional pipeline designed to strengthen the foundations of tribal life. The Native American Religious Freedom Act (1978), the Indian Child Welfare Act (1978), the Indian Gaming Regulatory Act (1988), the Native American Graves Protection and Repatriation Act (1990), the Indian Energy Resources Act (1992), and the Indian

Tribal Energy and Development and Self-Determination Act (2005)—among others—all demonstrated a national pledge to bury termination threats and encourage tribal economic, political, and cultural power.[11]

The judicial branch of the federal government also shifted gears. Increasingly, by the mid-1970s, judges considered tribal views regarding "the historical roots and true meanings of treaties and other laws" and decided in their favor. Such interpretations of treaties and other federal laws were essential for tribes to gain greater control of their resources and exercise sovereignty. Although it was not the first twentieth-century case to reinforce treaty rights and a tribe's right to use its land and resources, Judge Boldt's landmark 1974 decision in favor of treaty-based fishing rights was one that most clearly and dramatically signaled this sea change in federal support. The decision reverberated across the nation and underscored a commitment, though one not consistently attained, to validate both treaties and tribes' standing as governments.[12]

Through the 1970s and well into the 1980s, tribes prevailed in many Supreme Court decisions. For instance, the court concluded in *McClanahan v. State Tax Commission of Arizona* (1973) that Arizona could not tax tribal members' incomes earned on reservations. The decision, in other words, strengthened the concept that reservation-based Indians were free from state jurisdiction and taxes, and it reinforced the larger principle that state laws could not be applied to reservation Indians without explicit congressional approval because "state tax could not be 'reconciled with tribal self-determination.'" In 1982 the Court concluded that the Jicarilla Apache Tribe, as "a commercial partner" and in its "role as a sovereign," had the authority to levy taxes on energy companies that developed resources on their reservations. Interestingly, Justice Thurgood Marshall, a former civil rights attorney and the first African American on the Supreme Court, wrote both opinions. He considered himself a champion of Indian rights.[13] Such decisions would be challenged and tested. There would be backlash, compromise, and some outright losses. The alliance between William Rehnquist, Antonin Scalia, and Clarence Thomas, who all shared a strong states' rights agenda, turned the tide, particularly by the late 1980s. It remains to be seen how this will impact tribal sovereignty in the long term.

The more recent *Cobell* case, however, offers reason for optimism. The federal government agreed to pay a multibillion settlement for past mismanagement of Indian oil, gas, grazing and other leases. Hundreds of thousands of Indian people will receive substantial payment thanks to this suit, which was settled in December 2009. Congress approved it, President Barack Obama signed it into law, and a federal judge's required approval came in summer 2011. Of the $3.4 billion settlement, the largest ever approved by the United States government, $1.9 billion will be used to consolidate tribal lands by purchasing individual parcels of Indian land that had been "fractionalized" over generations.

Sometimes hundreds of people own a single parcel of trust land, a result of the nineteenth-century allotment policy, which divided reservations into homesteads, and consequent inheritance practices. Once the government purchases this land, it will turn it over to the appropriate tribe in an attempt to restore its cohesive land base. Almost fourteen thousand square miles of land are eligible for this program—about the size of Maryland. Activists advocated such a plan as one of the Twenty Points during the Trail of Broken Treaties occupation of the Bureau of Indian Affairs. It took forty years and an African American president to finally make it happen.[14]

As one historian put it, "History works, at times, like a ratchet and pawl. Although there is slippage backward, certain pushes forward cannot be reversed."[15] Such is the case with the more recent advances in the realization of Native Americans' rights and the national support for them. But it is not guaranteed. The trajectory can only continue, with broad, public understanding of and support for the distinctive, even "special," nature of Indian rights. Tribal leaders, Native American groups, and individuals must continue to articulate the historical, legal, and moral foundations of these rights. Non-Indians must continue to listen and learn.

NOTES

Introduction

1. Tom Wolfe, *The Electric Kool-Aid Acid Test* (New York: Bantam Books, 1969), 2; Fred Turner, *From Counterculture to Cyberculture: Stewart Brand, the Whole Earth Network and the Rise of Digital Utopianism* (Chicago: University of Chicago Press, 2006), 45–51.
2. Stewart Brand notebooks, May 3–20, 1963, and June 18, 1963, Stewart Brand Papers, Special Collections, Stanford University Library, Stanford, California (hereafter cited as SBP); Stewart Brand, interview with author, February 12, 2002; Wolfe, *Electric Kool-Aid Acid Test*, 224, 225, 231.
3. For a sampling of scholarship on the sixties see David Bruner, *Making Peace With the 60s* (Princeton, NJ: Princeton University Press, 1996); Morris Dickstein, *Gates of Eden: American Culture in the Sixties* (Cambridge, MA: Harvard University Press, 1977); David R. Farber, *The Age of Great Dreams: America in the 1960s* (New York: Hill and Wang, 1994); Todd Gitlin, *The Sixties: Years of Hope, Days of Rage* (New York: Bantam Books, 1987); Maurice Isserman and Michael Kazin, *America Divided: The Civil War of the 1960s* (New York: Oxford University Press, 2000); Arthur Marwick, *The Sixties: Cultural Revolution in Britain, France, Italy and the United States, c. 1958–1974* (New York: Oxford University, 1998); William L. O'Neill, *Coming Apart: An Informal History of America in the 1960s* (New York: Random House, 1971); Gerald J. DeGroot, *The Sixties Unplugged: A Kaleidoscopic History of a Disorderly Decade* (Cambridge, MA: Harvard University Press, 2008); and Terry H. Anderson, *The Movement and the Sixties: Protest in America From Greensboro to Wounded Knee* (New York: Oxford University Press, 1995). Although Anderson's title suggests Indian affairs will get significant coverage, only about five of over four hundred pages address Native American activism. Among the works that address the intersection of Indians and at least one other non-Indian support group, the counterculture, see Stewart Brand, "Indians and the Counterculture, 1960's–1970's," in *History of Indian-White Relations*, ed. Wilcomb Washburn, *Handbook of North American Indians*, vol. 4 (Washington, DC: Smithsonian Institution, 1980), 570–72; and Philip Deloria, *Playing Indian* (New Haven, CT: Yale University Press, 1998), 154–80.
4. John Bryan, "Buffy on Hippies—'They'll Never Be Indians,'" *Berkeley Barb*, June 30, 1967, 10. See also Don Strachan, "Buffy Sainte-Marie to Hippies," *East Village Others* 2, no. 17 (August 1, 1967), reprinted in *Our Time: Interviews from the East Village Other*, ed. and comp. Allen Katzman (New York: Dial Press, 1972), 211–15; Leslie Marmon Silko, "An Old-Time Indian Attack Conducted in Two Parts: Part One: Imitation 'Indian' Poems; Part Two: Gary Snyder's *Turtle Island*," in *The Remembered Earth: An Anthology of Contemporary Native American Literature*, ed. Geary Hobson (Albuquerque: University of New Mexico Press, 1979), 211–17; Geary Hobson, "The Rise of the White Shaman as a New Version of Cultural Imperialism," in *Remembered Earth*, 100–108. These last two essays were originally

published in the *Yardbird Reader* in 1976 and 1977 respectively. See also Deloria, *Playing Indian*, 154–80. Thank you to Michael Doyle for pointing me to several of these sources.
5. The definition of counterculture remains inevitably imprecise. Theodore Roszak's *The Making of a Counterculture* (Berkeley: University of California Press, 1995), originally published in 1969, remains useful for a contemporary attempt to define and explain it. For a collection of historians' assessments see Peter Braunstein and Michael William Doyle, eds., *Imagine Nation: The American Counterculture of the 1960s & 70s* (New York: Routledge, 2002). The editors define counterculture as "an inherently unstable collection of attitudes, tendencies, postures, gestures, 'lifestyles,' ideals, visions, hedonistic pleasures, moralisms, negations, and affirmations. These roles were played by people who defined themselves first by what they were not, and then, only after having cleared that essential ground of identity, began to conceive anew what they were. What they were was what they might become—more a process than a product—and thus more a direction or a motion than a movement," 10.
6. Doug Rossinow, *The Politics of Authenticity: Liberalism, Christianity and the New Left in America* (New York: Columbia University Press, 1998), 4–7. Though many contemporaries and commentators distinguished the counterculture from the New Left, Rossinow maintains that by the late 1960s/early 1970s the New Left came to see itself as part of a larger counterculture. The strongest link between them was their shared quest for authenticity. If they did not always function together harmoniously or operate as a "single movement" in Austin, Texas (his case study), there was genuine conviviality between them. He defines counterculture as "the loosely associated set of cultural rebellions among affluent white youth in the 1960s and 1970s," 247–52.
7. Rossinow, *Politics of Authenticity*, 6–8, 13–95. Rossinow noted that the Austin, Texas, New Left was notable for its tendency to view racial issues primarily as a matter of black and white, ignoring the burgeoning Mexican American movement in their state. The Native American movements rising up further west attracted some attention and support of Texas New Leftists, however. For a critique of the alienated's turn to culture and identity as antidote or as a de-alienation strategy see David Steigerwald, *Culture's Vanities: The Paradox of Cultural Diversity in a Globalized World* (New York: Rowman & Littlefield, 2004). For more on issues related to Indian authenticity see Deloria, *Playing Indian*; Paige Raibmon, *Authentic Indians: Episodes of Encounter from the Late Nineteenth-Century Northwest Coast* (Durham, NC: Duke University Press, 2005); and Paul Chaat Smith, *Everything You Know About Indians Is Wrong* (Minneapolis: University of Minnesota Press, 2009).
8. Vine Deloria Jr., *Custer Died For Your Sins: An Indian Manifesto* (Toronto: Macmillan, 1969), 101, 124.
9. John P. Adams, *At the Heart of the Whirlwind* (New York: Harper & Row, 1976), x.
10. For an example of two contrasting interpretations regarding interracial cooperation and conflict in California's civil rights history, see Sherna Bernstein, *Bridges of Reform: Interracial Civil Rights Activism in Twentieth Century Los Angeles* (New York: Oxford University Press, 2011); and Mark Brilliant, *The Color of America Has Changed: How Racial Diversity Shaped Civil Rights Reform In California, 1941–1978* (New York: Oxford University Press, 2011). Laura Pulido emphasizes cooperation among African American, Chicana/o, and Japanese radicals in 1960s and 1970s Southern California, while Neil Foley argues African Americans and Mexican Americans sometimes cooperated but other times regarded one another as competitors, including for jobs. He sees the history of these groups in postwar California and Texas as primarily one of missed opportunities and a failed promise of cooperation toward mutual goals of economic rights and equal education. See Laura Pulido, *Black, Brown, Yellow & Left: Radical Activism in Los Angeles* (Berkeley: University of California Press, 2006); and Neil Foley, *Quest for Equality: The Failed Promise of Black-Brown Solidarity* (Cambridge, MA: Harvard University Press, 2010). See also Daniel Martinez Hosang, *Racial Propositions: Ballot Initiatives and the Making of Postwar California* (Berkeley: University of California Press, 2010).
11. Deloria, *Custer Died For Your Sins*, 162, 168, 194–95. Deloria did find the Black Power movement more attractive than the civil rights movement, calling it a "godsend to the other groups" because it "clarified the intellectual concepts which had kept Indians and Mexicans

confused and allowed the concept of self determination suddenly to become valid. Stokely Carmichael [statements on black power] was the first black who said anything significant." But even here Deloria insisted that Indians backed off from "'power' as a movement." They knew they already had power. It was just a matter of figuring out how to deploy it effectively. Deloria, *Custer Died For Your Sins*, 102.

12. See Joanne Nagel, *American Indian Ethnic Renewal: Red Power and the Resurgence of Identity and Culture* (New York: Oxford University Press, 1996).
13. Thomas Sugrue, *Sweet Land of Liberty: The Forgotten Struggle for Civil Rights in the North* (New York: Random House, 2008), xviii.
14. Daniel M. Cobb, *Native Activism in Cold War America: The Struggle for Sovereignty* (Lawrence: University Press of Kansas, 2008), 14–21.
15. David Wilkins and K. Tsianina Lomawaima, *Uneven Ground: American Indian Sovereignty and Federal Law* (Norman: University of Oklahoma Press, 2008); George Castile and Robert Bee, eds., *State and Reservation: New Perspectives on Federal Indian Policy* (Tucson: University of Arizona Press, 1992); George Pierre Castile, *Taking Charge: Native American Self-Determination and Federal Indian Policy, 1975–1993* (Tucson: University of Arizona Press, 2006); Stephen Cornell, *The Return of the Native: American Indian Political Resurgence* (New York: Oxford University Press, 1988); Francis Paul Prucha, *The Great Father: The United States Government and the American Indian* (Lincoln: University of Nebraska Press, 1986); George Pierre Castile, *To Show Heart: Native American Self-Determination and Federal Indian Policy, 1960–1975* (Tucson: University of Arizona Press, 1999); Jeff Corntassel, *Forced Federalism: Contemporary Challenges to Indigenous Nationhood* (Norman: University of Oklahoma Press, 2009); and Jack Forbes, *Native Americans and Nixon: Presidential Politics and Minority Self-Determination, 1969–1972* (Los Angeles: American Indian Studies Center, 1981).
16. Corntassel, *Forced Federalism*, xiii–xvii.
17. Wilkins and Lomowaima, *Uneven Ground*, 249–63.
18. For overviews of Indian activism see Paul Chaat Smith and Robert Allen Warrior, *Like A Hurricane: The Indian Movement from Alcatraz to Wounded Knee* (New York: The New Press, 1996); Charles Wilkinson, *Blood Struggle: The Rise of Modern Indian Nations* (New York: W.W. Norton, 2005). For books that examine the pre–Red Power forms of activism see Cobb, *Native Activism in Cold War America*; Paul C. Rosier, *Serving Their Country: American Indian Politics and Patriotism in the Twentieth Century* (Cambridge, MA: Harvard University Press, 2009); Bradley G. Shreve, *Red Power Rising: The National Indian Youth Council and the Origins of Native Activism* (Norman: University of Oklahoma Press, 2011); and Daniel M. Cobb and Loretta Fowler, eds., *Beyond Red Power: American Indian Politics and Activism Since 1900* (Santa Fe, NM: School of Advanced Research Press, 2007).
19. Sugrue, *Sweet Land of Liberty*, xvii.
20. For a study of Indians who did fight for equal voting rights see Laughlin McDonald, *American Indians and the Fight of Equal Voting Rights* (Norman: University of Oklahoma Press, 2010).
21. Sharon Monteith, *American Culture in the 1960s* (Edinburgh: Edinburgh University Press, 2008), 45, 31.

Chapter 1

1. For information on fishing rights see American Friends Service Committee, *Uncommon Controversy: Fishing Rights of the Muckleshoot, Puyallup, and Nisqually Indians* (Seattle: University of Washington Press, 1970); Fay G. Cohen, *Treaties on Trial: The Continuing Controversy over Northwest Indian Fishing Rights* (Seattle: University of Washington Press, 1986); Alexandra Harmon, *Indians in the Making: Ethnic Relations and Indian Identities Around Puget Sound* (Berkeley: University of California Press, 1998); Charles Wilkinson, *Blood Struggle: The Rise of Modern Indian Nations* (New York: W. W. Norton, 2005), 160–73, 198–204; Charles Wilkinson, *Messages from Frank's Landing: A Story of Salmon, Treaties, and the Indian War* (Seattle: University of Washington Press, 2000); Paul C. Rosier, *Serving Their Country: American Indian Politics and Patriotism in the Twentieth Century* (Cambridge,

MA: Harvard University Press, 2009), 237–42; Bradley Shreve, *Red Power Rising: The National Indian Youth Council and the Origins of Native Activism* (Norman: University of Oklahoma Press, 2011), 156–82; and Roberta Ulrich, *Empty Nets: Indians, Dams, and the Columbia River* (Corvallis: Oregon State University Press, 1999).
2. Ken Kesey, *One Flew Over the Cuckoo's Nest* (New York: Signet, 1995). Originally published in 1962.
3. Ibid., 186–87. It is interesting that white women play primarily villainous roles in this book.
4. Ibid., 73, 142–43. It is noteworthy that reviews of the book did not acknowledge the Indian politics in it. For an example see R. L. Sassoon, *Northwest Review*, 6 (Spring 1963): 116–20.
5. Wilkinson, *Blood Struggle*, 160–66.
6. No author, *Kesey's Garage Sale*, introduction by Arthur Miller (New York: The Viking Press and Intrepid Trips, 1973), 14–15. Tom Wolfe took Kesey at his word, indicating that drugs and even an experiment with shock treatment inspired and helped flesh out Chief Broom's character. See Tom Wolfe, *The Electric Kool-Aid Acid Test* (New York: Bantam Books, 1969), 44; originally published in 1968.
7. Stewart Brand, of *The Whole Earth Catalog* fame, indicated Kesey first introduced him to Indians in the early 1960s, when he took Brand to the Warm Springs Reservation in Oregon. It seemed that Kesey had been there before. Stewart Brand, telephone interview with author, February 12, 2002, Berkeley, California. For a detailed account of the Columbia River fishing rights issues, including those pertaining to the Warm Springs Reservation, see Ulrich, *Empty Nets*.
8. Sherry L. Smith, *Reimagining Indians: Native Americans Through Anglo Eyes, 1880–1940* (New York: Oxford University Press, 2000).
9. Christopher Lehmann-Haupt, "Ken Kesey," *New York Times*, November 11, 2001. This was Kesey's obituary.
10. For details see Cohen, *Treaties on Trial*; Harmon, *Indians in the Making*; Wilkinson, *Messages from Frank's Landing*; and Daniel L. Boxberger, *To Fish in Common: The Ethnohistory of Lummi Indian Salmon Fishing* (Lincoln: University of Nebraska Press, 1989).
11. Paul Chaat Smith and Robert Allen Warrior, *Like a Hurricane: The Indian Movement from Alcatraz to Wounded Knee* (New York: The New Press, 1997), 42–46; Shreve, *Red Power Rising*, 119–38.
12. Although the *New York Times* did not print a story about Brando's fish-in participation, it did begin to cover the fishing rights controversy at this time. See "Indians Map Protest in Washington State," *New York Times*, March 1, 1964 (hereafter *NYT*).
13. For Brando's account of his involvement in social justice movements including Native American affairs see Marlon Brando with Robert Lindsey, *Brando: Songs My Mother Taught Me* (New York: Random House, 1994); and Lawrence Grobel, *Conversations With Brando* (New York: Hyperion, 1991), 43–7, 85, 105–25. Portions of the latter originally appeared in the January 1979 issue of *Playboy*, a periodical read by many non-Indians who probably would not have been considered among Indian activists' natural constituency. Brando agreed to be interviewed for *Playboy*, he said, because publisher Hugh Hefner contributed $50,000 bail money for Russell Means. He denied that he was "the spokesman for the American Indian. They have orators, poets, people who were giants, people who are able to talk better than most poets we know. Wonderfully articulate people." Unfortunately, *Playboy* never asked them to do an interview nor did the television show, *Sixty Minutes*. See Grobel, *Conversations With Brando*, 44, 111. For examples of local and regional media attention regarding Brando's fish-in activities see February 17, 1964, *Daily Olympian* (hereafter *DO*); March 2, 1964, *Tacoma News Tribune* (hereafter *TNT*); March 2 and 3, 1964, *Seattle Times* (hereafter *ST*); and March 3, 1964, *Seattle Post-Intelligencer* (hereafter *PI*). For Indian disagreements about tactics see Harmon, *Indians in the Making*, 233–34.
14. May 13, 1966, *ST*; February 7, 1967, *DO*; June 30, 1968, *ST*; American Friends Service Committee, *Uncommon Controversy*, 109–10. Governor Evans ordered the three tipis and four tents that made up the encampment dismantled on June 30, 1968. See June 30, 1968, *DO* and *ST*.
15. According to an undated SAIA proposal for "Inter-Community Organization & Cooperative Development Project," southern Puget Sound Indian fishermen organized the

group in 1964 "to affirm, fight for and secure our treaty fishing rights by various means and processes—on the riverbanks, in the courts, wherever." Hank Adams was the executive director. A copy of this proposal can be found in General Correspondence 1971 folder, box 80, Frederick T. Haley Papers, Special Collections, Suzzallo Library, University of Washington, Seattle (hereafter FH UW). For more on SAIA, see Gabriel Chrisman, "The Fish-in Protest at Frank's Landing," in "Seattle Civil Rights and Labor History Project," www.civilrights.washington.edu (accessed June 8, 2011).

16. See February 7, 1966, *DO*; February 7, 1966, *TNT*; February 16 and 18, 1966, *ST*; February 9, 10, 13, 15, and 16, 1966, *DO*; The Kalama quote is from February 17, 1966, *ST*. For *New York Times* coverage of Gregory and the fish-ins see February 15, 16, and 18, 1966; January 13, 1967; May 31, 1968; July 5, 12, and 26, 1968. See also Dick Gregory, *Up From Nigger* (New York: Stein and Day, 1976), 123–27; 173–76.

17. March 2 and 30, and November 11, 1966, *ST*; March 3 and 29, April 29, May 4, 1966, *DO*; McCloud's quote can be found in Chrisman, "The Fish-in Protest at Frank's Landing."

18. November 27, 1966, *ST*.

19. January 13, 1967; June 8, 19, and 30, 1968, *DO*; June 18 and 19, 1968, *Bremerton Sun*.

20. July and 14, 1968, *DO*; July 4, 1968, *PI*; "Gregory Booked at the 'Palace' For 90-Day Stay," 1968, *DO*, copy in Indian-Fishing-Rights-1968 file, Washington State Library, Olympia. This last article revealed that among the paperback books Gregory took with him to his cell were *Yoga Made Easy, American Astrology, Moon Sign Book, Horoscope*, and Alan Watts's *The Book: The Taboo Against Knowing Who You Are*—all titles one might expect to find in a counterculture library. For articles on Gregory's hospitalization during his incarceration see July 5 and 9, 1968, *DO*.

21. For coverage of Gregory's release from jail and the Culp visit see July 15, 16, and 17, 1968, *DO*; July 17, 1968, *ST*; July 18, 1968, *PI*. Robert Culp's arrival at the courthouse elicited a big photographic spread, including a full-body picture of France Nuyen in mini-skirt and boots.

22. Information on the non-Indians' experiences at Frank's Landing comes from the author's interview with Richard White, April 9, 2004, Palo Alto, California, and his unpublished, untitled autobiographical account, written soon after his time there. Copy in author's possession. This manuscript, over one hundred pages, is a particularly insightful account of an Indian-countercultural encounter, written from "within" that relationship. For a non-Indian outsider's perspective on Frank's Landing see Don Hannula, "Nisqually Fishing Confrontation Now 46 Days Old," October 20, 1969, *ST*. This reporter noted that Frank's Landing was the "nerve center of the militant Survival of American Indians Association." Housing for the encampment included a large tipi; plastic, see-through shelters; and even a tree house. The Landing, six acres of federal trust land, belonged to William Frank Sr. who at age eighty-nine was the oldest living Nisqually. He acquired this parcel in exchange for his allotment on the reservation which the government took over for use at Fort Lewis, an army post. For a history of the Frank family and the Landing see Wilkinson, *Messages From Frank's Landing*.

23. White, interview; Joseph Quinones, telephone interview with author, November 16, 2005. Although Quinones did not fish, he did man the bullhorn at one of the demonstrations and was arrested with those who did the fishing. Expecting to have the charges dismissed, since he had not fished, Quinones instead was tried, convicted, and sentenced to one year in jail or leave the state. He opted to leave Washington and thus ended his most direct involvement in fish-ins.

24. White manuscript, copy in author's files. The manuscript is written in short chapters or vignettes and does not contain consecutive pagination; thus, there are no page numbers to cite.

25. White, interview.

26. Ibid.

27. Ibid.

28. Ibid.

29. Stern's statement appeared in the Seattle underground newspaper the *Helix*, September 4, 1968; White, interview; Robby Stern, telephone interview with author, July 7, 2005; Hank

Adam's quote comes from Memorandum to Selected Indian Person, General Correspondence 1971 folder, box 80, FH UW. Stern claimed that in 1965–1966 there were 6,373 deaths among 472,000 American soldiers in Vietnam but 10,178 deaths among 400,000 Indians in the United States. For more on how people conceptualized the relationship between Vietnam and Indian models see Rosier, *Serving Their Country*, 244–53.
30. Stern, interview. For *Helix* coverage of the fish-ins see August 1, 1968; "Fish In Sep. 4," August, 1968; "Fish In," October 3, 1968; "Freedom Fish" and "Hi Noon Fish," October, 1968; "Indians Convicted," November 21, 1968; "Indian Trials," December 19, 1968; and "Indian Fishing," January 23, 1969. The fish-ins received much less coverage in other underground newspapers. For a rare example of a *Berkeley Barb* story see "You Can Help: Indians Fishing Rights at Stake," *Berkeley Barb*, December 1, 1972.
31. *Helix*, September 4, 1968.
32. Ibid.
33. Cobb, *Native Activism*, 173.
34. Ibid., 171–92; "High Court Building Stormed In Demonstration by the Poor," *NYT*, May 30, 1968; Ernesto J. Vigil, *The Crusade for Justice: Chicano Militancy and the Government's War on Dissent* (Madison: University of Wisconsin Press, 1999), 54–58.
35. Cobb, *Native Activism*, 178–83; "High Court Building," *NYT*, May 30, 1968. Participants did not always agree with one another about issues. For instance, Charlie Cambridge, Diné, told Reies Tijerina, whose primary concern focused on the theft of Spanish land grants, supposedly protected under the Treaty of Guadalupe Hidalgo, from Mexican Americans, that neither Spanish nor Mexican people had rights to the land. It was all Indian land. Cambridge claimed Tijerina "'got really pissed off.'" Quoted in Cobb, *Native Activism*, 178.
36. Vine Deloria Jr., *Custer Died For Your Sins: An Indian Manifesto* (Toronto: Macmillan, 1969), 182–83; Adams quoted in "March of Poor Held Failure for Indians," *NYT*, July 4, 1968.
37. White manuscript; "Freedom Fish," *Helix*, October, 1968; see Chrisman, "The Indian Fish-in Protest at Frank's Landing," for specifics on the fall 1968 demonstrations.
38. September 9, 1968, *DO*; Stern, interview. That these kinds of supporters did not win universal Indian support is apparent in the same article which quoted "some disgusted Indian leaders [who] were asking fisheries officials how they could become disassociated with their unwashed, bearded, bare-chested supporters from Seattle."
39. October 14, 1968, *DO*; October 14, 1968, *PI*.
40. August 13, 1970, *ST*. Another story, however, claimed that Bob Satiacum and Janet McCloud boycotted an October 1968 fish-in at Frank's Landing "because of the participation by the Peace and Freedom Party and Students for a Democratic Society," *Helix*, October, 1968.
41. Quinones, interview.
42. For a sampling of *New York Times* coverage of the fishing rights controversy and protests see "Tribe in Battle for Fishing Rights," October 17, 1965; "Indians Are Pitted Against Game Wardens in Great Fish War of Northwest," August 14, 1966; "Police and Coast Indians Clash Over Fishing Rights," September 10, 1970; "A Fishing Dispute Expands on Coast," September 22, 1970; and "Indians' Fish Rights Target of Protest," August 23, 1971.
43. September 18, 1970, *ST*; see also Wilkinson, *Blood Struggle*, 168–72; Chrisman, "The Fish-in Protest at Frank's Landing."
44. Thomas Sugrue, *Sweet Land of Liberty: The Forgotten Struggle for Civil Rights in the North* (New York: Random House, 2008), 221.
45. For a brief history of AFSC's involvement with Native American communities see "Community Relations Division Review for Board of Directors American Friends Service Committee," December 1962, in AFSC-Com. Rel.–INDIANS subject files cabinet, American Friends Service Committee Archives, Philadelphia, Pennsylvania (hereafter AFSC). By 1968 the AFSC became convinced this decentralized, localized approach was helping some individuals, but not changing more systemic problems. See memo from Pam Coe to Bob Gray, "Reactions to Bill Williams' San Carlos Evaluation," August 6, 1968, CRD-American Indian Affairs 1968 Projects: Pasadena-San Carlos Apache 15903 file, CRD 1968 Admin. & Justice American Indians box, AFSC.

46. "Summary of Orientation of Indian Program, Pacific Northwest Regional Office, Executive Committee Meeting—January 19, 1963," CRD American Indian Program 1963 Regional Office Seattle file, CRD American Indians 1963 box; Memo, Pam Coe to Barbara Moffett, April 29, 1966, CRD American Indian Program 1966 Correspondence MEMOS file, CRD 1966 Administration, Administration of Justice, American Indian Program, Education Program box, AFSC.
47. Mary Isely, Charles McEvers, and Pam Coe to Dear Friend, "Summary of Orientation;" September 1, 1966, CRD American Indian Program 1966 Projects Seattle—Fishing Rights file; and Pam Coe to Indian Program Staff, January 17, 1966, CRD American Indian Program 1966 Correspondence MEMOS file, both in CRD 1966 Administration box; and "Proposal to American Indian Civil Liberties Trust from AFSC Pacific Northwest Regional Office, September 3, 1968," CRD American Indian Affairs 1968 Project Seattle—Fishing Rights 51906 file, CRD 1968 Administration of Justice American Indians box, all AFSC. The AFSC paid $6,500 of the $7,500 total expenditure for this first edition, with the National Congress of American Indians contributing for the cost of paper and binding (estimated at about $1,000), and the Indian Rights Association contributing $500 to the expenses of the study group.
48. *Uncommon Controversy*, xviii, xxix. See also Robert Johnson, "Indian Fishing Controversy," *PI*, November 22, 1971.
49. AFSC, *Uncommon Controversy*, xxix.
50. John Belindo to Charles L. McEvers, November 22, 1967; Tandy Wilbur to Chuck McEvers, November 21, 1967; and Charles McEvers to Tandy Wilbur, November 27, 1967, all in CRD American Indian Affairs 1966 Project Seattle—Fishing Rights 53203 file, CRD 1967 Administration of Justice American Indian Affairs box, AFSC.
51. Indian Progress Roundup Report, in "Community Relations Indian News Memo #1–4 American Indian Program 1966–1967," Community Relations box, AFSC.
52. Memo, Arthur Dye to Helen Stritmatter, "Proposal to American Indian Civil Liberties Trust"; January 6, 1970, CRD American Indian Affairs 1970 Regional Offices Seattle—Pacific Northwest file, CRD 1970 American Indian Affairs to Economic & Rural Affairs box; and David H. Getches to Phillip Buskirk, February 28, 1974, CRD Native American Affairs 1974 Regional Offices—Pacific Northwest (Seattle) file, CRD Native American Affairs 1974 box, all AFSC; and Wilkinson, *Blood Struggle*, 170.
53. Memo from Arthur Dye to Marie Gilstrap, September 9, 1970; Memo from Arthur M. Dye to Barbara Moffett, "Che Guevara is Alive and Well in Tacoma," both in CRD American Indian Affairs 1970 Regional Offices Seattle—Pacific Northwest file, CRD 1970 American Indian Affairs to Economic & Rural Affairs box, AFSC. In the memo about the visit to the Puyallup fish-in camp, Dye said he talked to Roberta "Green" about the use of armed non-Indian supporters.
54. Ibid.; Rosier, *Serving Their Country*, 271; Chrisman, "The Fish-in Protest at Frank's Landing."
55. Arthur Dye to Phil Buskirk, September 22, 1970; Arthur Dye to Barbara Moffett, October 12, 1970; John Willard to Arthur Dye, October 14, 1970; and Arthur Dye to Phil Buskirk, October 19, 1970; all in CRD American Indian Affairs 1970 Regional Office Seattle—Pacific Northwest file, CRD 1970 American Indian Affairs to Economic & Rural Affairs box, AFSC.
56. Arthur Dye to Phil Buskirk, May 17, 1971; Hank Adams to George Loft of the Field Foundation, May 5, 1971; and Arthur Dye to Phil Buskirk, circa April 6, 1971, all in CRD American Indian Affairs 1971 Regional Office Seattle—Pacific Northwest file, CRD American Indian Affairs to Economic & Rural Affairs 1971 box; Arthur Dye to Phil Buskirk, March 23, 1972, CRD American Indian Affairs 1972 Regional Offices Pacific Northwest—Seattle file, CRD 1972 Administration of Justice (contd) American Indian Affairs box; and "A Proposal to Assist American Indians in Western Washington," CRD American Indian Affairs 1971 Regional Office Seattle—Pacific Northwest file, CRD American Indian Affairs to Economic & Rural Affairs 1971 box; all AFSC.
57. Arthur Dye to Bill Hayden, July 6, 1971, CRD American Indian Affairs 1971 Regional Office Seattle—Pacific Northwest file, CRD American Indian Affairs to Economic & Rural Affairs 1971 box, AFSC.
58. Wilkinson, *Blood Struggle*, 203–4; "Indians on Coast Upheld in Fishing," *NYT*, February 13, 1974; "Ruling Bolsters Fishing by Indians," *NYT*, December 26, 1974.

Chapter 2

1. Tom Wolfe, *The Electric Kool-Aid Acid Test* (New York: Bantam Books, 1969), 2. The book was originally published in 1968.
2. Ibid., 224, 225, 231.
3. Quoted in Virginia Morell, "Citizen Brand: 'Oh Wow! Yurt Man Goes High Tech,'" *Harrowsmith*, June–July 1984, copy in file 8, box 26, Whole Earth Access Papers, Special Collections, Stanford University, Stanford, California (hereafter WEAP).
4. Andrew G. Kirk, *Counterculture Green: The Whole Earth Catalog and American Environmentalism* (Lawrence: University Press of Kansas, 2007); Fred Turner, *From Counterculture to Cyberculture: Stewart Brand, the Whole Earth Network and the Rise of Digital Utopianism* (Chicago: University of Chicago Press, 2006).
5. Turner, *From Counterculture to Cyberculture*, 45–51.
6. See Stewart Brand's website, http://www.web.me.com/stewartbrand/SB_homepage.
7. Stewart Brand, interview with author, February 12, 2002.
8. Kirk, *Counterculture Green*, 38; Stewart Brand notebooks, 1955–56, and May 3–20, 1963 notebook, Stewart Brand Papers, Special Collections, Stanford University Library, Stanford, California (hereafter SBP).
9. Brand notebooks, May 20 and June 18, 1963, SBP.
10. Brand, interview.
11. "The Interview: Whole Earthling and Software Savant Stewart Brand," *SF Focus*, n.d., file 5, box 26, WEAP.
12. Stewart Brand, "Indians and the Counterculture, 1960s–1970s," in *History of Indian-White Relations*, Wilcomb E. Washburn, ed., *Handbook of North American Indians*, vol. 4 (Washington, DC: Smithsonian, 1980), 570–71. An earlier version of this can be found in "Indians and the Counter-Culture," *Clear Creek: The Environmental Viewpoint*, December 1972, 34–37.
13. Brand, interview.
14. Brand, "Indians and the Counterculture, 1960s–1970s," in *History of Indian-White Relations*; for Brand's comments on the peyote religion, see "Slambook Summer 1964," Brand notebooks, 111, SBP.
15. Brand, interview.
16. Ibid.
17. Brand notebooks, July 7, 8, 1964; April 21, 1963; May 6, 1963; April and May 1964 for consultation with "experts" including notes of meeting with Alvin Josephy; July 24, 1964, and August 4, 1964, all SBP.
18. "Slambook, 1964–65," Brand notebooks, July 22, 1964, 15, SBP.
19. Brand, interview. No scripts from "America Needs Indians" could be found. Brand suggested the papers he donated to Stanford University regarding *Whole Earth Catalog* might include something, but they did not. See also Charles Perry, *The Haight-Ashbury* (New York: Wenner Books, 2005), 19.
20. "AMERICA NEEDS INDIANS," July 27, 1964, included in letter from Stewart Brand to Alvin Josephy, December 11, 1964, December 1964 correspondence folder, box 2, Alvin Josephy Papers, coll. 14, Series II-Correspondence, Division of Special Collections and University Archives, University of Oregon, Eugene (hereafter AJP).
21. Ibid. Brand seemed particularly interested in the inflatable building, promising that crude approximations of his idea already existed in the "ephemeral airhouses" religious groups were using. He knew of two Christian ladies who barnstormed with a truck, a trailer, and a four hundred-seat inflatable auditorium, chairs, lectern sound system, compressors and the required fire exits. Local parishioners helped them set up in every town they visited. He assured his readers that blower systems, revolving doors, and cycling an HVAC system into the blower system would require study but not be difficult to resolve. More problematic would be anchoring the structure and dealing with variable pressure systems resistant to changes in wind pressure.
22. Stewart Brand to Alvin Josephy, February 2, 1965, Dec. 1964–Feb. 1965 folder, box 2; and Josephy to Brand, June 10, 1965, May–July 1965 folder, box 2, both AJP.

23. Michael Malone, "Stewart Brand: From Hippie Prince to Software Savant," *San Jose Mercury News*, September 16, 1984, file 6, box 26, WEAP. Also see Brand's web page http://www.web.me.com/stewartbrand/SB_homepage.
24. "Catch Him If You Can: An Interview With Steward Brand," *City Miner*, n.d., copy in file 7, box 26, WEAP.
25. For Brand's explanation of the inspiration and early years of the *Catalog* see *The Last Whole Earth Catalog: Access to Tools* (Menlo Park: Portola Institute, 1971), 439–441. For a complete list of the *Catalog*'s various editions and Brand's other publications see his website: http://web.me.com/stewartbrand/SB_homepage. For an interesting analysis of Brand and the *Catalog*'s significance see Andrew Kirk, "Appropriating Technology: *The Whole Earth Catalog* and Counterculture Environmental Politics," *Environmental History* (July 2001): 374–94. See also Andrew Kirk, "'Machines of Loving Grace:' Alternative Technology, Environment, and the Counterculture," in *Imagine Nation: The American Counterculture of the 1960s & 70s*, ed. Peter Braunstein and Michael William Doyle (New York: Routledge, 2002), 353–78; and Kirk, *Counterculture Green*. The Montgomery Ward analogy can be found in "Mail Order Catalogue of the Hip Becomes a National Best Seller," *New York Times*, April 12, 1970, 67; the profits party was reported in "A Party to Give Away $20,000," *San Francisco Chronicle*, June 14, 1970, copy found in Stewart Brand Biographical file, San Francisco History Center, San Francisco Public Library.
26. Christopher Lehman-Haupt, "The Whole Earth Is Disappearing," *San Francisco Chronicle*, September 5, 1971, copy in Stewart Brand Biographical File, San Francisco History Center, San Francisco Public Library.
27. *Whole Earth Catalog*, 1971 edition, 100, 217, 261, 275, 381.
28. Ibid., 382–83.
29. Ibid., 430. The eventual claim that Castaneda's work was fraudulent remained for the future. In the meantime, many young readers believed Castaneda's experiences were the real thing. For information on the controversy regarding Castaneda's veracity see Simon Romero, "Peyote's Hallucinations Spawn Real-Life Academic Feud," *New York Times*, September 12, 2003, http://www.nytimes.com/2003/09/16/science/16PEYO.html; and Dave Kehr, "The Shaman May Have Been Fake, but, Hey, the Drugs Were Real," *New York Times*, June 2, 2004, http://movies2.nytimes.com/mem/movies/review/html.
30. The Gereth Branwyn quote comes from Kirk, "Appropriating Technology," 384.
31. Quoted in "Stewart Brand: From the 60's To Software," clipping found in folder 5, box 26, WEAP.
32. Brand, "Indians and the Counter-Culture," *Clear Creek*, 37.
33. Ibid., 37.
34. Allen Cohen, "The San Francisco Oracle: A Brief History," in *The San Francisco Oracle*, facsimile edition, copy available at Bancroft Library, University of California, Berkeley.
35. Ibid., 161.
36. Ibid., 164, 161.
37. Ibid., xxxiii.
38. "The *East West* Interview," in *Gary Snyder: The Real Work, Interviews & Talks, 1965–1979*, ed. William Scott McLean (New York: New Directions Book, 1980), 92–93. For biographical information on Snyder see the chronology in *The Gary Snyder Reader: Prose, Poetry, and Translations, 1952–1998* (New York: Counterpoint, 1999), 611–12; and Timothy Gray, *Gary Snyder and the Pacific Rim: Creating Countercultural Community* (Iowa City: University of Iowa Press, 2006).
39. "The *East West* Interview," in *Gary Snyder: The Real Work*, 94.
40. Gary Snyder to Dad, November 13, 1949, file 9; December 29, 1949, file 11; April 21, 1951, file 18; and January 23, 1952, file 22, all in series II, box 2,3, Gary Snyder Papers, Special Collections, University of California, Davis (hereafter GSP).
41. Ibid., 94–5; "*Road Apple* Interview With Gary Snyder," in *Gary Snyder: The Real Work*, 17.
42. "*Road Apple* Interview," 15–16; "The Real Work," interview with Paul Geneson, Fall 1977, 68; and "Tracking Down the Natural Man," 86, all in *Gary Snyder: The Real Work*.
43. "Tracking Down the Natural Man," 86–7; "The *East-West* Interview," 107–8, 109, both in *Gary Snyder: The Real Work*.

44. "The *East-West* Interview," in *Gary Snyder: The Real Work*, 115–16.
45. "Knots in the Grain," 49; "The Real Work," 74, both in *Gary Snyder: The Real Work*.
46. "Introductory Note," *Turtle Island* (New York: New Directions, 1974).
47. "Prayer for the Great Family," *Turtle Island*, 24.
48. "The Bioregional Ethic," in *Gary Snyder: The Real Work*, 154, 155, 156, 157; Gray, *Gary Snyder and the Pacific Rim*, 275.
49. Gray, *Gary Snyder and the Pacific Rim*, 235, 277.
50. Cohen, "The San Francisco Oracle: A Brief History," in *The San Francisco Oracle*, facsimile edition, xlii.
51. *The San Francisco Oracle*, facsimile edition, 222–23.
52. Ibid., 219.
53. Ibid., xliv; Gary Snyder to Joanne, April 7, 1967, series 2, box 2, GSP.
54. Thomas Clarkin, *Federal Indian Policy in the Kennedy and Johnson Administrations, 1960–1969* (Albuquerque: University of New Mexico Press, 2001), 187–226.
55. "Indians for Sale," by Richard Honigman, in *San Francisco Oracle*, facsimile edition, 220–21.
56. "Kiva," ibid., 216–17.
57. Peter Coyote, *Sleeping Where I Fall: A Chronicle* (Washington, DC: Counterpoint, 1998), 41.
58. Ibid., 34, 64–5, 66, 71.
59. Peter Coyote, e-mail communications with author, February 26, 2002 and February 28, 2002.
60. Ibid.
61. "Baba Ram Dass," *Fountain of Light*, December, 1969. *Fountain of Light* was an underground newspaper published in Taos, New Mexico.
62. "Hopi Tape," Hippie Collection, folder 5, box 1, San Francisco History Center, San Francisco Public Library. This document is a partial transcript of the conversation at Hotevilla concerning the proposed Hopi-Hippie Be-In.
63. Ibid.
64. Ibid.
65. "Baba Ram Dass," no page numbers.
66. Alphonse Mittlestadt, "Hippies, Hippies, Hooray!!" *Hopi Action News* (September 29, 1967), 8; and "Doll Show to Offer Hopi Helping Hand," *Hopi Action News* (September 13, 1968), 7–9, reprinted from *Los Angeles Times*. Copies found in AZ 374, Hopi Traditionalist Papers, Main Library, Special Collections, University of Arizona, Tucson. Thank you to Leah Glaser who brought these articles to my attention.
67. Emmett Grogan, *Ringolevio* (United Kingdom: Heinemann, 1972), 367–80.
68. "Hopi-Hippie Be-In," Communication Company, San Francisco, April 29, 1967, copy found in Social Protest Collection, file 10, box 6, Bancroft Library, University of California, Berkeley.
69. Grogan, *Ringolevio*, 381–82.

Chapter 3

1. Sigurd Ozols, "Charlie Brown and the Peyote Road," *Berkeley Barb*, August 20, 1965, 3. See also W. J. Rorabaugh, *Berkeley at War: The 1960s* (New York: Oxford University Press, 1989), 134–35.
2. Walter H. Bowart, "An Eagle Without Claws," *Berkeley Barb*, May 20, 1966, 7.
3. Ibid., "P.S. by Charlie Brown." Brown wrote to *Berkeley Barb* readers, "The tipi is so beautiful and very beautiful things happen and the spirits that take care of me will take care of the medicine tipi so we'll still be here after this stupidity with the buildings dept. is over."
4. "The Earth Around You in Your Storehouse," interview with Sun Bear by Richard Ogar, *Berkeley Barb*, April 28, 1967, 8, 9, 10.
5. John Bryan, "Buffy on Hippies—'They'll Never be Indians,'" *Berkeley Barb*, June 30, 1967, 10.
6. "How the Hippies Turned Off Hopis," *Berkeley Barb*, May 26, 1967, 4; Richard Ogar, "American Indians In Trek to Coast," *Berkeley Barb*, September 15, 1967, 2; "Indians And Fall Equinox," *Berkeley Barb*, September 22, 1967, 2; and "Indian Like 'Free Men,'" *Berkeley Barb*, September 29, 1967, 5.

7. "Shoshones Say U.S. Can't Draft Them," *Berkeley Barb*, June 23, 1967, 3.
8. Ibid.
9. "Indian CO Ambushed by Army," *Berkeley Barb*, August 25, 1967, 7. See also another brief article on this case in *Berkeley Barb*, August 18, 1967, 7.
10. "The Earth Around You," 10.
11. "Committee Set Up To Help Whitemen," *Berkeley Barb*, January 3, 1969, 10.
12. For information on this case see "Indian Out to Zap U.S.," *Berkeley Barb*, December 5, 1968, 7. The use of stereotypical language in some of these stories is appalling. At the end of this article, for instance, the author indicates Bitsie's trial date, set for December 9, "should be a real gathering of the tribes . . . 'Honest Injun.'"
13. Rorabaugh, *Berkeley at War*, 154–57.
14. For one version of this poster see "Who Owns the Park?" *Berkeley Barb*, May 20, 1969, 2.
15. Rorabaugh, *Berkeley at War*, 158–66.
16. Adam Fortunate Eagle, *Alcatraz! Alcatraz! The Indian Occupation of 1969–1971* (Berkeley: Heyday Books produced in cooperation with the Golden Gate National Park Association, 1992), 15; Paul Chaat Smith, *Everything You Know About Indians Is Wrong* (Minneapolis: University of Minnesota Press, 2009), 131–32. Born on the Red Lake Indian Reservation (Ojibwa) in Minnesota, Adam Fortunate Eagle, also known as Adam Nordwall, attended Haskell Indian School and eventually migrated to San Francisco where he became a licensed termite inspector. By the late 1960s, he owned his own extermination business and lived in the East Bay area. Nordwall was one of the original organizers of the occupation, but being a middle-aged and middle-class person with a business and family, he did not live on Alcatraz and quickly lost his leadership position to younger occupants. Fortunate Eagle's account has been reprinted as *Heart of the Rock: The Indian Invasion of Alcatraz* (Norman: University of Oklahoma Press, 2009).
17. Fortunate Eagle, *Alcatraz!* 41. For an historian's account see Troy Johnson, *The Occupation of Alcatraz Island: Indian Self-Determination and the Rise of Indian Activism* (Urbana: University of Illinois Press, 1996). See also Troy Johnson, Joanne Nagel, and Duane Champagne, *American Indian Activism: Alcatraz to the Longest Walk* (Urbana: University of Illinois Press, 1997); and Dean Rader, *Engaged Resistance: American Indian Art, Literature and Film from Alcatraz to NMAI* (Austin: University of Texas Press, 2011).
18. For the complete text of the Indians of All Tribes' Alcatraz proclamation see "Indians of All Tribes November 1969 Proclamation," in *Red Power: The American Indians' Fight for Freedom*, 2nd ed., ed. Alvin M. Josephy Jr., Joanne Nagel, and Troy Johnson (Lincoln: University of Nebraska Press, 1999), 40–43.
19. Tim Findlay, "Alcatraz Reminiscences," in *American Indian Activism*, ed. Johnson, Nagel, and Champagne, 74–87.
20. Ibid., 72. Technically the second landing at Alcatraz occurred November 9, 1969, when a boat containing about fifty individuals circled the island and three of them jumped off, swimming to the island. The Coast Guard captured and removed those three men. Fourteen individuals returned that night and after reading the proclamation the next morning surrendered. The more significant, more lasting landing and occupation came ten days later. See Fortunate Eagle, *Heart of the Rock*, 73–89.
21. Peter Bowen and Brooks Townes, *The Sausalito-Indian Navy* (Weaverville, NC: Published by Peter Bowen and Brooks Townes, n.d.), 16, 22; Fortunate Eagle, *Heart of the Rock*, 94–101.
22. Bowen and Townes, *Sausalito-Indian Navy*, 7. *Father Knows Best* and *Ozzie and Harriet* were two television shows which featured suburban, Anglo American families of the 1950s and 1960s.
23. Ibid., 11.
24. Ibid., 15.
25. Candra Day, interview with author, January 19, 2002, Moose, Wyoming.
26. Ibid.
27. Ibid. Although Candra Day was not particularly involved in Alcatraz-related support activities, she did go over to the island on one occasion, finding it "scary, dangerous, and oppressive." Townes withdrew once he became disturbed by the factionalism he witnessed among

the occupiers. Talk of overpowering the white skippers and crews disheartened him, and he was drawn into a knife fight on the dock one morning. "While remaining fully in favor of the Indians owning Alcatraz, I felt then I'd done enough and had enough." See Brooks and Townes, *Sausalito-Indian Navy*, 21–2.

28. This description comes from the "Tupart Monthly Reports on the Underground Press," published by the National Media Analysis, Inc. in Washington, D.C., and printed as "CIA Lackeys Read TRIBE," *Berkeley Tribe*, September 2, 1971, 5. If the staff did not publish sex ads, they were not above printing stories that would appeal to more prurient interests. Above the newspaper banner on the November 27–December 5, 1969 issue is a headline: "SEX DOPE RITES See Page 3," a story about the Psychedelic Venus Church that hoped "to bridge the gap between suburban swingers and hippy heads" through orgies and marijuana smoking.

29. Kathy Williams, "Alcatraz Odyssey," *Berkeley Tribe*, Nov. 27–Dec. 5, 1969, 16–17.

30. "Victory at Sea," *Berkeley Tribe*, Nov. 27–Dec. 5, 1969, 17.

31. "Reese on the Rock," *Berkeley Tribe*, Dec. 26–Jan. 2, 1970, 7. This issue's front-page story was headlined "Earth People's Park Planned for 1970" and began with the words, "The decade ends with the Indians back on Alcatraz. And it ends with a communion at the Committee Theater in San Francisco." At this meeting the participants decided the Peoples Park would become the focal point for the new year and "a beachhead for a new order of civilization." Alcatraz was compelling, but Peoples Park remained in the forefront of action and interest.

32. This list comes from a boxed story "Indians on Alcatraz Need," *Berkeley Tribe*, Nov. 27–Dec. 5, 1969, 16.

33. "The Time Has Come," *Berkeley Tribe*, April 24–May 1, 1970, 15.

34. Sundog, "We Shall Live Again," *Berkeley Tribe*, April 24–May 1, 1970, 15.

35. Douglas Baker Jr. to Indians of All Tribes, February 13, 1970, box 4, file 3, "Promotional Schemes," Alcatraz Collection, San Francisco History Center, San Francisco Public Library (hereafter ACSFPL). Blue Cloud's handwritten comments appear on the copy of the poster included with this letter. Baker was not the only person whose entrepreneurial inclinations found inspiration from the Alcatraz takeover. The range of interest was remarkable, if a little screwy. Stuart A. Schwalbe & Associates offered their services for a national fundraising campaign on behalf of Indians of All Tribes. They would cover all initial expenses and be reimbursed only if successful. Profits would be split 20/80 with 80 percent going to the Indians and 20 percent to Schwalbe & Associates. Renaissance Press offered to print stamps and even Christmas cards with a special Alcatraz Indian Nation stamp and postmark. The cards could sell for fifty cents, of which Indians of All Tribes could keep thirty-four cents and Renaissance would earn sixteen cents to cover postage, design, and labor. "Every other sovereign nation does it . . . and at a profit from those who want mementos from the new state and from stamp collectors. (Your own money might be a gas too)." If they did not want to hire Renaissance Press, they were free to use the idea. "The main thing is that you continue your fight." See Stuart A. Schwalbe to Aubrey Grossman, January 9, 1970; and John Bryan, Kenneth Bowman, Joan Bryan, and Christopher Bowman of Renaissance Press to Alcatraz Indian Nation, December 1, 1969, both in box 4, file 3, ACSFPL.

36. "Hollywood Star Joins Indian Alcatraz Fight," *San Francisco Examiner*, December 15, 1969.

37. Stanley Eichelbaum, "Jane Fonda Visits Alcatraz Indians," March 2, 1970, I am unsure which newspaper, article found in Alcatraz Clippings file, San Francisco History Center, San Francisco Public Library (hereafter ACFSFPL). For Fonda's more recent commentary on this phase of her activism see Jane Fonda, *My Life So Far* (New York: Random House, 2005), 220–22, 235–36, 282. She visited not only Alcatraz but participated in demonstrations at Fort Lawton in Seattle (see chapter 5) and Pyramid Lake on the Paiute Reservation. Her activities related to Indian affairs, however, receive relatively little attention in the memoir. "Jane Fonda, Alcatraz Indians in Seattle Raid," March 9, 1970, newspaper unknown, copy found in ACFSFPL.

38. "A Treat for Legislators," March 6, 1970; and "Snub for Unruh on Alcatraz," May 21, 1970, newspaper unknown, copies found in ACFSFPL.

39. "Indians Get TV, Need Electricity," *San Francisco Examiner*, December 15, 1970, ACFS-FPL. Other celebrity visitors to Alcatraz included the comedian and actor Jonathon Winters and television talk show host Merv Griffin, who broadcast one of his shows from the island.
40. Krogh to Ehrlichman, December 11, 1970; and Garment to Ehrlichman, January 21, 1971, both in Alcatraz Policy Memos file, box 34, White House Central Files, Leonard Garment, Alpha Subject Files, Nixon Presidential Papers, National Archives, College Park, Maryland (hereafter WHCF NA). These documents are now housed at the Nixon Presidential Library, Whittier, California.
41. Smith and Warrior, *Like a Hurricane*, 25.
42. Gary Paxton to John [Trudell] and Friends, n.d., box 4, file 3, ACSFPL.
43. "Malvina's Alcatraz Ballad," *San Francisco Chronicle*, December 3, 1969, ACFSFPL.
44. Audiotape of the concert, "Benefit for the Indians on Alcatraz," Pacifica Radio Archives, North Hollywood, California.
45. Ibid.
46. Ibid.
47. Ralph Gleason, "Buffy Raps About Her Fellow Indians," *San Francisco Sunday Examiner and Chronicle*, n.d., box 3, file 25, ACFSFPL. For more on Buffy Sainte-Marie's life-long political activism, musical career, and dedication to Indian education see J. Poet, "Buffy Sainte-Marie: Voice of a Generation," *Native Peoples: Arts and Lifeways* (November–December 2008): 39–44; and her website http://www.creative-native.com/media.php (accessed February 17, 2010).
48. "Indian Land Calling," *Berkeley Barb*, December 26, 1969, 9; David Fuller to John Trudell and Al Silbowitz, "March 16, 1970, box 4, file 9, "KPFA-FM-Berkeley," ACSFPL. This file also contains Trudell and Silbowitz's original grant proposal.
49. Paul C. Rosier, *Serving Their Country: American Indian Politics and Patriotism in the Twentieth Century* (Cambridge: Harvard University Press, 2009), 245–46, 253–56.
50. A poster for the Glide Memorial Church Poetry Reading for Alcatraz can be found in box 4, file 10, "Church Support;" ACSFPL; letters from the United Theological Seminary, January 13, 1971; the United Presbyterian Church's Board of National Missions, January 11, 1971; the Palo Alto Society of Friends, December 21, 1969; and the Scarsdale Congregational Church, December 4, 1970 can be found in the same file.
51. Browne Barr to Shirley Keith, December 2, 1969, box 4, file 10, "Church Support," ACS-FPL.
52. See box 4, file 12, "Indian Organizations Support," ACSFPL.
53. Aran Ardaiz to Mrs. Richard Lallmang, Republican National Committee, December 8, 1969, box 4, file 12, "Indian Organizations Support," ACSFPL.
54. A press release from Congressman George Brown regarding this bill can be found in box 4, file 11, "Government Support," ACSFPL.
55. A press release about Senator Murphy's proposal can be found in Alcatraz: Political Leaders' Plans file, box 34, Leonard Garment, WHCF NA. The Alcatraz Indians' response can be found in "Alcatraz Indians Jibe at Murphy," *San Jose News*, December 19, 1969, box 34, Leonard Garment, WHCF NA.
56. Letter indicating ILWU monetary support can be found in "Dear Sisters and Brothers," written on ILWU letterhead, December 16, 1969; Joe Morris' flyer "TO ALL WORKING STIFFS," n.d.; copies of the Painter's Local Union #4 letters to Richard Nixon and others, all dated December 10, 1969; and other correspondence from unions can be found in box 4, file 16, "Union Support," ACSFPL.
57. Information on these union supporters comes from Grace Thorpe to Douglas Remington of United Auto Workers, Local #6, February 18, 1970, box 1, file 21, unnamed collection, San Francisco History Center, San Francisco Public Library (hereafter UCSFPL). This collection of papers was taken from Alcatraz Island after the federal marshals moved in, in June 1971. The papers first went to a federal records office, then to a lawyer working for the Indians of All Tribes. He tried to give them to the organization, but finally donated them to the San Francisco Public Library where they remain today. For more on union support see "Alcatraz Union Co-ordinator: Joseph L. Morris," *Indians of All Tribes Newsletter* 1, no. 2,

box 3, file 17, UCSFPL. For Joe Morris's memoir of his participation in the Alcatraz occupation see Joe Morris, *Alcatraz Indian Occupation Diary* (published by Joe Morris, 1988).
58. All quotes from letters found in box 1, file 23, UCSFPL.
59. Billie Flora to Grace Thorpe, March 20, 1970, box 1, file 23, UCSFPL.
60. These letters can be found in files 6; 7; 12; 16; 22; and 23 all in box 1, UCSFPL. According to American Indian Movement (AIM) leader Dennis Banks, Jim Jones was part Choctaw. Jones also raised money for Wounded Knee defendants' legal representation. See Dennis Banks and Richard Erdoes, *Ojibwa Warrior: Dennis Banks and the Rise of the American Indian Movement* (Norman: University of Oklahoma Press, 2004), 316. Letters from international correspondents also arrived on Alcatraz. See box 1, file 9, "Foreign Requests for Information," and box 1, file 10, "Inward—Foreign Support," both UCSFPL. For an example of a published column which criticized the occupation from the beginning see George N. Crocker, "The Alcatraz 'Invasion,'" *San Francisco Examiner*, December 1, 1969, copy in ACFSFPL. "Those Indians who seized Alcatraz Island had been well coached," he claimed. "Even their little speeches and their self-conscious bravura were part of a script already hackneyed in the San Francisco-Berkeley area, which has been a laboratory for the clinical propagation of group mischief these last five years." Suggesting the Indians were tools of some unnamed conspiracy, he went on: "The recruitment of real live Indians for this latest raid on property was a picturesque variation after the tawdriness of the Berkeley 'People's Park' episode of last June. We are learning that the scenario which has been written for the destruction of the American social order is imaginative, if nothing else. To keep the young, the neurotic and the naïve at fever pitch, the plans require that the successive defiances of civility take ever new forms." With each new defiance, Crocker claimed, the country was becoming increasingly demoralized and would eventually slide into chaos. Alcatraz was "just one small item on a long agenda." Further, he said, Alcatraz could not be given back to Indians because they never owned it. Historically Indians may have visited the Rock, but they did not inhabit it.
61. For a sample see files containing incoming correspondence regarding Indian Affairs, Gen In 10/1/69–12/3/69 file, WHCF NA. Paul Chaat Smith made the interesting observation that the Nixon White House was primarily responsible for making Alcatraz a long-lasting episode of national and international importance. "Without the drama of a White House envoy," he wrote, "that takeover would have been a mildly interesting one day story." See Smith, *Everything You Know About Indians is Wrong*, 57.
62. Alan G. Kirk, II, Assistant to the Secretary of the Interior, to Brad Patterson, June 16, 1970, Alcatraz Public Views file, box 34, Leonard Garment, WHCF NA.
63. The Marin County offer can be found in "Memorandum to Regional Council Members and Staff," July 16, 1970, Alcatraz Files: BANAC, CFOA 6398, box 33, Leonard Garment, WHCF NA. The people who participated in the meeting regarding this offer included the Nature Conservancy's Huey D. Johnson, Interior Department's William T. Davoren, and Barney Old Coyote, Area Director and Area Office of the Sacramento Bureau of Indian Affairs. The group concluded the only Indian group that had the stature, base, and license to function truly on behalf of all Indians was the National Council of American Indians and they did not support such a donation to the Indians of All Tribes. Brad Patterson wrote Leonard Garment that this offer "might take the pressure off the Alcatraz issue by really finding a place, not Alcatraz, for an Indian Cultural Center." But they would have to think carefully about the consequences of committing to such an ethnic center because "the Chicanos and blacks will be next—is this the way we want to move?" See memo, Patterson to Garment, August 8/26, 1970, Alcatraz files: BANAC files, box 33, Leonard Garment, WHCF NA. For the Atherton heiress's offer see Mitzi Briggs to President Nixon, n.d., GEN IN 7/1/70–9/30/70 file, WHCF NA. Her letter received further endorsement from Robert King, who had once worked for Richard Nixon and was a friend of Brad Patterson. King seconded Briggs's idea of selling the island for twenty-four dollars even though he realized such an act could be construed as condoning and rewarding forcible occupation of federal land. Still he believed if "skillfully handled" such objections could be overcome. It would be "a real psychological factor in restoring some vestige of pride in the Indian himself." This would earn a few "brownie points" for Nixon and accomplish something worthwhile. In

response, Brad Patterson promised King that he and Leonard Garment were watching things closely on Alcatraz, had not tried forcible removal, and were "wide open" regarding the future of the island. See Robert King to Brad Patterson, February 3, 1970, and Patterson to King, February 11, 1970, Alcatraz Public Views file, box 34, Leonard Garment, WHCF NA. The standard reply the White House sent out, however, was much less encouraging of the Indians on Alcatraz, offering the colorless, maddening, bureaucratic language we have all come to expect from such letters: "The Department of the Interior is presently studying possible uses of the island and we are withholding disposal at their request." See for an example, Daniel Kingsley of the General Services Administration to Bill Adair, n.d.; Kingsley to Robert Patterson, January 9, 1970, Alcatraz Public Views file, box 34, Leonard Garment, WHCF NA.

64. Louis T. and F. Pearl Jones to Rose Mary Woods, February 7, 1970, in GEN IN 1/1/70–3/3/70 file, box 5; and Aunt Ruth to Richard, June 2, 1970, GEN IN 4/1/70–6/30/70 file, box 5, both WHCF NA. Nixon also received a few letters in 1970 in support of Washington state Indians' fishing rights. See GEN IN 10/1/69–12/3/69 file, box 5, WHCF NA.

65. The Ohlone petition can be found in GEN IN 1/1/70–3/3/70 file, box 5, WHCF NA.

66. Harold Porter to Robert Robertson, March 21, 1971, copy forwarded from Robert Robertson to Brad Patterson, March 26, 1971, Alcatraz Public Views file, box 34, Leonard Garment, WHCF NA.

67. Copy of this column, n.d., can be found in Alcatraz Editorial Comment file, box 33, WHCF NA.

68. Bill Dauer, "Management's Corner," in *San Francisco Business*, April 15, 1970, copy sent from Robert Robertson to Brad Patterson, April 18, 1970, Alcatraz Editorial Comments file, box 33, WHCF NA. "A Good Deal," in *Hammond Times*, copy attached to memo from Bob Robertson to Brad Patterson, May 10, 1970, Alcatraz—Plan for Park file, box 34, WHCF NA. This editorial, which came from the author's hometown newspaper, indicates the White House was interested in editorial comment from any and all places.

69. See "Sodomy," in Alcatraz Beginnings file, box 33; and memos from Tod Hullin to Leonard Garment, December 16, 1970; and from Garment to John Ehrlichman, December 16, 1970, Alcatraz-Situation on the Island file, box 34; Bud Krogh, December 11, 1970, Alcatraz Policy Memos file, box 34; WHCF NA. Ehrlichman and others presumably hoped to use this alleged incident to discredit the occupation.

70. Garment to Ehrlichman, January 6, 1970, Alcatraz Policy Memos file, box 34, WHCF NA. Ehrlichman did not, to my knowledge, take Garment up on this suggestion.

71. Walter Hickel to Leonard Garment, March 10, 1970, Alcatraz-Plan for Park file, box 34, WHCF NA.

72. Garment to Ehrlichman, April 2, 1970; and Garment to Ehrlichman, September 14, 1970, both in Alcatraz Policy Memos file, box 34, Leonard Garment, WHCF NA; Leonard Garment, *Crazy Rhythm: My Journey From Brooklyn Jazz and Wall Street to Nixon's White House, Watergate and Beyond* (New York: Random House, 1997), xi. 225. See also Bradley Patterson Jr., *The Ring of Power: The White House Staff and Its Expanding Role in Government* (New York: Basic Books, 1980), 72–75.

73. Memo to John Ehrlichman [unsigned but probably from Garment], June 9, 1971, Alcatraz-June 1971 file, box 34, WHCF NA.

74. The *San Francisco Chronicle* described Alcatraz after the last occupiers had been removed, as "an unrelieved vista of squalor, filth, systematic pilfering, and mindless destruction." When the Indians first seized the island "it was romantic theater which excited sympathy throughout the world." Some traces of that idealism could still be found, in the school, for instance. But for the most part, the "squatters" had revealed little talent for colonizing the island. It was appropriate, then, for the federal government to take back control "after [displaying] nearly two years of exemplary restraint." The *Oakland Tribune* seconded the characterization of the government's "remarkable patience" but added that Alcatraz Island would remain a symbol of inspiration and hope to Native Americans. See columns and editorials dated June 14, 1971, from *San Francisco Chronicle*; and June 16, 1971, *Oakland Tribune* in Alcatraz-Editorial Comments file, box 33, WHCF NA. The previous December, Bud Krogh informed John Ehrlichman that the publisher of the *Chronicle* was cooling considerably on

his support of the Alcatraz Indians, admitting that the occupation had soured and that the present lot were "a filthy, drunken, drugged lot," memo from Krogh to Ehrlichman, December 11, 1970, Alcatraz Policy Memos file, box 34, Leonard Garment, WHCF NA.
75. "Alcatraz: 1 Yr. Manifesto," and "Rally," *Berkeley Tribe*, November 13, 1970, 9. This issue also contained information about the establishment of Deganawidah-Quetzalcoatl University near Davis, California. See chapter 5.
76. "Alcatraz Again," *Berkeley Tribe*, November 13, 1970, 9.
77. "Alcatraz," June 19, 1971, 9–11; "Indian Brothers," September 17, 1971, 6; "Alcatraz 3," March 3, 1972, 6; and front cover of November 19–26, 1971 issue, 1, *Berkeley Tribe*. See also "Adam is Red," November 20, 1970, 4–5, and an April 24, 1970, 16–17, two-page photo spread, *Berkeley Tribe*.
78. "Who Let the Indians Down?" *Berkeley Barb*, June 18, 1971, 3. The paper also briefly noted the copper case trial. See "Indians Face Paleface Law," *Berkeley Barb*, March 3, 1972, 5.
79. "Indians Mark '69 Culture Clash on 'The Rock,'" November 8, 1999, and "Occupation of Alcatraz: 30-Year Anniversary of Indian Coup," November 19, 1999, both in San *Francisco Examiner*, copies in ACFSFPL.
80. Richard Oakes, "Alcatraz Is Not an Island," December, 1972, *Ramparts* 37.
81. Garment, *Crazy Rhythm*, 225; Rosier, *Serving Their Country*, 258–59; and Charles Wilkinson, *Blood Struggle: The Rise of Modern Indian Nations* (New York: Norton, 1995), 196–97.
82. Vine Deloria Jr., "Alcatraz Activism and Accommodation," in *American Indian Activism*, ed. Johnson, Nagel, and Champagne, 46, 47, 50. At the time of the occupation, Deloria published a piece in the *New York Times Magazine* supporting the proclamation's demands. "I wish the government would give Alcatraz to the Indians now occupying it," he wrote in March 1970. "We would be given a chance to see what we could do toward developing answers to modern social problems." Reprinted as "This Country Was a Lot Better Off When the Indians Were Running It," in *Red Power: The American Indians' Fight for Freedom*, 2nd ed., ed. Alvin Josephy Jr., Joanne Nagel, and Troy Johnson (Lincoln: University of Nebraska Press, 1999), 28–38.

Chapter 4

1. Peter Coyote, *Sleeping Where I Fall: A Chronicle* (Washington, DC: Counterpoint, 1998), 130. Coyote's communal experiences took place in California.
2. Joe Sando met a young woman in Switzerland who told him she had been conceived at Jemez Springs, New Mexico, in the late 1960s when her mother moved to northern New Mexico as part of the hippie phenomenon. The mother returned to Europe, however, where she raised her daughter. Joe Sando, interview with author, April 21, 1999, Pueblo Cultural Center, Albuquerque, New Mexico.
3. Carol Hinton quote from *Flashing on the Sixties: A Tribal Document*, directed by Lisa Law (film documentary, 1994). A *Playboy* magazine reporter claimed the casualties of the failed Summer of Love dream "fled into the Indian country. A defeated people, they went to the Indians to learn how to live off the land. They saw no other way to survive." Jules Siegel, "West of Eden," *Playboy*, November, 1970, 240.
4. Iris Keltz, *Scrapbook of a Taos Hippie* (El Paso: Cinco Puntos Press, 2000), 25.
5. Lois Rudnick, *Mabel Dodge Luhan: New Woman, New Worlds* (Albuquerque: University of New Mexico Press, 1987); Mabel Dodge Luhan, *Edge of Taos Desert: An Escape to Reality* (Albuquerque: University of New Mexico Press, 1987); Flannery Burke, *From Greenwich Village to Taos: Primitivism and Place at Mabel Dodge Luhan's* (Lawrence: University Press of Kansas, 2008); Robert White, ed., *The Taos Society of Artists* (Albuquerque: University of New Mexico Press,1988).
6. Ben Wallace, "Bare Feet in the Snow: Experiments in Communal Living in Northern New Mexico," (unpublished manuscript), original privately held by Ben Wallace, Southern Methodist University (SMU), Dallas, Texas; *Sage*, February 19, 1969, 9–10. Several in the mainstream media attempted to explain hippie motives for coming to Taos, particularly the *Taos News*. For a relatively "retrospective" explanation see Susan Whaley, "Taos Used to Be . . . Cool," *Taos News*, May 5, 1971, A6.

7. Jack Loeffler, telephone interview with author, July 29, 2002.
8. Jack Loeffler interview with Lois Rudnick, August 5, 1988, copy of audiotape available at Harwood Foundation Library, Taos, New Mexico (hereafter HFL). See also Lois Rudnick, *Utopian Vistas: The Mabel Dodge Luhan House and the American Counterculture* (Albuquerque: University of New Mexico Press, 1998), 217–235. For another example of someone drawn first to peyote meetings in Nevada and eventually to community (if not commune) life in New Mexico, see told by Chris West to Iris Keltz, "Origins of Pilar Hill," in Keltz, *Scrapbook of a Taos Hippie*, 137–39.
9. John Kimmey, interview with Lois Rudnick, August 13, 1988, HFL. Kimmey also became close to Hopi elder David Monongye who, he claimed, gave him the Hopi prophecies and said he could pass along the information to whites. Many decades later, in 2000, Kimmey's continued interest in sharing these prophecies with non-Hopi people attracted censure from the Hopi Nation which asked him to stop telling non-Hopis about the sacred prophecies. See "Man Asked Not to Reveal Hopi Prophecies," *Dallas Morning News*, November, 2000, no page number, copy in author's possession.
10. Rick Romancito, "Hippie Communes," *Taos News*, January 5, 1995, Taos Communes file, Taos Public Library; Peter Rabbit, interview with Lois Rudnick, September 9, 1989, HFL. Dean Fleming, one of the founders of Libre, a Huerfano Valley, Colorado, commune started in 1968 also attributed the commune's philosophy to "the Indians." Intended as a community of artists, Fleming maintained the art was influenced by Indians as well: "The primary influence was Indian" and even the land itself "was full of the energy of Indians. Philosophically the Hopis had more to do with our shared philosophies ... the Hopis and of course many of the other Indians." Comanche, Cheyennes, Lakota and Teton Sioux, Utes and Navajos had all come through that area and left their imprint. In terms of art, the Indian influence was initially direct and literal: medicine wheels, circles, the four directions, and other similar imagery. See Dean Fleming, interview with Lois Rudnick, August 2, 1988, HFL. In his former wife's memoir of Libre, however, Indian interests play little importance. See Roberta Price, *Huerfano: A Memoir of Life in the Counterculture* (Amherst: University of Massachusetts Press, 2006). For an account of Drop City from the point of view of one of its founders see Mark Matthews, *Droppers: America's First Hippie Commune, Drop City* (Norman: University of Oklahoma Press, 2009). The only mention of Indians in this account relates to Peter Rabbit's promotional efforts to attract visitors to the commune by promising contact with Indian people.
11. Bill Gersh, interview with Lois Rudnick, August 7, 1988, HFL. "Chick Lansdorf," the pseudonym Ben Wallace used for the primary informant of his unpublished manuscript on Taos communes also came to Taos after becoming disillusioned with cities, particularly San Francisco. See Wallace, folder marked Veronica Friel reports & field notes, SMU. For others who moved to New Mexico to escape cities see "Hippies say, 'This Is Home,'" *New Mexican*, May 25, 1969, New Mexico Hippies vertical file, Santa Fe Public Library, New Mexico.
12. Gersh, interview. See also Keltz, *Scrapbook of a Taos Hippie*, 134. For examples of communitarians for whom the Indian element of Taos was tangential, at best, see Margaret Hollenbach, *Lost and Found: My Life in a Group Marriage Commune* (Albuquerque: University of New Mexico Press, 2004). Hollenbach moved to Taos in 1970 to join "The Family," a commune which emphasized group marriage, and had grown up in a home with San Ildefonso black pottery, Navajo rugs, and Pueblo and Cheyenne watercolors. She "was convinced that artists and Indians, mysteries and magic lived in Taos," but she did not seek out contact with native people during her rather traumatic time in Taos. Hollenbach, 18. See also Arthur Kopecky, *New Buffalo: Journals From a Taos Commune* (Albuquerque: University of New Mexico Press, 2004); and Arthur Kopecky, *Leaving New Buffalo Commune* (Albuquerque: University of New Mexico Press, 2006).
13. Lisa Law, interview with author, May 28, 2006; Lisa Law, interview with Lois Rudnick, August 2, 1988; Karen Evans, "Sixties Flashback: Photographer Lisa Law Followed the Counterculture Movement With a Keen Eye and a Beguiling Style," *Albuquerque Journal Magazine*, May 14, 1985, New Mexico Hippies vertical file, Santa Fe Public Library, New Mexico. See also Lisa Law, *Flashing On the Sixties* (Santa Rosa, CA: Squarebooks, 2000).
14. Coyote, *Sleeping Where I Fall*, 153, 155.

15. Ibid., 187–96.
16. Ibid., 197–98.
17. Ibid., 199.
18. Ibid., 205.
19. "Why Taos?" *Fountain of Light*, August, 1969. Copy found in the Center for Southwest Research, Zimmerman Library, University of New Mexico Library, Albuquerque.
20. For a critique of the various waves of middle-class people who moved to Taos hoping for happier, more meaningful lives—including the 1960s versions—see Arthur Martin, "Enchantment and Colonization: Modernity and Lifestyle Migrants in a New Mexico Town" (Ph.D. dissertation, University of New Mexico, 1998). Among Martin's criticisms of these migrants is they brought the "totalizing power of modern capitalist society" with them and consequently forced the abandonment of traditional, local, particularly Hispano, culture. In constructing Taos in a "romantic-bohemian mode," they celebrated ethnic diversity but simultaneously used their money to "disenfranchise Hispanos from their traditional lands" and appropriated "traditional Pueblo culture as a fantastic commodity-experience," 18–31.
21. Unohoo, Coyote, Rick, and the Mighty Avengers, *The Morning Star Scrapbook* (Occidental, CA: Morning Star Distributing, n.d.). This paperbound book, which sold for $3.95, is a scrapbook of photographs, news clippings, and commentary regarding the Morning Star Ranch commune. Copy available in Bancroft Library, University of California, Berkeley. The last articles in the scrapbook carry 1973 dates, so the scrapbook was printed sometime after 1973. See also Timothy Miller, *The 60s Communes: Hippies and Beyond* (Syracuse, NY: Syracuse University Press, 1999), 46–53. Miller says the name "Morning Star Ranch" stemmed from "an earlier owner's dedication of the land to the Virgin Mary." He emphasizes the commune's interest in Asian religions in his account. For an account of California commune Black Bear residents' relationships with local Native Americans see Don Monkerud, Malcolm Terence, and Susan Keese, eds., *Free Land: Free Love: Tales of a Wilderness Commune* (Black Bear Mining and Publishing, 2000), especially John Salter, "A Visit Down River," 162–71 and Michael Tierra, "Encounters with the Karuk," 172–80.
22. Unohoo et al., *Morning Star Scrapbook*., 7,8, 9.
23. Ibid., 15–18.
24. For more on the relationship between the two Morning Star communes and information on the New Mexico branch see Keltz, *Scrapbook of a Taos Hippie*, 81–85, 87–91, 93–97, 99–102. See also Miller, *60s Communes*, 78–81.
25. Unohoo et al., *Morning Star Scrapbook*, 29, 37, 47, 66, 40, 2, 169. Not all neighbors opposed the Morning Star commune. The Reverend Geoffrey P. Selth of the Unitarian Fellowship, Sonoma County, started a Friends of Morning Star group to help work on health problems on the property. The informal group consisted primarily of Sonoma State College and Santa Rosa Junior College professors and students. When the county tore down the commune's cooking facilities, neighbor Don Orr offered his ranch hands' dining room, one mile away. A letter to the editor (unclear from which newspaper) that appears in the scrapbook defends the Diggers and Morning Star commune. "It may well be that these young people do have something to offer our modern warring world. Can we say they do not?" The commune also sought protection from the local sheriff when the Gypsy Joker bikers came to visit, fired guns, and intimidated the hippies. 31, 33.
26. Rudnick, *Utopian Vistas*, 221; Miller, *60s Communes*, 80–81, 117–18. Contemporary underground newspapers regularly reported on communes, listing their philosophical orientations and basic attitude toward newcomers. For examples see "The Rural Communes," in Denver, Colorado's *Chinook*, June 4, 1970, 8–10; "The New American Indian Tribes," in Albuquerque, New Mexico's *Astral Projection*, December 1, 1968, 6; and *Astral Projection*, June 1969, 33–4, 23. The mainstream press also provided enormous publicity for these community experiments including Siegel, "West of Eden," 173–74, 240–53.
27. "Mama Lama: Told by Barbara Durkee to Iris Keltz," in Keltz, *Scrapbook of a Taos Hippie*, 128–29.
28. Stephen Fox, "Boomer Dharma: The Evolution of Alternative Spiritual Communities in Modern New Mexico," in *Religion in Modern New Mexico*, ed. Ference M. Szasz and Richard W. Etulain (Albuquerque: University of New Mexico Press, 1997), 145–57. Fox maintains

that Stewart Brand first encouraged the Durkees to settle in New Mexico. He also says the Durkees created the multimedia light show "Why America Needs Indians," which I attribute to Stewart Brand. See 152–53. For Woodstock see Michael Lang and Holly George Warren, *Road to Woodstock* (New York: Ecco/Harper Collins, 2009).

29. Rick Klein quoted in *Flashing On the Sixties: A Tribal Document*, directed by Law.
30. Siegel, "West of Eden," 242. Not all occupants of New Buffalo were interested in an Indian connection, however. For reminiscences of the place that do not mention Indians see Iris Keltz, "First Encounter With New Buffalo" and "Close Encounters with New Buffalo;" and Joyce Robinson, "Founding Settler of New Buffalo;" all in Keltz, *Scrapbook of a Taos Hippie*, 31–36, 39–44, and 47–52; Kopecky, *New Buffalo* and *Leaving New Buffalo*.
31. Rick Klein quotes are from *Flashing On The Sixties: A Tribal Document*, directed by Law; "Rick Klein," in Lisa Law, *Interviews With Icons: Flashing on the Sixties* (Santa Fe: Lumen, Inc. 2000), 209–14. In 1968 Steve and Barbara Durkee hired Henry Gomez, Little Joe's son, and a crew of Taos Pueblo Indians to help build adobe structures at Lama. Various people volunteered to help that summer including a group of black men who tried to convince the young Indian men they should not volunteer to fight in Vietnam. "They pointed out that dark-skinned men were more likely to be sent to dangerous fronts, that they had a greater chance of getting killed. But they could not crack the Indian's connection to the Marines. Little Joe Gomez lost seven of his sons in WWII. Henry was the only one of his sons who survived." See "Mama Lama," in Keltz, *Scrapbook of a Taos Hippie*, 129–30. For more on Pueblo Indian-Lama relations, see Jonathon Altman interview, November 12, 2005, folder 2; Sylvia Rodriguez interview, January 7, 2008, folder 54; and Saul Barodsky interview, October 21, 2006, folder 3, all in Oral History Interviews of the Lama Foundation, 1970–2009, Special Collections, Center for Southwest Research, University of New Mexico, Albuquerque. Thank you to Derek Kutzer for bringing this collection to my attention.
32. Fox, "Boomer Dharma," 152.
33. Keltz, *Scrapbook of a Taos Hippie*, 105–08. Joe's Restaurant, Taos' first alternative café, which operated from 1973 to 1977, was named in Little Joe Gomez's honor and whenever he and his wife came in, they ate for free. Little Joe, according to Keltz, was the hippies' "holy man and our shaman who taught us important spiritual lessons," 179, 181.
34. See Kopecky, *New Buffalo*, 18, 44, 114,135,157, 210 for examples of visits from Taos Pueblo people to the commune. For Kopecky's view of the New Buffalo peyotists see 161–62. Stuart Hardy indicated that Concha socialized with Beatniks, artists and hippies—all kinds of Anglo outsiders. He did not drive, so you had to pick him up, but he seemed to enjoy talking with the non-Indians. He was "very subtle" about his teachings. Moreover there was a subtlety to the interaction itself. He was open to outsiders but only on a non-obtrusive level. If you told people your knowledge too directly, you might lose it. People don't like to talk about the interaction with Indians for fear of appearing to "brag" about it. Stuart Hardy, interview with author, April 22, 1999, Taos, New Mexico.
35. Howard Bryan, "'Hippie Invasion' Stirs Turmoil in Taos," n.d., no newspaper name, article found in New Mexico Hippies Vertical File, Santa Fe Public Library, New Mexico.
36. Quoted in Olga Curtis, "Taos and the Hippie Invasion-Part 2: Too Much Hatred for Understanding," *Denver Post*, September 27, 1970, copy found in vertical file, HFL.
37. Rudnick, *Utopian Vistas*, 230.
38. This story appears in David Perkins, "Commune," *Spirit*, Spring–Summer 1996, 13, copy available at Harwood Museum Library, Taos, New Mexico. For another non-Indian view of Taos Pueblos' inclination to deal with the hippies through humor and teasing see Mabel Kuykendall, "Adobe Diggings," *Taos News*, March 3, 1971, A6. She wrote that the only time she ever saw Taos Pueblo people "retaliate" against people who misbehaved at the Pueblo was through the pranks, wit, and mimicry of the "chiffonetis," or clowns, during the pole climb of the San Geronimo Feast Day festivities. She writes about the clowns' treatment of a "very tall, scrawny hippie girl . . . sporting a feather (presumably representing an eagle feather which is very sacred to the Indians)." When the clowns pulled her out of the crowd, she resisted, screaming and wailing. After they released her, they mimicked her frantic display.

39. Larry Frank, "Caught," in *Train Stops* (Santa Fe, NM: Sunstone Press, 1998), 109–15.
40. Wavy Gravy [Hugh Romney], *The Hog Farm and Friends* (New York: Links Books, 1974), foreword by Ken Kesey, 20, 21, 25, 33. The descriptions of Wavy Gravy come from the press kit which accompanied publication of his 1992 book, *Something Good for a Change*. A copy of the press kit can be found in Wavy Gravy's biographical file, San Francisco History Center, San Francisco Public Library. He is also described as "the illegitimate son of Harpo Marx and Mother Theresa conceived one starry night on a spiritual whoopee cushion" and as "the official jester for Kesey's Merry Pranksters."
41. Wavy Gravy, *Hog Farm and Friends*, 64. Wavy Gravy's humor did not go over particularly well with Chicago's Black Panthers either. While in that city, in 1969, he spent time with the Panthers but found that people were criticizing him for not being a serious revolutionary. He dressed, for instance, like a duck and carried an inflatable banana. "I almost took it too far at a big demonstration for Bobby Seale and a bunch of people had gags on their mouths. I was gonna gag my banana but I didn't cause I knew it would offend a number of my brothers. But even thinkin' about doin' it made me laugh ... anger is steam and your head is a pressure cooker and your brains are beans. But the little valve on the top is for laughter and letting off steam. If you don't laugh a little every so often, you get beans on the ceiling," 99–100.
42. Sando, interview. For contemporary accounts which claim the springs could be meeting grounds for hippies and Indians see Stanley Kripper and Don Fersch, "The Rural Communes," *Chinook*, June 4, 1970, 9; Siegel, "West of Eden," 252.
43. Porfiero Montoya, interview with Dennis J. Stanford, December 5, 1967, tape no. 4, roll 10, American Indian Oral History Collection 1967–1972, Pueblo Transcripts, Special Collections, Zimmerman Library, University of New Mexico, Albuquerque; Sando, interview.
44. Montoya, interview; Sando, interview; and author interview with anonymous Taos Pueblo man, April 28, 1999, Taos, New Mexico.
45. Diane Reyna, interview with author, April 28, 1999, Santa Fe, New Mexico. Another source indicated hippie efforts to adopt Indian religions were not only superficial, but insincere. They were going through the motions, but not making any sacrifices. They also made their spirituality "too public." Anonymous, interview with author. This source also mentioned the hippies' "dirty" appearance and resented it. He had been a World War II prisoner of war, a situation that made personal hygiene nearly impossible. To choose to forego bathing, as he presumed many hippies did, was simply too difficult to comprehend.
46. Reyna, interview.
47. "Another Beatnik Invasion?" April 6, 1967, 1–2; Spud Johnson, "Invasion," April 6, 1967, 4; and "In Come the Hippies," June 1, 1967, 4; "Hippie-Hunt Bags Plentiful Comments, But No Hippies," July 6, 1967, B1; "'Psychedelic' Talk Scheduled," December 7, 1967, A3, all *Taos News*. The only mention of New Buffalo comes in a front-page photo of a donkey race between members of the commune. Front-page photo of the donkey race can be found on October 5, 1967, *Taos News*, 1.
48. "Taoseño Dislikes Hippies," and "Filming Here Next Week," May 23, 1969, 4 and 1; "As We See It ... The Hippie Problem," May 23, 1968, 4; "Police Raid 'Hippies,'" September 26, 1968, 1–2, all *Taos News*.
49. Spud Johnson, "Dream Come True," June 27, 1968, *Taos News*, 4. He first mentioned the Lama Foundation, though he originally assumed its name would be Solux in "Invasion," April 6, 1967, 4; and for his obituary see Claire Morrill, "Spud's Years Touched Many," November 7, 1968, 3, both *Taos News*.
50. Rudnick, *Utopian Vistas*, 228–30; "Here's What Those Hippies, Did," February 27, 1969; "'Hippie' Problem Stirs More Local Groups to Investigate," and "Those 'Hippies' Once Again," March 20, 1969, 1–2, 4; "Epidemic Reported in Hippie Communes," October 9, 1969, 1; "Do Hippies Love Us for Our Food Stamps," February 19, 1970, 1–2; "State Tightens Reins on Food Stamps," March 19, 1970, 1, 4; "The Hippie Problem," March 26, 1970, 4; "The Hippies," April 2, 1970, 4; "Youth Program Proposed to Counteract Hippies," April 17, 1969, 1; "Taos Drug Addicts Few, but Problem Grows," April 24, 1969, 1; "Food Stamps," May 14, 1970, 5; "Communes Face 'Red Tag' Threat," May 21, 1970, 1; all *Taos News*.

51. For examples see "Four Fines in Assault" and "El Prado Rape Alleged," April 16, 1970, 1–2; "Hippies Attacked," May 22, 1969, 1; "Taos Police Officer Charged With Misconduct," May 28, 1970, A2; and "4 Charged in Seco Incident," June 25, 1970, 1; all *Taos News*. The latter indicated four Taos men including Dennis Hopper and his brother, David, were arraigned for allegedly pulling guns on six Arroyo Seco youths. The newspaper also covered, in its "society pages," actor Dennis Hopper's open house at the Mabel Dodge Luhan home, which he purchased after coming to Taos to film *Easy Rider*. The proceeds from tickets sold to the event would go to the Taos Art Association. It also published an account of his wedding to singer Michelle Phillips. The story included all the trappings of a traditional society wedding story: a description of the bride's dress, bouquet, and wedding cake. See "Mabel Dodge Luhan House to Have Public Showing Through Courtesy of Dennis Hopper," October 1, 1970, B2; "Michelle Phillips, Dennis Hopper Are Wed in Double Ring Ceremony," November 5, 1970, B1, *Taos News*.
52. "Coming to Nuevo Mexico?" n.d., *Astral Projection*, vol. 1 no. 1–vol. 5, no. 1, box AN2A8, *Astral Projection* Collection, Special Collections, Zimmerman Library, University of New Mexico, Albuquerque (hereafter APC UNM). In the June 1969 edition, the paper reported in an article titled "The Communes of New Mexico," that most of the Taos townspeople were "very nice." The problems arose from the "more capitalistic outsiders (mostly from Texas) who are trying to drain off as much Taos money as they can get from the tourist trade." June 1969, 23.
53. Aaron Howard, "Hog Farm Summer Solstice," and Paul Prensky and Joyce Gardner, "Taos News: Heck of a Mecca," first published in the Austin, Texas *Rag* and reprinted in the San Francisco *Good Times*, both in Aug–Sept. 1969, *Astral Projection*, 17, 35, in folder vol. 1, no. 1–vol. 5, no. 1, box AN2A8, *APC* UNM.
54. "Effort to Talk To 'Hippies' Starts with Meet in Church," March 27, 1969, 2; "'Hippie Problem' Answers Sought by Committee Set Up by Town," April 3, 1969, 1; "Hippies, Straights Continue Dialogue," March 26, 1970, 1; and "Taos in Transition," December 23, 1969, 6, all *Taos News*.
55. "Violence Against the Hippies," April 23, 1970, 3; "Public Forum . . . Let's Cool It," April 30, 1970, 5, *Taos News*. In a variation on the call for rapprochement, Frank Lyon played the "gender card," defending mustaches and long hair as a way men can assert their masculinity—"just in the nick of time as the new woman's rights movement may otherwise stamp out the critters as members of the human race anyway." See "Hair!" *Taos News*, June 11, 1970, 5.
56. "Old Struggles & Newcomers," reprinted from *El Grito Del Norte* in April 1, 1970, *Fountain of Light*, copy found in private collection of Ben Wallace, SMU.
57. For this brief discussion of Chicano-hippie interactions I rely on Rudnick, *Utopian Vistas*, 231–35. Although not a hippie or communard, author and activist John Nichols, "a self-described semi-Marxist-Leninist propaganda arm for a group of quixotic Spanish-speaking septuagenarians locked in mortal combat with the United States government over the preservation of their water rights, their land, their culture, their very historical roots," did make Hispanic issues the focus of his interests and energies after moving to Taos in 1969. He published *The Milagro Beanfield War* in 1974. Nichols remains one of the fiercest critics of the hippies. As he put it, although a few remained and became serious citizens of the valley, "for the large part it was sort of an influx of . . . freaks, weirdos, who made no commitment to the area, to the culture, to the land, to the history . . . And they were gone in a few years. In the meantime, however, they . . . caused an awful lot of damage." See Rudnick, *Utopian Vistas*, 233–34; Rudnick interview with Nichols, September 5, 1989, HFL.
58. "Earth Peoples Park," February 1970, *Fountain of Light*.
59. Ibid.
60. Ibid. According to the newspaper, these smaller parcels of land could be purchased outside of Taos, in Albuquerque, Santa Fe, Carmel, Los Angeles, San Francisco, Denver, Omaha, and the Netherlands and Belgium.
61. For more contemporary examples of hippie-Hispano conflicts and attempts to communicate, see Paul Steiner and Meredith Steiner, *Chamisa Road* (New York: Random House, 1971); Jon Stewart, "Trucking; Towards Taos With Tootsie," October 1, 1970, *Chinook*, 5, 7

(reprinted from a San Francisco magazine called *Organ*); "Que Paso?" May 1, 1970, *Fountain of Light*, Ben Wallace Papers, SMU. This last piece lists a series of assaults and arsons directed against hippie property and indicates that police and judges were not pursuing the perpetrators or sentencing appropriately those brought to trial. Several articles offered advice on how to treat local cultures with sensitivity. See "Taos Bungle" and "Indian Calendar," both in July 1969, *Fountain of Light* that advised readers that they must ask permission before settling on land, realize that Pueblo Indians took pride in clean bodies and homes, contact the majordomo (water boss) before using water, and demonstrate tact and respect when attending ceremonial dances. An early attempt at cross-cultural communication can also be found in a Spanish language article, "Hablamos," *Fountain of Light*, June 1969, 5. For the most comprehensive, contemporary account of Taos-hippie relations see Olga Curtis, "Taos and the Hippie Invasion, Part 1 and Part 2," *Denver Post*, September 20, 1970 and September 27, 1970, copy found at HFL. For contemporary interviews which address hippie-Hispano relations see interview of Carmen Velarde by Ashley Marable, June 30, 1970; Loretta Paulson interview by Veronica Friel, June 23, no year [probably 1970]; "Ed" interview by Cary Harkaway, June 29, 1970, all in Ben Wallace, field notes, SMU. The latter indicated that many young Hispanos were friendly, stopping by his unnamed commune to visit or smoke dope. A few got drunk and started fights but most did not. He did, however, sense much more hostility from the older generation. Loretta Paulson assumed that eventually Lila and Lama communes would be able to teach "the right level of consciousness and harmony with all of nature" to the Spanish-Americans. In other words, the hippies would presumably teach the Hispanos what the Pueblos already knew before the hippies came. Velarde who taught weaving at New Buffalo assumed the locals distrusted the hippies because of drug use and fears they would scare away tourists.

62. For a detailed history of this complicated story see R. C. Gordon-McCutchan, *The Taos Indians and the Battle for Blue Lake* (Santa Fe: Red Crane Books, 1991). For an example of the American Friends Service Committee's involvement in the Blue Lake restoration legislation see "Testimony of Theodore B. Hetzel .... in Support of S. 3085 to Restore Certain Lands to Taos Indians," May 18, 1966, AFSC-Com. Rel-Indians file, American Friends Service Committee Archives, Philadelphia, Pennsylvania.

63. For a lengthy article on Blue Lake that also includes an overview of Pueblo and Indian history see "The Blue Lake Saga," *Fountain of Light*, February 1970. Although the article demonstrates a sincere interest in understanding the issue and its historical context, the "hippie" flavor comes through in comments such as: "The Indians learned from their Kachinas, as we are learning now from such psychedelics as LSD, that all life is not only sacred, but interrelated."

64. Gordon-McCutchan, *Taos Indians and the Battle for Blue Lake*, xvii.

65. Ibid., 136–37.

66. Ibid., 148–49.

67. Ibid., 186–87.

68. For a copy of the press release of Kim Agnew's visit issued by the Office of the Vice President and a memo to Leonard Garment from "Edgar," coordinator of the National Blue Lake Committee, July 22, 1970, see Blue Lake [CFOA 8695], box 100, Leonard Garment Alpha Subset Files, White House Central Files, Nixon Presidential Materials Staff, National Archives, College Park, Maryland.

69. "Hopi Call For Action," *Astral Projection*, issue 11, 24, APC UNM. See also "The Hopi Way of Life Is the Way of Peace," as told by Andrew Hermequaftewa, *Astral Projection*, August–September, 1969, box AN2A8, APC UNM. The latter also appeared in Denver's *Chinook*, February 5, 1970. For another story on Black Mesa see "Indian War," 1, no. 3, *The Tribal Messenger* [1970], copy available at Zimmerman Library, UNM.

70. Jack Loeffler, telephone interview with author, July 29, 2002.

71. Lois Rudnick interview with Jack Loeffler, August 5, 1988, HFL. In this interview Loeffler indicates that in 1972 he and another person discovered Edward Curtis's photographs of Indians. They were then "totally obscure" but their sale for over ten thousand dollars helped pay off the Black Mesa Defense Foundation's debt. Dennis Hopper purchased much of the collection. Lisa Law became active in the fight to halt relocation of Navajo people out of the land the federal government had once set aside for Navajo-Hopi joint settlement.

The Navajo-Hopi Land Settlement Act of 1974, however, set a deadline of July 6, 1986, for voluntary relocation of Navajos from lands now solely to be occupied by the Hopi and vice versa. Many more Navajos were affected, however, and consequently resisted. Law, using her skills as a photographer and organizer, worked to publicize the issue and encourage sympathy for the Navajos. For an example see "Navajos Make Their Voice Heard: Protestors Demand Repeal of Federal Act Mandating Division of Tribal Lands," October 29, 1985, (*Santa Fe*) *New Mexican*. Law helped organize this particular demonstration, which featured older Navajo women carrying signs that read "Removal is Genocide" and "Stop Strip Mining Navajos." This, too, failed to achieve the intended results. Navajo relocation continued unabated. Lisa Law, interview with author, May 28, 2006, Santa Fe, New Mexico. This issue, of course, proved more problematic for non-Indian sympathizers of Indian people as it pitted one tribe against another. For an extensive Hopi articulation of its position see *Hopi Tuto-veh-ni*, 1, no. 3 (Summer edition): 1—30. Copy given to author by Lisa Law. Perhaps the most well-known non-Indian support for the Navajos came with the film *Broken Rainbow*, which Robert Redford produced, that received the Academy Award for Best Documentary in 1986. For a sympathetic review of the film see Walter Goodman, "Film 'Broken Rainbow' Documentary," *New York Times*, April 11, 1986.
72. "Commune Life Around Taos Drops in Face of Reality," *New Mexican*, May 9, 1971, New Mexico Hippies vertical file, Santa Fe Public Library, New Mexico.
73. "New Buffalo Considers Cemetery, School," *Taos News*, February 20, 1986; "New Buffalo: From '60s Hippie Hang-out to Bed and Breakfast," *Taos News*, December 1992; Susan Salter Reynolds, "The Far Out Inn," *Los Angeles Times*, November 21, 1993; and Staci Matlock, "New Buffalo Ends an Era, Rick and Terry Klein, Tired of Reliving the 60s, Put Old Commune up for Sale," *Taos News*, January 9, 1997; all found in Taos Communes vertical file, Taos Public Library, New Mexico.

Chapter 5

1. Paul Chaat Smith and Robert Allen Warrior, *Like a Hurricane: The Indian Movement From Alcatraz to Wounded Knee* (New York: The New Press, 1996).
2. Vine Deloria Jr., "The American Indian and His Commitments, Goals, Programs: A Need to Reconsider," *The Indian Historian* 5, no. 1 (Spring 1972): 6. The American Indian Historical Society of San Francisco, California, began publishing this periodical in 1964. Its purpose was to present history and information about Indians in the past and present. "Friends of the Indian" were invited to join in but by "helping not leading, aiding but not pushing, taking part but not taking over." See *The Indian Historian: A Journal of American Indian History, Arts and Literature* 1, no. 1 (October 1964): 1. For a sample of an article regarding the Hank Adams shooting see "Hank Adams dedicated to his people's fight for rights," *Seattle Times*, January 24, 1971, A16.
3. Dee Brown, *Bury My Heart at Wounded Knee: An Indian History of the American West* (New York: Henry Holt, 1970), xviii, xvii.
4. Ibid., 137.
5. Helen Hunt Jackson, *A Century of Dishonor: A Sketch of the United States Government's Dealing with Some of the Indian Tribes* (New York: Harper & Row, 1881). For an historian's assessment of the book's influence at the time of publication see Francis Paul Prucha, *The Great Father: The United States Government and the American Indians*, Vol. II (Lincoln: University of Nebraska Press, 1984), 626–28.
6. The Vine Deloria, Jr., quote comes from advertisement copy for *Bury My Heart at Wounded Knee*, found in the *New York Times* (hereafter *NYT*), February 18, 1971; for Momaday's review see *NYT*, March 7, 1971; Thomas Lask's review of the book appeared in the *NYT*, February 2, 1971, one week after it was first noted in that newspaper under "new books." Nearly twenty-five years later the New York Public Library selected *Bury My Heart* as one of the most frequently requested and influential books of the twentieth century. See "The Most Requested of Library Books," *NYT*, June 29, 1995. For more on Indian Wars-Vietnam conflations see Paul C. Rosier, *Serving Their Country: American Indian Politics and Patriotism in the Twentieth Century* (Cambridge: Harvard University Press, 2009), 244–53.

7. For a sampling of *Bury My Heart at Wounded Knee*'s presence on the *NYT*'s best-seller list, see March 14, March 28, April 25, June 6, June 13, June 27, July 4, all 1971; April 9, 1972. The five million copies sold information comes from Douglas Martin, "Dee Brown, 94, Author Who Revised Image of West," *NYT*, December 14, 2002. Brown once indicated that he donated some of the royalties he earned from this highly successful book to Indian libraries. See Judy Kiemesrud, "Dee Brown," in the "Behind the Best Sellers," *NYT*, April 13, 1980.
8. Thomas Lask, "They Pulled Columbus Ashore," *NYT*, November 9, 1970. Author and environmentalist Edward Abbey reviewed *Custer Died For Your Sins* for the *NYT*, November 9, 1969. In the review Abbey notes the parallels between the war in Vietnam and wars against American Indians. He finds Deloria writes not with great bitterness but often with humor, and that the book offers some hope for justice. He concludes the book is not only about Indians and their troubles "but about us and our troubles. The two are the same." This newspaper also published a lengthy Deloria piece on contemporary Indian politics, "The War Between the Redskins and the Feds," December 7, 1969. In its obituary of Vine Deloria Jr., the *NYT* noted that he "burst into the American consciousness" with this book. Trained as a seminarian and a lawyer, "Mr. Deloria's real weapon, critics and admirers said, was his scathing, sardonic humor, which he was able to use on both sides of the Indian-white divide." See "Vine Deloria Jr., Champion of Indian Rights, Dies at 72," *NYT*, November 15, 2005.
9. Stan Steiner, *The New Indians* (New York: Harper & Row, 1968), xii, 61; Edgar S. Cahn, *Our Brother's Keeper: The Indian in White America* (New York: New Community Press, 1969), xii. Although not nearly as widely read as Brown's book, Steiner's work did garner two reviews in the *NYT*: Charles Poore, "Red Power," February 29, 1968, 35; and N. Scott Momaday, "Tribal Spirit," March 17, 1968, BR 22. *Our Brother's Keeper* was reviewed in the *NYT*, *Reader's Digest*, *Village Voice*, *Washington Post*, and *Times* (London).
10. Brown, *Bury My Heart at Wounded Knee*, xix.
11. Deborah Sue Brown to President Nixon, July 16, 1972, GEN IN 8/1/72—[12/31/72] file, box 7, White House Central Files (hereafter WHCF), Subject Files, IN (Indian Affairs), Richard Nixon Presidential Papers, National Archives, College Park, Maryland (hereafter NA).
12. Deloria, "The American Indian and His Commitments," 8, 10. Deloria did not hesitate to take this message to non-Indian audiences, as well. In a speech he presented at Temple University, he chastised the assemblage for ignoring Indians' contemporary problems, including the brutal murders of Indians in the West and elsewhere, which the Justice Department and the FBI refused to investigate and state governments refused to prosecute. "People are sorry about what happened at Sand Creek, but can't relate to what happens to the Nesqually [sic] people today ... *Bury My Heart at Wounded Knee* can be a best seller, and you can think you are sympathetic with Indians." If his audience remembered nothing else of what he concluded, he wanted them to remember this: Indians are a twentieth-century people. See "In Vine Veritas," *Indian Truth*, no. 211 (October 1973): 1, 6. This is the newsletter of the Indian Rights Association, headquartered in Philadelphia, Pennsylvania.
13. For brief notice of these takeovers and other actions see Paul Chaat Smith and Robert Allen Warrior, *Like a Hurricane: The Indian Movement from Alcatraz to Wounded Knee* (New York: The New Press, 1996), 88–89; Troy Johnson, Duane Champagne, and Joane Nagel, "American Indian Activism and Transformation: Lessons From Alcatraz," in *American Indian Activism: Alcatraz to the Longest Walk*, ed. Troy Johnson, Joane Nagel, and Duane Champagne (Urbana and Chicago: University of Illinois Press, 1997), 32; Joane Nagel, *American Indian Ethnic Renewal: Red Power and the Resurgence of Identity and Culture* (New York: Oxford University Press, 1996), 164–6. Robert Rundstrom counted thirty-four protest occupations between 1970 and 1978 "all of which refer to Alcatraz for their symbolic power in one way or another." See Rundstrom, "American Indian Placemaking on Alcatraz, 1969–71," in *American Indian Activism*, ed. Johnson, Nagel, and Champagne, 202. For Russell Means's account of the disruption of Plymouth Plantation's Thanksgiving, see Means, *Where White Men Fear to Tread* (New York: St. Martin's, 1995), 175–78. See also "Indians Protest Aboard 'Mayflower,'" *Washington Post*, November 27, 1970, copy found in Alcatraz Related Indian Takeover file, box 34, Leonard Garment, WHCF NA. These documents are

now housed at the Nixon Presidential Library, Whittier, California. For Means at Mount Rushmore in 1970 and 1971 see Means, *Where White Men Fear to Tread,* 167-70, 182-86.
14. Eva Nichols to Hon. Walter Hickel, September 20, 1970; Edward Hummel, Acting Director, NPS, to Wayne Colburn, Chief of Marshals Service, November 18, 1970, copies of both in Alcatraz Related Indian Takeover file, box 34, Leonard Garment, WHCF NA. For other examples of Indian non-support of activists' occupations see Smith and Warrior, *Like a Hurricane,* 87-88.
15. IFCO, "Administrative History," Inventory of Interreligious Foundation for Community Organization Papers, Schomburg Center for Research in Black Culture, New York Public Library (hereafter IFCO Papers.)
16. "IFCO Indian Task Force Meeting" minutes, May 2-3, 1969, file 25, box 9, IFCO Papers.
17. Vine Deloria to Lucius Walker, April 16, 1969, file 29, box 9, IFCO Papers. In a document, "Notes on American Indian Contacts," dated October 11, 1968, Deloria is described as "very active in Indian Circles," and as an Indian representative on non-Indian committees. His past association with the National Council of American Indians also made him a potential source for consulting on Indian community organizing. IFCO files also included a copy of his article, "Custer Died For Your Sins," which appeared in the August 1969 issue of *Playboy.* This piece reflected the same acerbic humor and caustic language that Deloria used in his correspondence with Walker. "The primary goal and need of Indians today is not for someone to study us, feel sorry for us, identify with us, or claim descent from Pocahontas to make us feel better. Nor do we need to be classified as semi-white and have programs made to bleach us further." What they did need was a congressional policy that acknowledged Indian intelligence and dignity. They also needed block grants and the opportunity to run their own schools, police, hospitals, and economic enterprises on reservations. Folder 6, box 9, IFCO Papers.
18. Vine Deloria to Lucius Walker, August 16, 1969, file 15, box 1, IFCO Papers.
19. Deloria, *Custer Died For Your Sins,* 163.
20. Walker to Deloria, August 20, 1969, file 15, box 1, IFCO Papers; Marilyn Clement, telephone interview with author, June 15, 2006.
21. "American Indian Task Force Transcript of Meeting, [May 2-3]. 1969," file 28, box 9, IFCO Papers.
22. Ibid., "IFCO-Indian Task Force Transcript of Meeting, [May 2-3], 1969," file 25, box 9, IFCO Papers. The first source is a literal transcript of the meeting; the second, a more formal (and sanitized) summary.
23. "IFCO-Indian Task Force Transcript of Meeting."
24. Ibid. The six people on the advisory committee were Jess Sixkiller, Margaret Nick, Robert Carr, Elizabeth Locklear, Charles Wilkins, and Harriet Skye Paul.
25. "A New Beginning: The Nike Missile Base" and "Pigs Raid Base," *Berkeley Tribe* (hereafter *BT*), June 19, 1971, 12. The *Berkeley Barb* also followed the story, reporting that "a horde of more than 100 pigs... Invaded Nike Indian Village... and ripped off their newly re-claimed land." See "Keepin' the Native Down," *Berkeley Barb,* June 18-24, 1971, 3.
26. Jack D. Forbes, "The Native Struggle for Liberation: Alcatraz," in *American Indian Activism,* ed. Johnson, Nagel, and Champagne, 134; "Davis," *BT,* November 13, 1970, 9; "Deganawide-Quetzalcoatl University (D-QU)," in *Red Power: The American Indians' Fight for Freedom,* 2nd ed., ed. Alvin Josephy Jr., Joane Nagel, and Troy Johnson (Lincoln: University of Nebraska Press, 1999), 194-95. The Nixon White House monitored events at Davis. See T. E. Hannon, Regional Administrator of the General Services Administration, to Brad Patterson, November 20, 1970, Alcatraz Related file, box 34, Leonard Garment, WHCF NA. Hannon reported that fifty Indians remained at the compound in the daytime, fifteen at night and that they were "orderly." He also told Patterson the D-Q University supporters sought an injunction to prevent turnover of the property to the University of California. Finally, he indicated that Colonel Potter believed they hoped to be arrested for trespassing in order to get publicity for their cause and if that happened, they would then leave the property. Dennis Banks served as chancellor of D-Q University in the late 1970s, appointed to that position by California Governor Jerry Brown. See Means, *Where White Men Fear to Tread,* 374; and Dennis Banks with Richard Erdoes, *Ojibwa Warrior: Dennis Banks and the*

Rise of the American Indian Movement (Norman: University of Oklahoma Press, 2004), 322–24. More recently, D-Q University has fallen upon hard times, losing its accreditation and one million dollars in funding in 2005. California's only college run for and by Indians shut down. Among the problems: mishandling of funds, impending financial collapse, inadequate college-level procedures for selection of courses and programs, and plummeting enrollment. See "D-Q University: End of the Road? State's Only Tribal College has Lost its Accreditation," *Sacramento Bee*, January 21, 2005, B1; and "Native American College Shuts Down; D-Q University, Which Opened in 1971, Lost Its Accreditation and $1 Million in Federal Funding," *Los Angeles Times*, February 20, 2005. For another example of Chicano-Indian cooperation in establishing an educational institution see information on the Chicano Indian Studies Center of Oregon (CISCO), which hoped to target Indian and Chicano high school dropouts: See Nicolas Rosenthal, "Repositioning Indianness: Native American Organizations in Portland, Oregon, 1959–1975," *Pacific Historical Review* 71, no. 3:422–34.

27. "Indians Invade, Lay Claim to Ft. Lawton," and "Army Disrupts Indian Claim on Ft. Lawton," *Seattle Post-Intelligencer* (hereafter *PI*), March 9, 1970; Lossom Allen, "By Right of Discovery: United Indians of All Tribes Retake Fort Lawton, 1970," in *Seattle Civil Rights and Labor History Project*, http://depts.washington.edu/civilr/FtLawton_takeover.htm (accessed March 1, 2010). See also Jeffrey C. Sanders, "The Battle for Fort Lawton: Competing Environmental Claims in Postwar Seattle," *Pacific Historical Review* 77, no. 2:203–35; and "Geronimo's Revenge," *Helix*, March 20, 1970. Sander's work emphasizes the split the invasion revealed within Seattle's postwar liberalism between environmental (open space and park advocates) and Native Americans, between mainstream liberals and "an increasingly boisterous youth movement," 205. For the place the Fort Lawton invasion takes in the larger context of Native American history in Seattle see Coll Thrush, *Native Seattle: Histories from the Crossing-Over Place* (Seattle: University of Washington Press, 2007).

28. "Jane Fonda 'Gripes' About Detention at Fort Lewis," and "Indian 'Attack' on Fort Fascinates World Press," *Seattle Times* (hereafter *ST*), March 9, 1970. For information on Bernie Whitebear see Lawney L. Reyes, *Bernie Whitebear: An Urban Indian's Quest for Justice* (Tucson: University of Arizona Press, 2006).

29. Allen, "By Right of Discovery"; "Indians Move on Fort Today," *PI*, March 10, 1970; "Indian 'Attack' on Fort Fascinates World Press," *ST*, March 9, 1970; "Indians Drum Up Support for Fort Claim," *ST*, March 10, 1970; "Indian Picket Line Remains at Ft. Lawton," *ST*, March 11, 1970; "Indians Picket Courthouse," *PI*, March 11, 1970; "County Studies 151-acre Claim to Ft. Lawton," *PI*, March 11, 1970; "Equality in Seattle is Indians' Message," no newspaper noted, March 12, 1970. All of these clippings can be found in Indians of North America: Land-General file, Special Collections, Suzzallo Library, University of Washington, Seattle. For more examples of sympathetic reporting see "Indians Add Tepee to Ft. Lawton Camp," *PI*, n.d., and "Big Jim Thorpe Was Great Dad," *ST*, March 15, 1970.

30. "Indians Want Nixon Powwow," *ST*, March 16, 1970; "77 Indians Arrested In Lawton Invasion," *PI*, March 16, 1970; "Indians Rally at Courthouse," *ST*, March 16, 1970; "Indians Plan Demonstration Today at Federal Courthouse," *PI*, March 16, 1970; "14 Indians Arraigned for 'Invasion,'" *PI*, March 17, 1970; "Park on Fort Land Reaffirmed," *PI*, April 3, 1970. Although the March 9, 1970, action received no notice in the *NYT*, the March 15 one warranted a short article. See "77 Indians Arrested Attempting to Camp Inside Seattle Fort," *NYT*, March 16, 1970.

31. "2 Indian Leaders Assail Fort Lawton Demonstration," *ST*, March 19, 1970; "On the Outside Looking Hopeful," *PI*, March 22, 1970; Herbert Barnes to Senator Jackson, January 27, 1971, file 17, box 113, Henry Jackson Papers, Special Collections, Suzzallo Library, University of Washington, Seattle (hereafter HJP).

32. "Message From Sky: 'Fort, Give Up,'" *ST*, March 19, 1970; "How Indians Would Use Fort," and "On the Outside Looking Hopeful," *PI*, March 22, 1970.

33. "Ft. Lawton Indian Invaders Jailed" and "MP Now Knows 'How Custer Felt,'" *PI*, April 3, 1970; "Indians Vote to Keep Vigil at Ft. Lawton," *PI*, March 23, 1970; "On the Outside," *PI*, March 22, 1970; Lawton Park Issues," *PI*, February 17, 1971. The third and last invasion led to a fire that burned one of the unused frame buildings on the fort campus. Colonel Palos,

whose response throughout the events had been relatively mild, indicated the FBI would have to investigate the fire. Had the picketing and invasions continued, it is quite likely the reportage would have turned negative and soured the UIAT's chances to obtain their goals. The Seattle underground newspaper, *Helix*, disagreed with the strategy to work with government officials on a negotiated outcome. "A growing number of Indians, notably younger ones, think this is bullshit," one reporter wrote. "Red power is what they want and they'll only get it with people power. You don't ask for change, you make it." Pistol, "Tonto Is Dead... Forever," *Helix*, April 16, 1970.

34. For letters Senator Jackson received regarding S.1708 and on Indian claims to Ft. Lawton see file 38, box 213; files 15 & 16, box 83; file 17, box 113; files 4 & 5, box 97; all in HJP. "Grandma" to Jackson, March 9, 1970; F.P. Hartnett to Jackson, May 13, 1970; Mrs. N.T. Whifford to Secretary of the Interior and copy to Jackson, June 15, 1970; all in file 4, box 97, HJP.

35. Blair F. Paul to Louis Bruce, December 7, 1970, Alcatraz Related Indian Takeover file, box 34, Leonard Garment, WHCF NA. Wes Uhlman to Fred J.Russell, December 14, 1970; Henry Jackson to Fred J. Russell, December 4, 1970; and Harrison Loesch to Henry Jackson, December 24, 1970, all in file 5, box 97, HJP; Fred Russell to Wes Uhlman, January 19, 1971, file 6, box 54, Mayor Wes Uhlman Papers, Series 5287-02, Seattle Municipal Archives, Washington (hereafter WUP). Whitebear charged Jackson with pressuring Louis Bruce and "heading 'an unethical, political power play' to thwart Indian efforts to obtain" the surplus land, and Jackson denied the charge. See Don Hammula, "Sen. Jackson Denies 'Pressure' on Bureau," *ST*, January 22, 1971.

36. Wes Uhlman to Fred J. Russell, December 17, 1970, file 15, box 97, HJP; Shelby Scates, "Whitebear Leads Indians to Victory in Ft. Lawton Battle," *PI*, December 5, 1971; Hilda Bryant, "Indians' Ft. Lawton Application Accepted," *PI*, April 16, 1971; interview with former Mayor West Uhlman, *Seattle Civil Rights and Labor History Project*, http://depts.washington.edu/civilr/FtLawton_takeover.htm (accessed February 25, 2010). For examples of the vast majority of letters to Mayor Uhlman that favored some Indian use of the new park see files 1, 4, 5, 7, and 8, box 54, WUP. Neither Whitebear nor his brother, Lawney Reyes, saw Uhlman as an ally in the early negotiations. Uhlman found the UIAT and Whitebear difficult, as well, in the early stages of the dispute.

37. "City, Indians Agree on Lawton Lease Plan," *ST*, November 15, 1971. For more information on the Daybreak Star Center see "Tribes Travel Upward from Fort Lawton," *ST*, March 4, 1985; "Facing the End, Activist Reflects on Life's Victories," *ST*, December 2, 1997; "Fort Lawton Takeover Recalled," *ST*, March 9, 2000; and "Indians Achieve a Dream: Lodge at Discovery Park," *ST*, July 20, 2003. In the years to follow, the United Indians of All Tribes oversaw construction of a $1.25 million Daybreak Star Center, using private donations as well as state money. The complex offered lunches to seniors and exhibited Indian art in several galleries. A downtown Indian Street Youth Center and an education complex on the east side of Lake Union addressed other urban Indians' needs. Overseeing it all was Bernie Whitebear, whose ambitious social-service agency received funding from eight federal agencies in the late 1990s with an annual budget of $4 million. Yet this satisfied neither Whitebear nor other board members. They aimed to construct a larger complex called People's Lodge. In 2003 the Foundation and Magnolia neighborhood residents finally reached an agreement on an architectural plan and the Indians began fund-raising. Unfortunately, Whitebear succumbed to colon cancer in 2000 and did not live to see this turn of events.

38. Interview with Lawney Reyes, *Seattle Civil Rights and Labor History Project*, http://www.depts.washington.edu/civilr/reyes.htm (accessed March 1, 2010).

39. Early Alcatraz occupier Edward D. Castillo made this point, as well, "Reminiscence of the Alcatraz Occupation," in *American Indian Activism*, ed. Johnson, Nagel, and Champagne, 127.

40. "Indian 'Raiders' Claim New Land," *San Francisco Chronicle* (hereafter *SFC*) June 5, 1970; "Indians Stand at Shasta," *SFC*, June 6, 1970; untitled article on Pit River action, *BT*, June 12, 1970; Johnson, Nagel, and Champagne, "American Indian Activism," in *American Indian Activism*, ed. Johnson, Nagel, and Champagne, 13.

41. Untitled, *BT*, June 12, 1970; "The Indians Stand," *SFC*, June 6, 1970.
42. "Indians Rousted at Shasta," *SFC*, June 7, 1970; Wavy Gravy, *The Hog Farm and Friends* (New York: distributed by Quick Fox, 1994), 121–22.
43. Wavy Gravy, *Hog Farm and Friends*, 123–24.
44. "Ousted Indians Head Back," *SFC*, June 8, 1970; "More Indians Arrested at Pit River," *SFC*, June 9, 1970; Wavy Gravy, *Hog Farm and Friends*, 124–25. The *Berkeley Tribe* passed along information on various ways readers could help the Pit River Tribe. Indians were encouraged to come to Pit River country and help reclaim land. Others were encouraged to send telegrams of support to President Nixon, the Cabinet, Commissioner of Indian Affairs Louis Bruce, the Indian Claims Commission, and all congressmen. They could also send or bring supplies such as food and cooking utensils for use in future occupations. Finally readers were encouraged to boycott PG&E "by paying us [the Pit River Tribal Council] instead of them. Make your PGE bill payable to Pit River Tribe, Hat Creek California; you'll receive a receipt and we will send a duplicate to PGE ... All responsibility will be on us." See untitled article, *BT*, June 12, 1970.
45. "Pit River Nation," *Indian Magazine*, circa 1970, Frederick Haley Collection, box 81, Special Collections, University of Washington Library, Seattle; Smith and Warrior, *Like a Hurricane*, 140, 245. The *Indian Magazine* was apparently a short-lived periodical, published in Healdsburg, California. This issue contained many photographs on the lumber industry, a dam, and of law enforcement using force to arrest the demonstrators at Burney, California. It also included information on how to make contributions to Pit River Legal Aid and Information.
46. Aubrey Grossman to President Nixon, December 9, 1972; telegram, Ross Montgomery, Chairman Pit River Tribe to President Richard Nixon, December 10, 1972, both in Indians-California file, box 18, Bradley Patterson, White House Central Files, Nixon Presidential Papers, National Archives, College Park, Maryland (hereafter Indians-California WHCF NA). The *Berkeley Barb* sympathetically covered the Pit River issues. See "Pitt Indians Tell Fears of Massacre," December 22, 1972; and "Indians Refuse Bribe as Court Accepts Claims," December 29, 1972. The Pit River Tribe consciously tried to attract press, television, and radio to their story and "to protect them against the possibility of the first Indian massacre in almost a century," but had limited success.
47. Memorandum, Bradley Patterson to Leonard Garment, December 1, 1972; Leonard Garment to Aubrey Grossman, December 5, 1972; Garment repeated his admonition against confrontation politics and tactics in another letter, Garment to Grossman, December 14, 1972, all in Indians-California, WHCF NA.
48. Aubrey Grossman to Leonard Garment, December 20, 1972; Leonard Garment to Aubrey Grossman, 26, 1973, both in Indians-California WHCF NA.
49. Kent Frizzell, Assistant Attorney General of the Land and Natural Resources Division, Justice Department, drafted Garment's response to Grossman. See Bradley H. Patterson to Kent Frizzell, December 27, 1972; Kent Frizzell to Bradley Patterson, January 5, 1973; all in Indians-California WHCF NA. Frizzell recommended to Patterson that the White House "give serious consideration to an explicit statement in the final letter that the executive branch does not intend to provide funds or land to the Pitt [sic] River Indians independent of judicial or legislative action." Patterson and Garment followed this advice.
50. The U.S. Forest Service kept the White House informed of Pit River activities designed to interfere with timber sales and logging through 1973. See "Early Warning Alert" re: "Pit River Indians may interfere with California timber sale," December 3, 1973, included with letter from Paul Grainger, Director of Budget and Finance, Forest Service, Washington, D.C., to Bradley Patterson, December 5, 1973. Grainger reported that the anticipated interference with timber sale operations did not occur on December 4. "There was lots of news coverage but only three Indians, a man, woman, and child, showed up to protest the sale." Other documentation on confrontations include a telegram from Aubrey Grossman to President Richard Nixon, December 3, 1973, warning that the Nixon administration was moving closer to a massacre of Indian people again, all of which could be avoided if the Justice Department would support, rather than oppose the Indians getting their day in court; Bradley Patterson to Aubrey Grossman, December 4, 1973, reminding him that

Leonard Garment's position, as stated in the January 1973 letter, still held; Grossman to Patterson, December 5, 1973, reminding the White House of his point: "How do you think the government will look if there is violence and all that was needed to avoid it was the government permitting the Indians to have their day in court—one day in court after 120 years of trying. There is no reason it should take two months to decide—two minutes might be sufficient." See also U.S. Forest Service "Early Warning Alert" re: "40 armed Indians representing the Pit River tribe entered timber sale area in Lassen NF . . . timber fallers vacated sale area," December 11, 1973; "Early Warning Alert," re: "Pit River Indian confrontation dissolves," December 13, 1973; "Early Warning Alert," re: "Pit River Indians return to Lassen NF timber sale site," December 14, 1973; and U.S. Forest Service "Status Report on Pit River Indians on Lassen National Forest," December 18, 1973, all in Indians-California WHCF NA.

51. Smith and Warrior, *Like a Hurricane*, 140–41; Charles Wilkinson, *Blood Struggle: The Rise of Modern Indian Nations* (New York: W.W. Norton, 2005), 139–41; George Pierre Castile, *To Show Heart: Native American Self Determination and Federal Indian Policy, 1960–1975* (Tucson: University of Arizona Press, 1998), 118–19; Means, *Where White Men Fear to Tread*, 222–25; Survival of American Indians Association, "Trail of Broken Treaties," n.d. [circa 1972]; and Ecumenical Metropolitan Ministry, "Information Sheet," October 5, 1972, both in Frederick Haley Papers, box 80, folder no. 1972–1973, Special Collections, University of Washington Library, Seattle (hereafter FH UW); Memorandum, Ecumenical Metropolitan Ministry to Survival of American Indians Association, October 20, 1972, box 80, folder no. 1/1, FH UW.

52. Ted Rising Sun's quote is from Nagel, *American Indian Ethnic Renewal*, 169.

53. Arthur Dye to Phil Buskirk et al., October 23, 1972, CWD American Indian Affairs 1972 Projects: Trail of Broken Treaties file, box CRD 1972, Admin of Justice, American Indian Affairs, American Friends Service Committee Archives, Philadelphia, Pennsylvania (hereafter AFSC).

54. Nagel, *American Indian Ethnic Renewal*, 169; Smith and Warrior, *Like a Hurricane*, 143–44; Means, *Where White Men Fear to Tread*, 225–26.

55. Wilkinson, *Blood Struggle*, 141; Smith and Warrior, *Like a Hurricane*, 144; Means, *Where White Men Fear to Tread*, 227–230; Josephy, Nagel, and Johnson, *Red Power*, 44–47.

56. Castile, *To Show Heart*, 118–29; Wilkinson, *Blood Struggle*, 142–43; Smith and Warrior, *Like a Hurricane*, 145–68; Means, *Where White Men Fear to Tread*, 230–35; Garment, *Crazy Rhythm*, 231–32; and Patterson, *Ring of Power*, 75–78. Information on the Hog Farm involvement came from author telephone interview with Wavy Gravy, February 25, 2002. Wavy Gravy indicated that Bob Dylan's manager, Al Grossman, got the Hog Farm a "gig" to show the films of police action at the BIA Building on *The Today Show*, a morning television program. However, the films disappeared and so the Hog Farmers never appeared on the television program. For Adams's reaction see Wilkinson, *Blood Struggle*, 143. For another difference of opinion regarding the outcome and significance of the BIA occupation see Castile, *To Show Heart*, 124–25. Castile disputes Ward Churchill's conclusion that the Trail of Broken Treaties' occupation of the BIA building "did more to bring Indians into the BIA than all the petitions and letters of 'more responsible' and 'legitimate' tribal officials over the preceding fifty years." Castile believes this "appraisal . . . is demonstrably untrue." A sweeping preference for Indian employees was already in place and the direct impact of the 1972 occupation was dismissal of Commissioner Louis Bruce, a Mohawk, and his young, activist Indian employees. The NCAI, National Tribal Chairmen's Association, and the National Council on Indian Opportunity also issued statements of denunciation.

57. For a copy of the White House response to the Twenty Points, see Leonard Garment and Frank Carlucci to Hank Adams, January 9, 1973, folder no. 1972–1973, box 80, FH UW; Castile, *To Show Heart*, 127–29; Garment, *Crazy Rhythm*, 236. The *Washington Post* reported that a government source characterized the White House response to the Twenty Points as "generally negative" and the cover letter as "hard line"—"a reminder, according to the source, 'that you can't get away with mass destruction.'" Donald P. Baker, "U.S. Rejects Indian Demands, Says Nixon Supports Reforms," *Washington Post*, n.d., copy found in TBT [Trail of Broken Treaties] Responses file, box 154, Leonard Garment, WHCF NA. This file

also includes a copy of the American Indian Press Association News Service's summary of the White House response to the Twenty Points: Karen Ducheneaux, "Response," n.d.
58. Hank Adams, Press Statement, January 11, 1973, folder no. News Releases 1971, box 80, FH UW; Hank Adams, Trail of Broken Treaties Press Statement, November 15, 1972, folder no. 1/1, box 80, FH UW. For his part, Adams took the offensive against the federal government on the issue of BIA records, writing President Nixon that he was "shocked" to discover no efforts had been made on the first and second floors of the BIA Building to recover and restore records that were essential to continuation of services to Indian people. "In fact," he wrote, "all papers are being exposed to greater disorder, disarray and damage under the practices adopted since the November 8 evacuation of that building." See Hank Adams to President of the United States, November 22, 1972, folder no. 1/1, box 80, FH UW. For an extended response to the White House's refusal to support resurrection of treaty making see "On the Restoration of Constitutional Treaty Making Authority," n.d., no author, folder no. 1972–1973, box 80, FH UW. This document "is written specifically for one purpose—to demonstrate to the people in Congress and the present administration that the proposal to reopen the treaty-making procedure is far from a stupid or ill-considered proposal but rather one which would place the United States in the forefront of civilized nations in its treatment of the aboriginal peoples of the continent—a problem which even Japan and the Soviet Russian Union have yet to solve." For a positive response to the White House reply to the Twenty Points see Glen A. Wilkinson to Leonard Garment, February 2, 1972, TBT file, box 154, Leonard Garment, WHCF NA. Wilkinson, who worked for a law firm that represented a number of Indian tribes for many years said, "This impresses me as a forthright, fair and scholarly reply to the 20 proposals submitted. Please accept my congratulations on this job."
59. A copy of Sid Mills's file can be found in 91W BIA Occupation [Bureau of Indian Affairs] file, box 79, John W. Dean III, WHCF NA. This file had contained the FBI files of Adams, the Bellecourts, and Russell Means, but they had been removed and were unavailable to researchers.
60. For examples of Justice Department *Civil Disturbance Information* booklets, see those dated October 27, 1972; October 31, 1972; November 1, 1972; November 20, 1972; "FBI Summary of Extremist Activities," December 13, 1972, all in 91W BIA Occupation file, box 79, John W. Dean III, WHCF NA. During the occupation itself, the acting director of the FBI sent John Dean, counsel to the president, as well as the attorney general and deputy attorney general, a confidential telegram advising that among those supporting the occupation were the American Independence Movement Press, "a liberal political splinter group of the Democratic Party." A representative from this group, who was in the BIA Building with the Indians was attempting to contact members of Viet Nam Veterans Against the War, as well as antiwar and "revolutionary groups" for the purpose of encouraging them to caravan to Washington and join the protest. The FBI source also indicated the Indian occupants were asking for help from the Black Panther Party in Washington—a group which "advocates the use of guns and guerrilla tactics to bring about the overthrow of the United States government." A copy of this telegram, dated November 4, 1972, can be found in 91W BIA Occupation file, John W. Dean III, WHCF NA.
61. Mrs. Harold Turner et al. to President Richard Nixon, November 17, 1972; and Sunday Experience Program participants to President Nixon, telegram, November 5, 1972, both in GEN IN 8/1/72 [12/31/72], box 7, Subject Files, IN, WHCF NA. In November and December 1972, the White House received over thirty letters and telegrams about the Trail of Broken Treaties events, judging by the number of carbon copies of the White House form response letters found in this file. Unfortunately, not all the constituents' letters are available in this file. The White House form letter was devoid of much content. For a transcript of Charles Trimble's press conference statement re: TBT see Press Conference, Charles E. Trimble, Executive Director, National Congress of American Indians, National Press Club Building, Washington, D.C., November 10, 1972, folder no. News Releases 1971, box 80, FH UW.
62. Many of these newspaper editorials can be found in Trail of Broken Treaties [TBT] Editorial Reactions file, box 152, Leonard Garment, WHCF NA. Rowland Evans and Robert

Novak, "The Nixon Permissiveness," *Washington Post*, November 27, 1972, in 91 W BIA Occupation file, box 79, John W. Dean III, WHCF NA.
63. TBT Editorial Reactions file, box 152, WHCF, Leonard Garment, WHCF NA.
64. Richard Margolis, "A Long List of Grievances," *NYT*, November 12, 1972. The Jack Anderson columns related to the stolen documents can be found in Indians TBT 1972 file, box 39, John W. Dean, III, WHCF NA. These columns appeared in the *Washington Post* on December 11 and 12, 1972. When Hank Adams attempted to return some of the documents to the FBI, he was arrested by the agency for possession of stolen documents. For criticism of this move, see Les Whitten and Vine Deloria Jr., "Old Indian Refrain: Treachery on the Potomac," *NYT*, February 8, 1973, copies in Adams' Arrest [CFOA 909] file, box 99, Leonard Garment, WHCF NA. The 91W BIA Occupation file also contains some Department of Justice summaries of post-TBT editorial responses. See "Indian Protest Aftermath," U.S. Department of Justice, *Civil Disturbance Information*, November 24, 1972, 91W BIA Occupation file, box 79, John W. Dean III, WHCF NA. Alvin Josephy, who was in the BIA Building on November 6, 1972, as an observer at a meeting of the "Steering Committee" in Louis Bruce's occupied office, as well as at the general assembly of all the Indians in the building's auditorium, supported the White House's decision to resolve the crisis without resort to violence. Several days later he wrote Leonard Garment that the situation was so dangerous that he concluded "every attempt should be made, as a first and immediate step, to defuse what could well become a major national tragedy ... I had no hesitancy then—nor do I have now—in stating my belief that the situation would have become another 'Attica,' with possibly many deaths and injuries and the destruction of part or all of the B.I.A. building ... In hindsight, I am convinced that ... the Administration ... followed the wisest courses, and avoided—by not attempting a forcible ejection of the Indians—a certain catastrophe with terrible and lingering consequences and far-reaching repercussions." Alvin Josephy to Leonard Garment, November 13, 1972, TBT Editorial Reaction file, box 152, Leonard Garment, WHCF NA.
65. Wayne N. Aspinall to Mr. Dean, November 13, 1972; and John W. Dean to Mr. Chairman, November 22, 1972, both in 31W BIA Occupation file, box 79, John W. Dean III, WHCF NA; memo, Frank Carlucci to Dave Wilson, Bud Krogh, Len Garment, and Dick Cook, November 22, 1972, TBT Congressional Hearings file, box 152, Leonard Garment, WHCF NA.
66. "Statement of Frank Carlucci ... Before the House Subcommittee on Indians Affairs," TBT Congressional Hearings file, box 152, Leonard Garment, WHCF NA. The *NYT* and *Washington Post* briefly covered the hearings. See Paul Ramirez, "Morton Testifies On Takeover Role," *Washington Post*, December 5, 1972; and "Indians' Capital Protest Has Not Resolved Any of Their Grievances," *NYT*, December 7, 1972. Hank Adams was apparently not invited to testify, although he wanted to. He sent Representative James Haley, chairman of the Subcommittee on Indian Affairs, a lengthy statement about the Trail of Broken Treaties caravan, BIA occupation, and aftermath. See Adams to Haley, November 30, 1972, folder no. 1/1, box 80, FH UW.
67. James Harvey to the President, November 14, 1972, CRD American Indian Affairs 1972 file, AFSC.

Chapter 6

1. Paul Chaat Smith and Robert Allen Warrior, *Like a Hurricane: The Indian Movement from Alcatraz to Wounded Knee* (New York: The New Press, 1996), 207; Leonard Garment, *Crazy Rhythm: From Brooklyn and Jazz to Nixon's White house, Watergate, and Beyond* (New York: Da Capo Press, 2001), 238.
2. Smith and Warrior, *Like a Hurricane*, 191–92; Charles Wilkinson, *Blood Struggle: The Rise of Modern Indian Nations* (New York: W.W. Norton, 2005), 144–45; see also Akim Reinhardt, *Ruling Pine Ridge: Oglala Lakota Politics from the IRA to Wounded Knee* (Lubbock: Texas Tech University Press, 2007) for more on the tribal council system of government, the political history of Pine Ridge, and the Wilson regime.
3. Smith and Warrior, *Like a Hurricane*, 194–201. Leonard Garment claimed that, according to Hank Adams, AIM had decided long before this February 1973 meeting that Wounded

Knee would be an ideal location for a demonstration. That may be, but this episode sprung from the particular events at play in winter 1973. Garment gave Colonel Warner, "informal military liaison for the crisis," and Hank Adams credit as the people who did most to prevent "the second Wounded Knee from ending like the first one." See Garment, *Crazy Rhythm*, 238–42. See also Bradley J. Patterson, *The Ring of Power: The White House Staff and Its expanding Role in Government* (New York: Basic Books, 1990), 78–81; and "Bradley H. Patterson, Exit Interview," September 10, 1974, http://nixon.archives.gov/virtual library/documents/exit interviews/patterson.php (accessed March 9, 2010).

4. The "toward deep history" quotation is from Wilkinson, *Blood Struggle*, 145; Smith and Warrior, *Like a Hurricane*, 201–5.

5. For examples of letters and telegrams citizens, including political leaders, sent to the White House regarding Wounded Knee II and for Patterson's comment on AIM, Bradley Patterson to James Abdnor, August 3, 1972, Letters (Wounded Knee) files; and for Garment on the special Indian Mass see Leonard Garment to Kenneth Cole, March 26, 1973, News Clippings Wounded Knee file, both box 76, Bradley Patterson, White House Central Files, Nixon Presidential Papers, National Archives, College Park, Maryland (hereafter WHCF NA). These documents can now be found at the Nixon Presidential Library in Whittier, California. The Rev. Vine Deloria gave a sermon at the mass, calling on the federal government to send a peace-making mission rather than federal marshals to Pine Ridge. Folksinger Buffy Sainte-Marie sang and dedicated a song to the Wounded Knee occupiers. Michael Butler, the producer of the counterculture Broadway musical *Hair*, purchased her airline ticket from Hawaii so she could participate. A variety of religious organizations donated funds so busloads of northeastern Indians could attend the mass. See "Indians Celebrate Special Mass Here," *New York Times*, March 25, 1973.

6. John P. Adams, *At the Heart of the Whirlwind* (New York: Harper & Row, 1976), 101.

7. Alvin M. Josephy Jr., "Wounded Knee and All That—What the Indians Want," *New York Times Magazine*, March 18, 1973.

8. Wilkinson, *Blood Struggle*, 146–47; memo, Bradley Patterson to Jerry Warren, "Wounded Knee-Situation Report," March 1, 1973; and memo, Brad to Ken, March 13, 1973, both in Policy Opinions and Discussions (Wounded Knee) file, box 76, Bradley Patterson, WHCF NA. The March 13 memo included a partial transcript of a Nixon press conference wherein the president described the occupiers as "a small group of interlopers totally unrepresentative of the American Indian people and of their elected leaders." But he went on to acknowledge that "the real grievances and needs of American Indian people—those on reservations and those in our cities—are not being well met." Lawlessness had to stop, but so too did inaction on Indian reform. He promised his administration "will take counsel not just on the sideshow at Wounded Knee, but much more important, on the lack of action on our part, and on that part of the Congress, on what legitimate Indian needs are and how we can meet them effectively." Among the Nixon administrators who preferred more immediate action and a harder line was Casper Weinberger. See memo, Weinberger to Garment, March 14, Policy Opinions and Discussions (Wounded Knee) file, box 76, Bradley Patterson, WHCF NA. Weinberger believed "we are rapidly being pushed into a kind of ridiculous position particularly with the media jumping up and down with excitement every night" and feared unless it was stopped immediately and followed up with arrests and trials, "we are going to have a series of [occupations] all over the country."

9. "Building the Nation," in "Wounded Knee, 1973," 7, 5. A copy of this pamphlet can be found in, carton 18, file 37F, Social Protest Collection, Bancroft Library, University of California, Berkeley. The pamphlet does not contain information on authorship or place of publication.

10. Ibid., 7, 8, 21.

11. Ibid., 8.

12. Ibid., 9, 10. The pamphlet explained that the Wounded Knee occupiers, as oppressed people, had the right to bear arms against their oppressors. They used their guns for self-defense. Police inside the compound did not carry weapons "as in China and Cuba."

13. Ibid., 22–23.

14. Flyers advertising these events can be found in Native American Student Association folder 37B, 1969–1979, carton 18, Social Protest Collection, Bancroft Library, University of California, Berkeley. The variety of interests that supported such rallies was also in evidence following a January 8, 1974, Wounded Knee demonstration at the San Francisco federal building. After the march, participants moved on to Dolores Park for a powwow, skits of La Cucarachas, and a presentation for the Prisoner's Union.
15. Marcus Dinsmore, "Wounded Knee For Me: Great Spirits Power," *Berkeley Barb*, March 25, 1973, 8–9.
16. Ibid.
17. Sgt. Pepper, "Sioux Seen Same as Septembrists," March 9, 1973, 2; Sgt. Pepper, "Oglala Start Much Like Irish in Soviet," March 16, 1973, 3; Sam Silver, "Chaos Reigns as Whites Show Colors," March 16, 1973, 3, all *Berkeley Barb*.
18. Sam Silver, "Support Growing Here for Oglalas," "Superstars Back Sioux," and "Oglala Benefit," all March 23, 1973, 2; John Hurley, "Help on Way to Sioux Under Siege," 2, 14; George Kauffman, "Brando a Winner," 3; "Demo for Knee" and "Indian Rock Benefit," 14, all March 30, 1973; John Hurley, "Nation Behind Oglala," 2; "Indian Festival's Grim Reminders," 2, 14; "Council Backs Oglalas," April 6, 1973, 15; and "Come to Wounded Knee! Easter March Set," April 13, 1973, 6; "Clearwater's Widow: 'Bury Him at Wounded Knee,'" April 27, 1973, 5; all *Berkeley Barb*. For another example of an underground press that highlighted Wounded Knee coverage see Albuquerque's *Tribal Messenger*, including "400 Support Wounded Knee," April 2, 1973, 1; and a special Wounded Knee Supplement, April 13, 1973, with a map of tank and gun emplacements, roadblocks, and Indian bunkers; a timeline of events related to the occupation; about twenty-five photographs; and a notice of a benefit concert for the Wounded Knee Defense Fund.
19. Ernesto Vigil, *The Crusade for Justice: Chicano Militancy and the Government's War on Dissent* (Madison: University of Wisconsin Press, 1999), 201–8, 276–79, 281–82. One of Vigil's major themes in this book is FBI surveillance of the Crusade for Justice and AIM.
20. Bill Zimmerman, *Airlift to Wounded Knee* (Chicago: Swallow Press, 1976), 5–7, 49, 68–71,181, 309–10. For more extensive coverage of Zimmerman's entire career as an activist, including Wounded Knee, see Bill Zimmerman, *Troublemaker: A Memoir from the Front Lines of the Sixties* (New York: Doubleday, 2011).
21. Dennis Banks with Richard Erdoes, *Ojibwa Warrior: Dennis Banks and the Rise of the American Indian Movement* (Norman: University of Oklahoma Press, 2004), 196–201. In his 2011 memoir Zimmerman explained that he and the other airlift participants felt intense guilt over Clearwater's death until Wounded Knee occupier and Oglala Sioux tribal member Glady Bissonette assured him she held the FBI and federal marshals responsible, not the airlifters. *Troublemaker*, 353–54.
22. "The American Indian Movement," April 2, 1983, copy included with memo from Geoff Shepard to Fred Malek, April 12, 1973, A.I.M./American Indian Movement file, box 35, Leonard Garment, WHCF NA.
23. Ibid.
24. For correspondence regarding IFCO grants to AIM see Marilyn Clement to Clyde Bellecourt, March 19, 1970, file 13, box 9; Marilyn Clement, "The American Indian Movement Evaluation," October, 1969, file 13, box 9; Clyde Bellecourt to Ann Douglas, July 13, 1972, and Ann Douglas to Clyde Bellecourt, January 6, 1973, file 16, box 9; information on IFCO support for AIM Survival Schools can be found in files 17 and 20, box 9; an agreement between IFCO and AIM, St. Paul, Minnesota for a twenty-five thousand dollar grant to fund the Red School House can be found in file 3, box 12. For IFCO frustrations with AIM see memo from Marilyn Clement to Lucius Walker, February 5, 1970, file 22, box 9; letter, Lucius Walker to Clyde Bellecourt, May 27, 1970, file 13, box 9. For IFCO's continued support of AIM see: no author noted, "IFCO Project Evaluation and Recommendation" re: AIM, March 30, 1972, file 6, box 10; Marilyn Clement to Nawaz Dawood, January 25, 1974, file 20, box 9; and no author, "IFCO Evaluation," May, 1974, file 1, box 10; no author, "IFCO Evaluation," April, 1975, file 19, box 9, all Interreligious Foundation for Community Organization Papers, Schomburg Center for Research in Black Culture, New York Public Library (hereafter IFCO Papers). In an undated "American Indian Projects Evaluation

Summaries," Marilyn Clement reported that AIM had achieved "major successes" with the police and judicial systems and had helped find jobs for hundreds of men. AIM was not, however, the only Native American group to capture IFCO attention and funds. Other Indian groups that had, or intended, to apply for IFCO support, included the Alaska Federation of Natives, Upper Midwest Indian Center, American Indians United, Coalition of American Indian Centers, Diné Ahilmdaalnish, Inc., Gallup Indian Center, American Indian Organizing Committee, National Indian Youth Council, Project Black Mesa, Choctaw Legal Defense Association, Diné Baa-Hani, Coalition of Indian Controlled School Board, Inc., Indian Pueblo Cultural Center, and League of Nations Pan-Am Indians, for just a few examples.

25. "Supplement Information: AIM 1971 Activities Report. American Indian Movement 'Challenges to the Churches,'" file 14, box 9, IFCO Papers.
26. Ibid.
27. "Minutes for the 1969 Lutheran Council in the U.S.A. Indian Ministry Conference and 1969 Annual Assembly of Lutheran Church and Indian People," file 13, box 9, IFCO Papers.
28. "Summary 1969 Lutheran Council in the U.S.A. Conference on American Indian Concern, [sic] July 29–30, 1969, Sioux Falls, South Dakota," file 13, box 9, IFCO Papers.
29. "Supplement Information AIM 1971 Activities Report. American Indian Movement 'Challenges to the Churches,'" file 14, box 9, IFCO Papers.
30. Ibid. Russell Means, *Where White Men Fear to Tread* (New York: St. Martin's Griffin, 1995), 150–53. This was Means's first involvement with an AIM event and because of their success he decided to join the organization full-time thereafter.
31. John P. Adams, *At the Heart of the Whirlwind*, 100–103.
32. Details of the role Hank Adams played in negotiations between the Wounded Knee occupiers and the White House can be found in Memorandum, Hank Adams to Vine Deloria, Jr., May 16, 1973, Policy Opinions & Discussions (Wounded Knee) file, box 76, Bradley Patterson, WHCF NA. Hank Adams's efforts eventually failed, an outcome he attributed at least in part to ten members of the Wounded Knee Legal Defense/Offense Committee (WKLDOC) team who advised against an "early settlement." He found attorney Mark Lane to be the "person most adverse to peaceful settlement along the lines already proposed by Wounded Knee."
33. John P. Adams, *At the Heart of the Whirlwind*, 111, 113–36.
34. James A. Christison, Jr., to the Honorable David Ross Williams, January 31, 1974, folder 21, box 12; and Dean Kelley to President Gerald Ford, April 5, 1976, copy sent to Lucius Walker, folder 27, box 11, all IFCO Papers. That not all Baptists agreed with the Baptist Board of National Ministries' position on AIM is clear from a letter Arnold M. Kramer, a pastor of First Alliance Church in Alliance, Nebraska, wrote to James Christison: "I hope that when you met in St. Paul to vindicate Wounded Knee defendants that you were doing it on your own time, and not at our A.B.C.U.S.A. expense or salary, for a good many of us would consider that a villainous misappropriation of funds. My next question is: Were you doing this on your own time (for instance, while you were on vacation) or while you were supposed to be on the job?" Kramer to Christison, October 29, 1974, folder 21, box 12, IFCO Papers. The NCC contribution is noted in "Minutes for January 14," in Meetings Minutes, WKLDOC, Jan.–May 1974 file, box 96, Wounded Knee Legal Defense/Offense Committee Papers, Minnesota Historical Society, Minneapolis (hereafter WKLDOC Papers).
35. Quote found in Rolland Dewing, *Wounded Knee: The Meaning and Significance of the Second Incident* (New York: Irvington, 1985), 184. In one of the interesting, though very minor coincidences of history, WKLDOC attorney Beverly Axelrod and White House staffer Leonard Garment had been law school classmates and engaged in "a long-running sporadic love affair" at Brooklyn Law School in the late 1940s. See Garment, *Crazy Rhythm*, 43–44.
36. Ibid., 225.
37. The best source on the Wounded Knee Legal Offense/Defense Committee is John William Sayer, *Ghost Dancing the Law: The Wounded Knee Trials* (Cambridge: Harvard

University Press, 1997), 45–7; Paul Chaat Smith, *Everything You Know About Indians Is Wrong* (Minneapolis: University of Minnesota Press, 2009), 151–155. Hank Adams complained about Mark Lane and some of the other WKLDOC lawyers, believing they were "most adverse to peaceful settlement along the lines [Adams] proposed at Wounded Knee." He claimed, in a memo to Vine Deloria, that Ramon Roubideaux also noted "some discernible hardening of Wounded Knee positions as probable result of some of the most recent non-Indian attorney advices." See Hank Adams to Vine Deloria, "Memo: Participation in Negotiations for the Wounded Knee Settlement, May 16, 1973," Policy Opinions & Discussions (Wounded Knee) file, box 76, Bradley Patterson, WHCF NA.

38. Sayer, *Ghost Dancing the Law*, 51, 48.
39. Ibid., 46. Once the group decided that lawyers would forego all fees, several lawyers apparently withdrew their services.
40. Ibid., 54; for examples of the individuals and organizations WKLDOC solicited for funds see Correspondence: Fund Raising, etc. 1973" file, box 95, WKLDOC Papers.
41. "Wounded Knee 1973," Statement by the American Indian Movement, November 1973, in "Wounded Knee Information Booklet," box 98, WKLDOC Papers.
42. "Wounded Knee Information Booklet," 19–28, includes biographical vignettes of some of the defendants, box 98, WKLDOC Papers. For information on the Wounded Knee airlift participant case, which WKLDOC also took on, see Zimmerman, *Troublemaker*, 361, 364–65. Zimmerman brought his fundraising skills to WKLDOC, raising the initial seed money to support a direct-mail campaign and using a portion of the proceeds for the airlift defense and donating the rest to the organization. "Public sympathy for the Indians remained high," Zimmerman claimed: "We delivered thousands of dollars to the airlift lawyers and tens of thousands to WKLDOC, which then developed its own direct-mail team." The federal government dropped all charges against the airlift defendants in February 1975. See *Troublemaker*, 365, 393.
43. Marius Spanier to Dear Sir, n.d.; Nick Phillips to Dear Friends, n.d.; Dagomir Marquezi to Wounded Knee Legal Defense/Offense Committee, October 30, 1974; Sean O. Cionnaith to Wounded Knee Legal Defense Committee, December 5, 1973; Sean O. Cionnaith to Roger Blacklow, February 6, 1974; and Wounded Knee Legal Defense/Offense Committee to the Irish Committee for the Defense of Wounded Knee, February 23, 1974; all Correspondence: Foreign Fund Raising: Solidarity & Info Request file, box 95, WKLDOC Papers.
44. Arline Abdalian to Candy, March 15, 1974; Emilio Alvarez, Jr., to Dear Friends, July 1, 1974; and Jean Allen to My dear sirs, May 15, 1974, all in Correspondence: Fundraising-A file, box 95, WKLDOC Papers.
45. Gwenne Ellen Freiman to Dear Committee Members, May 6, 1973, Correspondence: Fund Raising, etc. 1973 file, box 95, WKLDOC Papers.
46. Foundation contributors proved as eclectic and varied as individual contributions. Among the foundations which contributed to WKLDOC were the Cambium Fund of the Genesis & Ecumenical Center in San Francisco; Third World Fund from San Francisco; Prison Law Collective from San Francisco; and the Boston-Cambridge Ministry in Higher Education which was an American Baptist, United Church of Christ, United Methodist Church, and United Presbyterian Church organization in Cambridge, Massachusetts. See Foundations file, box 97, WKLDOC Papers.
47. Joe Jaqua to Dear Committee, January 15, 1975; Reine Kram to Joe Jaqua, March 21, 1975; Joe Jaqua to Dear Reine, February 24, 1975; all in Correspondence: Fund Raising, 1975 file, box 95, WKLDOC Papers; Charles Davis to Dear AIM, n.d.; and WKLDOC to Charles Davis, May 18, 1974, box 95, WKLDOC Papers.
48. Memorandum, Paul E. Boe to Board of Social Service and Dr. David Preus, Acting President of the American Lutheran Church, March 7, 1973, Correspondence: Misc (Other than Fund Raising), March–June, 1973 file, box 96, WKLDOC Papers. In this letter, Boe reminded his readers that the Division of Social Service had given financial support to the Minneapolis chapter of AIM since 1969. They had made four grants of $5,000, $8,000, $12,000 and $12,000 to support the organization's basic expenses. The board reviewed the

division's involvement with AIM on several occasions and as recently as December 5, 1972, voted to continue to support the organization. He also acknowledged not all Lutherans shared this enthusiasm for AIM, attaching a letter written by one pastor who objected to the Division of Social Service's support.
49. John P. Adams, *At the Heart of the Whirlwind*, 5.
50. Alfred C. Ames to Bronson Clark, March 24, 1973 [Ames mistakenly dated the letter 1972], CRD American Indian Affairs 1973, General: Wounded Knee file, box CRD 1973 American Indian Indians, American Friends Service Committee Archives, Philadelphia, Pennsylvania, (hereafter AFSC).
51. J. Philip Buskirk to Alfred Ames, April 3, 1973, CRD American Indian Affairs 1973 General: Wounded Knee file, box CRD 1973 American Indian Indians, AFSC.
52. Memo, Warren Witte to North Central Board and Staff, February 22, 1974, CRP Native American Affairs 1974 General Program Description file, box CRD Native American Affairs 1974, AFSC.
53. Robert Johnson, "News Release," March 13, 1973; Memo, Barbara Moffett to All Community Relations Staff and Regional Office Executive Secretaries, Subject: Wounded Knee, March 15, 1973; Memo, Barbara Moffett and Lyle Tatum to Regional Office Executive Secretaries, Community Relations Staff, and Peace Education Staff, Subject: Wounded Knee, March 23, 1973; Memo, Arthur Dye to Barbara Moffett, RE: Wounded Knee, March 31, 1973; Ben Richmond to Ray Hartsough, April 19, 1973; and Phil Buskirk, "Native Americans Are Speaking to Us," a summary of the AFSC position on Wounded Knee and Indian affairs, April 5, 1973; all in CRD American Indian Affairs 1973, General: Wounded Knee file, box CRD 1973 American Indian Affairs, AFSC.
54. Robert S. Johnson, "News Release," January 8, 1974; "Proposal for AFSC Response to Wounded Knee Trials," January 24, 1974; Memo, Warren Witte and Barbara Moffett to All AFSC Offices, Subject: Wounded Knee Trials, January 31, 1974; Memo from Bob Johnson to Barb Moffett et al., RE: Wounded Knee, n.d.; "Jurors and Others For Reconciliation" statement of purpose, n.d.; Memo, Barbara Moffett to National Community Relations Committee, re: Proposal from Jurors, October 24, 1974; Ed Nakawatase to Mark Lane, October 29, 1974; "Religious Leaders, Jurors and Deans of Law Schools to Meet With Attorney General's Office," n.d.; Laurence Strong, Chairperson, Executive Committee, AFSC to William Saxbe, November 14, 1974; and Memo, Ed Nakawatase to Barbara Moffett, RE: Jurors and Others for Reconciliation, November 11 and 12, 1974, dated November 26, 1974, all in CRD Native American Affairs 1974 General Wounded Knee file, box CRD Native American Affairs 1974, AFSC.
55. David H. Getches to Philip Buskirk, February 28, 1974; J. Philip Buskirk to David H. Getches, March 29, 1974; for information on AFSC's understanding that much work remained to turn this favorable decision into real benefit and their role in it see Memo, J. Philip Buskirk to Asia Bennett, Fred Lane, Barbara Moffett, July 30, 1974; CRD Native American Affairs 1974, Regional Offices—Pacific Northwest (Seattle) file, box CRD Native American Affairs 1974, AFSC. Buskirk made it clear that AFSC's role should be to "help the treaty right tribes use the Boldt decision to attain the ends *they* [my emphasis] want." Essentially he believed they should do all they could to support the Small Tribes of Western Washington (STOWW) organization and the Treaty Right Fishing Commission. He was particularly concerned about helping the small tribes, currently the least able to take on the responsibilities linked to the Boldt decision, participate fully and fairly in the operation of just fishing regulations and development of fisheries and related income-producing enterprises. Buskirk also penned a new preface to the 4th edition of *Uncommon Controversy* that linked fishing rights to the Trail of Broken Treaties and the Wounded Knee occupation, indicating all three made clear "the core of the movement is the issue of treaty rights, the recognition and honoring of historic agreements." He also repeated Charles McEvers's 1969 hope that Indians' voices would be increasingly heard and that the AFSC book's purpose was the increased awareness of knowledge about these issues—something only Indians themselves can fulfill. Draft of this preface can be found in CRD Native American Affairs 1974 General Uncommon Controversy file, box CRD Native American Affairs 1974, AFSC.

56. Rex Weyler, *Blood of the Land: The Government and Corporate War Against the American Indian Movement* (New York: Everest House, 1982), 96. See also Wilkinson, *Blood Struggle*, 147–49.
57. Garment, *Crazy Rhythm*, 242–43.

Epilogue

1. Angela Davis, "Keynote Address To the Founding Conference for a National Defense Organization Against Racist and Political Repression," copy found in REORG—Extraneous Input I-A-2 Addressed to founding conference on defense organization against racist and political repression file, box 98, Wounded Knee Legal Defense/Offense Committee Papers, Minnesota Historical Society, Minneapolis (hereafter WKLDOC Papers).
2. Ibid. Tom Oliphant, a *Boston Globe* reporter, who accompanied the Wounded Knee airlift pilots on their mission to cover the story and counter potential government arguments the airlift dropped weapons rather than food, faced prosecution. The government quickly dropped the charge, however, when the nation's journalists condemned the Justice Department for arresting a newsman covering a story. As it turned out, Oliphant's role went beyond mere observation. See Bill Zimmerman, *Troublemaker: A Memoir from the Front Lines of the Sixties* (New York: Doubleday, 2011), 323, 339–41, 356–57.
3. Davis, "Keynote Address."
4. Ibid.
5. "NASC Organizing Nationwide," *Native American Solidarity Committee Newsletter* 1, no. 1, October 1975, copy in folder 36a, carton 18, Social Protest Collection, Bancroft Library, University of California, Berkeley (hereafter BL).
6. Ibid. *NASC News* 1, no. 2, n.d., file 36a, carton 18, Social Protest Collection, BL. For examples of how AIM attempted to solicit money and other forms of support from non-Indian groups, during this same period, see "American Indian Movement, Inc.," file 37F, carton 18, Social Protest Collection, BL.
7. *NASC News* 1, no. 2, n.d., file 36a, carton 18, Social Protest Collection, BL. For more information on the San Francisco chapters' activities see file 36a, carton 18, Social Protest Collection, BL. For an Interreligious Foundation for Community Organization, Inc. (IFCO) effort to hold a "consultation" between church decision-makers and Native American leaders, also inspired by the looming bicentennial see "The Bi-Centennial/Justice for Native Americans," file 20, and "Native American Consultation with the Churches-Planning Meeting 1975," file 22, both box 11, IFCO Papers, Schomburg Center, New York Public Library. The "Native American Consultation With the Churches" took place October 1–3, 1975 on the Rosebud Sioux Reservation in (ironically) Mission, South Dakota. Participants included tribal leaders, AIM leaders, and representatives from about one dozen church organizations. CBS provided national television reportage on the Consultation.
8. This outcome mirrors historian Doug Rossinow's assessment of the New Left's ultimate achievements in late twentieth-century American life. In cultural terms the New Left realized "amelioration not transcendence;" in political terms "reform not revolution." Doug Rossinow, *The Politics of Authenticity: Liberalism, Christianity and the New Left in America* (New York: Columbia University Press, 1998), 294.
9. Charles Wilkinson, *Blood Struggle: The Rise of Modern Indian Nations* (New York: W.W. Norton, 2005), 205.
10. Ibid., 197.
11. For a case study of how legislative change and judicial decisions worked favorably for the Jicarilla Apache see Garrit Voggesser, "The Evolution of Federal Policy for Tribal Lands and the Renewable Energy Future," in *Indians and Energy: Exploitation and Opportunity*, ed. Sherry L. Smith and Brian Frehner (Santa Fe, NM: School of Advanced Research Press, 2010), 75–83. See also the Southern Ute example in the introduction to Smith and Frehner, *Indians and Energy*, 7–8.
12. Wilkinson, *Blood Struggle*, 198–205. For an excellent history of an earlier and important case that established the legitimacy of Indian land claims on the basis of longtime occupancy as well as treaty rights see Christian W. McMillan, *Making Indian Law: The Hualapai*

Land Case and the Birth of Ethnohistory (New Haven, CT: Yale University Press, 2007). For another interpretation of why this case matters see Sherry L. Smith, "Reconciliation and Restitution in the American West," *Western Historical Quarterly* 41 (Spring 2010): 5–25.

13. Wilkinson, *Blood Struggle,* 243–48, 249–51.
14. "Judge Approves $3.4 Billion in Indian Royalties Settlement," *New York Times*, June 20, 2011; "Tribes, Feds Seek New Start with $3.4B Deal," *Jackson Hole Daily*, July 16, 2011.
15. McMillian, *Making Indian Law,* xvii.

INDEX

Abernathy, Ralph, 10, 30–31, *31–32*, 183, 199, *199*
Adams, Hank, 20–34, *31–32*, 40–42, 172–78, 183, 188, 198–99, 217, 251n64, 254n37
Adams, John P., 9, 198–99, 207
African Americans
 Native American activism and, 6, 9–10, 22–26, 30, 152–55, 179, 183, 188–89, 191, 194, 199, 207, 218–19
 political action infrastructure and methods of, 21, 42, 105, 155, 201, 207
Agnew, Spiro, 97, 142
Alaskan Native Land Claims Settlement Act, 182
"Alcatraz Again" (coyote2), 109
Alcatraz Island
 hippies' history with Native Americans and, 45, 141
 lessons of, 156–58, 165–66
 occupation of, 16, 79, 84–112, 92, 146, 217
Alpert, Richard, 55, 73–77, 126
American Civil Liberties Union (ACLU), 23, 42, 140–41, 201
"America Needs Indians" (Brand), 4–5, *5*, 45–46, 50–52, 55–56, 116, 124, 217
American Friends Service Committee (AFSC), 17, 34–41, 140, 173, 183, 207–11, 215–16, 226n45, 256n55
American Indian Citizenship Act, 81
American Indian College Committee, 157
American Indian Council of Santa Clara Valley, 101
American Indian Medicine (Vogel), 54
American Indian Movement (AIM)
 founding of, 151
 fundraising of, 153, 156, 195–200, 202, *204*, 216, 253n24
 political strategies of, 143, 175–79, 186–87, 202

 Trail of Broken Treaties and, 172–82, 248n56
 Wounded Knee and, 4, 10, 93, 183–212
Ames, Alfred, 207–8
Anderson, Mad Bear, 49, 168
Anglo Americans
 authenticity and, 63, 115, 192, 214, 222n6
 exchanges with Native American culture, 45–77, 115–44
 as media consumers, 22–23, 78–82
 in racial politics, 12, 15, 28, 32, 64–65, 80–81, 147–50, 215–16
Apache Tribes, 148
Arapahoe Tribe, 78–79
Arizona Republic, 180
Artman, Charlie Brown, 78–79
Association on American Indian Affairs (AAIA), 11, 114, 140–41
Astral Projection (newspaper), 135, 142
authenticity, 7–8, 63, 80–81, 93, 119, 138–39, 222n6

Baker, Douglas, Jr., 95, 232n35
Banks, Dennis, 151, 172–74, *176*, 182–86, 194–98, *199*, 202–11, 245n26
Banyacya, Thomas, 49, 83, 142
Beeler, Joe, 201–2
Be Here Now (Dass), 55
be-ins, 44, 56, 73–76, 81, 95
Bellecourt, Clyde, 178, 196–98, 202
Bellecourt, Vernon, 178, 202
Bennett, Ramona, 34, 40
Berkeley Barb (newspaper), 78–82, 88, 90, 109, 192–93, 230n3
Berkeley Tribe (newspaper), 90–91, 93, *94*, *106*, 108–9, 156–57, 166, 248n44
Betts, Dickie, 193
Black, Shirley Temple, 107
Black Bear Ranch, 120
Black Elk, Wallace, 202

259

Black Elk Speaks (Neihardt), 54, 72
Blackfoot Tribe, 50, 101
Black Mesa strip mine, 142–43, 241n71
Black Panther Party, 10, 26, 33, 90–95, 119, 161–65, 191, 194, 215, 240n41
Blue Cloud, Peter, 95, 232n35
Blue Lake (territorial issue), 12, 112, 114, 135, 139–44
Boe, Paul, 203, 207
Boldt, George, 42, 211, 218
The Book of the Hopi (Waters), 47, 54, 65
Brand, Stewart
    "America Needs Indians" and, 3–5, 45–46, 49–52, 55–56, 116, 124, 142, 217, 228n21
    drugs and, 47–48
    Ken Kesey and, 3–4, 45, 52, 224n7
    Whole Earth Catalog and, 3–4, 43–44, 52–55
Brando, Marlon, 22, 22, 23, 33, 95, 183, 192, 215, 224n13
Bridges, Al, 25–30, 160
Bridges, Maiselle, 27–28
Brown, Dee, 17, 145, 147–50, 183, 186
Bruce, Louis, 163–64, 181–82
Bureau of Indian Affairs
    in negotiations with Native activists, 164
    occupation of, 13, 145–46, 171, 175–82, 186, 248n56
    policies of, 73–75, 91, 149, 198, 217
    tribal governments and, 142, 183–85
Burnette, Robert, 172, 174–75
Bury My Heart at Wounded Knee (Brown), 17, 145, 147–50, 186
Buskirk, J. Phillip, 38, 208, 211, 256n55

Cambrium Fund, 99–100, 255n46
Carlucci, Frank, 177–78
Carmichael, Stokely, 24, 175, 191, 194, 201, 222n11
Castenada, Carlos, 55, 229n29
celebrities, 22–25, 95–100, 107, 126, 158–60, 183, 192–93, 215
    See also specific people
A Century of Dishonor (Jackson), 148
"Challenge to the Churches" (AIM document), 197–98
Cherokee Tribe, 29
Cheyenne Autumn (Sandoz), 72
Cheyenne Tribes, 148, 173
Chicanos. *See* Mexican Americans
Chivington, John, 148
churches. *See* Lutherans; Native Americans; Quakers; religion and religious groups
Civil Disturbances Information (Justice Department), 179
Clearwater, Frank, 194, 214, 253n21
Cohon, Peter. *See* Coyote, Peter
Collier, John, Jr., 21–22, 67–68

Colville Tribe, 159
Comanche Tribe, 57–58
communes, 53, 113–44, 238n25, 239n31
Confederated Tribes of Warm Springs, 46
Costanoan Tribe, 83–84
counterculture. *See* hippies
Coyote, Peter, 17, 70–72, 85, 113, 120–23
Craft Manual of North American Indian Footwear (White), 54
Crazy Horse, 93, 190
Crocker, George N., 234n60
Crow Dog, Leonard, 189, 200
Crusade for Justice (group), 10–11, 29–30, 101, 183, 193
"A Curse on the Men in Washington, Pentagon" (Snyder), 68–69
Custer, George Armstrong, 93, 148
Custer Died For Your Sins (Deloria), 9, 17, 54, 147, 153–54, 244n8

Davis, Angela, 10, 195, 213–14, 216
Day, Candra, 87–88, 231n27
Daybreak Star Center, 158, 247n37
Dean, John W., 181, 250n60
Deganawida-Quetzalcoatl University, 157, 245n26
Deloria, Vine, Jr.
    Custer Died For Your Sins, 9, 17, 54, 72, 145, 147, 149, 153–54, 244n8
    on Dee Brown, 147–48, 150
    political experience of, 54–55, 111, 236n82
    racial coalitions and, 10–11, 31–32, 151–55, 222n11, 244n12
The Dharma Bums (Kerouac), 56
Diggers (group), 69, 71–72, 76, 120, 124
Dinsmore, Marcus, 191–92
Disciples of Thunder (commune), 121
Douthit, Peter. *See* Rabbit, Peter
Drop City (commune), 117–18
drugs, 3, 45–48, 50, 55, 57, 71–80, 116, 126–34
Durkee, Steve and Barbara, 116, 126, 134, 239n31
Dye, Arthur, 38–40

Economic Development Administration (EDA), 163
Ecumenical Metropolitan Ministry (E.M.M.), 172–73
Ehrlichman, John, 97, 107–8, 181
The Electric Kool-Aid Acid Test (Wolfe), 45
Elgin, Al, 153, 156

Federal Bureau of Investigation (FBI), 178–79, 187, 193, 209
Feinstein, Max, 116, 118, 126
Findley, Tim, 86–87
fishing rights, 10, 13, 16, 18–42, 27, 47, 62, 79, 87, 99, 111, 173, 218

Flathead Tribe, 21–22
Fonda, Jane, 96, 158–60, 215
Fools Crow, Frank, 186
Ford, Gerald, 200
Fort Lawton, 145–46, 157–59, *160*, 161–65, 167, 169, 217
Fort Phil Kearny (Brown), 147
Fountain of Light (newspaper), 123, 241n61
Frank, Billy, 21, 25–26, 33
Frank's Landing, 16, 25–26, 28–42, 111, 159
Fulbright, William, 186
Future Shock (Toeffler), 149

The Galvanized Yankees (Brown), 147
Garment, Leonard, 17, 97, 107–11, 142, 170–71, 175–87, 211–12, 234n63
gender, 13, 27–28, 49, 58, 60, 190
General Services Administration (GSA), 163–64
The Gentle Tamers (Brown), 147
Geronimo, 83–84, 158
Gersh, Bill, 118–19
Gimmell, Mickey, 165–66
Ginsberg, Allen, 57, 60
God is Red (Deloria), 154
Gomez, Little Joe, 47, 117–18, 120, 128–29, 239n31
Gonzalez, Corky, 10–11, 29–30
Gonzalez, Rodolfo Cortez, 101
Goodbear, Harvey, 49
Good Morning, Tellus, 47, 120, 128
Gottlieb, Lou, 124–26
Gravy, Wavy, 17, 131–32, 167–68, 175, 240nn40–41, 248n56
The Greening of America (Reich), 149
Gregory, Dick, 10, 17, 23, 25, 33, 87, 183, 202
Grogan, Emmett, 70, 76–77
Grossman, Aubrey, 95, 170–71

Haley, James, 140–41
Heurta, Dolores, 213
Hickel, Walter, 97, 100, 105, 108, 152
Hidatsa Tribe, 29
hippies
  be-ins and, 44, 56, 73–76, 81, 95
  communal living and, 113–44, 239n31
  definitions of, 222n5
  effect of associating with Native American causes and, 33–34
  Native American idealization and, 6–7, 43, 48–56, 65, 70–77, 80, 120, 240n45
Hog Farm (group), 131–32, 136, 166–68, 175, 248n56
Hollenbach, Margaret, 237n12
Hoopa Tribe, 120
Hopi Tribe, 35, 50, 59, 65, 70, 73–77, 81, 114, 117, 120–23
Hopper, Dennis, 126, 241n51, 242n71

Independent Oglala Sioux Nation, 188
Indian Child Welfare Act, 217
Indian Claims Commission (ICC), 111, 140, 165–66, 169, 171, 177
Indian Crafts and Lore (Hunt), 54
Indian Energy Resources Act, 217
Indian Gaming and Regulatory Act (1988), 14, 217
Indian League of the Americas, Inc., 101
Indian Reorganization Act (1934), 185
Indian Resources Development Act (1967), 69
Indian Rights Committees, 26, 29
Indian Self-Determination and Indian Education Act, 111, 217
Indians of All Tribes (group), 86–112, 217
The Indian Tipi (Laubin), 53–54
Indian Tribal Energy and Development and Self-Determination Act, 217–18
International Foundation for Advanced Study, 3, 46
Interreligious Foundation for Community Organizing (IFCO), 152–56, 195–96, 245n17, 253n24

Jackson, Helen Hunt, 148
Jackson, Henry "Scoop," 158, 163–64
Jaqua, Joe, 206–7
Jemez Pueblo, 132
Jennings, Lois, 45, 49, 53, 116
Jones, Peter, 90–91
Jook Savages (group), 119, 126
Josephy, Alvin, 50–52, 55, 187–88

Karok Tribe, 120
Keith, Shirley, 98, 101
Keltz, Iris, 115, 129
Kennedy, John F., 20, 79, 96, 200
Kerouac, Jack, 56, 60
Kesey, Ken, 3, 18–20, 43, 45, 52, 59, 131, 136, 224n7
Kimmey, John, 47, 116, *118*, 121, 237n9
King, Martin Luther, Jr., 199, 201, 207
King, Robert, 234n63
Klamath Tribe, 36
Kleindienst, Richard, 209
Kunstler, William, 190, 195, 201

labor unions, 102–3, 105, 233n57
Lakota Tribe, 183–212
Lama (commune), 116, 126, 143, 239n31
Lane, Mark, 190, 195, 200, 202, 210, 254n37
La Raza, 138–40
Laskowich, Gloria, 168
Laubin, Reginald, 53–54
Law, Lisa and Tom, 119–20, *120*, 126, 131
Leary, Timothy, 57, 73, 126
Little Big Man (film), 145

Loeffler, Jack, 47, 50, 116, *117*, 142–43, 241n71
Loesch, Harrison, 164, 175, 181–82
Long Beach Indian Youth Council, 101
Los Angeles Times, 135, 180
The Lost Universe (Weltfish), 54
LSD, 3, 45–47, 57, 77, 126, 132–33
Luhan, Mabel Dodge, 115, 134
Lummi Tribe, 18
Lutherans, 196–97, 203, 207, 210, 215

Magic Tortoise Foundation (commune), 119
Makah Tribe, 18
Mandan Tribe, 29
McCarren Act, 80
McClanahan v. State Tax Commission of Arizona, 218
McCloud, Janet, 24–25, 34
McEvers, Chuck, 37, 256n55
McNickle, D'Arcy, 21–22
Means, Russell, 151, 173–86, 198, *199*, 202–3, 206, 210–11, 224n13
media
  mainstream, 17, 86, 95, 99, 103, 107, 125, 127, 135, 141, 143, 147, 149, 158, 164–67, 179–80, 184, 187
  spectacle and, 22, 85–87, 90–91, 103, 169, 179, 184–85, 248n46
  underground, 17, 29, 78–80, 82, 88, 90, 93, 99–100, 108–9, 123, 135, 142, 156–57, 166, 183–84, 192–93, 230n3, 248n44
Merry Pranksters, 3, 20, 45, 52, 131, 136
Methodists, 198, 210
Mexican Americans, 6, 9–11, 29–30, 42, 137–38, 157, 183, 188–89, 193–94
Millbrook (commune), 126
Mills, Sid, 159–60, 178–79
Modoc War, 148
Momaday, M. Scott, 64, 148–49
Monongye, David, 49, 121, 142, 237n9
Montgomery, Ross, 170–71
Montoya, Porfirio, 132–33
Morning Star (commune), 124–26, 238n25
Morris, Joe, 89, 102
Mount Rushmore, 145, 151–52
Muckleshoot Tribe, 21–23, 36, 39

National Association for the Advancement of Colored People (NAACP), 23, 42
National Association of Criminal Defense Lawyers (NACDL), 201
National Committee for Restoration of Blue Lake Lands to the Taos Pueblo, 114, 140
National Congress of American Indians (NCAI), 11–15, 21, 37, 55, 114, 140, 161, 175
National Council of Churches (NCC), 114, 140–41, 183, 195, 198–200
National Indian Lutheran Board, 197

National Indian Youth Council (NIYC), 15, 21–22, 54–55, 153
National Lawyers Guild (NLG), 201
Native Alaska Claim Act, 111
Native Alliance for Red Power, 101
Native American Church, 8, 43, 47, 78, 80, 116, 128–29
Native American Graves Protection and Repatriation Act, 217
Native American Religious Freedom Act, 217
Native American Rights Fund (NARF), 41, 180, 211
Native Americans
  in the Anglo imaginary, 18–20, 36–37, 43, 48–49, 51–56, 58, 61–63, 65–68, 78–79, 83–84, 88, *94*, 96, 115, 117–19
  church support for, 6, 8–9, 32–41, 100, 145, 152–56, 172–73, 183, 195–200, 203, 207–10, 253n24
  exchanges with hippies and, 43–44, 48–56, 117–18, 120–34, 240n45
  FBI harassment of, 178–79, 187, 193, 209, 251n64
  intergenerational tensions among, 13, 16, 133–34, 216
  international support for, 147, 168, 187, 205
  intertribal politics and, 40, 101, 151–52, 215
  labor union support for, 102–3, 105, 233n57
  legal aid for, 200–203, 210, 254n37
  media focus on, 78–80, 90–99, 103, 107–10, 135, 141, 143, 145, 147, 149, 164–66, 170, 179–80, 183–85, 187
  militancy of, 13, 15–16, 93–95, 150–52, 156, 159–65, 175–79, 183–212, 216
  Poor People's Campaign and, 29–31
  radical alliances of, 10, 22–26, 30–35, 78–81, 84–112, 145–46, 159, 164–65, 171, 175, 183, 188, 191–95, 199–207, 213–15, 234n60
  self-determination issues and, 5, 75, 188, 217–18
  termination policies and, 5, 87, 93, 146, 166
  treaty rights as central focus of, 13–42, 112, 114, 135, 139–46, 172, 184–86, 192, 198–203, 211, 215
  tribal sovereignty and, 8, 11–15, 62, 69, 83, 93, 110, 183–86
  U. S. political and legal structures and, 12–13
  Vietnam War and, 6, 81–82, 99–100, 107, 135, 188–94, 216
Native American Solidarity Committee (NASC), 184, 214
Navajo Tribe, 35, 47, 50, 62, 76, 114, 148
New Buffalo (commune), 116, 119, 126–27, *127*, 128, *128*, 129–30, 143, 239n34
New Harmony (commune), 124
The New Indians (Steiner), 149
New Left, 6–7, 143, 222nn6–7

New York Times, 103, 135, 141, 180, 187
Nez Perce War, 148
Nike Missle Base, 151, 156
Nisqually Tribe, 18, 21, 24, 26–27, 27
Nixon, Richard
    Alacatraz occupation and, 96–97, 101–2, 105–8, 111
    BIA Building occupation and, 171, 174, 176–82, 184, 249n57, 250n58
    Blue Lake issue and, 140–44, 169
    Fort Lawton occupation and, 160
    Native American policies of, 17, 111, 146, 171–72, 188, 200, 211, 217, 234n63
    Pit River tactics and, 169, 248n50
    Watergate and, 181, 211
    Wounded Knee and, 187, 198–99
Nobody Loves a Drunken Indian (film), 96
Nordwall, Adam (Fortunate Eagle), 86, 110, 191, 231n16
North American Indian Arts (Whiteford), 54
North American Indian Club, 101

Oakes, Richard, 98, 104, 110, 146, 165, 167–69, 172, 188
Obama, Barack, 218–19
occupations. *See specific actions and sites*
Office of Economic Opportunity (OEO), 80, 163, 176
Oglala Sioux. *See* Lakota Tribe; Sioux Tribes
Oglala Sioux Civil Rights Organization (OSCRO), 185–86, 188, 200
Ohlone Indians, 107
Ojibwa Tribe, 80, 98
Olema (commune), 120–23
Omaha Tribal Council, 101
One Flew Over the Cuckoo's Nest (Kesey), 18–19, 43
Oracle (newspaper), 44, 57–58, 65, 66, 68–69, 77, 79
Ortiz y Pino, Gerald, 137
Our Brother's Keeper (Citizens Advocacy Group), 149

Paiute Tribe, 4, 46–47
Palos, Stuart, 160, 162–63
Patterson, Bradley, 17, 170, 175–77, 181, 186–87, 234n63
Peace and Freedom Party, 26, 28
Peoples Park, 83–84, 105, 138
peyote, 43, 47–50, 71, 73, 76, 78, 80, 116, 128–29, 132
Pima Tribe, 29
Pine Ridge Reservation, 4, 16, 62, 161, 183–212
Pit River Tribe, 146, 165–71, 248n44
Playboy magazine, 127, 135, 224n13
Poor People's Campaign (SCLC), 29–30, 30, 31–32, 162, 172

protests. *See specific protests and sites*
Pulido, Laura, 222n10
Puyallup Tribe, 18, 21, 27, 34, 38–39
Pyramid Lake Tribal Council, 101

Quakers, 6, 24, 26, 34–42, 173, 183, 207–10, 215–16
    See also American Friends Service Committee (AFSC)
Quinault Reservation, 20
Quinones, Joseph, 25–26, 33–34, 71, 225n23
Rabbit, Peter, 117–18
race
    authenticity and, 7–8, 80–81, 93, 119, 138–39
    civil rights movement and, 18, 24, 90–91
    movement leadership and, 12, 147–50, 215–16
    political activism and, 9–13, 29, 31, 79, 90–93, 152–55, 164–65, 189–94, 216, 222n10
    scholarly attention to, 5–6
Radio Free Alcatraz, 100
Ramparts Magazine, 96, 110
Reality Construction Company (commune), 119, 138
religion and religious groups
    Buddhism and, 55, 57
    civil rights era and, 7
    communes and, 124–29
    Native American practices and, 6, 43, 47, 51–55, 59, 61, 63, 240n45
    political activism and, 6, 8–9, 32–39, 41, 100, 145, 152, 172–73, 193, 195–200, 203, 207–10, 215–16, 253n24
reservations (as political spaces). *See* Native Americans; *specific reservations*
Reyna, Diane, 133–34
Reyna, Tony, 129–30
Rincon Band of Mission Indians, 101
Rolling Thunder, 25, 71–72, 81–83, 121
Romney, Hugh. *See* Gravy, Wavy
Rosebud Reservation, 62, 172, 189
Rossinow, Doug, 222nn6–7, 257n8
Roubideaux, Ramon, 200, 254n37
Rudnick, Lois, 126, 130
Rush to Judgment (Lane), 200

Sage (publication), 115–16
Sainte-Marie, Buffy, 6, 29, 80–81, 98–99
Salish Tribe, 59
Samora, Frank, 128–29
Sand Creek Massacre, 100, 107, 148
Sanders, Jeffrey C., 246n27
Sando, Joe, 132–33, 236n2
Sandoval, Joe Sun Hawk, 120, 128–29
San Francisco Chronicle, 86–87, 166–67
San Francisco Mime Troupe, 45, 70
Santa Ana Pueblo, 132
Santa Clara Pueblo, 131

Santo Domingo Pueblo, 76, 121
Satiacum, Bob, 21–22, 22, 34, 160–61
Seattle Liberation Front, 34, 159, 161
Seattle Post-Intelligencer, 33, 164
Seattle Times, 159, 165
self-determination (of Native Americans), 5, 37, 111, 172, 188, 217–18
Seneca Tribe, 29
A Separate Reality (Castenada), 55
Shoshone Reservation, 25, 64, 78–79, 81–82
Silbowitz, Al, 99–100
Silko, Leslie, 63
Sioux Tribes, 58, 86, 93, 148, 152, 173–74, 212
    See also Lakota Tribe
Small Tribes of Western Washington (STOWW), 36, 40–42, 161, 256n55
Smith, Paul Chaat, 86, 145, 184, 186, 201
Snyder, Gary, 43–44, 56–70, 100
Society of Friends. *See* Quakers
Sohappy v. Smith (decision), 41
Soldier Blue (film), 145
Southern Christian Leadership Conference (SCLC), 10, 29–30, 33, 199
Spaceship Earth (Ward), 53
Stern, Robby, 28, 32–33, 37
Students for a Democratic Society (SDS), 26, 28, 32–33, 191, 195
Survival Arts of the Primitive Paiutes (Wheat), 54
Survival of American Indians Association (SAIA), 23–24, 34, 38, 40–41, 172, 183, 198

Tanner, Jack, 23–25
Taos News, 134, 137
Taos Pueblo, 12, 47, 112, 117, 120–29, 139–44, 169–71, 182, 217
Tax, Sol, 50, 103
The Teachings of Don Juan (Castenada), 55
termination (policy), 5, 11–12, 69, 87, 93, 111, 146, 166
Tesuque Pueblo, 126, 131, 136
Thom, Mel, 153–54, 156
Thorpe, Grace, 96, 103, 158, 160, 167
Tijerina, Reies, 30, *31–32*, 138, 140, 226n35
Time magazine, 125, 147
Times of London, 100
Townes, Brooks, 87–88
Trail of Broken Treaties, 146, 170–84, 187–88, 208–9, 217
Treaty of Fort Laramie (1968), 212
Treaty of Medicine Creek, 111
treaty rights
    definitions of, 14–15, 150
    land reclamation and, 12, 112, 114, 135, 139–44, 146, 158–71
    as political focus, 13–42, 146, 172, 184, 186, 192, 198, 200, 202–3, 211, 215

tribal sovereignty, 8, 11–15, 62, 69, 83, 93, 110, 183–86
Trips Festival, 4, 45, 124
Trudell, John, 95, 97, 99–100, 110, 151, 156
Tulalip Tribe, 36
Turtle Island (Snyder), 62–63
Tuscarora Tribe, 29
"Tuwaqachi--The Fourth World" (Grossinger), 65
Twenty Points (TBT document), 174–77, 179, 182, 211, 217

Udall, Stewart, 52, 69, 73, 140
Umatilla Tribe, 20
Uncommon Controversy (AFSC), 36–39, 41, 256n55
United Indians of All Tribes (UIAT), 146, 158–59, 162–64, 246n33, 247n37
United States
    draft policies of, 80–82
    imperialism of, 7–11, 145, 188–92, 215
    termination policies and, 5, 11–12, 69, 87, 93, 111, 146, 166
University of Washington Law Review, 41
Unruh, Jesse, 96, 102
U.S. v. Washington (decision), 41–42, 211, 218
Ute Reservation, 21

Vietnam Veterans Against the War (VVAW), 193, 195, 250n60
Vietnam War
    American imperialism and, 145
    antiwar activism and, 79–81, 85
    church organizations' relation to, 34
    Native American activism and, 6, 25, 28, 68, 71, 99–100, 107, 188–94, 216
    in Native American communities, 49, 82, 135

Walker, Lucius, 153–55, 196
Wall Street Journal, 179
Wampanoag Tribe, 151
Warm Springs Reservation, 4, 20, 46–47, 50, 60
Warrior, Robert Allen, 145, 184, 186
Wasco Tribe, 4, 46
Washington Post, 107, 180
Washoe Tribe, 47, 116
Waters, Frank, 47, 54, 65, 115
The Way of Zen (Watt), 57
We Talk, You Listen (Deloria), 149
White, Richard, 25–28, 33, 225n22
Whitebear, Bernie, 159–60, *162*, 163–65
"Who Is An Indian" (Collier), 67
Whole Earth Catalog (Brand), 3–4, 43–44, 52–55
"Why Taos?" (*Fountain of Light*), 123
Wilkinson, Charles, 42, 217

Williams, Edward Bennett, 96–97
Williams, Richard, 81–82
Wilson, Dick, 185–86, 192, 198–200, 211
Wind River Reservation, 78–79
Winnebago Tribal Council, 101
Wishram Tribe, 61
"Wounded Knee, 1973" (pamphlet), 188–90
Wounded Knee Legal Defense/Offense Committee (WKLDOC), 17, 184, 190, 200–206, 209–10, 213, 254n37
Wounded Knee (massacre), 100, 107, 148
Wounded Knee (occupation of), 4, 10, 12, 16, 92–93, 146, 183–212

Yakima Tribe, 41, 169
Yaqui Tribe, 25, 55
Yaryan, John, 22, 34
Yellow Thunder, Raymond, 185, 188
Yurok Tribe, 120

Zen Buddhism, 55, 60
Zimmerman, William, 193–94, 253n21

E98.T77 S57 2012